Enhanced Methods in Computer Security, Biometric and Artificial Intelligence Systems

Enhanced Methods in Computer Security, Biometric and Artificial Intelligence Systems

Edited by

Jerzy Pejaś

Andrzej Piegat

Technical University of Szczecin, Poland

 Springer

Library of Congress Cataloging-in-Publication Data

A C.I.P. Catalogue record for this book is available
from the Library of Congress.

Pejaś, J.
    Enhanced Methods in Computer Security, Biometric and Artificial Intelligence Systems/ edited by
Jerzy Pejaś, Andrzej Piegat
        p.cm.

ISBN   1-4020-7776-9   e-book   0-387-23484-5   Printed on acid-free paper.

Printed in the United States of America.

9 8 7 6 5 4 3 2 1   SPIN 11053675 (HC)

springeronline.com

Table of Contents

Chapter 2
Biometric Systems

Chapter 3
Methods of Artificial Intelligence
and Intelligent Agents

Preface

The book contains mainly (but not only) works of European scientists investigating problems in the area of computer science.

The works give a picture of the present state and progress concering this field of science and show directions of contemporary research investigations. Authors present new scientific methods and show how these methods and other well known methods could be used to solve some particular practical problems.

All papers contained in the book were assembled into 3 chapters:
1. Methods of Artificial Intelligence and Intelligent Agents,
2. Information Technology Security,
3. Biometric Systems.

Chapter 1 contains 13 papers comprising various areas of artificial intelligence such as: fuzzy set theory, predicate logic, neural networks, fuzzy arithmetic, expert systems, evolutionary computations, clustering, data mining and others. The 7 of all 13 papers present applications of artificial intelligence in solution of such practical problems as: requalification of contaminated sites, training of aviation pilots, ship control, firm bankruptcy, stock market, soil erosion, and flight control.

All papers are interesting but especially I would like to draw the reader attention to some particular papers, beginning from **Chapter 1**.

A very interesting paper in this chapter is the paper "*A fuzzy expert approach for comparing alternative end uses for requalification of contaminated sites*" prepared by a group of Italian scientists: G. Facchinetti, I. Mannino, G. Mastroleo, and S. Soriani. To make the decision "how a contaminated site of a country should be used after their remediation" is very difficult, because many features of the site and many future possible destinations of it have to be taken into account. The features and destinations mostly can not be evaluated numerically (ie.: using the numeric values) but only with use of linguistic, fuzzy evaluations. The authors show how multi-dimensional fuzzy problem can be solved by its decomposition and application of fuzzy logic.

In the paper "Choosing representative data items: Kohonen, Neural Gas or Mixture Model?- A case of erosion data" by A. Bartkowiak and co-authors accomplish an interesting comparison of various neural models used as representatives of a big data sets. It is a very practical problem - how effective are various types of neural networks? This effectiveness can probably be evaluated only by specific experimental investigations - and the authors applied this method.

I would like also draw the reader attention to a very important but underestimated problem of the neural model extrapolation outside the region covered by measurement data. The problem is presented in the paper "*Algorithm for automatic definition of validated and non-validated region in multi-dimensional space*" written by P. Klęsk. The extrapolation problem is generally not noticed by users of neural models and other types of models, what results in many errors, mistakes and false evaluation of neural networks. The author shows a method, which allows to detect in which region of the problem space calculations delivered by a model can be trusted and where can not.

The problems and their solutions presented in the **Chapter 2** "Information Technology Security" belong to three important areas of security engineering in information systems: analysis of software security, public key infrastructure, and development/design of new cryptographic algorithms and protocols.

Analysis of software security aims mainly at detection of software errors, construction of appropriate techniques of software creation (e.g. of an error-robust ones) and at evaluation of the software influence on security of the whole information system. From this point of view of the software user the software itself and generally the whole information system has to be secure and has to realize only such tasks, which are compatible with its specification. Thus a prerequisite of the information system is the trust of its users that the system is able to contribute to the achievements of the business objectives of users, to bring them some benefits. The problem of the IT-trust analysis and of increasing the trust was presented in the papers "*How to justify trust in software based systems?*" by J. Górski and "*Tool support for* detecting *defects in object-oriented models*" by J. Górski and co-authors.

The technology of the public key infrastructure has no more been treated as a technical novelty since a long time. There exist many proves that its practical application gives many benefits and considerable savings. One of such examples is given in the paper "*Integrated payment system for public key infrastructure services*" by I. E. Fray and J. Pejaś. The nEPSKIP-system proposed in the paper may be used not only to account the PKI-services but also to other doubled services as e.g. bank clearing. However, construction of that services must be supported by other PKI-components, such as by service of the certificate status verification and devices for secure signature signing. Proposals of a novelty solution of the two components enable an easier usage of the PKI-technology and increase its usefulness for creation of e-society.

Cryptographic algorithms have to guarantee a high resistance level against break and a high speed of coding/decoding operations. The high speed can be achieved not only by application of appropriate calculation and information processing methods but by parallelization of operations as well. In the paper by V. Beletskyy and D. Burak "*Parallelization of the data encryption standard (DES) algorithm*" the authors show that also classical algorithms as DES can be parallelized, though its structure is not based on operations of parallelization. A new cryptographic algorithm is also presented in the paper of T. Hebisz and E. Kuriata "*The capacity of ciphers fulfilling the accessibility of cryptograms*". The authors propose a new cipher algorithm based on the techniques of error correction coding, which enable detection of changes and manipulations on cryptograms. They present also the VAST-system, which ensures WWW-users' confidentiality in the network.

Chapter 3 "Biometric Systems" is devoted to problems of processing and analysis of human features for person recognition and identification. It contains description of chosen algorithms and their implementations for personal computers, in form of introductory descriptions and ready software systems as well. The chapter comprises 11 papers dealing mainly with the face picture analysis (6 papers) and recognition systems (3 papers). Analysis of the presented papers shows that investigations connected with biometric systems are going towards a few directions. The first of them is the design of new models, the second one is the usage of known and sometimes even classical methods of biometric problems solution, and the third direction is an implementation of the methods in form of active computer systems.

A complex model of a human face was presented in the paper "Częstochowa's precise model of a face based on the facial asymmetry, ophthalmogeometry, and brain asymmetry phenomena: the idea and algorithm sketch" by L. Kompanets and co-authors. The model is based on temporary knowledge about asymmetry, ophtalmogeometry, brain hemispheres functioning asymmetry phenomena and delivers tools useful in techniques of identity verification and person identification. It is also useful in investigation of human-computer interactions and person evaluation with respect to his/her cognition-psyche type.

The works "*An experimental criterion for face classification*" by K. Saeed and P. Charkiewicz present novel approaches to classification and to recognition. The approaches use eigenvalues obtained from Toeplitz matrices and have high effectiveness in comparison with other methods.

Application of the picture processing and recognition was presented in few papers. The first of them "*An environment for recognition system modeling*" by G. Kukharev and A. Kuźmiński describes a simulation system, which allows for planning of investigations and practical verification of many different methods. It is a valuable tool for scientists investigating different systems of picture recognition (not only in biometric tasks).

The paper "*The PCA reconstruction based approach for extending facial image databases for face recognition*" by L. Chen and co-authors presents application of the known PCA-method to improve operational effectiveness of face recognition systems. This method can be especially used in face databases, which includes incomplete information (e.g. missing picture of the face front or missing the side picture). In such difficult cases the method is able to reconstruct the missing picture data.

Implementation of chosen biometric algorithms is also the subject of the work:"*Modified gradient method for face localization*" written by G. Kukharev and co-authors. They propose a method that enables face localization in very complex pictures. An elaborated computer program allows for work in real time and guarantees high efficiency of the face localization independently from the scale and from the neighborhood conditions.

Remaining works presented in Chapter 3 refer to subjects closely connected with biometrics and methods that can find biometrical application. Their characteristic feature is the approach originality and possibility of practical implementation.

The works contained in presented book surely make you, Dear Reader, enable to keep pace with the siginificant development of computer science. I wish you a great satisfaction from the reading.

Professor Andrzej Piegat
Editor

explicit. However, it is possible to point to situations where the validity of those assumptions is not obvious, unless supported by some additional evidence (e.g. in a military hospital environment where patients are suspects of terrorist attacks). The virtue of the trust case is that it brings such assumptions into the surface and provides for their explicite *management*.

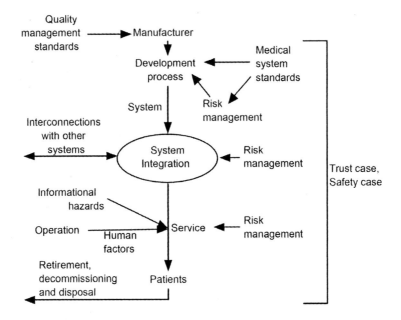

Fig. 4. Trust Case within the scope of lifecycle

CL_0.1	Therapy Prescription (TP) for a Patient (P) made by Health Professional (HP) is consistent with the Patient's health status and the present state of the Pharmaceutical Knowledge (PhK)	
ARG_0.1	The scope of the trust case is restricted to drug application and does not include quality of medical treatment	
	CL_0.1.1	TP is consistent with PhK
	A_0.1.1	HP is competent to assess the health status of P
	A_0.1.2	HP intends to assess the health status of P
	CL_0.1.2	TP is consistent with the health status of P as assessed by HP

Fig. 5. Example assumptions in the trust argument

How can we justify trust in software based systems?

JANUSZ GÓRSKI
Department of Software Engineering, Gdańsk University of Technology
Narutowicza 11/12, 80-952 Gdańsk, e-mail: jango@eti.pg.gda.pl

Abstract: The paper introduces the notion of *trust case* and explains its meaning within the context of IT systems. It reports on the experiences gained during development of a trust case for a complex IT system for drugs distribution and application. Several open research problems related to development, management and use of trust cases are identified and enumerated.

Key words: trust, modeling, safety, security, composability, medical applications.

1. INTRODUCTION

Stakeholders consider an IT system as an enabler of their business objectives. For instance, a merchant involves itself in the procurement of an e-commerce solution to improve the access to the customers and/or to increase the rate of transactions. And only if he/she trusts that the system can help in achieving those goals she/he invests in its procurement. Thus a prerequisite of the IT system being applied is the *trust* (or confidence) of its users that the system is able to contribute to the achievement of their business objectives (brings them some benefits). In many cases such trust is mostly subjective (has no objective justification) and is based on beliefs, influences by other people and expectations rather than on evidence. A noticeable exception is the domain of safety critical systems where there are recommendations, guidelines and sometimes regulations governing the extent and quality of evidence that must be collected to justify trust in a system before it is eventually commissioned for being used. Another domain is that where security matters and we expect that the integrity of security policies and mechanisms is demonstrated and/or justified before we entrust to the system our valuable assets. Openness of contemporary systems, integration of services and ubiquitous computing paradigms result in the situation where the systems with safety and security implications are becoming increasingly popular and the trust (or distrust) in those systems is a dominating factor of their acceptance (e.g. the feeling of

insufficient security is presently among the main factors preventing people and companies from getting involved in e-commerce).

Computers and related software found their way to numerous systems, including those where a system failure could put into risk human lifes, cause a huge property damage or lead to severe environmental pollution. This led to the notion of *computer safety* and launched an extensive research effort to understand and control the risks associated with the use of software intensive systems in safety related applications. The effort primarily focused on the use of computers in control and/or protection systems and the related research has been driven by the requirements of such systems. The underlying assumption was that enough control can be excercised over the whole *safety lifecycle*, including early conceptualization, development, installation, operation, maintenance and decommissioning. Numerous guidelines and standards were developed that advice which criteria are to be applied while building systems with possible safety consequences (e.g. [1,2]). They are associated with a broad range of methods and techniques aiming to provide more assurance throughout the whole safety lifecycle. In some some applications where safety is the primary concern (e.g. nuclear, avionics, medical) licencing the system for being used is conditioned by the need to present and maintain a *safety case*, the structured argument that collects the evidence supporting the claim that the system is sufficiently safe for its intended environment.

The paper investigates the notion of *trust* and introduces the concept of *trust case* that is analogous to the notion of safety case for safety critical systems. Trust case is an explicit argument that collects and marshals evidence justifying and supporting trust in a given system. The paper presents this concept referring to a case study in developing trust case for a complex e-health application. It also points to a number of open issues and research problems related to application of trust cases.

2.   MODEL OF TRUST

Let us assume an object O that is of interest to a subject S. Let us consider a property P postulated for O. By T(S,O,P) we denote that S trusts that O actually exhibits the property P. This situation is shown in Fig.1.

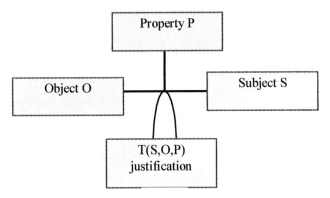

Fig. 1. The trust relationship

T(S,O,P) is a ternary relationship. If the domain $D_p(O)$ of the properties of O that are of interest is fixed and for each P in $D_p(O)$, T(S,O,P) holds, then we can write T(S,O) which means that S trusts O. Otherwise the trust is conditional and related to P.

With each relationship T(S,O,P) we associate an attribute '*T(S,O,P) justification*' as is shown in Fig.1.

Even with this simple model of trust we can ask a number of questions (to be more specific let us assume that our trust model is related to a medical application).

Which objects are of interest? Within the context of medical applications the object of interest can be any IT enabled system, device or service, e.g. a medical device, a medical procedure, a whole hospital IT system.

Which subjects are of interest? In general the subject can be any stakeholder of the object under consideration. The primary group are the patients but we should also consider doctors, nurses, hospital authorities, external regulatory bodies and any other subject that can have interest in the considered medical system.

Which properties are of interest? The properties would depend on the objectives and concerns of a particular subject or subjects group. Nevertheless we can easily identify a number of categories of properties that would be particularily important, like patient's safety, patient's privacy, privacy of health professionals, accountability of all actions that have potential impact on the patients' health and the like.

What are the needs for trust justification? The needs can vary from the regulatory requirement to establish the justified trust relationship between a licencing authority and the system before the system is being commissioned for use, through commercial motivations where the trust relationship is needed e.g. to convince customers to get them involved in transactions, to ethical constraints where we need to justify that the norms and values respected by the society would not be violated.

What are the criteria to be met during trust justification? In some cases such criteria are explicitly stated and documented, e.g. the need to demonstrate the required SIL (*Safety Integrity Level*) for a safety critical system or the need to meet the required CMM (Capability Maturity Model) level to bid for a government contract. They can be also more vague like the need to follow "best practices" or even more elusive like the need to meet (sometimes unspoken) expectations.

3. TRUST CASE – WHAT IS THIS?

A trust case is developed by making an explicit set of claims about the system and then collecting and producing the supporting evidence and developing a structured argument that the evidence justifies the claims. The ontology describing trust case elements and showing their interrelationships is shown in Fig. 2 (the

arrows show the direction of reading the association names). This model is based on the results of the research into safety cases [3,4].

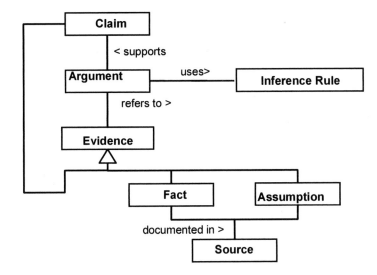

Fig. 2. Trust Case ontology

Trust case is a structured collection of *claims* where each claim is supported by an associated argument. Arguments refer to *evidence* that includes: *facts, assumptions* and/or (more specific) *claims.* Facts and assumptions are linked to data *sources.* For a given fact, these data can e.g. demonstrate adherence to established principles, document design decisions, contain results of performed analyses, etc. For an assumption the associated data source can document who and when introduced the assumption and how it was justified. Sub-claims are developed further down by giving arguments that support them.

The inference rules used in arguments are of three basic types: *quantitative* (e.g. justifying the failure probability postulated by a claim from the probabilities given by the supporting evidence), *logic* (establishing the validity of a claim from the logical assertions given by the supporting evidence) and *qualitative* (establishing the validity of a claim by referring to the common acceptance of good practices that were adhered to as demonstrated by the evidence supporting the claim). The qualitative argumentation can in particular refer to accepted standards, guidelines or so called "engineering judgement".

Trust case develops top-down starting from the topmost claim and recursively working towards more specific claims, facts and assumptions. It results in a tree-like structure, as shown in Fig.3 (or multi tree, in case we have multiple trust targets).

If we deal with several trust targets we have to consider the mutual consistency of the resulting argument trees. If inconsistencies do exist, this means that some of the trusted properties are in conflict and such conflicts must be resolved either by modifying the properties or by accepting a weaker arguments that justify their trustworthiness. As an example consider a medical system where from the privacy point of view a patient related data should be strictly access controlled and restricted and at the same time should have a very high availability with the relaxed access

control in emergency situations (the safety point of view). In such applications the trust case should cover both, safety and security viewpoints, and in addition it should consider possible conflicts and their resolutions.

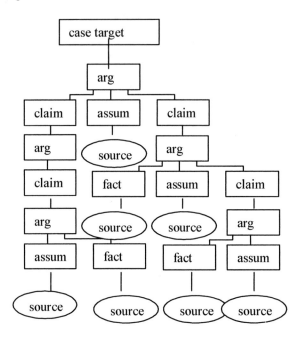

Fig. 3. Trust Case structure

4. RELATIONSHIP TO THE LIFECYCLE

Although in most cases the stakeholders have their primary interest in the operational properties of a particular system, to justify those properties it is necessary to assume the broad scope that potentially covers the whole lifecycle of the system. An example of the scope for trust justification for medical devices is shown in Fig.4 (derived from [10]). Depending on the properties of interest this scope can vary. For a generic properties like safety and security, controlling the scope is supported by the existing standards (e.g. [2,6] for safety, [7,8,9] for security).

It should be noticed that in case of a particular system, it may happen that we do not have access to some evidence or the evidence does not exist at all. In such situation to justify trust we have to make assumptions, as shown in Fig.5 (derived from [10]).

In the example shown in Fig.5 the claim CL_0.1 depends on two assumptions: A_0.1.1 and A_0.1.2. The former asserts that Health Professional is competent enough to correctly diagnose the patient whereas the latter asserts that HP is positively motivated to diagnose the patient. Although those assumptions seem obvious and are made with respect to most medical systems, they are rarely made

Chapter 1

Information Technology Security

5. BUILDING A TRUST CASE

To define claims we need a language. A natural language (e.g. English) is the first choice, but due to its obvious limitations (the lack of precision and possible ambiguities), the natural language expressions can sometimes be misinterpreted. Another problem is that while specifying claims in a natural language it is difficult to control the scope and it is easy to mix the levels of abstraction a given claim refers to. In consequence the soundness of the supporting argumentation can be adversely affected.

To overcome those difficulties we decided to control the language used to express trust cases by introducing the Claim Definition Language – CDL [10]. The structural components of CDL are shown in Fig.6.

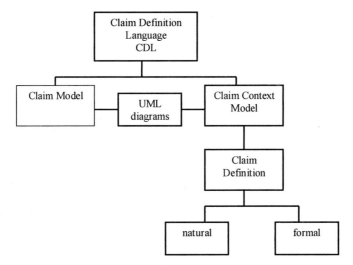

Fig. 6. Structural components of CDL

CDL includes two main components that help in building a trust case: (1) a graphical language that provides constructs to represent claims, arguments, facts and assumptions and to show how they are combined into a *claim model,* and (2) a graphical language that provides for representing, for each claim, its associated *context model* showing all the (physical and logical) objects that are referred to in the claim together with their relationships.

Both, claim models and claim context models are expressed as UML diagrams (with some extensions towards business process modeling as proposed in [12]).

Each claim *definition* is given by referring to the components introduced in the corresponding claim context model. To avoid possible ambiguities, in addition to its natural language expression, each claim definition is also given in as a formal expression.

An example of a claim model is given in Fig.6.

More information on CDL and examples of its use can be fouind in [13].malized ion aoduced in a claim context model

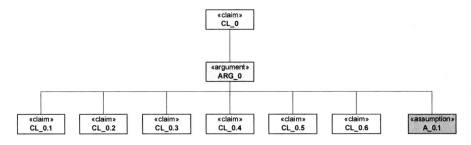

Fig.6. Example of claim model

6.   COMPOSABILITY

A question of high importance is the composability of trust cases that is illustrated in Fig. 7. At some level of detail, the system trust case refers to the claimed properties of component A1 that are justified by referring to some evidence related to A1. Now, let us assume that, for some reasons, A1 is being replaced by A2, and A2 has its own trust case, developed independently. The question is under which conditions we can replace the trust case of A1 by the trust case of A2.

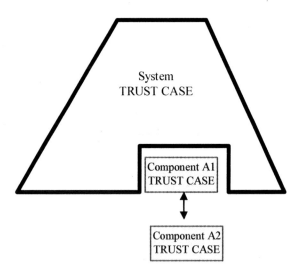

Fig.7. The idea of Component-based Trust Case

Answering this question would help e.g. in:
- replacing one component with another of the same type (but for example from other vendors);
- evolutionary system development (when new components and functions are added to the system);
- upgrading system components.

To achieve the goal of trust case composability we need to address the following issues (see Fig. 8):

- identify a system trust case structuring method that reflects the actual structure of the system in terms of its components;
- elaborate a system trust case development and management method that follows this way of trust case structuring;
- identify the criteria to be met by the "component related" part of the system trust case to be detached and considered in isolation (component trust case interfacing criteria);
- elaborate component trust case development and management method that maintains validity of the component trust case interfacing criteria;
- identify and develop tools supporting generating, collecting and maintaining evidence in trust cases.

The issue of trust case composability is actually broader in scope than just interfacing the component trust tase to a system trust tase. In covers as well the issue of relating two different trust cases developed for the same system/component to justify two different (but not necessarily disjoint) claimed properties (e.g. safety and security). It may also be relevant if we have e.g. two trust cases for two systems that were developed independently but from now on will be considered together.

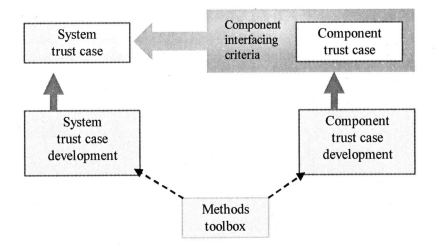

Fig.9. Component based trust case strategy

7. OPEN ISSUES

The following issues (among others) have been found of interest during an ad hoc discussion on trust and safety cases for medical systems arranged during the

EWICS TC7 (European Workshop on Industrial Computer Systems, Technical Committee 7) Medical Workshop [14]:

* How do trust cases fit in -scope, roles and responsibilities;
* What is the role of the manufacturer of a medical device (does not produce operational part of trust justification; could include a way the device is used);
* Is there a need for a third party trust case? (but is this feasible for a hospital? easier to put obligation on supplier);
* The role of standards compliance as trust argument;
* Trust case as a means to support communication, negotiation and review between stakeholders;
* Trust case as a means to provide visibility of what has been done;
* Using trust cases to win user acceptance;
* Using trust cases to support risk management, e.g. of legal risks;
* The role of trust cases to enhance reviewability, management of change of components, documenting assumptions and helping to catch problems.

REFERENCES

[1] European Workshop on Industrial Computer Systems, Technical Committee 7 http://www.ewics.org/
[2] IEC61508:1998 and 2000, part 1 to 7: Functional Safety of Electrical, Electronic and Programmable Electronic Systems
[3] EU EUREKA SHIP (Safety of Hazardous Industrial Processes) Project http://www.csr.city.ac.uk/csr_city/projects/ship/ship.html
[4] Górski J., 'Developing Safety Cases for Software Intensive Systems', Proc. Conf. on Risk Analysis and Safety Management of Technical Systems, Gdansk, 25-27 June, 2001, pp. 111-120
[5] EWICS TC7 (European Workshop on Industrial Computer Systems, Technical Committee 7) Medical Devices Subgroup, Edinbourgh, UK, 23 September, 2003
[6] Safety Case Assessment Criteria http://www.hse.gov.uk/railway/criteria/
[7] Common Methodology for Information Technology Security Evaluation, version 1.0, 1999
[8] Common Criteria for Information Technology Security Evaluation version 2.1, 1999 (Parts 1,2,3)
[9] ISO/IEC Information Security Management, 2000
[10] Trust Case Development, WP11 Report, Project IST DRIVE (Drugs In Virtual Enterprise), D11.1-3, January 2003
[11] Eriksson, H.-E., Penker, M.: Business Modeling with UML, J. Wiley, 2000
[12] Górski J., Jarzębowicz A., Leszczyna R., Miler J., Olszewski M. , 'An approach to trust case development', LNCS 2788, Springer-Verlag, 2003, pp. 193-206
[13] R. Bloomfield, J. Gorski, B. Bibb, 'Cases Discussion', EWICS Medical Workshop, Edinbourgh, UK, September 2003

The capacity of ciphers fulfilling the accessibility of cryptograms

TOMASZ HEBISZ, EUGENIUSZ KURIATA
Uuniversity of Zielona Góra, Institute of Control and Computation Engineering
ul. Podgórna 50, 65-246 Zielona Góra, Poland
e-mail: {T.Hebisz, E.Kuriata}@issi.uz.zgora.pl

Abstract: The attempt of using the techniques of error correction coding for building the cryptographic system, which can detect the manipulations on cryptograms, is shown in the paper. Presented approach to generating cipher, generating redunant ciphertexts, which are resistant to manipulations, allows to fulfilling the accessibility as well as confidentiality and authenticity. The capacity of obtained ciphertexts, by mean of statistical tests' results, is also presented.

Key words: cryptography, error correction, security, accessibility of information

INTRODUCTION

The security is defined as fulfillment of the confidentiality, authenticity and accessibility. Most cryptosystems fulfill the confidentiality and authenticity, but ignore or even completely neglect the property of accessibility. There is possible to construct the cryptosystem that gives the accessibility by means of manipulations correction using error correction coding [1, 2].

Error correction codes and cryptography are connected very close and have many common applications. There are a lot of cryptosystems using error correction codes, for example McEliece cryptosystem or Niederreiter cryptosystem [8, 9, 10, 15].

The manipulations on cryptograms are defined as a change of cryptogram contents made by opponent in communication channel. Generally, there is no difference between the transmission errors and manipulations. This justifies the using error correction coding for construction of cryptographic system.

There is possible to apply the non-systematic codes in cryptosystem, which fulfills the accessibility of information. Various modes of operation of such system, and the statistical analysis of cryptograms generated by it, are presented.

1. CRYPTOGRAPHIC ALGORITHM

Proposed cryptosystem de facto generates blocks of ciphertexts, which are vectors of cyclic, non-systematic Reed-Solomon code, and correctional properties of cipher are connected with the parameters of used code.

1.1 Encryption and decryption procedures

Presented cryptographic algorithm is based on using coding and decoding procedures of cyclic Reed-Solomon code. These procedures can be applied for constructing the symmetric-key block cryptosystem, consisting of the pair of transformations $\{E_K, D_K: K \in \mathbf{K}\}$, where $E_K: \mathbf{M} \to \mathbf{C}$, $D_K: \mathbf{C} \to \mathbf{M}$ such that

$$(\forall\, K \in \mathbf{K},\ \forall\, M \in \mathbf{M}:\quad C = \mathrm{E}(M + K))$$

and

$$(\forall\, K \in \mathbf{K},\ \forall\, C \in \mathbf{C}:\quad M = \mathrm{D}(C) - K).$$

E denotes encoding procedure of non-systematic cyclic Reed-Solomon code over $GF(q)$, consisting in computing n-symbol code vector C, representing k-symbol information vector $M + K$.

Similarly, D denotes decoding procedure of this code, therefore $\mathrm{D}(C) = \mathrm{D}(\mathrm{E}(M + K)) = M + K$. The symbols + and – denote addition and subtraction in $GF(q)$, respectively. The Fig. 1. shows the block scheme of such system.

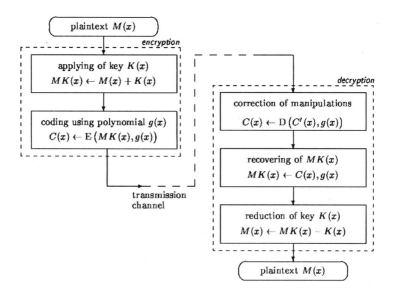

Fig. 1. Block scheme of cryptosystem with using Reed-Solomon code

1.2 Computing in isomorphic finite fields

As the matter of fact, during the encryption procedure the information is coded using nonsystematic Reed-Solomon code. Therefore, the use of different representations of elements of $GF(p^m)$ instead of standard finite field arithmetic devices or routines in the implementations of cryptographic algorithms makes the cryptoanalytic work much more difficult. Several essential methods of computing in isomorphic finite fields may be shown [6, 7].

- **"Natural" isomorphism**
  This possibility of computing in isomorphic Galois field consists in using different irreducible polynomials while constructing a field. This approach gives

$$N_q(m) = \frac{1}{m} \sum_{e|m} p^{m/e} \mu(e),$$

different representations of elements of $GF(p^m)$ [11]. The symbol $\mu(x)$ denotes the discrete Möbius function described by the following equation

$$\mu(x) = \begin{cases} 1 & \text{if } x = 1, \\ (-1)^k & \text{if } x \text{ is product of } k \text{ different primes}, \\ 0 & \text{if } x \text{ is divided by the square of prime}. \end{cases}$$

- **The application of affined transformations**
  Since $GF(p^m)$ is an m-dimensional vector space over $GF(p)$, then any element of $GF(p^m)$ represented using canonical basis can be transformed into the other vector by means of an affined transformation. In this case

$$N_T = p^m \cdot q^{(m-1)m/2} \prod_{i=1}^{m} q^i - 1$$

isomorphic fields $GF(p^m)$ can be constructed.

- **The application of "general" isomorphism**
  This approach uses an arbitrary permutation P mapping elements of $GF(p^m)$ onto the elements in the isomorphic $GF(p^m)$. This method is rather practical for software implementation of operation in finite fields of smaller order gives $(p^m)!$ isomorphic representations of elements.

The presented methods can be easily applied for fast software encryption and in constructing the cryptographic hardware, offering in result more secure level of privacy at some expense of speed of operations.

1.3   Modes of operation of cipher

For proposed cipher two modes of operation are possible: electronic codebook (ECB) or cipher-block chaining (CBC). Algorithm of ECB mode of operation is shown on Fig. 2. It consists of two procedures:

- **Encryption:**
  Input: k-symbol key K, k-symbol plaintext blocks M_1, M_2, ..., M_s.

  for $1 \leq i \leq s$ $C_i \leftarrow E(K + M_i)$.

  Output: n-symbol ciphertext blocks C_1, C_2, ..., C_s.

- **Decryption:**
  Input: k-symbol key K, n-symbol received ciphertext blocks C'_1, C'_2, ..., C'_s, certain blocks may have some symbols changed by an intruder or by channel noise.
  for $1 \leq i \leq s$

  $M_i \leftarrow D(C'_i) - K$.

  Output: k-symbol plaintext blocks M_1, M_2, ..., M_s.

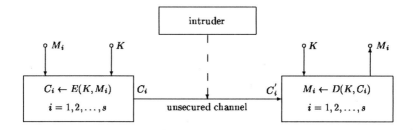

Fig. 2. ECB mode of operation of cipher

This is a simplest approach, where a message is partitioned into k-symbol blocks and each block is encrypted individually using the same key. Blocks are encrypted independently of other blocks. Assuming that proposed cipher can correct t symbols in one block, a change of t or less symbols in a single ciphertext block does not affect decipherment of that block at all. Only when the number of manipulations on the symbols of ciphertext is greater than t and when these manipulations are detectable, deciphering procedure does not work properly, and this fact may be signaled.

Rearranging ciphertext blocks in the channel results in the correspondingly re-ordered plaintext blocks at the receiver. Moreover, identical plaintext blocks are encrypted into identical ciphertext blocks. Ciphertext blocks are independent; therefore, malicious substitution of ciphertext blocks by the intruder does not affects the decryption of adjacent blocks. For these reasons the ECB mode is recommended for encrypting data no longer than one block.

The CBC mode of operation of presented cipher presented on Fig. 3. is more complicated and offers more new possibilities than ciphers with the same length of ciphertext and plaintext, since it is quite different. In comparison with ECB mode, the CBC mode applies additional elements, namely, memory elements symbolized by squares, in which one n-component vector over $GF(q)$, representing one block of ciphertext, can be stored, and a block, performing the operation of function f_K. The cryptographic procedures in this mode of operation result directly from Fig. 3. and are the following:

- **Encryption**:
  Input: secret function f_K, n-component initialization vector (I_V), k-symbol plaintext blocks $M_1, M_2, ..., M_s$.

  $$C_0 \leftarrow I_V,$$

  for $1 \le i \le s$

  $$K_i \leftarrow f_K(C_{i-1}),$$
  $$C_i \leftarrow E(K_i + M_i).$$

  Output: n-symbol ciphertext blocks $C_1, C_2, ..., C_s$.

- **Decryption**:
  Input: secret function f_K, n-component initialization vector (I_V), n-symbol received ciphertext blocks $C'_1, C'_2, ..., C'_s$, certain blocks may have some symbols changed by an intruder or by channel noise.

  $$C_0 \leftarrow I_V,$$

  for $1 \le i \le s$
  $$K_i \leftarrow f_K(C_{i-1}),$$
  $$C_i \leftarrow D^*(C'_i),$$
  $$M_i \leftarrow D(C'_i) - K_i.$$

  Output: k-symbol plaintext blocks $M_1, M_2, ..., M_s$.

It should be noted that D^* function carries out the correction of possible manipulations on C'_i and must always be calculated, as an intermediate stage of decrypting procedure D.

Since CBC mode is more sophisticated than ECB mode, its properties are also more rich than those of the latter. When the same plaintext of s blocks is enciphered under the same key and initialization vector, identical ciphertext blocks will be obtained. If one wants to obtain different ciphertexts for the same message, encrypted two times, he must change I_V or first plaintext block.

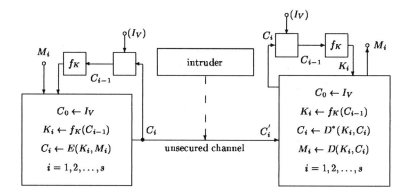

Fig. 3. CBC mode of operation of cipher

The application of chaining mechanism makes the ciphertext C_i dependent on M_i and all preceding plaintext blocks. Rearrangement of the order of ciphertext blocks in the channel by an intruder causes then mistakes in decryption. Correct decryption of block C_i requires a proper C_{i-1} block.

It follows from the properties of shown cipher that after changing in ciphertext C_i more than t symbols, the decipherment of block C_i and C_{i+1} will be erroneous.

The CBC mode is self-synchronizing in the sense that if in ciphertext block C_v the manipulations cannot be corrected but C_{v+1} has less than $(t+1)$ manipulations, then ciphertex block C_{v+2} is correctly decrypted to M_{v+2}.

2. ANALYSIS OF CIPHERTEXTS

The cryptographic hardness of proposed method depends to a large degree of the key space size. Generally, in presented method the message is coded using redundant code. Thus the appreciating of cryptographic strongness of ciphertexts is verified by analysis of three problems:

- computation complexity of analytic cryptoanalysis,
- defining the key space,
- analysis of statistical properties of ciphertexts.

In presented cryptosystem, first criterion is based on complexity of decoding cyclic codes without the knowledge of generator polynomial. This approach is based on syndrome decoding problem and it has successfully resisted more than 20 years of cryptoanalysis effort, because it is still NP-problem.

The key space is depending on the way of computation in isomorphic finite field. For example, for "general" isomorphism, the size of key space consists of:

- number of polynomial $K(x)$ added to the message, which is equal to

$$(p^m)^k$$

where (p^m) — size of used *GF*, k — number of information symbols in codeword,

- number of permutations used for generate isomorphic Galois fields applied for coding/decoding procedure, which is equal to

$$(p^m)!$$

Thus, for established parameters of code, such as p, m, n and k,

$$|\mathbf{K}| = (p^m)^k ((p^m)!).$$

For example, let us use the $GF(2^8)$, because of very huge popularity of the *ASCII* alphabet, and let $k = 100$, $n = 257$ ($t = \lfloor 257 - 100 \rfloor / 2 = 78$), we obtain:

$$|\mathbf{K}| = (2^8)^{100} (2^8)! = 256^{100} (256!)$$

For analysis of statistical properties of ciphertexts one can use the statistical tests and histograms of character occurrence frequency in ciphertext.

During the computer experiment, many attempts of ciphering were performed. A task of computer experiments was to prove the correction advantages of the system. A text file and an audio-wave file were used as plaintext files, because of its characteristic frequency of character occurrence. The size of used files was about 8MB. The cryptograms files were bigger then the plaintexts files and they took about 11 MB space of hard disk.

Fig. 4. presents an example of the histograms of character occurrence frequency in plaintexts and ciphertexts obtained during enciphering text file and wave-audio file. As one can see, the characters of ciphertexts have almost proportional distribution. Much better results give the CBC mode of cipher. A cryptogram resembles the random set of characters.

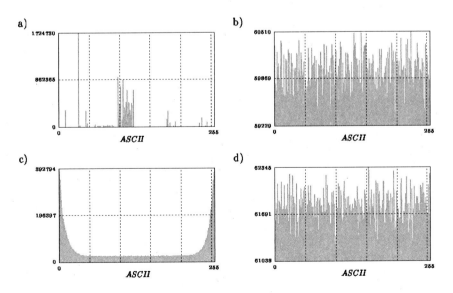

Fig. 4. Histograms of character occurrence frequency a) in text file,
b) in ciphertext of text file, c) in wave-audio file and d) in cipher-text of wave-audio file

Test	Max	a	b	c	d	e
BIRTHDAY SPACINGS	1	1	1	1	1	1
THE OVERLAPPING 5-PERMUT.	2	0	2	1	2	1
BINARY RANK for 31 × 31 mat.	1	1	1	1	1	1
BINARY RANK for 32 × 32 mat.	1	1	1	1	1	1
BINARY RANK for 6 × 8 mat.	1	1	1	1	1	1
THE BITSTREAM TEST	20	0	20	16	19	20
OPSO	23	0	22	22	22	22
OQSO	28	0	27	28	28	28
DNA	31	0	30	30	30	30
COUNT-THE-1's on a bytes stream	2	0	2	1	2	2
COUNT-THE-1's for spec. bytes	25	22	25	24	25	22
THE PARKING LOT	1	1	1	1	0	1
THE 3DSPHERES	1	0	1	1	1	1
SQEEZE	1	1	1	1	1	1
THE OVERLAPPING SUMS	1	0	1	1	1	0
THE RUNS	4	4	4	4	3	4
THE CRAPS	1	1	1	1	1	1

Tab. 1. Results of DIEHARD tests of cryptograms
a) cryptograms for text file generated in ECB mode, b) cryptograms for text file
generated in CBC mode, c) cryptograms for wave-audio file generated in ECB mode,
d) cryptograms for wave-audio file generated in CBC mode, e) cryptograms for text file
encrypted using T-DES algorithm in ECB mode.

There are few packets of statistical tests available for cryptographic applications. The Diehard tests packet appears to be most popular [12]. Tab. 1. shows the results of Diehard's tests of cryptograms obtained for enciphered textfile and wave-audio file.

Unfortunately there is not the measure which allows to reliably compare of statistical properties of various cryptographic algorithms. The only possibility is to compare the results of individual tests results. To compare obtained results with other cryptosystems, the text file used in the above example was encrypted using the T-DES method which is often applied in practice. Fig. 5. shows the histograms of character occurrence frequency and the Tab. 1(e) shows the results of Diehard's tests for the obtained ciphertext. As one can see, the obtained results for the method T-DES is similar to the results of case using Reed-Solomon code.

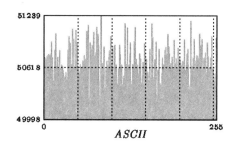

Fig. 5. Histogram of character occurrence frequency for ciphertext
obtained using T-DES algorithm

3. CONCLUSIONS

Presented cryptosystem allows verifying the correctness of obtained codewords, what gives an opportunity to fulfill the confidentiality, authenticity and accessibility, using the properties of cyclic Reed-Solomon code.

Unfortunately there is no measure, which allows to reliably comparing of statistical properties of various cryptographic algorithms. But in consideration of Diehard tests' results and histograms of character occurrence frequency of obtained ciphertexts, one can say, that the statistical properties of ciphertexts are sufficient and hard enough to cryptoanalysis. Long enough key space is guaranteed by using computation in isomorphic *GF*. Especially worth mentioning is CBC mode of shown cipher. A cryptograms produced in this mode have very good statistical properties however the computational complexity is bigger than in ECB mode, but the difference seems to be insignificant.

The presented method are equally suitable for the software and hardware implementations as well, but the hardware implementation seems to has much more practical applications for the sake of speed of ciphering and deciphering procedures.

REFERENCES

[1] T. Hebisz, Cz. Kościelny. *A method of constructing symmetric-key block cryptosystem resistant to manipulations on ciphertext.* Bulletin of the Polish Academy of Sciences, Technical Sciences, Vol. 50, No. 4, 2002.

[2] T. Hebisz, E. Kuriata, M. Jackiewicz. *Fulfilment of computer security and safety by using symmetric-key block cryptosystem resistant to manipulations on ciphertext.* International Conference on Computer Information Systems and Industrial Management Applications CISIM '03, 2003.

[3] A. Kiayias, M. Yung *Polynomial Reconstruction Based Cryptography.* SAC 2001. ICALP 2002. LNCS 2259. pp. 129-133. Springer-Verlag. 2002.

[4] A. Kiayias, M. Yung *Cryptographic Hardness Based on the Decoding of Reed-Solomon Codes.* Springer-Verlag. ICALP 2002. LNCS 2380. pp. 232-243. 2002.

[5] L. Knudsen, B. Preneel *Construction of Secure and Fast Hash Function Using Nonbinary Error-Correcting Codes.* IEEE Trans. on Information Theory. Vol. 48. No. 9. pp. 2524-2537. 2002.

[6] Cz. Kościelny. *Computing in the composite GF(q^m) of characteristic 2 formed by means of an irreducible binomial,* International Journal of Applied Mathematics and Computer Science, Vol. 8, No. 3, pp. 671-680, 1998.

[7] Cz. Kościelny, T. Hebisz. *More secure computing in finite fields for cryptographic applications.* Mathematical Theory of Networks and Systems MTNS 2000, The fourteenth International Conference, Perpignan, 2000, CD-ROM.

[8] E. Krouk. *A new Public Key Cryptosystem.* Proc. of Sixth Joint Swedish-Ruppian Intern. Workshop on Information Theory, 1993.

[9] E. Kuriata. *Error correction codes in crytography.* VI Intern. conference "Wojskowa Konferencja Telekomunikacji i Informatyki", 1997 (in polish).

[10] Y. X. Li, R. H. Deng, X. M. Wang. *On the equivalence of McEliece's and Niederreiter's public-key cryptosystems.* IEEE Trans. on Information Theory. Vol. 40. pp. 271-273. 1994

[11] R. Lidl, H. Niederreiter. *Introduction to finite fields and their applications.* Cambridhe University Prepp, 1986.

[12] G. Marsaglia. *Statistical tests Diehard.* http://stat.fsu.edu/~geo/diehard.html.

[13] R. J. McEliece. *A Public Key Cryptosystem Based on Algebraic Coding Theory.* JPLDSN Progrepp Rept., pp. 42-44, 1978.

[14] A. J. Menezes, ed. *Application of Finite Fields.* Kluwer Academic Publishers, 1993.

[15] H. Niederreiter. *Knapsak-type cryptosystems and algebraic coding theory*, Probl. Control and Inform. Theory, Vol. 15, 1986.

Parallelization of the Data Encryption Standard (DES) algorithm

V. BELETSKYY, D. BURAK

Faculty of Computer Science & Information Systems, Technical University of Szczecin,
49, Żołnierska st., PL-71210 Szczecin, Poland,
e-mail: vbeletskyy@wi.ps.pl, dburak@wi.ps.pl

Abstract: In this paper, we present the results of parallelizing the Data Encryption Standard (DES) algorithm. The data dependence analysis of the loop iterations was applied in order to parallelize this algorithm. The OpenMP standard is used for presenting a parallel algorithm. The classic DES algorithm can be divided into parallelizable and unparallelizable parts. As a result of our experiments it was stated that most of the „*for*" loops of the DES algorithm are well suitable for parallelization. The experiments with the parallel part of the algorithm against the sequential one using two- processors machine has shown that the speed-up is about 1.95. However, the rest code, containing I/O functions, is unparallelizable that reduces the speed-up of the parallel program running on multiprocessor computers.

Key words: cryptography, Data Encryption Standard, OpenMP API, data dependence analysis

1. INTRODUCTION

Considering the fact that the relatively large part of the sequential DES algorithm source code is filled in with the „*for*" loops and the most of computation is comprised in these loops, it is possible and useful to parallelize this algorithm. The parallel DES algorithm will permit us to reduce the time of running cryptographic tasks on multiprocessor computers. This problem is also connected with the current world tendency to the hardware implementation of cryptographic algorithms (just because we also need parallel algorithms in this case). The major subject of this paper is to present the parallel DES algorithm. The paper is organized as follows. In Section 2, we in brief describe the DES algorithm. Section 3 contains the description of the parallelization of the sequential DES algorithm. Section 4 presents experimental results (regarding efficiency) obtained for a parallel DES algorithm.

2. DESCRIPTION OF THE DATA ENCRYPTION STANDARD ALGORITHM

The Data Encryption Standard (DES) algorithm, adopted by the U.S. government in 1977, officially described in FIPS PUB 46 [1], widely used for many applications, is a symmetric block cipher algorithm that transforms 64-bit plaintext blocks under a 56-bit secret key, by means of permutation and substitution [1].

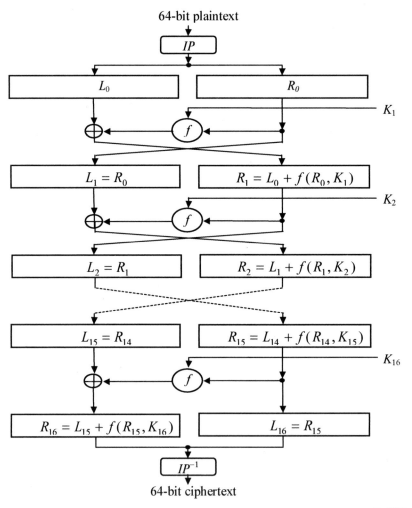

Fig.1. Block Diagram of the DES algorithm

Figure 1 shows the block diagram of the DES algorithm.

It consists of the following steps:

1. Take 64-bit input block of plaintext and permute it with Initial Permutation (IP) [1].
2. Split the permuted block into two halves: the first 32 bits is named L_0 and the last 32 bits- R_0 [1].
3. Take 64-bit key, discard its parity bits and permute it with Permuted Choice 1 (PC-1) [1].
4. Split the permuted key into two halves: the first 28 bits is named C_0 and the last 28 bits is named D_0.
5. Starting with i=1, calculate the sixteen 48-bit subkeys ($K_1 \div K_{16}$).
5.1. Perform one or two (it depends on the number of the iteration) circular left shifts on both Ci-1 and Di-1 to get Ci and Di.
5.2. Permute the concatenation Ci Di with Permuted Choice 2 (PC-2) [1].
5.3. Go back to 5.1 until K_{16} has been calculated.
6. Starting with i=1, apply these sixteen different 48-bits subkeys to the data block ($K_1 \div K_{16}$).
6.1. Expand the 32-bit sub-block Ri-1 into 48 bits according to the Expansion function (E) (Fig.2) [1].
6.2. Perform exclusive-or E(Ri-1) with Ki (Fig.2).
6.3. Break E(R[i-1]) $\oplus$ Ki into eight 6-bit blocks (B1÷B8) [1].
6.4. Starting with j=1, substitute the values found in the S-boxes for all B_j (S-Boxes-Substitution Boxes) [1].
6.4.1. The value of the 1st and the 6th bits B_j (called m) indicates the row in S[j] to find the substitution [1].
6.4.2. The value of the $2^{nd} \div 5^{th}$- bits B_j (called n) indicates the column in S[j] to find the substitution [1].
6.4.3. Replace B_j with S[j][m][n].
6.4.4. Go back to 6.4.1 until all 8 blocks have been replaced.
6.5. Permute the concatenation of $B_1 \div B_8$ with Permutation (P) (Fig.2) [1].
6.6. Perform exclusive-or the resulting value with L_{i-1}. $R_i \equiv L_{i-1} \oplus f(R_{i-1}, K_i)$, where $f(R_{i-1}, K_i) \equiv P(S[1](B_1) \ S[1](B_1) \ S[2](B_2) \ S[3](B_3) \ S[4](B_4) \ S[5](B_5) \ S[6](B_6) \ S[7](B_7) \ S[8](B_8))$ and where B_j is a 6-bit block of E(R_{i-1}) $\oplus$ K_i [1].
6.7. $L_i \equiv R_{i-1}$ [1].
6.8. Go back to 6.1 until K_{16} has been applied.
7. Permute the block $R_{16} \ L_{16}$ with the Final Permutation (IP^{-1}). IP and IP^{-1} permutations are inverses of one another [1].

The DES algorithm encrypts 64-bit input block of plaintext by means of the algorithms above (p.1÷7). In order to decrypt the ciphertext, we have to use the same algorithm and the keys K_i in the reverse order (because, it is a symmetric algorithm).

The DES algorithm turns a 64-bit input block of plaintext (M) into a 64-bit output block of ciphertext (C). To encrypt or decrypt more than 64 bits, there are four official modes. If each 64-bit block is encrypted individually, then the mode of encryption is called the Electronic Code Book (ECB) mode [1].

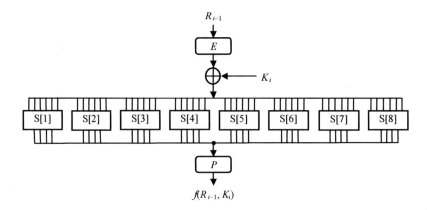

Fig.2. Block Diagram of the *f* function in the DES algorithm

3.   PARALLELIZATION OF THE ALGORITHM

A C source code of the sequential DES algorithm in the ECB mode [1] contains nine „*for*" loops (including no I/O function). As a result of the detailed analysis of these loops, we have come to the conviction that seven of them are suitable for parallelization.

Five of them are presented in the deskey() function, which sets the internal key register according to the hexadecimal key contained in the 8 bytes of the hexkey, according to the DES algorithm, for encryption or decryption [1]. One of them is presented in the des_enc() function, which encrypts blocks in the ECB mode and the last is presented in the des_dec() function, which decrypts blocks in the ECB mode.

First, we present five „*for*" loops included in the deskey() function.

Below, the declarations of variables of the deskey() function [1] are given:

```
register int      i, j, l, m, n:
unsigned char pc1m[56], pcr[56];
unsigned long kn[32];
short            edf;
unsigned char *key;
```

There are the following forms of the „for" loops included in the deskey() function [1]:

3.1.
```
for ( j = 0; j < 56; j++) {
    l = pc1[j];
    m = l & 07;
    pc1m[j] = (key[l >> 3] & bytebit[m]) ? 1 : 0;
}
```

3.2.
```
for( j = 0; j < 28; j++ ) {
    l = j + totrot[i];
    if( l < 28 ) pcr[j] = pc1m[l];
```

```
                      else pcr[j] = pc1m[l - 28];
                   }
```

3.3.
```
                   for ( j = 28; j < 56; j++) {
                      l = j + totrot[i];
                      if( l < 56 ) pcr[j] = pc1m[l];
                      else pcr[j] = pc1m[l - 28];
                   }
```

3.4.
```
                   for ( j = 0; j < 24; j++ ) {
                      if( pcr[pc2[j]] ) kn[m] |= bigbyte[j];
                      if( pcr[pc2[j+24]] ) kn[n] |= bigbyte[j];
                   }
```

3.5.
```
                   for ( i = 0; i < 16; i++) {
                      if(edf == DE1 ) m = (15 - i) << 1;
                      else m = i << 1;
                      n = m + 1;
                      kn[m] = kn[n] = 0L;
                      for( j = 0; j < 28; j++ ) {
                         l = j + totrot[i];
                         if( (l < 28 ) pcr[j] = pc1m[l];
                         else pcr[j] = pc1m[l - 28];
                      }
                      for ( j = 28; j < 56; j++) {
                         l = j + totrot[i];
                         if( l < 56 ) pcr[j] = pc1m[l];
                         else pcr[j] = pc1m[l - 28];
                      }
                      for ( j = 0; j < 24; j++ ) {
                         if( pcr[pc2[j]] ) kn[m] |= bigbyte[j];
                         if( pcr[pc2[j+24]] ) kn[n] |= bigbyte[j];
                      }
                   }
```

Now, we present the „for" loops included in the des_enc() and des_dec() functions.

Below, the declarations of the variables of the des_enc() and des_dec() functions are presented [1]:

```
                   int            i, blocks;
                   unsigned long  work[2], ek[32], dk[32];
                   unsigned char  *cp;
```

There is the following form of the „*for*" loop included in the des_enc() function [1]:

3.6.
```
                   for(i=0; i < blocks; i++) {
                      scrunch(cp, work);
                      desfunc(work, dc->ek);
                      unscrun(work, cp);
                      cp++;
                   }
```

The form of the „*for*" loop included in the des_dec() function [1] is as follows:

3.7.
```
for(i=0; i < blocks; i++) {
    scrunch(cp, work);
    desfunc(work, dc->dk);
    unscrun(work, cp);
    cp++;
}
```

We have used Petit to parallelize the loops above and the OpenMP standard to present parallel loops.

Developed at the University of Maryland under the Omega Project and freely available both for DOS and Linux systems, Petit is a research tool for analyzing array data dependences [4], [5].

Petit has the following basic features [4]:

* not perfectly nested loops analysis;

* memory- and value-based dependence analysis based on the Omega test;

* nonlinear dependence analysis based on uninterpreted function symbols;

* scalar / array expansion and privatization;

* an interface that allows browsing programs and dependence relations, etc.

Petit operates on programs in a simple Fortran-like language that has the following features [5]:

* one input file has to include the only one procedure;

* do not operates on complex data structures (s. a. unions, structures);

* do not accept expression containing indexes, etc.

The OpenMP Application Program Interface (API) supports multi-platform shared-memory parallel programming in C/C++ and Fortran on all architectures including Unix and Windows NT platforms. OpenMP is a collection of compiler directives, library routines and environment variables that can be used to specify shared memory parallelism. The OpenMP directives extend a sequential programming language with Single Program Multiple Data (SPMD) constructs, work-sharing constructs, synchronization constructs and help us to operate on private data. An OpenMP program begins execution as a single task (master thread). When a parallel construct is encountered, the master thread creates a team of threads. The statements within the parallel construct are executed in parallel by each thread in the team. At the end of the parallel construct, the threads of the team are synchronized. Then only the master thread continues execution. To build a valid parallel code, it is necessary to foresee all dependences, conflicts and requirements regarding parallelism of the program [2], [3].

The process of the DES algorithm parallelization can be divided into the following stages:

* carrying out the dependence analysis of a sequential source code in order to detect parallelizable loops;

* finding the dependence vectors for loops using Petit;

* selecting parallelization methods;

- constructing the parallel forms of the source loops in accordance with the OpenMP API requirements.

There are the following basic types of the data-dependences that occur in „*for*" loops [6], [7]:

A Data Flow Dependence indicates a write-before-read ordering that must be satisfied. This dependence cannot be avoided and limits possible parallelism. The following loop yields these dependences:

```
for(i=0; i<n; i++) {
    a[i] = a[i - 1];
}
```

A Data anti-dependence indicates a read-before-write ordering that should not be violated when performing computations in parallel. There are techniques for eliminating these dependences [7]. The loop below produces anti-dependences:

```
for(i=0; i<n; i++) {
    a[i] = a[i + 1];
}
```

An Output Dependence indicates a write-before-write ordering. There are techniques for eliminating these dependencies [7]. The following loop yields output dependences:

```
for(i=0; i<n; i++) {
    a[0] = a[i] ;
}
```

The substitution technique [7] was used for the loops specified in p.3.1÷3.5 in order to eliminate dependences preventing the loops parallelization. The following loop forms are received as the result of applying the substitution technique:

3.1 „*for*" loop:
```
for ( j = 0; j < 56; j++) {
    pc1m[j] = (key[pc1[j] >> 3] & bytebit[pc1[j] & 07]) ? 1 : 0
}
```

3.2 „*for*" loop:
```
for( j = 0; j < 28; j++ ) {
    if( (j + totrot[i]) < 28 ) pcr[j] = pc1m[j + totrot[i]];
    else pcr[j] = pc1m[(j + totrot[i]) - 28];
}
```

3.3 „*for*" loop:
```
for( j = 28; j < 56; j++) {
    if( (j + totrot[i]) < 56 ) pcr[j] = pc1m[j + totrot[i]];
    else pcr[j] = pc1m[(j + totrot[i]) - 28];
}
```

3.5 „*for*" loop:
```
for ( i = 0; i < 16; i++) {
    if(edf == DE1 ) m = (15 - i) << 1;
    else m = i << 1;
    kn[m] = kn[m + 1] = 0L;
```

```
for( j = 0; j < 28; j++ ) {
    if( (j + totrot[i]) < 28 )
    pcr[j] = pc1m[j + totrot[i]];
    else pcr[j] = pc1m[(j + totrot[i]) - 28];
}
for( j = 28; j < 56; j++) {
    if( (j + totrot[i]) < 56 )
    pcr[j] = pc1m[j + totrot[i]];
    else pcr[j] = pc1m[(j + totrot[i]) - 28];
}
for ( j = 0; j < 24; j++ ) {
    if( pcr[pc2[j]] ) kn[m] |= bigbyte[j];
    if( pcr[pc2[j+24]] ) kn[m + 1] |= bigbyte[j];
}
}
```

There is no possibility to use the substitution technique in the case of the 3.4 „*for*" loop.

The loops above were converted from the C language to the Petit language and the iteration dependence analysis for each loop was performed using Petit.

There are no iteration dependences in the case of the 3.1 „*for*" loop and all loop iterations can be performed in parallel. Using suitable OpenMP directives, the following parallel 3.1 „*for*" loop form (in accordance with the OpenMP API) is obtained:

3.8.   #pragma omp parallel private (j)
```
#pragma omp for
for ( j = 0; j < 56; j++) {
    pc1m[j] = (key[pc1[j] >> 3] & bytebit[pc1[j] & 07]) ? 1 : 0;
}
```

There are also no iteration dependences in the case of the 3.2 „*for*" loop. The following parallel 3.2 „*for*" loop (in accordance with the OpenMP API) is got:

3.9.   #pragma omp parallel private (j)
```
#pragma omp for
for( j = 0; j < 28; j++ ) {
    if( (j + totrot[i]) < 28 ) pcr[j] = pc1m[j + totrot[i]];
    else pcr[j] = pc1m[(j + totrot[i]) - 28];
}
```

There are also no iteration dependences in the case of the 3.3 „*for*" loop. The following parallel 3.3 „*for*" loop (in accordance with the OpenMP API) is received:

3.10.   #pragma omp parallel private(j)
```
#pragma omp for
for ( j = 28; j < 56; j++) {
    if( (j + totrot[i]) < 56 ) pcr[j] = pc1m[j + totrot[i]];
    else pcr[j] = pc1m[(j + totrot[i]) - 28];
}
```

Petit detected the following iteration dependences in the case of the 3.4 „for" loop: flow- dependences, anti dependences, and output dependences. In order to parallelize this loop, the OpenMP directive „reduction" for the variable „kn" using

the „ | " operator was used (the variable reduction technique). The following parallel
3.4 „for" loop (in accordance with the OpenMP API) is obtained:

```
3.11.        #pragma omp parallel private( j )
             #pragma omp parallel for reduction( | : kn )
             for ( j = 0; j < 24; j++ ) {
                 if( pcr[pc2[j]] ) kn[m] = kn[m] | bigbyte[j];
                 if( pcr[pc2[j+24]] ) kn[m + 1] = kn[m + 1] | bigbyte[j];
             }
```

Petit detected the output dependence in the case of 3.5 „for" loop. In order to
parallelize this loop, the private variables „i" and „m" are used (the variables
privatization technique). The following parallel 3.5 „for" loop (in accordance with
the OpenMP API) is received:

```
3.12         #pragma omp parallel private (i,m)
             #pragma omp for
             for ( i = 0; i < 16; i++) {
                 if(edf == DE1 ) m = (15 - i) << 1;
                 else m = i << 1;
                 kn[m] = kn[m + 1] = 0L;
                 #pragma omp parallel private(j)
                 #pragma omp for
                 for( j = 0; j < 28; j++ ) {
                     if( (j + totrot[i]) < 28 ) pcr[j] = pc1m[j + totrot[i]];
                     else pcr[j] = pc1m[(j + totrot[i]) - 28];
                 }
                 #pragma omp parallel private(j)
                 #pragma omp for
                 for ( j = 28; j < 56; j++) {
                     if( (j + totrot[i]) < 56 ) pcr[j] = pc1m[j + totrot[i]];
                     else pcr[j] = pc1m[(j + totrot[i]) - 28];
                 }
                 #pragma omp parallel private( j )
                 #pragma omp parallel for reduction( | : kn)
                 for ( j = 0; j < 24; j++ ) {
                     if( pcr[pc2[j]] ) kn[m] = kn[m] | bigbyte[j];
                     if( pcr[pc2[j+24]] ) kn[m + 1] = kn[m + 1] | bigbyte[j];
                 }
             }
```

Next, let us consider the 3.6 and 3.7 *„for"* loops. Taking into account the strong
similarity of these loops (there is the only difference between them- the first loop
operates on variable „ek", the second does on „dk"; variables „ek" and „dk" are of
the same type), we examine only the 3.6 *„for"* loop. However, this analysis is valid
also in the case of the 3.7 *„for"* loop.

First, we have to fill in the loops by the bodies of the corresponding functions
(otherwise, we cannot apply the data dependence analysis). The 3.6 *„for"* loop is
obtained after this operation.

Second, to permit us to carry out dependence analysis, we have replaced all
pointer operations with suitable array indexing.

Now, we can detect the iteration dependences existing in the considered loop. In order to parallelize this loop, the private variables „i", „keys", „work", „left", „right", „work1", „block", „into", „outof", „into1", „outof1" are used (the variables privatization technique).

The 3.7 „*for*" loop was parallelized in the same way.

4. SPEED-UP MEASUREMENT

In order to study the efficiency of the parallelization proposed, the Intel C++ compiler (supporting the OpenMP 2.0 API) has been used to run the DES sequential and parallel algorithms. Using two processors versus the only processor, the following speed-ups were received for the encryption and decryption of the same 14,5 megabytes file of plaintext (see Table 1).

The number of processors used for encryption and decryption plaintext	Total time of the DES sequential algorithm (Seconds)	Total time of the DES parallel algorithm (Seconds)	Total speed-up	The des_enc() time of sequential algorithm (Seconds)	The des_enc() time of parallel algorithm (Seconds)	The des_enc() speed-up	The des_dec() time of sequential algorithm (Seconds)	The des_dec() time of parallel algorithm (Seconds)	The des_dec() speed-up
One	24,6	24,6	1.86	11,5	11,5	1,95	11,5	11,5	1,95
Two	24,6	13,2		11,5	5,9		11,5	5,9	

Tab. 1. Speed-ups of the DES parallel algorithm

The total speed-up of the DES parallel algorithm depends heavily on two factors: the degree of *"for"* loops parallelization and the method of writing data to a file (reading a data file operation is significantly faster, so it is not such important factor). The results confirm that the whole DES algorithm and particularly- data encryption and decryption functions are suitable for a high degree of parallelization and it was used a proper C language function writing the data block of 512 bytes to the file (fwrite(&data[i], sizeof(unsigned char), 512, outfile). It is very important to use this function, because in case of applying fprintf function we got 43.7 seconds of total time for the DES parallel algorithm (and 55.0 seconds for the sequential one).

5. CONCLUSION

In this paper, we describe the parallelization of the classic DES algorithm. The DES algorithm was divided into parallizable and unparallelizable parts. We have shown that the „*for*" loops included in the functions responsible for the encryption and decryption processes are parallelizable. In order to parallelize these loops, the substitution technique, the variables privatization technique and the variable reduction technique were used. In order to permit us to carry out dependence analysis, we have replaced all pointer operations with suitable array indexing. The experiments carried out on a two-processors machine show that the application of the parallel DES algorithm for multiprocessor computers would considerably boost the time of the data encryption and decryption. We believe that speed-ups received for these functions (it is about 1.95) are satisfactory.

However, the code containing I/O functions is unparallelizable, because the access to memory is, by its very nature, sequential. Hence, the total speed-up received on PC computer is about 1.86. Nevertheless, using the memory with more latency (for example, using the interleaving technique) we can even increase the speed-up of the whole parallel program. The hardware synthesis of the DES algorithm will depend on appropriate adjustment of the data transmission capacity and the computational power of hardware. We plan to study other platforms such as SGI and Cray to verify whether they are well situated for the parallel execution of the DES algorithm.

REFERENCES

[1] Bruce Schneier, 1995. 'Applied Cryptography: Protocols, Algorithms, and Source Code in C, Second Edition', John Wiley & Sons.
[2] OpenMP C and C++ Application Program Interface. Ver.2.0. 2002
[3] http://www.openmp.org/
[4] W. Kelly, V. Maslov, W. Pugh, E. Rosser, T. Shpeisman, D. Wonnacott, 1996. 'New User Interface for Petit and Other Extensions. User Guide.'
[5] http://www.cs.umd.edu/projects/omega/
[6] D. I. Moldovan, 1993. 'Parallel Processing. From Applications to Systems', Morgan Kaufmann Publishers, Inc.
[7] R. Allen, K. Kennedy, 2001. 'Optimizing compilers for modern architectures: A Dependence- based Approach', Morgan Kaufmann Publishers, Inc.

Linked authenticated dictionaries for certificate status verification

WITOLD MAĆKÓW
Technical Uuniversity of Szczecin
ul. Żołnierska 49, 71-210 Szczecin, e-mail: wmackow@wi.ps.pl

Abstract: There's presented a proposal of a new certificate revocation scheme using linked authenticated dictionaries in the note. It was mainly basis of idea of Certificate Revocation Trees linking, but it's more generall. This scheme prevents Certification Authority doing some possible frauds. This way the neccessery trust level to CA is decreased.

Key words: certificate revocation, authenticated dictinary, dictionaries linking

1. INTRODUCTION

Certificate revocation and certificate status verification are very important problems in Public Key Infrastructure (PKI). There're many, practical and theoretical only, solution of those problems. Most common is usage of Certificate Revocation List (CRL). Many improvements, like Delta CRLs, Segmented CRLs or Over-issued CRLs help to increase efficiency of CRLs, but it wins against other solutions thanks to implementation simplicity rather then efficiency.

New group of efficient certificate revocation methods are based on Authenticated Dictionaries (AD). Dictionaries are common data structures that support search, insert and delete operations. Authenticated Dictionaries are dictionaries which contain additionally authentication information. In this manner trusted publisher (Certification Authority) may spread information by untrusted means (Directories). End entities (Users) may verify correctness of received data. The Merkle hash tree scheme was used to implement simplest static AD – Certificate Revocation Tree (CRT)[1]. Skip List [2] and 2-3 tree [3] were used for dynamic implementations of AD. In this paper it bases on general model of authenticated data structures creation and data verification presented in [4].

Main advantages of AD usage to certificate revocation are as follows: 1) small portion of data in response to certificate status query (it's not necessary to send whole data structure), 2) possibility of an online/real-time certificate status verification using untrusted parties (not only trusted CA), 3) possibility (in limited range) of positive statement response to certificate status query.

In earlier note it was proposed new scheme [5] – Linked Certificate Revocation Tree (LCRT). LCRT is standard CRT with some time stamping techniques[6] used on it. This scheme prevents to order changing attack (user and CA cooperation) and decrease necessary trust level to CA thanks to usage of mass media as a mean for proof data publication. This proposal was changed finally to Linked Authenticated Dictionary (LAD), which is more general, efficient and flexible solution.

1.1 Simplified model of PKI environment

LAD scheme is a generalize extension of LCRT, proposed in [5]. Both, LAD and LCRT are schemes of certificate revocation, and are embedded in theoretical PKI model (for example in Simplified Reference Model presented in [6] by S. Micali). This standard model was extended by some extra elements, and some functions of original elements were changed. In this model CA (Certification Authority) issues certificates to the Users(U) and certificate information to the Directories (D). The Directories are responsible for distribution of certificates information to the Users (or more in general to the Requestors). Simplified model is presented in Fig.1.

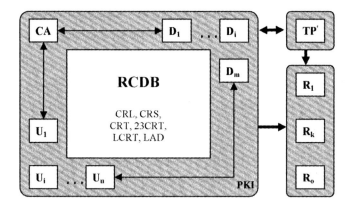

Fig. 1. Simplified model of PKI environment

The following entities are involved:
- **CA** (Certification Authority), a trusted agent that issues and revokes certificates;
- **D** (Directory) , a non-trusted agent that receives certificates information from CA and handles requester queries (in on-line and off-line manner);
- **U** (User), a non-trusted owner of certificate issued by CA;
- **R** (Requester), a non-trusted agent who receives certificates information from Directories, a not necessarily bounded with local CA;
- **TP** (Publisher), a non-trusted agent responsible for publication in mass media some verification information; used only in LCRT and LAD schemes;

‒ **RCDB** (Revoked Certificates Database) ‒ data structure (or structures) with some specific mechanisms and protocols used for revoked certificates collecting;

The scheme presented in Fig.1 is sufficient for considering certificate revocation and certificate status verification. The elements known from more detailed models, like e.g. Registration Authority, have no influence on certificate revocation, and furthermore, on RCDB implementation.

1.2 Authenticated dictionaries

The dictionary type data structure is a dataset with three basic operations implemented on it. The operation of interest includes: 1) inserting of new data into dataset, 2) removing of specified data and 3) searching for data having a given key. Sometimes bigger quantity of data is placed into dataset on the creation stage ‒ it may be considered as an initialization of dictionary. Next elements will be inserting and removing in the standard way.

On the bases of formal dictionary definition from [3] mentioned above proposal may be written as given below. There is data structure DS_S representing set S, where S is subset of space U ($S \subseteq U$). There're following operations defined for this structure:

‒ *Search(DS_S, e)* ‒ searching of element with key e in DS_S data structure. The logical value $ans \in \{true, false\}$ is returned in response, according to the scheme: $e \in S \Rightarrow ans = true$; $e \notin S \Rightarrow ans = false$

‒ *Insert(DS_S, e)* ‒ the assumption $e \in U \setminus S$ is made. Data structure $DS_{S'}$ created as a result of this operation will represent the set $S' = S \cup \{e\}$

‒ *Remove(DS_S, e)* ‒ the assumption $e \in S$ is made. Data structure $DS_{S'}$ created as a result of this operation will represent set $S' = S \setminus \{e\}$

‒ *Initialize(DS_S, I)* ‒ the assumptions set $S = \varnothing$ and set $I \neq \varnothing$ are made. Data structure $DS_{S'}$ created as a result of this operation will represent set $S' = I$

Definition 1 Dictionary DS_S is a data structure representing set S with operations *Search, Insert, Remove* and *Initialize* implemented on it.

New operation of authenticated search (*AuthSearch*) can be derived from ordinary search.

‒ *AuthSearch(DS_S, e)* - searching of element with key e in DS_S data structure. There's returned pair $\langle ans, pr \rangle$ in response. Value *ans* is set according scheme

$e \in S \Rightarrow ans = true$; $e \notin S \Rightarrow ans = false$. Value pr is a proof of *ans* response authenticity, prepared by DS_S data structure creator.

Definition 2 Authenticated dictionary ADS_S is a data structure representing the set S with operations *AuthSearch, Insert, Remove* and *Initialize* implemented on it.

There's new element in scheme with authenticated dictionary ‒ untrtusted mediator, placed between trusted data holder and requestor. The trusted data holder shouldn't serve requestors *Search* queries directly ‒ it's responsible only for data structure updates. Updated authenticated dictionary (or authenticated update package) is spread by holder among mediators. Authenticity proof is generated by holder after each update and it's the integral part of the authenticated dictionary.

1.3 Authenticated dictionaries linking

There's also a proof (or proofs set) for whole structure authenticity and integrity, which can be verified with specific protocol. For example in CRT: value of any leaf, hashes needed for path recovery from this leaf to the root and finally signature of a structure holder on a root – that's a proof of leaf value authenticity and also proof of authenticity and integrity of a whole structure. In the case when there are created some more data structures mentioned above there is a possibility to linked and published the proofs of authenticity.

In the some cases data in DS_S could become outdated. In the first scenario data is not needed any more, there's certainty that wouldn't be any more queries for this data (the turning point may be different for each data). Solution is very simple – redundant data would be removed to keep efficient size of structure. The second scenario occurs when probability of search queries for some particular data decrease rapidly – but queries are still possible.

The set of revoked certificates may be considered as a good example of second scenario. Certificate status verification is usually made only to the moment of certificate expiry, but verification of an archival signature may require information about certificate revocation long time after certificate expiry date. We shouldn't remove information about any revoked certificate then, even if probability of demand for this certificate is extremely low. Structure size (and of course searching time) will increase during data structure lifetime, but size of a subset of most useful (not expired) certificate revocations will be similar.

The solution may be closing the structure after some period of time, saving it as a current one and constructing the new one. It will be constructed with some elements of higher probability of revocation. Each archival structure will be connect with the proof of authenticity published after closing the structure. Next proofs will be linked between successive ones. This way we make impossible to fraud with the archival sets by a CA what decreases absolutely necessary trust level to the CA.

2. SCHEME PROPOSAL – THE BASICS

2.1 Certificates space

Sets and structures mentioned below will be only depend on one Certification Authority (CA) – in other words there's no possibility to find certificates from different sources placed in one structure. The assumption is that CA creates certificates with increasing serial numbers (1,2,3...,n). Serial numbers of the first and the last (last one created) issued certificates could be retrieved by users - separated protocol will be used for positive statement verification. Let A be set of all issued certificates:

$$A = \{ a1, a2, ...\}$$

Let set A^{lim} be an extension of A:

$$A^{lim} = A + \{l_0, l_\infty\}$$

where l_0 i l_∞ are symbolic elements, meeting following condition:

$$\forall a : a \in A^{lim} \Rightarrow (l_0 < a < l_\infty)$$

Size of A^{lim} set is depend on time, each newly issued certificate increases size of set by one. With n issued certificates it will be:

$$\overline{\overline{A^{lim}}} = n + 2$$

Serial numbers of all revoked certificates with elements l_0 i l_∞ create subset S of A^{lim} ($S \subseteq A^{lim}$).Size of S is also depend on time and with k revoked certificates it will be:

$$\overline{\overline{S}} = k + 2$$

Set S could be divided to subsets S_1, S_2, ..., S_j, where each subset includes certificates revoked in independent time period, as folows:

S_1 – certificates revoked between t_0(t = 0) and t_1 moments
S_2 – certificates revoked between t_1 and t_2
...
S_j – certificates revoked between t_{j-1} and t_j

The periods of time t_1, t_2, ..., t_j will be called closing stamps/indicators. Each closing stamp determines moment of closing of the old set and opening of the new one.Mentioned above periods of time are disjoint – there's no possibility to find one certificate placed into two different subsets S_i i S_j. In other words intersection of all subsets S_t is two elements set $\{l_0, l_\infty\}$. Time periods will be called rounds. The round RND_i will represent time period for t_i closing stamp.

On the bases of idea from 1.3 section it can be defined set of up-to-date revoked certificates for each round. This set $S_i{}'$ includes certificates revoked before t_i closing stamp and not expired before t_{i-1}.

It can be defined simpler format of revocation information for our scheme – (a_m, tr_m, te_m) – where: a_m is a serial number of revoked certificate, tr_m is a revocation time and te_m is an expiry time. Definitions of subsets S_i and $S_i{}'$ mentioned above may be now presented as follows:

$$a_m \in S_i \Leftrightarrow t_{i-1} < tr_m < t_i$$
$$a_m \in S_i{}' \Leftrightarrow tr_m < t_i \wedge te_m \geq t_{i-1}$$

2.2 Example of certificate subsets creation

The revocation of four certificates with serial numbers a_1, a_2, a_3 i a_4 is shown in Fig.2. For example certificate with serial number a_1 was revoked at a moment tr_1 and it's valid untill te_1.

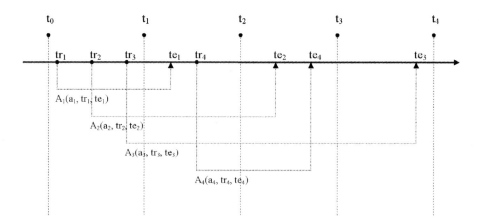

Fig. 2. Certificate revocations – time relationships

On the bases of S_i i S_i' definitions from 2.1 section it can be written as below:

$S_1 = (a_1, a_2, a_3)$ $S_1' = (a_1, a_2, a_3)$

$S_2 = (a_4)$ $S_2' = (a_1, a_2, a_3, a_4)$

$S_3 = \varnothing$ $S_3' = (a_2, a_3, a_4)$

$S_4 = \varnothing$ $S_3' = (a_3)$

2.3   Data structures proposal

For further consideration the most important are sets of up-to-date revoked certificates S_i'. Each set of that kind has a defined dictionary type data structure DS_i. Contents of a currently opened structure (closing time not occurred yet) is variable – next revocations may happen. Contents of archival structures (closing time occurred) is invariable. Two different data structure types are defined for these two different scenarios – Temporary Authenticated Dictionary (TAD) and Permanent Authenticated Dictionary (PAD).

Let RND_j be a current round and t_{j-1} be a opening time for this round. Starting from t_{j-1} all revocations are placed into a TAD_j. At the end of round RND_j all data from TAD_j will be used for archival PAD_j structure creation and TAD_j will be destroyed.

Temporary Authenticated Dictionary is a structure for most recent revocations. This dictionary is constructed successively with *Insert* function calls. The new proof is calculated after each insertion. Each insertion may cause necessity of rebalancing of the whole structure. Only two functions: *AuthSearch* and *Insert* are called during whole lifetime of TAD structure. Self-balancing structures (for example based on Skip List or RBST) should be used for this dictionary. The key is a certificate serial number. Additionally elements in TAD_j are organized on the list according revocation order.

Permanent Authenticated Dictionary is used for archival revocations storage. This dictionary is built with all elements at once (*Initialize* function). Also the authenticity proof (or proofs set) is generated on the beginning – after initialization stage. Only one function *AuthSearch* is called during the whole lifetime of PAD structure (after initialization). Balanced structure doesn't change – successfully we may use for it Merkle hash tree based on BST. On the PAD_j creation stage we used data from two sources: current (just closed) TAD_j and previous PAD_{j-1}. All elements from TAD_j (also with information about revocation order – revocation list) were taken. Only valid certificates (not yet expired) were taken from PAD_{j-1}. Data taken from PAD_{j-1} doesn't include revocation order information. Fig.3 shows the example of PAD.

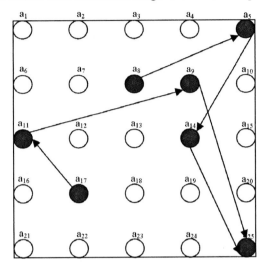

Fig.3. Example of elements dependencies within PAD_j. All elements are arranged with serial numbers: a_1, a_2, a_3, … White rings are revocations from PAD_{j-1}, black ones are revocations from TAD_i (with revocation order information)

2.4 Time division - rounds and subrounds

Every time when the new PAD structure is created the new authenticity proof is also generated. Each proof is linked with successive ones and then published. There's a conflict – on the one hand rounds should be long enough to collect many revocation into one structure and to prevent creation of too many archival structures, on the other hand proofs generated during structure closing should be published as frequently as possible. The solution may be dividing rounds into subrounds. Intermediate proof is generated and published in subround beginning. Subround end doesn't entail necessity of a current structure reconstruction.

The first of all time is split into rounds. The round duration isn't determined a priori - the end of each round is appointed by occurrence of specific events (length of each round probably will be different). Each round is split again into smaller pieces – subrounds. All subrounds should have the same length. The one and only exception is a case of CA key change - subrounds including this event may be shorter. An amount of subrounds in different rounds will be variable. This conception was shown in Fig.4.

In further consideration we will use four different sings for time points:

- t_r – it's a time of round RND_r closing
- $t_{r,s}$ – it's a time of subround $SRND_{r,s}$ closing (s subround of r round)
- $t_{r,s,c}$ – it's a time of revocation $REV_{r,s,c}$ creation (c revocation in s subround of r round)

- t_x' – round-independent time sign
  There's a dependency: $t_{r,0} = t_{r-1} = t_{r-1,last}$. For example in Fig.4: $t_{j,0} = t_{j-1} = t_{j-1,p}$.
  Subround ends if:
- maximum lifetime of subround was reached; or
- CA key pair was changed.

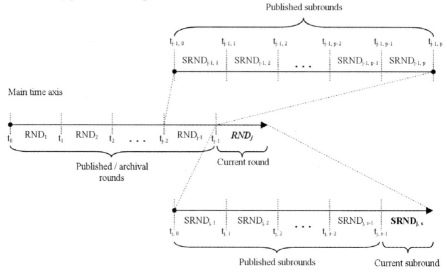

Fig.4. Division of time into rounds and subrounds

New intermediate proof $IP_{r,s}$ is calculated and published at the beginning of each subrond $SRND_{r,s}$. This proof is calculated mainly with the most recent revocation. Neither beginning nor end of a subround causes changes in data structures.

Round ends if end of current subround was reached and one of the following conditions was fulfilled:

- there's enough certificate revocations collected through all subrounds of current round for archival structure (PAD) creation; this account limit is the same for all rounds (exact way of limit determination is a bit more complex); or
- maximum lifetime of round was reached; or
- CA key pair was changed.

The empty TAD_r structure is created on the beginning of each round RND_r. The archival PAD_r structure is constructed with data from closed TAD_r when RND_r ends. Proof of an authenticity of PAD_r is used for calculation of Super Hash Value (SHV_r), which is published.

2.5 Data structures linking

The scheme of data structure linking is shown in Fig.5. Super Hash Value (SHV) calculated from recent PAD structure is published and used as an initial value on the list of revocation hashes created in TAD. Each newly added revocation is linked with previous value according scheme: $L_{r,s,c} = H(H(REV_{r,s,c}) \mid L_{r,s,c-1})$. At the beginning of each subround last linked hash value is published as an intermediate proof: $IP_{r,s} = L_{r,s-1,last}$. New SHV value will be created as follows: $SHV_r = H(P_r \mid L_{r,last,last} \mid SHV_{r-1})$

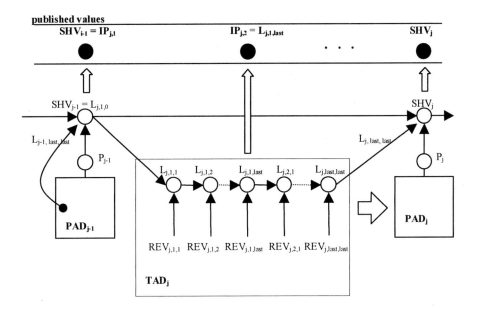

Fig.5. Linking scheme

3. SCHEME PROPOSAL – PROTOCOLS

3.1 Generation of public proofs

3.1.1 Super Hash Value generation

New structure PAD_j is created at the end of a round RND_j. Proof of an authenticity of this PAD_j with addidtional information is send from CA to Publisher:

$$CA \rightarrow TP: Sign_{SKCA(j)}\{P_j, L_{j,last,last}\}, CER_{CA(j+1)}$$

where: SKCA(j) is a CA secret key valid in RND_j round, P_j is an authenticity proof of PAD_j, $L_{j,last,last}$ is a linked hash value of a last revocation of last subround of j round, $CER_{CA(j+1)}$ is a CA certificate valid in new round RND_{j+1}.
Then TP calculates new SHV_j value:

$$SHV_j = H(P_j \mid L_{j,last,last} \mid SHV_{j-1})$$

After all TP publishes package ($SHV_j, CER_{CA(j+1)}$).

3.1.2 Intermediate Proof generation

At the subround $SRND_{j,s}$ beginning CA sends to the TP linked hash $L_{j,s-1,last}$ value of most recent revocation: $L_{j,s-1,last} = H(HV_{j,s-1,last} \mid L_{j,s-1,last-1})$. This value will be treated as Intermediate Proof for this subround ($IP_{j,s} = L_{j,s-1,last}$):

$$CA \rightarrow TP: Sign_{SKCA(j)}\{IP_{j,s}\}$$

Then TP publishes $IP_{j,s}$ value.

3.2 Certificate revocation

User U sends to the CA signed certificate CER_m:

$$U \rightarrow CA: Sign_{SKU}\{CER_m\}$$

Then CA creates revocation information REV_m' for supplied certificate CER_m:

$$REV_m' = \{a_m, te_m, tr_m, r, s, c\} = REV_{r, s, c}$$

This information consist of: revoked certificate serial number (a_m), certificate validity time (te_m), revocation time (tr_m), current round number (r), current subround number (s) and revocation number within current subround (c). Then CA calculates hash of revocation information:

$$HV_m' = HV_{r,s,c} = H(REV_{r,s,c})$$

and linked this value with previous one:

$$L_m' = L_{r,s,c} = H(HV_{r,s,c} \mid L_{r,s,c-1})$$

where $L_{r,0,0} = SHV_{r-1}$ and $L_{r,s,0} = IP_{r,s-1} = L_{r,s-1,last}$.

CA places revocation info REV_m with values L_m' and HV_m' into a current TAD_r (*Insert* operation). The proof of authenticity of this new element and proof for whole structure are generated. Actualization package for TAD_r is spread among directories.

Then CA sends to the user U a proof of revocation in the same form as in certificate status verification (exactly it's a proof a presence of certificate revocation of a_m serial number in TAD$_r$):

$$CA \rightarrow U: \{a_m, pr_m\}$$

where a_m is a serial number and pr_m is a presence proof. CA may also send list of hashes needed for order verification. List starts from newly revoked certificate and it ends on first hash generated after recent IP issue (reversed order):

$$CA \rightarrow U: \{HV_{r,s,c}, HV_{r,s,c-1}, \dots, HV_{r,s,1}\}$$

3.3 Certificate status verification

Let t_j' be a current time and t_{j-1} be a beginning of a current RND_j round. Requestor R sends to Directory D serial number a_m of wanted certificate:

$R \rightarrow D: a_m$

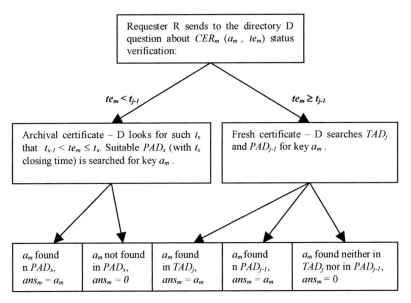

Fig.6. Certificate status verification scheme

Directory D looks for this certificate and first of all checks its validity time te_m. Further proceedings are shown in Fig.6.

After all directory D returns to the requester R package:

$D \rightarrow R: \{ans_m, pr_m\}$

where ans_m is an answer (serial number of looked for certificate or value 0) and pr_m is a proof for this answer (proof of presence or absence). Proof pr_m was generated after *Initialize* (in PAD) or after *Insert* (in TAD) by CA and it's an integral part of authenticated dictionary (see 1.2 section).

3.4 Certificate revocation order verification

Let t_j' be a current time and t_{j-1} be a beginning of a current RND_j round. Requestor R sends to Directory D serial number a_m of wanted certificate:

$R \rightarrow D: a_m$

First of all directory D looks for an REV_m information in possessed data structures and proceed according scheme shown in Fig.7.

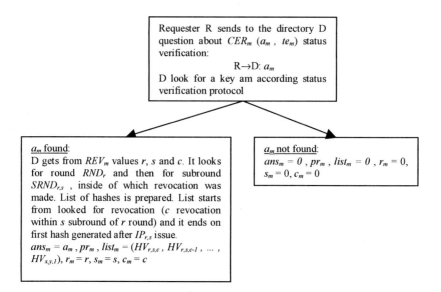

Fig. 7. Certificate revocation order verification scheme

After all directory D returns to requester R package:

D→R: $\{ans_m, pr_m, r_m, s_m, c_m, list_m\}$

REFERENCES

[1] Paul Kocher. *A Quick Introduction to Certificate Revocation Trees*(CRTs). Technical report, ValiCert, 1999.

[2] Michael T. Goodrich, Roberto Tamassia. *Efficient Authenticated Dictionaries with Skip Lists and Commutative Hashing.* Technical Report, Johns Hopkins Information Security Institute, 2000.

[3] Moni Naor, Kobbi Nissim. *Certificate Revocation and Certificate Update.* Proceedings 7th USENIX Security Symposium (San Antonio, Texas), 1998

[4] Chip Martel, Glen Nuckolls, Prem Devanbu, Michael Gertz, April Kwong, Stuart G. Stubblebine. *A General Model for Authenticated Data Structures.* Technical Report CSE-2001-9, 2001

[5] Włodzimierz Chocianowicz, Witold Maćków, Jerzy Pejaś. *Protocols of revocation and status verification methods for public key certificates.*, RSA Conference, Paris. 2002

[6] Silvio Micali. Efficient Certificate Revocation. Technical report, Massachusetts Institute of Technology, 1996

[6] Ahto Buldas, Peeter Laud, Helger Lipmaa, Jan Villemson. *Time-Stamping with Binary Linking Schemes.* Advances on Cryptology --- CRYPTO '98. 1998

Integrated Payment System for Public Key Infrastructure Services
Network Electronic Payment System for Public Key Infrastructure Service Providers (nEPSKIP)

IMED EL FRAY, JERZY PEJAŚ
Faculty of Computer Science & Information Systems, Department of Programming Techniques, Technical University of Szczecin, 49, Żołnierska st., 71-210 Szczecin, Poland, phone (+48 91)449 56 62, e-mail: {ielfray, jpejas}@wi.ps.pl

Abstract: Public Key Infrastructure (PKI) service providers need a simple, open, flexible and secure payment system. There are many transactions related with the PKI services, which are characterized by low unit price. Therefore it is obvious the mechanisms of a client's service used by any PKI service provider should cost no more than expected cash receipts. This paper examines the types of payment system used nowadays, the PKI payment system requirements, an overview of the Network Electronic Payment System for Public Key Infrastructure Service Providers (nEPSKIP) that has been developed, and a summary of how this system meet the requirements.

Key words: public key infrastructure, electronic payment system, secure network system

1. INTRODUCTION

Issuing a certificate (including also a qualified certificate) for a public-key of any entity allows him or her the generation of electronic signatures. The electronic signatures are the proofs of signed documents authenticity and make the authentication of signing entity possible, but on other hand make many troubles for the signature recipient (and also the verifier of its authenticity). The signature verification procedure is computationally difficult and usually time consuming[1] and

---

[1] They require the gathering of all needed public-key certificates and certificate revocation lists (CRL), which allow firstly to build the certification path leading from so called trusted point to verified signing entity certificate in mind, and then to verify the validity of each

this is the reason why it should be expected, that this procedure will determine the main bounds in commercial using of electronic signatures. Fortunately, the ideas and also ready for use solutions are developed parallely to simplify the signature verification process. Generally the market needs the new type of PKI service providers which will render services such as time stamping, certificate status and certification path verification, electronic signature validation, etc. Accessibility of such services should make easier the design processes of electronic signature applications and their implementation in practice. Consequently, this should result in increasing the amount of persons using the electronic signature and being also the customers of certification service providers. Assuming the most of certification service transactions will be offered for extremely small fee, the service provider will be in trouble: the running provider's costs must be low, it means the payment process should be arranged in such a way that settlement accounts of widely used PKI services must cost significantly less than the total payments of all service users and should not involve essential difficulty in usage of this services (e.g. there is no need for user to register as a legal user of PKI services).

It is obvious that PKI Service Providers require a payment system to support their financial applications. Such system should be [HOG96]:

- flexible (not limited to monetary payments),
- *free* (usage of the system not dictated by the owners),
- simple - (no complex protocols involved),
- secure (resistant to theft of money),
- offered a high degree of privacy for the consumer,
- maintained enough records for auditing purposes.

Additionally the payment system can be a component of a provider's service infrastructure or can be managed by independent party, conducting the financial clearing on behalf of many PKI service providers.

The general assumptions mentioned above concern the majority elements of proposed payment system called Network Electronic Payment System for Public Key Infrastructure Service Providers (nEPSKIP). Our target is to obtain the system covering four the most common means used in payment systems:

- electronic coins,
- remote micro payments,
- electronic cheques,
- electronic transfers.

Taking into account the features stated above, the nEPSKIP payment system is extremely flexible and the size of the payments could range from cents to several hundred dollars or more.

The further feature of the system is its clearing and settlement mechanism, which is used between user, vendor and banks. The traditional method of billing involves billers generating a paper bill and posting it to their customers, via mail, for

---

certificate belonging to this path. The similar operation should be performed in the case when the signature is related with time-stamp token, non-repudiation of delivery token, etc.

review and payment. In contrary, Network Electronic Payment System for Public Key Infrastructure Service Providers (nEPSKIP) delivers bills from billers to customers via a digital delivery channel (e.g. Internet). Additionally, to be able to view the bill electronically, the customer can also settle the bill using existing electronic payment methods. The nEPSKIP system removes the costly 'paper delivery' of today's billing process, saves billers money and ensures the convenience for the customer.

In the paper the idea of micro payments for the settlement of mass used PKI services with low unit price was proposed as well. This idea is closely related to PayWord protocol published in 1996 by R. Rivest and A. Shamir [RSH96]. The user must set up a financial account with a broker (pays real money) and then a broker issues to a user a "virtual card" (public key certificate with payment limit). This certificate authenticates user to vendor and is a guaranty due to which a broker assumes responsibility for paying user's debts.

From that moment the user generates the chain of micropayments (payments token) with value needed and attaches it to the request each time when he or she requires an access to some PKI service. In result, if the token is legitimate, a vendor accepts the request for a service and PKI service provider issues the proper response.

The main advantage of such a solution is that there is no need to make registration with PKI service provider: the user should have the proper certificate only.

2. PAYMENT MODELS[2]

There are three types of players in our scheme: issuers, users and vendors. An issuer (a broker, a bank) is an entity that operates the payment service and holds the items that the payments represent (for example cash held in regular bank accounts). The users of the payment service are making payments, while the vendor is receiving payments.

2.1 Electronic Coin Model

The objective of electronic coin systems is to emulate physical cash. An issuer attempts to do this by creating of digital token monies (usually called coins), which are then purchased (or withdrawn) by the users, who then redeem (deposit) them with the issuer at a later date. In the interim token monies can be transferred between users in order to trade them for goods or services.

In order that the token monies can take on some of the attributes of physical cash, techniques can be used so that when a token money is deposited, the issuer cannot determine the original withdrawer of the token money. This provides the electronic token monies with unconditional untraceability [CFN88].

---

[2] This description of payment models (excluding the micropayment model) is based on the work of Howland [HOG96].

Electronic coin systems can be hard to implement in practice, due to the overheads of solving the *double spending* problem (to prevent the double deposit of the same coin by the user).

2.2   Remote electronic micropayments model

Remote electronic micropayments model can be considered as a special case of the electronic coin model applicable when payments for services are small, e.g. cents per transaction. To support micropayments the cash generation, withdrawal and deposit must be significantly simplified hence the computational overhead is not expensive.

Parties involved in a micropayment protocol are users, vendors and issuers (brokers). Brokers authorize users to make micropayments to vendors and redeem the payments collected by the vendors. A user always adds a micropayment to a service request. All micropayments (in a form of independent or linked tokens) are collected by a vendor and are a foundation for the clearing between the vendor and the broker.

2.3   Electronic Cheque Model

Electronic cheque systems reflect "real cheques" quite well, and therefore are relatively simple to understand and implement. A user fills an electronic cheque out, which is the signed digitally payment instruction. This is transferred to another user, who then deposits it with the issuer. The issuer verifies the user's signature on the payment, and transfers the funds from the user's account to the vendor's account.

2.4   Electronic Transfer Model

Electronic transfer systems are the simplest one among the four payment models considered. The user simply creates a payment transfer instruction, signs it digitally and sends it to the issuer. Then the issuer verifies the signature on the request and performs the transfer.

3.   REQUIREMENTS

Developed payment system nEPSKIP fulfils the following assumption:
- Settlements for services are made with accuracy to an individual person (individual settlements).
- Each client of PKI services provider has an application (which particularly is essential to contact with nEPSKIP system only or is integrated with other more complex application).
- Before the usage of PKI services each user has to be registered in nEPSKIP system or has to possess micropayment tokens set up with broker (from home or external payment domain); an individual or group registration (see Section 4.1) is performed electronically.

- When the registration of an user or a micropayment token is completed propitiously the system issues to a user a special public-key certificate used in the process of her or his authentication by means of SSL/TLS protocol; this certificate contains entries bounding their use to an identity identification and total payment limit per some defined period; the private key can be stored in a trusted place (e.g. a smart card with crypto processor or protected key storage).
- SSL/TLS protocol should be used for mutual authentication; when mutual authentication is completes positively then the user's application is allowed to send requests for PKI services.

Firstly, all four payment models defined in Section 2 have been considered. Finally it was decided to reject the electronic coin payment model (for the reasons presented in Section 2.1). The features of three payment models selected for an implementation has been used for the resultant composition of nEPSKIP system, which helps the user to perform:

- electronic/traditional funds transfer from the user's account to the vendor's account against the electronic/paper invoice for each user that use PKI services,
- traditional funds transfer to the vendor's account (based on an electronic invoice for a PKI service subscription),
- filling out an electronic cheque, which is an instruction to pay money to a vendor,
- micropayments using a mobile phone, electronic micropayments schemes (credit-based or prepayd schemes), etc.

4.   ARCHITECTURE OF nEPSKIP SYSTEM

The nEPSKIP system consists of the following functional modules (see Fig.1):

- registration module – an element that is responsible for a registration of new system users, micropayment tokens and PKI services provided by system,
- authentication and authorization module – limits the access to system resources to users with proper permissions only and controls (authorizes) the PKI services which are rendered accessible for their benefit,
- database module – maintains the data related to registered system users and micropayment tokens, types of services, unit prices per service, PKI service providers, user's outstanding payments and theirs remittances,
- accessible services – contains the current PKI services table that describes the type of service, its PKI service provider and the way that service can be accessed (e.g. URL address),
- billing module – manages the services settlement process, the issuing electronic invoices and acceptance of fund transfers (including pre·payments), electronic cheques or micropayments prepared in cooperation with a broker's module (optionally with GSM operator),
- broker's module – on the base of user's approval makes the payments for services on his or her behalf, i.e. makes out the funds transfer request from a user's account to a PKI service provider's account, carries out the clearing

between brokers from other payment domain, issues public key certificates for registered users.

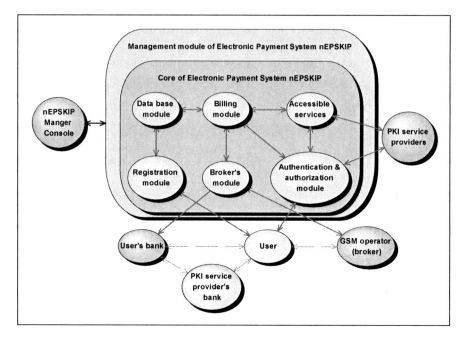

Figure 1. Architecture of the nEPSKIP system

All modules of nEPSKIP system are managed using a manager's console, tightly coupled with the management module.

PKI services users, PKI service providers, GSM operators (as the brokers) and users' banks interact directly with nEPSKIP system. The only active subject is a user, which forces an information exchange with another subjects existing in an environment of nEPSKIP system.

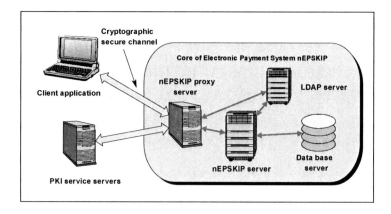

Figure 2. Client-server model of the nEPSKIP system

The implementation of nEPSKIP system is based on a client-server model (Fig.2). A client is directly connected to *nEPSKIP proxy server*, which authenticates user, checks his or her permissions and finally permits (after positive authorization) the access to the requested service.

4.1 Registration

There are two categories of payers defined in nEPSKIP system: personal payers and group payers (e.g. organizations, companies, etc.). A personal payer registers himself or herself in the system, nEPSKIP system administrator registers a group payer on the basis of previously signed agreement (in a paper or an electronic form, the latter is made using the qualified certificate [DEP93, DSF00]). This administrator acts due to the permission of a group payer and is responsible for a further administration of group payer members accounts, e.g. for registration of a new group member (a member's registration request should be confirmed by an authorized representative of a group payer). Thereafter, each member's request for access to some PKI service will be associated with a member's account, but payments will be associated with a group payer only.

The nEPSKIP system requires the following data to be registered: a login and a pass phrase, a name of the user and his/her address, contact details (a mobile phone number, an email address), personal details, preferred payment models, authentication types (see Section 4.2).

Once the user completes the registration process, nEPSKIP server generates asymmetric key pair and issues a public key certificate for him. A certificate is published in LDAP directory, which belongs to an owner of this one and then is delivered together with a private key (encrypted using a key derived from a pass phrase) to a user for his/her e-mail address. After reception of e-mail a user can decrypt a private key and then write it into well-protected memory or a smart card with crypto processor.

The user comes to an agreement with the nEPSKIP system owner at the registration stage. This agreement can be signed electronically (if the user has the qualified public key certificate) or handwritten (when the paper-agreement can be sent to the user's contact address). The signing of an agreement activates the user's account and all services he/she needs.

We assume that the user's personal data are not verified in nEPSKIP system. A user is worthy of belief in so far as his/her pays bills regularly. To reduce the risk of potential losses nEPSKIP system locks a user's account when his/her debt exceeds a predefined limit and unlocks it when debt is paid. Additionally, for users who don't pay their bills, new certificates for the next payment period won't be issued.

4.2 Authentication and authorization

Two various authentication methods are implemented in nEPSKIP system: basic mutual authentication and auxiliary unilateral authentication.

Basic mutual authentication is carried out by SSL/TLS protocol using X.509 certificates, which are exchanged between communicating machines (client and server) when they initiate connections. The authentication is carried out by the server attempting to verify its identity to the user, and is requested by the server to prove user's identity as well. As the result mutual authentication establishes trust and cryptographic channel between the user (more correctly, between a client acting on behalf of the user) and the server. The server can confirm the source of the certificate and, providing the source is reputable, client has the confidence that the server user is sending his/her private details to the intended recipient.

Unilateral authentication is based on the SASL mechanisms (both ISO/IEC 9798-3 authentication scheme [ZNY01] and the one-time-password system [NEW98]). The purpose of this is to establish the authentication and to prove the identity of the user only.

In this case when nEPSKIP system user works in an administration mode, basic mutual authentication and unilateral authentication are used always together, i.e. the user checks the state of his/her payments, performs operations based on a broker's module, activates/deactivates the PKI services, etc. Such combination of the user authentication mechanisms enables a server which user deals with to establish confidence in the case when user don't store a private key (see Section 4.1) in a smart card with a crypto processor.

Basic mutual authentication is used in an operational mode only. Therefore, nEPSKIP proxy server doesn't make any modification of a service request, e.g. a request for a time stamp token is sent to Time Stamping Authority (TSA, see [ZNY01]) and is forwarded (of course, this concerns the request after authorization only) directly to the intended PKI provider.

Each request for any operation running in an administrative or operational mode is authorized. In an operational mode PKI service can be allowed only if an authorization system has checked that a user was in possession of proper rights and has been paying bills regularly or has registered a valid payment token (see Section 4.3). Note that here having no valid public key certificate issued by the nEPSKIP system means a negative authorization of any user's operations (including these one which are making in an administrative mode). An essential problem of a request authorization in an administrative mode is related with monitoring of operations undertaken by nEPSKIP system administrator and legal payers.

Also the default account is defined in nEPSKIP system. This account allows users to provide the commitment to a new user-specific and vendor-specific mircopayment scheme (see Section 4.3) and his/her certificate issued by any trusted broker. A user with registered commitment can send (after mutual authentication) an access request for a service like any other registered system user. A user account clearing is based on the information exchange between the home domain and the external domain broker's modules.

4.3   Payments (billing and broker)

The following payment scenarios are possible with the nEPSKIP system: (a) an electronic invoice creation, e.g. monthly, (b) a prepayment transfer directly to a service provider account, (c) a money transfer for micropayments using mobile phones.

An electronic invoice is filled out for the registered system user or the broker from an external domain (in the case of micropayments). When the user or the broker makes the money transfer for proper accounts of PKI service providers, nEPSKIP system issues and sends an invoice in the paper form. There is possible to use another solution: the broker's module sends the payment request to the user's bank or the broker from the external domain. Then, the bank or the external broker sends this request to the client's (i.e. the user's or the broker's) mobile phone with a feature enabling a client to make an electronic signature of a request and confirm his/her acceptance of a money transfer to the provider's (the vendor's) account.

A value of the user's account is increased each time when a prepayment is transferred by the service user to nPSKIP system and is decreased while a user spends money for some PKI service. A small debt doesn't block the user's access to his/her account: further requests for services are sold on a credit and must be cleared immediately after the reception of an invoice.

In third scenario an access to a desired service is possible only if the user confirms a payment sent to his/her mobile phone. This confirmation has SMS form and must be delivered to a special info number. Then, PKI service provider and GSM operator are involved into a financial clearing between them.

The broker's module plays an important role in the designed payment system. The importance of this role can be shown especially in the case of micropayments. Let us assume, that two different instances of nEPSKIP system are working in a global network, each one being owned by two different PKI service providers (e.g., Provider A and Provider B). Let Provider B provides time-stamping services not offered by Provider A. The client, which is already registered in nEPSKIP system of Provider A and wants to use time-stamping services without necessity to be registered again by Provider B should follow the steps presented below:

- Using the proper application the user builds two-layered accumulated linear linking mircopayment scheme[3] (see Fig.3), where all payments (H_i, $i = 1, 2, ..., n$) are divided into rounds of equal degree (i.e. they should contain the same, e.g. N, number of payments per round).
  To generate the values of L_i and H_j the following two relation are used, respectively (l_0 and s_0 – two arbitrary chosen random number, r_{max} – the number of rounds):

$$L_i = \begin{cases} l_o, & i = 1 \\ h\left(L_{i-1}, H_{n-(N-1)(i-1)+1}\right), & i = 2,\ldots,r_{max} \end{cases} \tag{1}$$

$$H_j = \begin{cases} s_0, & j = n \\ h\left(H_{j+1}, h\left(L_i, H_{j+1}\right)\right), & j = n-(N-1)(i-1), i = 1,\ldots,r_{max} \\ h\left(H_{j+1}\right), & j = n-1,\ldots,0 \wedge j \neq n-(N-1)(i-1) \end{cases} \tag{2}$$

---

[3] The concept of this scheme type was inspired by a similar scheme used, for example, in the systems of unforgeable time-stamping tokens creation (see [LIP99])

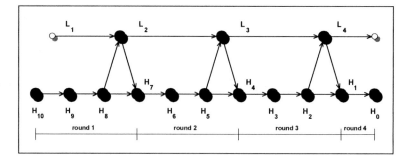

Figure 3. A two-layered accumulated linear linking mircopayment scheme for N = 4

- The created payment tokens permit the user to get PKI service subscription (e.g. a time-stamping service), delivered by Provider B; to achieve this goal a user computes his/her commitment for that service:

$$M = \left\{ V, C_U, H_0, L_1, \ldots, L_{r_{max}}, D, I_M \right\}_{sigU} \tag{3}$$

where: V – a vendor name (Provider B), C_U – a user's public key certificate issued by a broker which belongs to Provider A domain (this certificate may contain a credit limit per vendor to be applied), D – expiration date of the commitment, I_M – extra information (n – a number of a payment unit, N – a number of a payment unit per round, r_{max} – a number of rounds), sigU – a user's digital signature.

A commitment is a user's declaration to pay Provider B for any of the payment token H_i, that Provider B redeems with a broker from Provider A domain before date D.

- Now, a user must attach a succeeding payment token from some payments sequence to each request which will be sent to Provider B, where jth payment consists of the pair (H_j, j); a vendor can verify this payment using H_{j-1} payment and optionally a checkpoint L_i to ensured H_{j-1} payment belongs to ith round.

An algorithm (called TL-ALLMS algorithm) for creation of a two-layered accumulated linear linking mircopayment scheme is described below.

Algorithm: Two-Layered Accumulated Linear Linking Mircopayment Scheme (TL-ALLMS)
INPUT: n – a total number of payment tokens, N - a constant known to the user and vendor, means the number of payment tokens per round, h – a collision resistant hash functions.
OUTPUT: a sequence of the pairs (H_i, i), $i = n-1, .., 0$ which are used as a payment tokens and checkpoints $L_j, j=1, .., r_{max}$, where r_{max} means a number of rounds.
Let $i = 1$.
For $j = n-1, n-2, \ldots, 0$ execute
if $j = n - (N-1)(i-1)$ then

$$H_j = h(H_{j+1}, h(L_i, H_{j+1}))$$
$$i = i + 1$$
$$L_i = h(L_{i-1}, H_{j+1})$$
else
$$H_j = h(H_{j+1}).$$

Store a number of rounds $r_{max} = i$; this value should fulfil the following inequality:

$$n - r_{max}*(N - 1) \leq 0$$

End of Algorithm.

When all payment tokens are spent by the user, at the end of each day (or other suitable period) the vendor sends broker from domain of Provider A the redemption message which consists of the commitment (eq. (3)) received from user and last payment $P_m = (H_m, m)$. This rule is similar to those used in PayWord micropayment scheme (see [RSH96]), but the verification mechanism applied in TL-ALLMS algorithm is faster. The verification of last payment P_m in PayWord system always requires m calculation of hash function values; particularly, when $m = n$, then the verification process requires n and maximum $N-1$ calculation of hash function values for PayWord and TL-ALLMS schemes, respectively.

3.1 Messages exchange protocol

Now, all communications with nEPSKIP system are established over secure HTTP (HTTPS protocol) connections and should allow many corporate users access from behind their company firewall. The user applies this protocol in an administration and an operational mode as well.

HTTPS protocol is used to deliver requests and pass receipts, and other information (from and to the user). All requests and receipts are kept by nEPSKIP system.

With the structure of information headers presented on the Fig.4 nEPSKIP proxy server is responsible directly for receiving and redirecting requests from the user to the proper PKI service providers and responses to user as well.

```
Content-Type: application/timestamp-query
    <<the ASN.1 DER-encoded Time-Stamp Request message>>
```

Figure 4. The time-stamp request based on HTTP protocol

4. SECURITY

The information exchange between nEPSKIP system and environment components which the system interacts with, is carrying on always via cryptographically secure channels based on SSL/TLS protocol. These channels are built between a user's application and nEPSKIP proxy server when both parts are positively mutually authenticated before. There is only one case when cryptographic channel is created after unilateral authentication – it concerns the remote registration of a personal payer.

A mutual authentication is intended to protect against a user's false denial of the usage of the particular services – a nobody who doesn't possess a user's private key, which belongs to the same pair as a public key issued to him/her as a public key certificate, is not able to gain access to a user's account. To obtain a higher assurance level a user should digitally sign all information (requests), e.g. according to CMS requirements [CMS02]. Because all responses created by nEPSKIP system are signed too, hence the user has evidences which can be useful if a dispute arises as to whether the user has signed a request (caused by either a lying signer trial to repudiate a created signature, or by a fraudulent claimant); in such cases an unbiased third party should be able to resolve the matter equitably, without requiring access to the user's secret information.

5. CONCLUSIONS AND FUTURE WORK

It is shown in the paper that a network payment system nEPSKIP can be integrated with PKI services with different unit prices (but rather small, on a level close to micro payments). Thanks to such approach the user can gain access to all services provided by a system and trace her or his payments as well. The proposed solution allows also PKI services provider to decrease its operating costs, especially these related to charge payments from PKI services users.

The nEPSKIP system needs not be treated as a component of PKI service provider infrastructure. This means, that also independent third parties (e.g. a broker) can manage nEPSKIP system. Nevertheless, a TL-ALLMS micro payment mechanism embedded into a system allows to make it open to another users beyond domain of a given third party.

The nEPSKIP system requires further works. Particularly, we see the need to embed the electronic coin model into a service system. To realize this feature the nEPSKIP system should be more (than currently) integrated with bank systems as well as changes should be introduced into national regulation concerning legal acceptance of such payment model in different countries. Using Simple Object Access Protocol (SOAP) we plan also to redesign the system protocols.

The experiences with nEPSKIP system show that a centralized payment system for PKI services is not a right solution; instead of this we should built distributed payment systems rather and the solution more focused on the user of such a system.

ACKNOWLEDGMENTS

The author would like to thank Unizeto Ltd. (Poland) for its permission to publish the partial results of the work we have done together up to date and to many people from this company for a great deal to the work presented in this paper, especially for their useful comments and advice.

REFERENCES

[HOG96] **Howland G.** *Development of an Open and Flexible Payment System*, November 1996, http://www.systemics.com/docs/sox/overview.html

[CFN88] **Chaum** D., **Fiat** A., & **Naor** M. *Untraceable Electronic Cash*, Advances in Cryptology CRYPTO '88, S. Goldwasser (Ed.), Springer-Verlag, pp. 319-327.

[DEP93] **EC** *Directive 1999/93/EC of the European Parliament and the of the Council of 13 December on a Community framework for electronic signatures*

[DSF00] **ETSI** *Digital Signature Format*, European Telecommunications Standards Institute (ETSI), Technical Specifications, ETSI TS 101 733 V1.2.2, October 2000

[ZNY01] **Zuccherato** R., **Nystrom** M. *ISO/IEC 9798-3 Authentication SASL Mechanism*, RFC 3161, August 2001

[NEW98] **Newman** C. *The One-Time-Password SASL Mechanism*, RFC 2444, October 1998.

[SHS93] **FIPS Publication** 180 *Secure Hash Standard (SHS)*, National Institute of Standards and Technology (NIST), May 11, 1993.

[LIP99] **Lipmaa** H. *Secure and efficient time-stamping systems*, PhD Thesis, Departament of Mathematics, University of Tartu, Estonia, 1999

[RSH96] **Rivest** R.L., **Shamir** A. *PayWord and MicroMint:Two simple micropayment schemes*, CryptoBytes,Vol.2, No 1 (RSA Laboratories, Spring 1996), pp 7-11, http://theory.lcs.mit.edu/~rivest/RivestShamir-mpay.pdf

[CMS02] **Housley** R. *Cryptographic Message Syntax (CMS)*, RFC 3369, August 2002

Some methods of the analysis and risk assessment in the PKI system services providers

JERZY PEJAŚ, IMED EL FRAY
Uuniversity of Szczecin, Faculty of Computer Science
ul. Żołnierska 49, 71-210 Szczecin, Poland, e-mail:{jpejas;ielfray}@wi.ps.pl

Abstract: The PKI systems are one of the main components in the information exchange between employees and customers of the enterprise, and firms as well. Depending on current routing boards, the information which needs to be send can be transferred using many different telecommunication systems. To ensure the confidentiality of the information, the uniform safety policy for the whole enterprise should be defined. Correctly prepared and implemented security policy comprises the rules of authorization for physical access to rooms and objects, and the rules of authorization for access to the network resources as well. As the technical infrastructure introduces the uniform policy, the cryptographical systems can be used, with PKI systems in particular. The PKI system requires the creation of a suitable infrastructure for generation, storage and distribution of keys and certificates. In this article, authors will try to analyze vulnerabilities and threats for the individual components of the PKI infrastructure based on MEHARI method of the risk analysis, which are estimated on a real example. Since even the best system will not guarantee the confidence of users' keys issued by the Certification Authority, the analysis and assessment is not restricted only to PKI components, but also to the working environment. When subsidiaries of this infrastructure are able to compromise the keys, the whole infrastructure becomes a useless equipment and software storage

Key words: PKI systems, risk analysis

1. INTRODUCTION

The growth of the interest in issuing the public key certificates (as being a safe infrastructure in case of increasing danger, which comes out from the use of the internet) has had a great impact on numerous efforts undertaken by government institutions and companies for the implementation as well as creation of commercial solutions in this field. It is well known, that the security is like a chain - it is as strong as its weakest element [1]. Therefore, security of the PKI system encounters many problems, which from their nature are not always connected with the cryptography. It's mostly the people, who are involved in majority of the problems. The following question appears: does the solution relay too much on the people and on their honesty and ability to predict all undesirable situations? Except on the dependence on the people, many solutions relays on the computer systems. Therefore, the next question arises: whether those systems are sufficiently safe and do they continuously collaborate with each other? All these and other questions give some picture of the system and show what is the risk relevant to the usage of the PKI services.

The nature of the risk related to the PKI infrastructure is different. Part of them is of technical significance and is based on various technical aspects, another in turn, is based on the problem of mutual trust between participating parties as well as confidence to the substantial technological solutions. The only and not trivial problem in this case will be the risk assessment as well as his estimation. The risk can be calculated from the mathematical methods, which use some basic concepts related to them, such as: assets, vulnerabilities, threats, countermeasures, etc. It can also be based on perception of some threats not necessarily evidenced by the analysis (as a result of conducted audit). It is hard to neglect any of these methods, therefore the solution complying both of these approaches is necessary. One of the methods considering presented attitude is the MEHARI method [2]. The result of use of this method is the assignment of the areas, which pose a threat for the PKI system.

2. METHODOLOGY USED IN THE RISK ANALYSIS

The MEHARI risk analysis method uses knowledge concerned identification and determination of the value of the resources, determination of threat level and susceptibility of resources to such threats. The analysis is concentrated mainly on three areas connected with the security (integrity, confidentiality and availability). The strategy of the risk analysis according to MEHARI consists of three phases [2]:

–   *Strategic security plan* – its aim is to set security objectives for the company, so that all actions which are undertaken and implemented throughout   the company, work toward the same objectives and protect resources depending on their classification,
–   *Security operational plan* – realization of security objectives defined in previous phase, by performing tasks suggested in present plan in given organizational unit, which come off a risk analysis either through analytical approach or through global approach in every autonomous unit (services audio or security measures assessment as show in Fig. 1,
–   *Company operational plan* – it concerns the consolidation of security actions undertaken in every unit. It is the phase where security indicators must be implemented in order to follow the trends in the overall company security level and monitor company's sensitive and sore points.

Two approaches suggested in the operational security plan are necessary to perform correct risk analysis. The analytical approach is based on detailed audit of the security of the firm. As a result, the direct conclusions and recommendations related to the security needs for every kind of threat can be obtained. In turn, the global approach depends on the potentiality and impact of the envisaged scenario (the set of questions related to risk factors). From the values of risk seriousness associated with each scenario, the security needs are concluded in this approach.

From the analysis of two values derived from the analysis, risk seriousness is determined:

- *Impact value* – it is the function of resource value (based on classification) and the effect of operations which decrease (reduce) the impact of threat on resources with respect to every security criteria (availability, integrity and confidentiality).

- *Potentiality value* - is solely dependant on the efficiency of planned operations with respect to eg. an environment of given resource (natural, being as a result of the mistake or malignity).

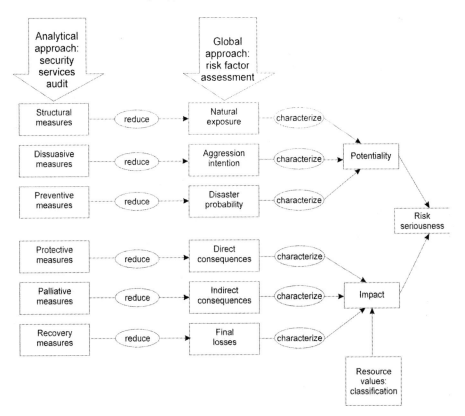

Fig. 1. Representation of the analytical and global approaches in the risk analysis [2]

3. PROJECT OF THE COMPUTER NETWORK WHICH PROVIDES PKI SERVICES

The PKI structure consists of three main elements [3]:
- *Registration Authority – RA,* verifies user information and registers them.
- *Certification Authority - CA,* issues numerical certificates. This action is proceeded by the identification of the applicant. Positive verification of the application is finished along with issuing certificate signed with the date of its examination.
- *Repository Keys, Certificate Revocation Lists - CRLs.* Typical implementation which enables to access the CRL certificates based on the LDAP, X.500, HTTP and FTP protocols.

Based on the structure mentioned above, an exemplary PKI network was created. The main problem of the project was to separate the three parties, which take part in issuing process and main the operation on qualified certificates afterwards. It concerns mainly the Certification Authority (CA), the Registration Authority (RA) and Trusted Third Part (TTP) as well. The network is designed in order to safely service certificates and the internet is used for communication between all required party. This situation is presented in Fig. 2 (in our project we concentrated basically on the Certification Authority network, CA).

As it is illustrated in Fig. 2, an exemplary CA network is a bisegmental internal network. The first segment is the part of a network, where WWW and LDAP servers are located. This is the only part of CA which can be accessed from the outside and which every user can connect to. All servers situated in this zone can communicate between each other without any obstacles. However, the network movement to and from the Internet, as well as the movement to the CA server is suitably limited. A so called 'logs server' which records all information from the servers as well as administrator's console was connected to all servers in this zone. In the second segment of a network, the main server issuing certificates is located. This is the most safe fragment of a network and nobody from the outside can access it. The main server issuing certificates and so called, the time gauge server (TS) is located in this segment. Similarly to the external segment, the log server and the administrator's console can also be found. Presented in Figure 2, when [nie wiem do końca czy to jest dobrze?] designing the network we applied the requirements of communication with the use of "security lockage" between WWW servers and the Internet. In our exemplary network we separetly used 'hardware firewalls' and the routers with an option of filtration of the network movement.

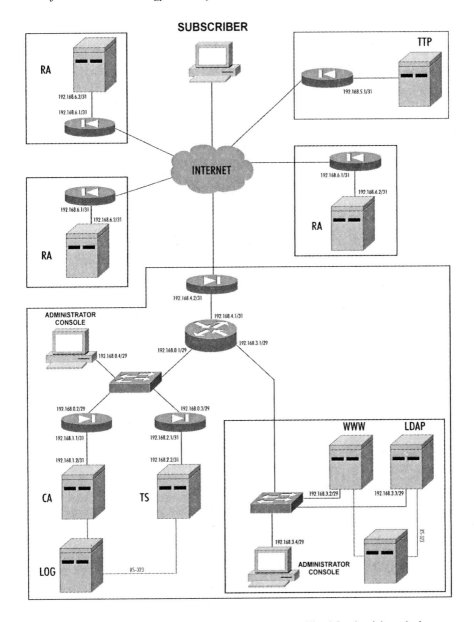

Fig. 2. An exemplary computer network of the CA utilized for the risk analysis

For the purpose of the risk analysis, the interface of Internet supplier is directly connected to the firewall which will protect the entire CA network against improper access. Right after the first "firewall", the main router is located. It is configured in a way, that it only allows trafic directed to the web server, while rejecting other packages. The WWW and LDAP servers are connected to the router through the switches, while the main CA server and the time gauge server are connected through the internal firewalls. Both servers have independent firewalls. The console of administrators of CA server and TS server is also connected to the router. However, differently from the external segment, the administrator has an access to the CA server through the firewall.

Additionally:

- In our project the subscriber's computer is not secured by any devices filtrating the movement in its direction, because we assume that this kind of the safety devices is his private matter and we can not intervene,
- other two servers, the Registration Authority (RA) as well as the server of the Trusted Third Party (TTP) are protected with standard firewalls (the security level corresponds to E3 or EAL4 level according to ITSEC),
- the personnel operating the network in the individual departments has to be trained and adopted to the recommendations arising from the obligatory procedures and security policy of the firm (they sign an appropriate declaration),
- internal and external location (building, rooms for staff and servers) match requirements posed to firms providing certification services (access control based on electronic cards, systems of internal and external monitoring, fire-fighting systems, ultimate power supply,...).

4. RISK ANALYSIS AND ASSESSMENT FOR DESIGNED PKI NETWORK

From the technical point of view, analysis of the Public Key Infrastructure (implementation of the network structures which accomplishes individual functions of the PKI as demonstrated in section 3) as well as considering additional elements which are components of this infrastructure (politic, procedures,...), the disturbances and abnormalities in functioning of individual components can be result of various factors, such as[4,5]:

- *disclosure of private key* - possible in case of: workers disloyalty, poor quality key, gaps in cryptographical devices storing private keys, incorrect configuration of devices, improper level of computers storing the subscribers private keys,
- *disturbances in the work of servers which are components of the PKI infrastructure* - possible in case of incorrect configuration of servers, placing physically too many services on one server, improper monitoring of the state of security of individual servers,
- *falsification of broadcast data* - possible in case of improper safety level, when communication channels between subscriber and server or registration point does not exploiting the encryptment process or are using weak encryption algorithms,
- *disturbances of work of the network* – possible in case of excessive loading, or the carrying out the attacks of refusal services (the attacks of DDoS),
- *physical damage of hardware* - possible in case of workers disloyalty, as result of unaware mistake disabling continuation of the work etc.,

Complete list of threats, reasons for their appearance and their influence on the individual PKI component is presented in Tab. 1.

Threat	Reason	RA	CA	SUB	RP
Disclosure of the key during its generation or utilization	– Improper safety level (eg. electromagnetic fleeting) – disloyal personnel – key of poor quality – incorrect configuration – unsuitable security level	*	*	*	-
Lack of the admission to the CRL or verification services regarding certificate status	– breakdown of the net – breakdown of the supply – breakdown of the LDAP server – overloading of the server (Spam's, DOS attacks)	-	-	*	*
False verification of identity	– false identity rekord – disloyal personnel (usurpation of key or certificate of another person) – incorrect procedure of identity verification (based on the electronic signature)o	*	*	-	*
Lack of the possibility of complete verification of certificate status	– time gap between publication of first and second CRL – overloading of CA disabling certificate's actualization – unpredicted mistake in the software (eg. in repository)	*	*	*	*
Data manipulation (incorrect information about the time tagging)	– falsification of transmitted data with use of NTP protocol – disynchronization of the nuclear time standard – falsification of markers (reordening)	-	*	-	-
Destruction of hardware and software	– downfalls (fire, flooding) or accident – terroristic sabotage (explosives) – modification or removal of data from permanent carriers (CA server, logs, LDAP...) by disloyal employees – accidental physical destruction of hard drive, software	*	*	*	-

Tab. 1. List of threats, reasons of their appearance and the influence on the individual components of the PKI infrastructure

Introduced in Tab.1 threats as well as their influence on individual components of the PKI infrastructure have a direct relationship with the resources of the PKI system. In order to estimate the risk seriousness, and to determine the needs of safety arising from individual threats acting on the system, the first activity should be focused on the classification of resources (evaluation of the sensitivity of resources according to provided services) with respect to the risk in case of the loss of accessibility, integrity or confidentiality. In the next step, as it is shown in Figure 1, the risk seriousness is determined on the ground of two values derived from the analysis (impact and potentiality values). Both values in this analysis are calculated on the ground of the set of scenarios available in the MEHARI method, which may threaten function of the PKI system [2]. An exemplary scenario, which may threaten the PKI can be: the illegal disclosure, spread or accessibility of data (eg. the disclosure of the key, snooping of authentic communicates of the network and lining under them), temporary inaccessibility of supplies (eg. the lack of access to CRL or verification of certificate's status services), the manipulation of the data (the incorrect information about the time labeling, false verification of the identity), the destruction of hardware and software or loss of data set, etc.

Based on the scenarios introduced above, an estimation of risk seriousness according to guidelines of the method was executed. A cumulative Tab. 4 for all scenarios was created. In this table, being a basis of the risk analysis, three measures assigned to potentiality (the structural measures, dissuasive measures, preventive measures) as well as three measures assigned to impact (the protective measures, palliative measures, recovery measures) according to drawing 1 are considered. Both, the potentiality and impact are the average values from the individual opinions assigned to them. In turn, every measure is also an average from the individual factors being its component (evaluation of current situation according to the functions executed by the PKI system, including the evaluation of sensibility of subsystems, susceptibility to changes, implemented mechanisms of the access control, utilized security subsystems, procedures etc.) for every factor being a component of a given scope of activity.

The final value of impact is calculated from Tab. 2 (cross-section between calculated average value of impact from measures (preventive measures,….) for every threat and resources value.

Resources value Impact from measures	1	2	3	4	impact
1	1	1	1	1	
2	1	2	2	2	
3	1	2	3	3	
4	1	2	3	4	

Tab. 2. Predefined table of impact

Taking into account all of those measures, for example "the lack of the access to CRL list because of the breakdown of the LDAP server in result of breakdown of software " we receive Structural Measures = 2, Dissuasive Measures = 2, Preventive Measures = 3, Protective Measures = 3 and Palliative Measures = 3. After rounding to the full number in the range from 1 to 4, the average values for measures as well as for impact and potentiality, we can obtain impact value from measures = 3 and the potentiality value = 2. To determine the final risk seriousness it is necessary to determine the final impact value. Considering resources value, for axample as = 3 and impact value from measures as = 3, we can receive from Table 2 the final impact value as = 3.

The last stage of risk seriousness assessment consists of determination of the final risk seriousness for every threat. Risk seriousness (lack of the accessibility to the CRL list because of....) is determined from Tab. 3 (the cross-section between the potentiality and impact value).

Potentiality Impact	0	1	2	3	4	Risk seriousness
1	0	0	0	1	1	
2	0	1	2	2	3	
3	0	2	3	3	3	
4	0	3	4	4	4	

Tab. 3. Predefined table of risk seriousness

Value of risk seriousness equal 4 is umbearable. In case when it is equal 3, it is considered as permissible but impossible for acceptation. Value equal 2 is acceptable but it is necessary to endeavor to decrease it. Values 1 and 0 are the only acceptable.

5. CONCLUSIONS

Usually, deciding about the selection of a given system we have a confidence that used security systems are sufficient for protection of our supplies. What is this confidence? Confidence can be defined as presumption that given system will behave in a way that is defined and well-known for us. However, the ascertainment " I trust" is always burdened with some risk. This risk is much higher compared to complexity of the PKI system. Even if we will became familiar with such a system and if we will understand how this system works assuming that any procedure will not be smashed, we can not be sure about the security of the information exchange. It can be thousands of reasons - from bad mood of employee and resulted negligence to the gaps in procedures smartly utilized by hackers etc. If the pathway of mutual dependencies based on the confidence will be created, but at least one element will fail, then the whole network becomes destructed because the confidence will practically not be regained. The system behaving in such a way is defined as structurally unstable. This is a very unfavourable situation, especially considering the security of the PKI infrastructure which is intended to become a basis for functioning of the e-business.

REFERENCES

[1] Carlisle Adams, Steve Lloyd: "Podpis elektroniczny. Klucz publiczny" Biblioteka problemów, Wyd. Robomatic 2001
[2] PresentationMehari_11-2003, www.clusif.asso.fr
[3] www.signet.pl

[4] Peter Herrmann: „How to Integrate Trust Management into a risk Analysis Process" 2nd Internal iTrust Workshop on Trust Management in Dynamic Open Systems, London, September 2003

[5] Carl Ellison, Bruce Schneier: „Ten Risks of PKI: What You're not Being Told about Public Key Infrastructure"; Computer Security Journal Volume XVI, Number 1,2000

No of scenario	Scenario	Cause	Origin: type of aggressor/action	STRUCTURAL MEASURES	DISSUASIVE MEAS.	PREVENTIVE MEAS.	PROTECTIVE ACTEAS.	PALLIATIVE MEAS.	RECOVERY MEAS.	POTENTIALITY	IMPACT	RISK SERIOUSNESS
1	Destruction of hardware and software	Accidental or severe damage of resources	water damage (flooding) or accident (sewage system failure)			2	2	3		2	2	2
		Natural or incidental situations, preclusion of PKI services	breakdown of external electrical installation (eg. storm, rupture of power supply,...)						2	0	2	0
		Fire	accidental fire	1		2	2	3	2	1	3	2
			short circuit of power supply	1		2	2	3	3	1	3	2
		Data modification or removal from hardware (eg. software modification on CA server, repository server, LDAP,...)	malignance (logic bomb) by authorized person	2	2	3	3	2	3	2	3	3
			malignance of non-authorized person	2	2	2	3	3		2	3	3
2	Unabilkity to access the CRL or verification services regarding certificate status	Lack of connection	breakdown of telephony and information network	2			3	3		2	3	3
			breakdown of telephony and information operator	3		1	3	3	2	2	2	2
			natural catastrophe			2	2	3	2	2	2	2
		Breakdown of LDAP	conscious attack of third person or personnel	2	3	2	3	3	3	2	3	3
			software crash	2	2	3	3	3		2	3	3
			overloading of server	2	2	1	2	2		2	2	2
			breakdown of hardware discs	2	2	2	3	2		2	2	2
		Breakdown of repository server	of directory file service LDAP crash (CRL, keys, certificates)	3	3	2	2	3		3	3	3
3	Disclosure of private key	Access to the system and copy files	through intruder	3		2	2			2	3	2
			through software programmer (back entrance)	2	2	3	2		2	2	2	2
			through inlegally authorized personnel	2	2	3	2		3	2	2	2
		Interception of authorized communication	through telecommunication personnel (utilization of minitoring devices)	2	2	3	2		2	2	3	2
		Interception of unstable information	through electromagnetic techniques	2	1	2	1			2	2	1
4	Data manipulation (incorrect information about the time tagging)	Falseness of transmitted data	by outside intruder			3	2	2		3	2	2
			through personnel member manipulating network devices	2	1	2	2	2	3	2	3	3
		Falseness of markers	through personnel member			3	3	2	3	3	3	3
		Destruction or asynchronization of the atomic time pattern	destruction of the atomic time pattern	3			2	2		3	2	2
			asynchronization of the nuclear time standard	3			2	2	3	3	3	3
5	False verification of identity	Software modification	malignant modification by programmists (eg. Software modification of CA server, repository server, LDAP, which can result in issuing of incorrect certificates)	2			3	2	2	2	3	3
		Rewriting error	false declaration (false identity card)	2		3	3	3	3	3	3	3
			by authorized, disloyal personnel	2	3	3	3	2	3	3	3	3

Tab.4. Assessment of risk seriousness for the PKI infrastructure acc. MEHARI

VAST: Versatile Anonymous System for Web Users

IGOR MARGASIŃSKI, KRZYSZTOF SZCZYPIORSKI
Warsaw University of Technology, Institute of Telecommunications
ul. Nowowiejska 15/19, 00-665 Warsaw, Poland
e-mail: {I.Margasinski, K.Szczypiorski}@tele.pw.edu.pl

Abstract: This paper presents an original method of providing versatile anonymity for Web users – VAST. It includes an introduction to the current techniques of providing anonymity in WWW system, both popular Third Party Proxy Servers and enhanced systems based on Chaining with Encryption. Limitations of these systems are discussed. In Third Party Proxy Servers – concentration of personal Web activity data; in Chaining with Encryption – low performance and high costs of network realization. Both classes of solutions do not eliminate all the risks of traffic analysis. The new method described – VAST – overcomes mentioned weaknesses and provides versatile anonymity for all parties involved in data exchange based on the WWW system. In this paper we also introduce a draft of the method implementation in Java language.

Key words: anonymity, privacy, anonymous web browsing, privacy-enhancing technology

1.   INTRODUCTION

When leading their lives into the digital dimension, people have the right not to change their behaviours, and ways of fulfilling their needs. The moulding of our world, the creation of new environments of existence should belong to men not machines. The World Wide Web, which along with the e-mail is the most popular Internet application, lacks privacy protection. Privacy in the Web can be achieved using tools which provide **anonymity**. It is one of the ways to create a digital environment similar to our reality.

We can distinguish two kinds of anonymity: **person anonymity** and **message anonymity**. Person anonymity may be classified into: **sender anonymity** and **receiver anonymity**. It is of significance that the term "anonymity" is usually associated with some particular **point of view**. For example, anonymity of a poet generally means withholding his identity only from his readers and not from his publisher. The protection can be achieved by **hiding** (an access to crucial data is protected) or **masking** (the possibility to distinguish crucial data is protected – often by masking in so called **dummy traffic** – fake data). We should also mention the term "**unlinkability**", which means that it is known that both sender and receiver participate in some communication, but they cannot be identified as communicating with each other. In this paper we concentrate on **receiver anonymity from all parties' point of view**. Our aim is not to hide identity of user (receiver) from the anonymity service provider, but to hide his Web activity. Therefore, what we have in mind is the unlinkability of user and destination Web servers. We introduce a solution to a problem of the lack of Web privacy – VAST – *Versatile Anonymous SysTem for Web Users.*

2.   RELATED WORK

Third Party Proxy Servers providing anonymity for Web users are gaining more and more popularity. Proxy is a distant machine – a middleman between a client and a server, which forwards user's requests to destination Website and resends its content. This architecture creates the possibility of hiding all information about client from server (for example IP address). Additionally, it is possible to encrypt transmission between client and proxy server. Then all user Web activity will be hidden from parties who have an access to transferred Web transactions (for example from Internet Service Providers or from LAN administrators). Third Party Proxy Server also provides wide range of possibilities of control of transferred resources: it is likely to control HTTP State Management Mechanism – *Cookies* [8] and to block discarded additional elements (for example pop-up windows), and also to remove scripts and programs. Proxy can perform any filtering of transmitted documents. The advantages of proxies, responsible for their high popularity are: filling the technical loop-hole in WWW system related to lack of user's privacy protection [7], high efficiency in hiding user's identity data, easy access to the service, supported by no additional requirements from users (only an Internet access and standard Web browser needed), simple usage, insignificant delays of Web navigation, simplicity, relatively low costs required for system realization and no demands to modify existing network nodes and protocols – system implementation based on current well known standards. However, there are also serious disadvantages to Third Party Proxy Servers. Currently employed proxy servers have access to information about user's Web activity. Anonymity service providers induce the belief that this data is not collected, used or shared. The user has to face the risk of concentration of personal Web activity in one place. If the anonymity service provider attempts to exercise this possibility, the user will be exposed to an even greater risk than in traditional Web browsing, because information collected by different Websites is much more difficult to put together. Furthermore, proxy servers do not protect against tracking by traffic analysis. An eavesdropper can observe the volume of transmitted data and correlate inputs and outputs (proxy server request). A very serious risk also exists here, because it is possible for third parities to track and profile users. The next disadvantage of proxy servers is the limitation of sets of elements which can be downloaded. Some of HTML standard enhancements (like JavaScript) can create high risks for the whole system [9]. It is possible and easy to perform powerful attacks using these technologies. The mentioned attacks can completely compromise proxy sever systems.

Having security limitations of single proxy servers in mind, the natural way to improve these systems is to disperse localization of information about user's Web activity. This is being done by replacing one server with many nodes. Each of these proxies has a partial knowledge about transferred data – it can be realized by public key cryptography – **Chaining with Encryption**. By repeatedly encrypting a message (for example, request to Web server) with public keys of succeeding nodes, we can transmit data from user's computer to destination server without disclosing the identity of both sender and receiver to every proxy. Routing among accessible nodes should be random. Thanks to this, packets alternate mutually, which in effect leads to an elimination of traffic analysis attack. This idea dates back to David Chaum's theory [2] of providing anonymity for electronic mail – MIXNET, where the enhanced proxy servers are the so-called MIXes. Their name has its origin in their characteristic role which is the mixing of delivered items. Before a MIX sends a message, it waits until it receives a batch of messages. Then it sends the messages outputting them in random order. Examples of systems based on MIXNET include: *Onion Routing* ([6], [11]), *Crowds* [10], *Freedom* [5] (first profitable system of this kind). Systems based on a network of many proxies require construction of expensive infrastructure. This brings in a discouraging factor for potential investors. The use of network of proxies is a great technique for providing anonymity during e-mail correspondence. However, serious delays, which are not inconvenient in sending e-mails, are a serious obstacle in Web browsing. To increase system's performance speed, it is necessary to employ powerful and fast computers as proxies. Yet, they are expensive. The authors of *Crowds* project presented an analysis of delays caused by sequent proxies of their system. We employ this data to illustrate the increase in time needed to receive a page – as a function of number of proxies. Presented results (table 1) show that the cost of providing anonymity in systems based on a network of proxies is a significant increase of waiting time. Moreover, Crowds system contains serious simplifications in comparison to MIXNET – which role is to increase the performance speed. In spite of these costly – from the security point of view – differences, performance is not satisfactory.

Number of proxies	Page size [kB]					
	0	1	2	3	4	5
2 + 1	20,8%	35,0%	23,7%	13,7%	17,8%	26,3%
2 + 2	42,1%	43,4%	32,3%	22,8%	18,6%	28,2%
2 + 3	73,1%	72,1%	60,7%	40,0%	36,6%	45,0%

Tab. 1. Delays as a function of number of proxies and
page size in Crowds system (0% delay is for two proxies)

To accomplish encryption and decryption of exchanged data these systems use additional client-side software applications. This software takes over all communication with the Internet and reroutes packets to anonymous service servers. But a system which requires that a user installs additional software decreases his trust. Downloaded applications able to communicate with a public network may constitute so-called Trojan Horses. The user does not have the ability to check what really goes to the service server. This requirement also narrows the group of users, because it means dependency on a specific hardware and operating system. Systems based on chaining with encryption do not eliminate all risks of traffic analysis attacks. Anonymity is still dependent on a third party – information about user's Web activity was only dispersed between many proxies. However, there is no certainty that proxies do not collaborate with each other. In our opinion, WWW service requires an individual approach. When designing a system providing anonymity for Web browsing, concentrating on different aspects and parameters unlike in e-mail, should proof beneficial. Today more than ever, the WWW service increases its multimedia character. The users expect texts and graphics to be available immediately. Today's solutions though, still require very high financial investments. What is more, anonymity service provider cannot submit a proof that system proxies do not collaborate. Originators usually omit this fact and only mention curtly that each of proxies should belong to a different infrastructure provider. Is this a reason enough to support a belief that proxies do not collaborate? Nowadays we can see many examples of cooperation between independent companies in the process of tracking Web users and profiling them. Why would it be any different in this case? Implementation of this class of methods is not widely spread. We can only presume that in case of their popularization and implementation of proxies by many different companies, this possibility could be misused.

3.   VAST OVERVIEW

Our goal was to design a method dedicated to WWW system specifics, which can take advantage of them. We have set the following principles for our solution:
- preservation of all advantages of single third party proxy servers,
- providing versatile anonymity (including service provider and also preventing risks of traffic analysis attacks),
- retention of speed (minimalization of performance differences between VAST usage and traditional browsing),
- accessibility – no additional requirements from users,
- facility to implement outside laboratories – relatively low costs.

VAST system contains only one proxy node. To achieve anonymity from proxy server's point of view and also to disable traffic analysis attack we are placing **specific kind of dummy traffic generation mechanism between distant proxy and local agent**. More pages than actually requested by user are transferred from proxy to client. Information about which content is the object of interest to the user stays with him. An agent (JAVA applet) cooperates with user's browser. At the time when the user is familiarizing himself with the page content, the agent simulates users Web activity – by requesting random Websites from proxy. The basis of this solution is the observation of a typical Web navigation. User does not request Websites at all times. Requests get sent in various time intervals and in between them, the user reads the content. VAST utilizes this fact. Additionally, VAST takes advantage of the simplicity of generating dummy traffic in WWW system – we mean that a wide range of Internet resources is indexed in Web search engines. We can simulate user's activity using it. The VAST system, unlike other existing solutions, does not conduct additional major activity while the transaction takes place, but it utilizes free time to take actions providing versatile anonymity. A source code of agent applet would be available to all. Then users would be able to check if it is not a *trojan horse*.

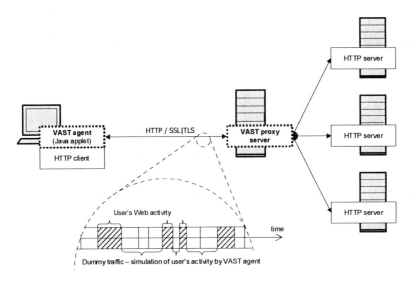

Fig. 1. VAST system scheme

VAST consists of two primary elements: **agent** placed in Web browser environment and **proxy** placed between the agent and a destination Web server.

Agent is an Java applet residing in user's Web browser. Primary functions of VAST agent include: communication with proxy server secured by SSL/TLS protocol (Secure Socket Layer / Transport Layer Security [3]), simulation of user Web activity, generation of URL (Uniform Resource Locator) addresses as a background for addresses requested by user, receiving configuration parameters from user and transmitting them to proxy, requesting pages selected by user and pages selected by simulator, receiving resources from proxy, dividing resources between group of pages chosen by user and dummy traffic pages, presentation of pages chosen by user (skipping dummy traffic pages), analysis of a level of user anonymity as a result of a proportion between resources downloaded by user and resources downloaded by simulator, presentation of actual anonymity level and communication with user by graphic interface.

Proxy server which is a part of the VAST system is very similar to popular anonymous proxy systems – the main difference is an absence of user interface. This function was moved to VAST agent. Primary functions of VAST agent are: hiding all user's identifiable data from destination Web server – IP address among others, encrypting all data transmitted between VAST agent and VAST proxy – resources' URL addresses among others, optional encrypting communication between VAST proxy and destination Web server, blocking cookies from destination Web server, blocking scripts and programs from destination Web server and blocking Java applets from destination Web server.

4.   DESIGN AND IMPLEMENTATION

For the purposes of this paper the following two descriptions are introduced:

- *Web transaction* – a series of HTTP client requests and correspondent server responses, which represent a single Web page (HTML files and contained elements, i.e. graphic files),
- *Subject session* – collection of Web transactions generated by user – where all transactions can be connected with each other by links from transactions pages. In the rest of this paper a shorter name – *session* – will be used.

We presume that potential eavesdropper, who has an access to transmitted data is able to separate each transactions and sessions from communication. The dummy traffic generation complies with establishment of additional sessions. Transactions which belong to these sessions typically take place while the user is familiarizing himself with the content of pages already received. Agent generates dummy traffic requests assigned to user's session as well. Thanks to this, the reliable distinction as to which session comes from the user is not possible to make. Specific properties of session generated by human – thematic relations between transactions – are then lost. When user starts a new session, the agent also restarts dummy sessions. An eavesdropper (who knows the algorithm of agent applet – open source), can not distinguish if a particular request comes from user or from simulator. The anonymity service provider – the strongest possible attacker – is only able to separate particular sessions. The provider may know than that one of these sessions is of an interest to the user, but he does not know which one. The provider also does not know which requests from particular session come from the user. The user can configure the number of dummy sessions. Having the bandwidth of Internet connection and the frequency of requests in mind, one can select appropriate level of anonymity, which can be represented by the probability (P) of the fact that the user is interested in the subject of selected session.

$$P \leq \frac{1}{Number\ of\ dummy\ sessions\ +\ 1} \tag{1}$$

We should mention here that conducting only one dummy session provides anonymity called *probable innocence* [10]. Closer analysis of VAST security is presented in section 5. The user will have to configure the system before he starts using it – this is necessary to input a list of search engines preferred by user. The agent will then employ them to generate dummy traffic. The agent will use a **dictionary** of queries downloaded from VAST proxy server. It is important for the dictionary to contain a large number of queries. If the user enters a query which is not in the dictionary, the VAST agent will inform about it and warn that the VAST service provider may infer that the query was not generated by the simulator. A request of a page trough a search engine means the beginning of a new session. The same rules apply to the beginning of dummy sessions. At first user's requests are not immediately ran. The choice which transaction is executed first is random. In subsequent transactions user's requests have priority of execution by an agent. However, if their frequency is higher than the frequency of dummy transactions, the user gets an appropriate message. The agent displays a warning, based on higher frequency of certain transactions, that eavesdropper may presume that requests came from the user. The graphic representation of a sample communication between VAST agent and VAST proxy server is shown in figure 2. In this example two dummy sessions were used. Cuboids represent WWW transactions in particular sessions. The arrows point to the user's transactions.

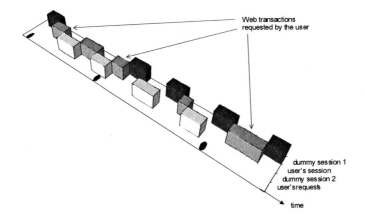

Fig. 2. Sample of communication between VAST agent and VAST proxy server. The cuboids represent single WWW transactions

Performance

The presented system had been designed to provide high performance – similar to performance in traditional Web browsing. Additional operations focused on providing anonymity neither take place at the time of realization of user's requests nor at the time of data downloading. They occur when the user is familiarizing himself with the requested page. A question remains: how does the dummy traffic actually delay browsing? Sometimes the user browses briefly through the page's content. How long will he be forced to wait? VAST may block data which originates in third party servers (i.e. AdServers). It means the disabling of all third party banner ads often published on various Web pages. The statistics analysis conducted by authors showed that size of ads published on most popular Web pages and Web portals often exceeds 50% of total page size. The number of requests necessary to download pages is often a multiple number of requests to destination server. In the VAST system requests to the third party servers may be replaced by dummy requests. Users allow downloading of numerous advertising elements. So we are justified in thinking that replacement of ads with dummy traffic which provide privacy protection would be also acceptable.

The volume of dummy traffic should be maintained on a certain level in order to perform effective masking of user's activity. The number of transactions performed in appropriate sessions should be approximately equal. Let t_d be average time of downloading of single Webpage; t_f – average time of familiarizing with page content; t_w – average delay in Webpage downloading induced by VAST system in comparison to traditional proxy server; n – number of dummy sessions. Then, the delay t_w can be described as follows:

$$t_w = 0.5\, t_d \qquad \text{for } t_f \geq n\, t_d \tag{2}$$

(average time required to finish current transaction)

$$t_w = n\, t_d - t_f + 0.5 t_d \qquad \text{for } t_f < n\, t_d \tag{3}$$

(nt_d of dummy transactions have to be performed to provide proper level of anonymity). We can sum it up as:

$$t_w = \frac{|\, n\, t_d - t_f \,| + (n+1)\, t_d - t_f}{2} \tag{4}$$

Figure 3 shows t_w delays a function of average Webpage downloading time t_d and average time of user's familiarizing with content t_f, suitable for $n = 1$ (A) and $n = 2$ (B) dummy sessions. The following results can be obtained for a typical downloading time $t_d = 8$ [s]:

n	t_f [s]	0	1	2	3	4	5	6	7	8	9	10	11	12	13	14	15	16	17	18	19	20
1	t_w [s]	12	11	10	9	8	7	6	5	4	4	4	4	4	4	4	4	4	4	4	4	4
2	t_w [s]	20	19	18	17	16	15	14	13	12	11	10	9	8	7	6	5	4	4	4	4	4

Tab. 2. Delays introduced by VAST (t_w) system as a function of
user's familiarizing with Web content time

According to our expectations, these results shows that acceptable delays (similar to delays present in traditional anonymous proxy server systems) occur when users spend some time ($t_f \approx nt_d$) familiarizing with Webpage content.

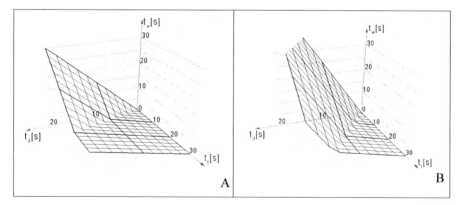

Fig. 3. Delays induced by VAST system in comparison to traditional proxy server
(A – one dummy session, B – two dummy sessions)

5.   SECURITY

The communication between user's computer and proxy server is secured by SSL/TLS protocol. It means that parties from the local environment do not have an access to transmitted data. Anonymity **from the local environment parties point of view** is accomplished through hiding. The security in this area is based on the strength of the SSL/TLS protocol itself and cryptographic algorithms utilized in it. Because both agent and proxy server are elements implemented by anonymity service provider, it is possible to choose appropriate cryptographic algorithms (i.e. SSL version 3). In the intervals between user's transactions dummy traffic is being generated. It constitutes a very effective barrier against traffic analysis attack. As we mentioned above, the communication between agent and proxy server is very effectively guarded against sniffing attack or the possibility of correlation of requests and servers answers based on timing relations. In the communication between proxy server and destination Web server encryption is not a key. Eavesdropping of this data results only in the interception of information about the VAST proxy server's activity. If the system is employed by many users the information is worthless. In the extreme case, when there is only one VAST active user and when the eavesdropper has the possibility of interception of all requests realized by proxy server, the security **from others Internet users point of view** is the same as from the VAST service provider's point of view (still satisfied).

Let's consider the anonymity **from the VAST service provider's point of view** next. Referring to the figure of a sample communication between the VAST agent and the VAST proxy server (figure 2), attacker may only correlate particular requests such as it is shown in figure 4. We can observe that the proxy server may differentiate between particular sessions (three session noted in the picture with different shades). An attacker may not determine which shades represent user's activity. He also keeps in mind that user's requests correspond only to some blocks represented by the same (unknown) shade. Therefore, it is possible, after conducting an analysis of transactions content, to determine that data transmitted from sections: A, G, I, L, M is one session. B, D, F, J, M – second, and C, E, H, K is the third. The potential attacker knows that the topic of one session is of interest to the user. He is neither able to determine which one nor separate user's requests (in this example: B, F, M). Presented illustration is a schematic simplification. The regular blocks should not be identified with the volume of transmitted data. We should also consider the attack where VAST service provider resends fake pages or fake dictionary to find out if they have been requested by an applet or by a human being. In this case the attack can be successful, but its result is the lost of reliability by service provider. After detection of this attack – what is easy and unavoidable – his service is compromised and worthless to users. Therefore this attack can not be utilized to perform widespread profiling. The cost of the attack is higher than its profit.

From the destination Web server point of view there is no ability to identify the system's users. To the destination Web server the only available data is about proxy server which forwards user's requests. Active elements placed on pages, which can communicate with destination server are removed by the VAST proxy server.

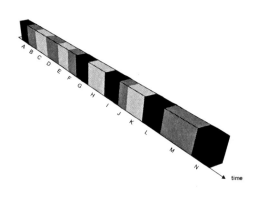

Fig. 4. Illustration of communication between agent and proxy server – from the proxy
server's point of view (compare with fig. 2).

Until now no system providing effective protection against all of well known
types of **traffic analysis attack** (like timing attack, message volume attack, flooding
attack, linking attack) has been implemented. Systems based on David Chaum's
theory, which are an accurate realization of MIXNET, provide an effective
protection against timing attack or message volume attack. Below we are going to
discuss the protection offered by the VAST system against each of the attacks.
Timing attack is based on the observation of communication time through linking
of potential end points and searching for correlations between beginning and/or
ending of an event in each possible end point. The VAST system provides a total
protection against this type of attack thanks to specific dummy traffic generation
mechanism. An eavesdropper is not able to differentiate between particular requests,
because right after the finalization of one transaction the next one begins. Therefore,
it is not possible to establish if a request belongs to a particular transaction. Of
course, in case where there is only one active system user (extreme case),
eavesdropper can presume that all proxy requests come from the user. However,
even in this case the anonymity of user is not compromised and it is the same as the
anonymity of user from the VAST proxy server's point of view. **Message volume
attack** is based on the observation of the transfer volume (i.e. message volume) and
correlation of input and output. As mentioned above, the VAST system fills periods
of user's inactivity with dummy traffic. Separation of particular messages from
encrypted link between agent – proxy server is then practically impossible. **Flooding
attack** is based on sending a large number of messages – flooding – or messages
with certain characteristics by other system users. This is done in order to separate
user's message. The VAST system protects against this attack because of the form
of the message sent to the proxy server itself. Even after an effective isolation of
user's message, it is still unknown which requests are generated by machine and
which come from human. The VAST system, as presented above, does not offer an
effective protection against **linking attack** which is based on a long-term
observation. This attack uses changes in traffic related to presence of connection or
its absence. In our VAST system concept, in order to maintain simplicity, we did not
take into consideration these types of risks. However, it is possible to enhance the
VAST system and include a mechanism providing effective protection against long-
term linking attack (compare to section 6).

6. FUTURE WORK

The presented system introduces a concept which in its practical implementation requires additional mechanisms. When implementing this system for public use we should consider the possibility of an **long-term linking attack** (statistical profiling) conducted by proxy server or party which can eavesdrop on the communication of proxy. The risk originates in the possibility of separating recurring requests during the course of many sessions. To provide an effective protection against this class of attacks a mechanism of registering recurring requests should be used in the agent program. This would allow an introduction of dummy traffic simulating activity not only in the course of one session but during a longer time. It is important for the information gathered by the agent to be appropriately protected. The agent will record recurring user requests. The agent's program does not share this data with other parties. Recurring requests are accompanied by dummy traffic, which also simulates user's activity in the course of many sessions. The potential attacker will only be able to decide that the user is browsing through his favorite pages, but the attacker will not be able to determine through which one. We should consider the transformation of agent Java applet into a Java program which would be called local proxy. This will allow saving files locally on user's computer. It will be possible to save user's activity history. This will also permit storage of dummy traffic files and their usage as a cache memory. The user may choose page already downloaded during a dummy transaction. This greatly increases the navigation speed.

7. CONCLUSION

In this paper we have introduced an original method – VAST – which provides protection of Web user's privacy by granting versatile anonymity. This solution evolved from popular in WWW single proxy systems. It is a comprehensive technique which overcomes weaknesses of existing systems such as: serious, noticeable delays, access of service provider to user's private date and high costs of service implementation. The novel idea in this system – utilization of Web search engines resources to generate dummy traffic in the relation between local agent and distant proxy – may be in some cases viewed as its weakness. For users, whose fees for the Internet access are based on the amount of downloaded data, it means higher costs. We should stress that the system can block third party servers advertisement elements. It means that the graphic files from third parties are exchanged for dummy traffic. As usual – there is also a price for anonymity – to preserve full security, the user can not start navigating from direct URLs but from queries put into popular search engines. Another factor impacting the comfort of usage is that the requested phrases should be included in VAST's dictionary (which can be indeed very vast). It means that sometimes the user would have to take a moment to think how to change his request to find what he is really looking for. Anonymity from the VAST service provider's point of view is accomplished through masking. Therefore, the provider may with certain probability (chosen by the user) presume that particular requests come from user. We should note that total elimination of this weakness would mean the accomplishment of absolute WWW anonymity achieved by technical means, which seems to be practically impossible.

REFERENCES

[1] Berners-Lee, T., Fielding, R., Frystyk, H. Hypertext Transfer Protocol – HTTP/1.0. RFC 1945, 1996.

[2] Chaum, D. Untraceable Electronic Mail, Return Addresses, and Digital Pseudonyms. Communications of the ACM Vol. 24 no 2,1981, pp. 84 - 88.

[3] Dierks T., Allen C. The TLS-Protocol Version 1.0. RFC 2246, 1999.

[4] Fielding, R., Gettys, J.,Mogul, J., Frystyk, H., Masinter, L., Leach, P., Berners-Lee T. HyperText Transfer Protocol – HTTP/1.1. RFC 2616, 1999.

[5] Goldberg, I., Shostack, A. Freedom Network 1.0 Architecture and Protocols. Zero-Knowledge Systems. White Paper, 1999.

[6] Goldschlag, D. M., Reed, M. G., Syverson, P. F. Onion Routing for Anonymous and Private Internet Connections. Communications of the ACM Vol. 42 no 2, 1999, 39-41.

[7] Krane, D., Light, L., Gravitch D. Privacy On and Off the Internet: What Consumers Want. Harris Interactive, 2002.

[8] Kristol, R., Montulli, L. HTTP State Management Mechanism. RFC 2965, 2000.

[9] Martin, D., Schulman, A. Deanonymizing Users of the SafeWeb Anonymizing Service. Privacy Foundation, Boston University, 2002.

[10] Reiter, M.K., Rubin, A.D. Crowds: Anonymity for Web Transactions. ACM Transactions on Information and System Security, 1998, pp. 66-92

[11] Syverson, P. F., Goldschlag, D. M., Reed, M. G. Anonymous Connections and Onion Routing. IEEE Symposium on Security and Privacy, 1997.

Cryptography and Steganography: teaching experience

BARTOSZ SOKÓŁ[1], V. N. YARMOLIK[2]
Bialystok University of Technology, Wiejska 45A street, 15-351 Bialystok, Poland,
[1] *bsokol@ii.pb.bialystok.pl*
[2] *yarmolik@gw.bsuir.unibel.by*

Abstract: In this article we present overview of work with cryptography and steganography techniques, which refers to information hiding and providing secrecy. Article contains cryptography and steganography teaching results and experiences. First chapter contains information about steganography and its history. Next chapter provides information about hiding methods. We present there the most known, simple, computer-based steganographic techniques which our students mastered during studies. Third chapter includes information about few laboratory projects and results to the cryptography and steganography point. This chapter makes a review of several interesting steganography and cryptography approaches, which were implemented and become a subject of meticulous studies aimed at the development of new software.

Key words: Steganography, information hiding, cryptography, watermarking

1. INTRODUCTION

An important subdiscipline of information hiding is steganography which is a mean of providing secrecy and can be viewed as akin to cryptography. Steganographia (Trithemius, 1462-1516) assumed from Greek στεγνό-ς, γραφ-ειν literally means "covered writing" [2]. While cryptography is about protecting the content of message by scrambling a message so it cannot be understood, steganography is about concealing their very existence - "camouflages". A cryptographic message can be intercepted by an eavesdropper, but the eavesdropper may not even know a steganographic message exists [1].

The goal of steganography is to avoid drawing suspicion to the transmission of a secret message. Our students tried to design new software, hide secret data in it and be sure of security (chapter 3). Other students tried to detect and remove embedded code. Detecting the secret data relies on the fact that hiding information in digital media alters the carriers and introduces unusual characteristic or some form of degradation to the carrier. In general, attacks against embedded data can include various combinations of cryptoanalysis, steganalysis, and image processing techniques. These attacks may reveal a steganographic message. Analysis of data hiding techniques involves investigating available tools and techniques for hiding information, classifying these techniques and understanding the impact steganography software has on various carriers. These problems were considered during lectures and had an influence on projects and designed software.

Fig. 1 Science about secret writing and main branches [3].

1.1   Steganography history

Although steganography has been used since ancient times, little is generally understood about its usage and detection. Many ingenious methods of message hiding have been invented [4,5]. Among these methods are null ciphers, covert channels, code words, forms of digital signatures, hidden tattoos, covered writing, invisible inks, microdots, character arrangement, and spread-spectrum communications. Steganography can be applied in many ways to digital media. One method of applying steganography is hiding information within images (photographs or drawings), text files, audio, video, and data transmission. A common method for concealing information in an image is to store information bits within the least significant bits of the pixels comprising the image (see chapter 2.3).

Steganographic history starts from the Histories of Herodotus [6]. Herodotus tells how Demeratus, a Greek at the Persian court, warned Sparta of an imminent invasion by Xerxes, King of Persia: he removed the wax from a writing tablet, wrote his message on the wood underneath and then covered the message with wax.

The latest steganography achievements are from 1999. Researchers at Mount Sinai School of Medicine in New York encoded a hidden message in strand of human DNA using a technique described as "genomic steganography" [8,9]. Short description of this technique is in [1]. Further exploration into the application of DNA for storage, encryption, and steganography is explored in [10].

A widely used method of linguistic steganography is the acrostic. The most famous example is probably Giovanni Boccaccio's (1312-1375) *Amorosavisione* which is said to be the "world's hugest acrostic" [12].

Although steganography is different from cryptography, we can take many of the techniques and practical wisdom from the latter. In 1883, Auguste Kerckhoffs enunciated the first principles of cryptographic engineering, in which he advises that we assume the method used to encipher data is known to the opponent, so security must lie only in the choice of key [13]. Applying this wisdom, we obtain a tentative definition of secure stego-system: one where an opponent who understands the system, but does not know the key, can obtain no evidence (or even grounds for suspicion) that a communication has taken place. It will remain a central principle that steganographic process intended for wide use should be published, just like commercial cryptographic algorithms and protocols [2].

The general model of hiding information in other data and main steganographic techniques will be reviewed below.

2.   METHODS OF INFORMATION HIDING

Information hiding techniques can be used in situations where plausible deniability is required. "The obvious motivation for plausible deniability is when the two communicating parties are engaged in an activity which is somehow illicit, and they wish to avoid being caught" [14] but also for more legitimate motives include fair voting, personal privacy, or limitation of liability.

A number of applications of information hiding have been proposed in the context of multimedia applications. In many cases they can use techniques already developed for copyright marking directory, in others, they can use adapted schemes or shed interesting light on technical issues. They include the following: automatic monitoring of copyrighted material on the Web, automatic audio of radio transmissions, data augmentation, and tamper proofing [2].

Computer-based steganographic techniques introduce changes to digital carriers to embed information foreign to the native carriers. Carriers of embedded messages may resemble: text, disk and storage device [15], network traffic and protocols [16], the way software or circuits are arranged [17], audio, images, video, or any other digitally represented code or transmission.

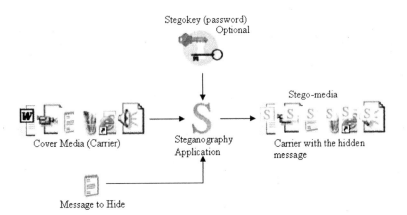

Fig. 2 Steganography Model [1].

Above figure provides an illustration of a steganographic model or process. The cover carrier and the embedded message create a stego-carrier. Sometimes hiding information may require a *stegokey* or password that is additional secret information and may be used to select cover regions to hide or encrypt the embedded message [1].

In literature there are basically three types of steganographic protocols: pure steganography, secret key steganography, and public key steganography.

Pure steganography is a steganographic system which does not require the prior exchange of some secret information (like a stego-key)..Embedding process can be described as a mapping E: C x M → C, where C is the set of possible covers and M the set of possible messages. The extraction process consists of a mapping D: C → M, extracting the secret message out of cover.

Definition 1 (pure steganography): The quadruple G = <C,M,D,E>, where C is the set of possible covers, M the set of secret messages with $|C| \geq |M|$, E: C x M→ C the embedding function and D: C → M, the extraction function, with the property that D(E(c,m)) = m for all m ∈ M and c ∈ C is called a pure steganographic system [2].

A secret key steganography system is similar to a symmetric cipher: the sender chooses a cover c and embeds the secret message into c using a secret key k. If the key used in the embedding process is known to the receiver, he can reverse the process and extract the secret message.

Definition 2 (secret key steganography): The quintuple G = <C,M,K,D_K, E_K>, where C is the set of possible covers, M the set of secret messages with $|C| \geq |M|$,.K the set of secret keys, E_K: C x M x K → C and D_K: C x K → M with the property that $D_K(E_K(c,m,k),k) = m$ for all m ∈ M and c ∈ C and k ∈ K, is called a secret key steganographic system [2].

As in public key cryptography, public key steganography does not rely on the exchange of a secret key. Public key steganography systems require the use of two keys, private and public key; let one is stored in a public database. Whereas the public key is used in the embedding process, the secret key is used to reconstruct the secret message.

Below we will present few the most known steganography techniques and systems.

2.1   Data hiding in text

Many ways have been proposed to store information directly in messages. We can hide information in documents by manipulating position of lines and words [18]. One technique proposed by Maxemchuk consists in use the distance between consecutive lines of text or between consecutive words to transmit secret information. In line-space encoding, the positions of lines in the document are moved up or down according to secret message bits, whereas other lines are kept stationary for the purpose of synchronization One secret message bit is encoded in one line that is moved; if a line is moved up, a 1 is encoded, otherwise a 0.

Another way, we can modify HTML file by adding spaces, tabs, "invisible" characters, and extra line breaks are ignored by web browsers. These "extra" spaces and lines are not perceptible until revealing the source of the web page.

Another technique is known as a null cipher or open code. The main idea is to camouflage the secret message in an innocent sounding message. Secret message emerges by taking for example the third letter in each word from "innocent message".

Likewise, the way language is spoken may encode a message. Pauses, enunciations may all be used to pass on hidden messages to an intended listener. Additional text-based hiding techniques are described in [19].

2.2 Data hiding in disk space, network packets, and executable files

Other ways to hide information rely on finding unused space that is not readily apparent to an observer. Taking advantage of unused or reserved space to hold covert information provides a means of hiding information without perceptually degrading the carrier [1]. The way operating system store files results in unused space that appears to be allocated to files. This "allocated" but available space is known as slack space and can be used to hide information without showing up in the directory. Another method of hiding data in file systems is to create a hidden partition. These concepts have been expanded in a novel proposal of a steganographic file system [15].

Characteristic inherent in network protocols can be taken advantage of to hide information [16, 20]. An uncountable number of data packets are transmitted daily over the Internet. For example, TCP/IP packets can be used to transport information across the Internet. These headers have unused space and other features that can be manipulated to embed information. More information about hiding information TCP/IP packet header is in [1].

Executable files contain lots of redundancies in the way independent subsequent instruction are scheduled or an instruction subset is chosen to solve a specific problem. Code obfuscation techniques, primarily developed to protect re-engineering of software, can be used to store additional information in executable files. Such techniques try to transform a program P into a functionally equivalent program P' which is more difficult to reverse-engineer; in steganographic applications the secret data lies in the sequence of transformation applied [2].

2.3 Data hiding in Audio and Images.

There are many different methods for hiding information in audio and images. In images, we can modify properties such as contrast, colors or luminance to hide secret messages. Proposed methods hide data in audio and images with virtually no impact to the human sensor system. When considering an image in which to hide information, one must consider the structure of the image as well as the palette. The most popular method to hide information in the image is least significant bit (LSB) insertion or manipulation. This is a common, simple approach to embedding data in a cover. Unfortunately, this approach is vulnerable to even a light image distortion. When we want to hide an image in the LSBs of each byte of a 24-bit image, we can store 3 bits in each pixel. To the human eye, the resulting stego-image will look identical to the cover image. On average LSB requires that only half the bits in an image be changed. Data can also be hidden in more significant bits and still the human eye would not be able to discern it. 8-bits images are not as forgiving to LSB manipulation because of color limitations [1]. Next example shows this situation:

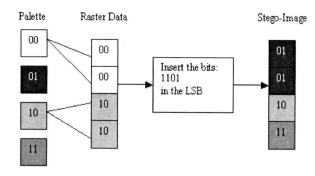

Fig. 3 Example of a palette shift causing visible noise [1].

Steganography software processes LSB insertion to make the hidden information less detectable. Several approaches have been applied in steganography software to hide information in images (EzStego [21], S-Tools [22], StegoDos [23], Mandelsteg [24], White Noise Storm [25] etc.). LSB manipulation is an easy and quick way to hide data but is vulnerable to small changes resulting from image processing or lossy compression. High color quality images can be stored in relatively small files using JPEG compression methods (JPEG images are very popular on the Internet).

Another way to hide information is in more significant areas of an image. It relies on manipulating image properties such as luminance. These techniques are appropriate when the embedded information needs to survive such processing and are commonly used in methods for digital watermarking.

2.4   Summary of steganographic techniques.

Many different steganographic methods have been proposed during the last few years. Most of them can be seen as substitution systems. Such methods try to substitute redundant parts of a signal with a secret message; their main disadvantage is the relative weakness against cover modifications. There are several approaches in classifying steganographic systems. Here is a classification according to the cover modifications applied in the embedding process: substitution systems (substitute redundant parts of a cover with secret message – LSB coding, manipulation of image or compression algorithm, modification of image properties); transform domain techniques (embed information in a transform space of the signal – hide messages in significant areas of the cover image which makes them more robust to attacks, such as compression, cropping, etc.); spread spectrum techniques; statistical methods (encode information by changing several statistical properties of a cover and use hypothesis testing in the extraction process-statistical steganography); distortion techniques (store information by signal distortion and measure the deviation from the original cover in the decoding step); cover generation methods (encode information in the way a cover for secret communication is created) [2]. Most of presented techniques left some sort of "fingerprints" in the data. Steganography problems must be addressed when designing a new system.

3. TEACHING EXAMPLE EXPERIENCE.

In this chapter we present few projects aimed at the development of new software. Students work with cryptography starts from hash functions and algorithms through DSS standard, a suite of algorithms which can be used to generate a digital signature; elliptic curve algorithms; steganography; obfuscation; watermarking; tamper-proofing and other cryptography problems and techniques. The main idea is to find out cryptography techniques and to develop a new software which will execute new algorithms.

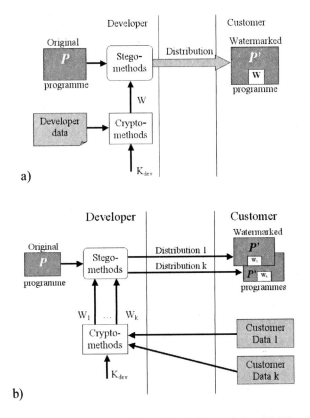

Fig. 4 Software watermarking (a) and fingerprinting (b) [7].

First projectis about steganography. Students have to prepare software, which willrealize simple steganography text-based hiding technique proposed by Maxemchuk (see chapter 2.1). In text file, by manipulating the distance between consecutive words, they had to transmit secret information (software owners name). First of all we have to know the binary representation of the secret data. If the bit equals to "0", we have one space between consecutive words, if the bit equals to "1", we have two spaces between consecutive words. Activity is repeated to.the end of the file. If we reach the end of the binary representation, we start from the first bit again. This algorithm was.used to hide information about authors of this article in a text in this chapter. Of course, it.is very simple to destroy hidden information or change the meaning (modification of one space lead up to disturbance of the hidden information). More difficult algorithm relies on data hiding in images (see chapter 2.3). This technique refers to experienced in image processing students and will be the next steganography theme considered during studies.

Next problem was, how to put static as well as dynamic watermark into software. Software watermarking embeds a copyright notice in the software code to allow the owners of the software to assert their intellectual property rights. Students have to prepare new software which will realize watermarking and fingerprinting techniques in connection with the following transformations.

Static watermarks are stored in the application executable itself. In the case of Java, information could be hidden in any of the many section of the class file format: constant pool table, method table, line number table, etc. There are two basic types of static watermarks code watermarks which are stored in the section of the executable that contains instruction, and data watermarks which are stored in any other section, including headers, string section, debugging information section, etc. Static data watermarks are very common since they are easy to construct and recognize. Students tried to embed static data watermark in the initialized data (string) section:
CONST C = "Copyright..."
or in the text (code) section of the program. As an example may be the following code:

```
char v;
switch e {
    case 2 : v = 'C';
    case 5 : v = 'O';
    case 6 : v = 'P';
    case 8 : v = 'Y';
    ... }
```

Static watermarks suffer from being easily attacked by semantic-preserving transformations. In contrary dynamic watermarks are stored in a program's execution state, rather than in the program code itself. There are three kinds of dynamic watermarks. In each case, the application program P is run with a predetermined input sequence $X=X1,...,Xn$ which makes the application enter a state which represents the watermark. The methods differ in which part of the program state the watermark is stored, and in the way it is extracted. Namely, there are Easter Egg Watermarks, Data Structure Watermarks and Execution Trace Watermarks. The defining characteristic of an Ester Egg watermark is that it performs some action that is immediately perceptible by the user, making watermark extraction trivial. Typically, the code will display a copyright message or an unexpected image on the screen. Next example shows situation when watermark is embedded in the unexpected behaviour (an "Easter Egg") of the program P when it is run with input X.

X → if Input = = X { Display(Software Author Picture)}.

The main problem with Ester Egg watermarks is that they seem to be easy to locate. Once the right input sequence has been discovered by other student, standard-debugging techniques will allow him to trace the location of the watermark in the executable and then remove or disable it completely.

Dynamic data structure watermark usually being embedded within the state (global, heap, and stack data, etc.). The watermark is extracted by examining the current values held in P's variables, after the end of the input sequence has been reached. This can be done using either a dedicated watermark extraction routine, which is linked in with the executing program, or by running the program under a debugger. In the next example the watermark gets embedded in the global variables V when the program P is run with input X.

```
String V;
if Input ==X {
V[1] ='C'; V[3] ='P';
V[2] ='O'; V[4] ='Y';
V[6] ='I'; V[5] ='R';
...
}
```

Dynamic execution trace watermark within the trace (either instruction or addresses, or both) of the program as it is being run with a particular input X. The watermark is extracted by monitoring some (possibly statistical) properties of the address trace and/or the sequence of operators executed.

Another example is the technique of watermark embedding in the execution trace when the programme P is run with input X.

X → [programme P] → push 'C'; ...; push 'O'; push 'P'; ...; push 'Y'; push 'R'; ...

Lots of software were implemented with steganography techniques and static as well as dynamic watermarks. Students tried to hide various kinds of information start with name, address, and end with nickname, picture, etc. Proposed techniques were interesting and up to date and students will use experienced techniques with all designed software. An effective watermarking scheme is one of possible solutions that can in future resist most attacks against software products. We hope, prior and next projects will arouse interest with new students too and they will try to add own ideas and algorithms to cryptography discipline.

4. CONCLUSION

Steganography and watermarking is a very interesting technique. In connection with cryptography, steganography supplies students with new subjects, new techniques, and new challenges. They are very interested in creation of a new software, cognition new techniques and methods. These techniques and a lot more (including obfuscation, digital signature, tamper-proofing, HASP keys, etc.) will be future topics to work with students.

The success of steganography is dependent upon selecting the proper media and hiding techniques. This paper provided basic information to steganography techniques. To date, a general detection technique applicable to digital image steganography has not been devised.

Steganography applies not only to digital images but also to other media such as: voice, text and binary files, and communication channels. During our work with students new software was created to hide and detect hidden data. Development in the area of covert communications and steganography will continue.

Acknowledgements - This work is supported by Bialystok University of Technology - grant S/WI/3/03

5.   REFERENCES

[1] N.F. Johnson, Z. Duric, S. Jajodia: Information Hiding Steganography and Watermarking – Attacks and Countermeasures; Kluwer Academic Publishers, 2001.

[2] S. Katzenbeisser, F.A.P.Petitcolas: Information Hiding – techniques for steganography and digital watermarking; Artech House, 2000

[3] S. Singh: The code book. The science of secrecy from ancient Egypt to quantum cryptography. Swiat Ksiazki, 2003, pp. 19-21, 45.

[4] D. Kahn: The Codebreakers. 2nd edition; Macmillan, 1996.

[5] B. Norman: Secret Warfare; Acropolis Books, 1973.

[6] Herodotus: The Histories, London, England: J.M. Dent & Sons, Ltd, 1992.

[7] V.N.Yarmolik, Proceedings of CISIM 2003, Obfuscation, watermarking and tamper-proofing: modern approaches for software ownership protection.

[8] C. Bancroft: Genomic Steganography: Amplifiable Microdots. Talk provided at Biomomolecular Computation Workshop: Its Potential and Applications, National Science Foundation, Arlington, Virginia, 1999.

[9] C.T. Clelland, V. Risca, C. Bancroft: Hiding Messages in DNA Microdots. Nature, 399 (6736):533-534, 1999.

[10] A. Gehani, T.H. LaBean, J.H. Reif: DNA-based Cryptography, in [11], 2000

[11] E. Winfree, D.K. Gifford (eds.): DNA Based Computers V, Massachusetts Institute of Technology, June 1999, DIMACS Series in Discrete Mathematics and Theoretical Computer Science, vol. 54, American Mathematical Society, 2000.

[12] E.H. Wilkins: A History of Italian Literature, London: Geoffrey Cumberlege, Oxford University Press, 1954, pp. 105-106.

[13] A. Kerckhoffs: La Cryptographie Militaire, Journal des Sciences Militaires, vol. 9, Jan. 1883, pp. 5-38.

[14] M. Roe: Cryptography and Evidence, Ph.D. thesis, University of Cambridge, Clare College, 1997.

[15] R.J. Anderson, R.M. Needham, A. Shamir: The Steganographic File System, in Proceedings of the Second International Workshop on Information Hiding, vol. 1525 of Lecture Notes in Computer Science, Springer, 1998, pp. 73-82.

[16] T.G. Handel, M.T. Stanford: III. Hiding Data in the OSI Network Model, in.Proceedings of the First International Workshop on Information Hiding, vol. 1174 of Lecture Notes in Computer Science, Springer-Verlag, 1996, pp. 23-38.

[17] J. Lach, W.H. Mangione-Smith, M. Potkonjak: Enhanced Intellectual Property Protection for Digital Circuits on Programable Hardware, in.Proceedings of the Third International Workshop on Information Hiding, vol. 1768 of Lecture Notes in Computer Science, Springer-Verlag, 1999.

[18] J. Brassil, L. O'Gorman, N.F. Maxembchuk, S.H. Low: Document Marking and Identification using Both Line and Word Shifting, Infocom, Boston, 1995, pp. 853-860.

[19] P. Wayner: Disappearing Cryptography. Chestnut Hill, MA: Ap Professional, 1996.

[20] C.H. Rowland: Convert Channels in the TCP/IP Protocol Suite, 1996.

[21] R. Machado: "EzStego, Stego Online. Stego", 1997.

[22] A. Brown: "S-Tools for Windows", 1996.

[23] "StegoDos-Black Wolf's Picture Encoder v0.90B," 1993.

[24] H. Hastur: "Mandelsteg", 1994.

[25] R. Arachelian: "White Noise Storm", 1994.

Analysis of non-linear pseudo-noise sequences

MAREK JACKIEWICZ, EUGENIUSZ KURIATA
*University of Zielona Góra, Institute of Control and Computation Engineering,
ul. Podgórna 50, 65-246 Zielona Góra, Poland,
e-mail: {M.Jackiewicz, E.Kuriata}@issi.uz.zgora.pl*

Abstract: In this paper method of generating keys for a stream-cipher on the base of non-linear pseudo-noise sequences is presented. The most important task, ensuring suitable security of the cryptographic system, is an appropriate key selection. There exist many key generation systems but they usually posses properties, which do not allow to design a safe system. In the paper, a method of performance analysis of sequences for cryptographic application is shown. To verification of this methods of keys generation is applied by statistical tests DIEHARD and linearity test, proposed by NIST.

Key words: Latin squares, quasigroups, cryptography, pseudo-noise sequences.

1. INTRODUCTION

The most important task of cryptographic systems is to ensure the best possible safety. Through suitable algorithms and secret keys. Fulfillment of such requirements is possible by means of an appropriate management on cryptographic keys. Whilst cryptographic algorithms and transformation of a plain text into a cryptogram are known (they are for public use) the required safety relies on the ciphering key. They have to posses appropriately long period and maximum entropy [7]. Perfect secrecy is possible to attain only when the number of possible keys is as large as the number of possible plain texts. In general, the key has to be as long (or even longer) as the message length and no keys can be used more then once. Such a system is called "one-time pad". Thus, in order to fulfill the above conditions it is necessary to develop algorithms generating pseudo-random sequences.

The problem is important in cryptographic symmetrical systems, and in particularly for stream ciphers (for example with one-time pad) where for the enciphering and deciphering function the same key has to be used. Obtaining a good key is very complex problem therefore the generation of specific length of sequence in most cases does not assure its maximum entropy. That is why cryptographical systems [8, 17] will not provide a proper data protection. For this reason it is necessary to work out the new techniques of a key generation. The quasigroup can be employed for that purpose as its provides a large number of a latin squares of order more than 10 [4].

2.   QUASIGROUPS

An algebraic system

$$Q = \langle A, \bullet \rangle \tag{1}$$

consisting of q-elements of a set A and a binary operation denoted by $\bullet$, which applies on the elements from this set, is called a quasigroup [1, 5], when some two elements from the following equations

$$a \bullet x = b$$
$$y \bullet a = b \tag{2}$$

having exactly one solution. Thus, a quasigroup is rather simple algebraic system with one operation which needs neither be commutative nor associative. According to (2) the operation table in a quasigroup must be a latin square.

A square matrix of size $q \times q$, whose elements belonging to set A are placed in the way, that in each column and in each row any symbol occurs only one is called a latin square of order q. For the representation purposes of q-element set one can assume that a set A is composed of positive integers:

$$A = \{0, 1, ..., q-1\} \tag{3}$$

A quasigroup

$$R = \langle A, \bullet \rangle \tag{4}$$

in which there exists an identity element $e \in A$ satisfying

$$\forall x \in A \quad x \bullet e = e \bullet x = x \tag{5}$$

is called a *loop*. A latin square of order q is said called a normalized or reduced if both elements of its first row and its first column are in natural order.

For each $q \leq 2$ the total number $L(q)$ of latin square of order q [4, 10] is given by

$$L(q) = q!(q-1)!T(q) \tag{6}$$

where:

q – number of elements in a quasigroup,
$T(q)$ – number of reduced latin squares of order q.

In Tab. 1 a number of reduced latin squares $T(q)$ of $q \leq 10$ [1, 4, 6, 10] is presented. The number of latin squares $T(q)$ rises very rapidly with q and is indeed large even for rather small q. For the sake of large number of latin squares for $q > 10$ its value can only be estimated [4] by formula

$$\prod_{k=1}^{q}(k!)^{\frac{q}{k}} \geq L(q) \geq \frac{(q!)^{2q}}{(q)^{q^2}} \tag{7}$$

q	$T(q)$	$T(q)$
3	1	1
4	4	4
5	56	56
6	9 048	$9.05 \cdot 10^3$
7	16 942 080	$1.69 \cdot 10^7$
8	535 281 401 585	$5.35 \cdot 10^{11}$
9	377 597 570 964 258 816	$3.78 \cdot 10^{17}$
10	7 580 721 483 160 132 811 489 280	$7.58 \cdot 10^{24}$

Tab.1. Number of reduced latin squares $T(q)$ versus q

For example the number of all latin squares $L(q)$ for $q = 128$ and $q = 256$ elements are given bellow

$$1.64 \cdot 10^{21090} \geq L(128) \geq 3.38 \cdot 10^{20665},$$
$$7.53 \cdot 10^{102804} \geq L(256) \geq 3.05 \cdot 10^{101723}.$$

3. PSEUDO-NOISE SEQUENCES

There exist many key generating programs of stream-ciphers, but only a few at them fulfil conditions described by Shannon [18]. He affirm that safe cipher should have entropy similar to maximum possible one [7, 18]. The same concerns keys, if larger entropy then larger safety. This means that the keys should employed provide near uniform distribution. One of the simplest key generators generating uniform sequence is linear feedback shift register associated to primitive polynomial over $GF(q)$ of m degree [11]. As a consequence a linear pseudo-noise sequence with period $M = q^m - 1$ is obtained. Such sequences posses many interesting properties which are very important from the point of view of cryptographic applications, i.e. in constructing the cryptographic key. The only shortcoming of such a sequence is its repetition which allows to recover all the sequence based on its $2m$ elements only.

That is why linear pseudo-noise sequences cannot directly be applied as a cryptographic key [11].

3.1   Non-linear pseudo-noise sequences

The linear pseudo-noise sequences cannot be applied as a cryptographic key. Thus, one can apply simple quasigroup to get the sequence with better statistical parameters.
Let

$$a = a_0 a_1 ... a_{q^m - 2} \tag{8}$$

be an arbitrary sequence of elements from $GF(q)$, and let

$$R = \begin{bmatrix} a_i & a_{i+1} & \cdots & a_{i+m+c-1} \\ a_{i+1} & a_{i+2} & \cdots & a_{i+m+c} \\ \cdot & \cdot & \cdots & \cdot \\ \cdot & \cdot & \cdots & \cdot \\ \cdot & \cdot & \cdots & \cdot \\ a_{i+m+c-1} & a_{i+m+c} & \cdots & a_{2(i+m+c-1)} \end{bmatrix}$$

be an $(c+m) \times (c+m)$ matrix over $GF(q)$, the rows of which are consecutive elements from the sequence (8). The subscript i, $0 \le i \le q^m - 2$, are taken modulo $q^m - 1$.
If

$$\exists i, \ 0 \le i \le q^m - 2, \ \exists c \ge 1 \left[\det(R) \ne 0 \right] \tag{9}$$

and if in the sequence only one element of $GF(q)$ occurs $q^{m-1} - 1$ times, while every other element from $GF(q)$ occurs q^{m-1} times, a sequence (8) is called non-linear pseudo-noise sequence (NLPN).
Let

$$q = p^k > 2 \tag{10}$$

where p – prime, k – positive integer ≤ 1 and a and a^i denote a linear pseudo-noise sequence of length $q^m - 1$ over $GF(q)$ and its cyclic shift i places to the right, respectively.
The sequences

$$a \bullet a^i, \ a^i \bullet a \tag{11}$$

are non-linear pseudo-noise sequences (NLPN), if

$$i \cong \left(\frac{q^m - 1}{q - 1} \right) \qquad (12)$$

3.2   Modification of NLPN

The above mentioned mathematical apparatus makes possible generating of non-linear pseudo-noise sequences according to the block diagram shown in Fig. 1. In every generators the seed allows to generate the same sequences. In this case the seed ingredients are as follows:

- coefficients of a primitive polynomial over $GF(q)$ of m degree used for generating linear pseudo-noise sequence (LPN),
- initial condition of linear feedback shift register (LFSR),
- operation table in a quasigroup or three q–element permutations,
- delay i.

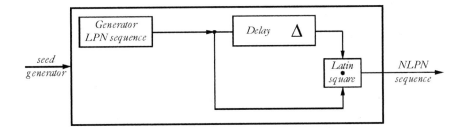

Fig. 1. A scheme of generating non-linear pseudo-noise sequences.

Thus if one establishes parameters of a seed, every time will be generated the same sequence of key. Then the seed should be send by a safe channel (if such exists) to a recipient. This implies that each data transmission requires sending a new seed.

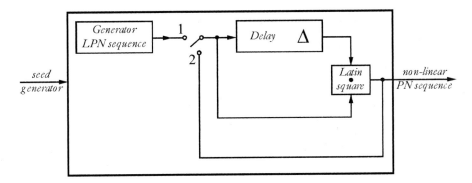

Fig. 2. A scheme of generating non-linear sequences in feedback loop

To overcome this problem we can propose a modification of this method consisting in applying feedback (Fig. 2). It makes it possible to generating many different keys based on one seed only.

4.   ANALYSIS OF QUALITY OF SEQUENCE KEY

The problem of generating number sequences is relatively complex. Thus in most cases quality assessment of generators (or sequences generated by this generators) is based on statistical tests. Another possibility is to check entropy, that is the investigation of frequency of signs occurrence in a sequence. Fig. 3 presents results of these tests as well as the histograms of linear and non-linear pseudo-noise sequences.

For the sake of presentation purposes the number of elements in histograms from Fig. 3 is appropriately restricted.

While testing non-linear pseudo-noise sequences (with full period) the distribution of signs of ASCII codes is almost uniform.

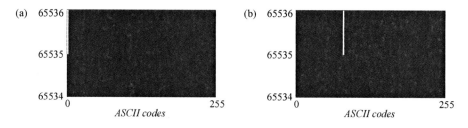

Fig. 3. Histograms of linear and non-linear pseudo-noise sequences generated with primitive polynomial over $GF(q)$ of third degree: (a) for LPN; (b) for NLPN.

5.   MUTUAL CORRELATION AND AUTOCORRELATION OF SEQUENCE

The above sequences [11] posses cryptographic properties. These properties are connected with their robustness to analysis and prediction if sequence elements by statistical methods. Such a property is an autocorrelation function (Fig. 4, Fig. 5), where autocorrelation function and mutual correlation were presented. These characteristics allow to think that between consecutive iterations there is a lack of any relationship, which may contribute weak point of keys generator.

The autocorrelation function permits to distinct from linear pseudo-noise sequences and non-linear sequences. The autocorrelation function $\rho(i)$ of pseudo-noise sequences with length $M = q^m - 1$ can be defined as follows

$$\rho(i) = \frac{A - D}{M} \tag{13}$$

where:

  A – number of places, in which pseudo-noise sequence a and its cyclic shift a^i, for any $i \in \{0; M\}$, have the same values in identical positions,
  D – number of places, in which theses values are different $A+D = M$.

  The autocorrelation function for $i = 0$, $i = M$ and its multiple are always equal 1.

  For pseudo-noise sequences generated by linear recursive dependent sequences associate with any primitive polynomial, every autocorrelation function will be the same. However for non-linear pseudo-noise sequences the autocorrelation function in every case is different [6].

6.   STATISTICAL TESTS NLPN SEQUENCES

  For the proposed generators of pseudo-noise sequences conducted statistical tests [16, 20], where conducted and received results are presented in Tab. 2. These tests are taken from DIEHARD [12] package and they are the used for testing binary sequences. The test for pseudo-noise sequences generated with primitive polynomial over *GF*(256) of third degree (16777215 elements) [12].

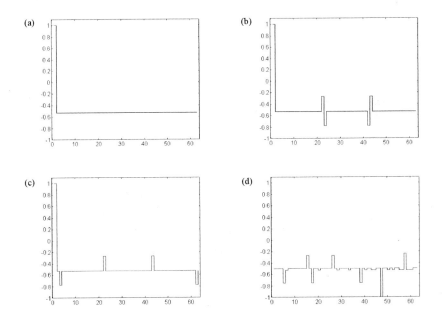

Fig. 4. Autocorrelation function of linear and non-linear pseudo-noise sequences and mutual correlation for linear and non-linear pseudo-noise sequences: (a) LPN; (b) NLPN; (c) NLPN; (d) mutual correlation for NLPN and LPN sequences.

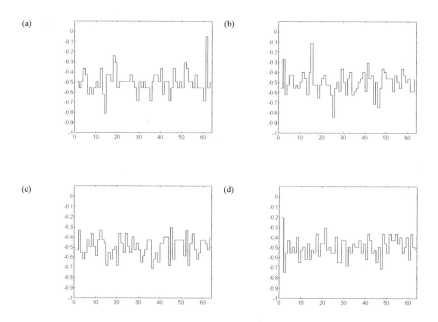

Fig. 5. Mutual correlation for non-linear pseudo-noise sequences (NLPN) and sequences obtained by feedback: (a) NLPN and NLPN1; (b) NLPN oraz NLPN2; (c) NLPN oraz NLPN25; (d) NLPN oraz NLPN50.

Test names and number of its results		LPN	NLPN	number sequences					IDEA
1		2	3	4	5	6	7	8	9
Birthday Spacings	*1*	+	+	+	+	+	+	+	+
Overlapping Permutations	*2*	+	+	+	+	+	+	+	+
Ranks of 31x31 matrices	*1*	1	+	+	+	+	+	+	+
Ranks of 32x32 matrices	*1*	1	+	+	+	+	+	+	+
Ranks of 6x8 Matrices	*1*	+	+	+	+	+	+	+	+
Monkey Tests on 20-bit Words	*20*	20	1	+	2	1	1	3	1
Monkey Tests OPSO	*23*	23	2	1	2	1	1	1	1
Monkey Tests OQSO	*28*	28	+	+	+	+	2	+	2
Monkey Tests DNA	*31*	31	3	1	1	2	1	1	1
Count the 1`s in a Stream of Bytes	*2*	+	+	+	+	+	+	+	+
Count the 1`s in Specific Bytes	*25*	2	+	4	4	2	2	1	3
Parking Lot Test	*1*	+	+	+	+	+	1	+	+
Minimum Distance Test	*1*	1	+	+	+	+	+	+	+
Random Spheres Test	*1*	+	+	+	+	+	+	+	+
The Sqeeze Test	*1*	+	+	1	+	+	+	+	+
Overlapping Sums Test	*1*	+	+	+	+	+	+	+	+
Runs Test	*4*	1	+	+	1	+	+	+	+
The Craps Test	*1*	+	+	+	+	+	+	+	+

Tab. 2. The results of statistical test for linear and non-linear pseudo-noise sequences as well as sequence generated with feedback.

Sequences	result
Linear pseudo-noise sequence	20
Nonlinear pseudo-noise sequence	+
Nonlinear sequence with feedback 25 iteration	+
Nonlinear sequence with feedback 50 iteration	+

Tab. 3. The results of linearity test proposed by NIST.

In Tab. 2 the name of a test in presented in the first column as well as the number. In next columns was written (+), when all tests were classified as correct or numerical values denoting a number of failed tests. Results in the second column were introduced for linear pseudo-noise sequence. These results do not allow to use these sequences, because of the linearity property [11]. Third column presents results for non-linear pseudo-noise sequence. In column denoted from 4 to 8, results for sequences generation with feedback after 1, 2, 25 as well as 50 iteration are shown. The last column presents the results for cryptograms obtained with the IDEA algorithm. This cryptogram is recognized as a safe one, therefore the results for NLPN suggest that it can be treated as safe. Generally one can assume that generating non-linear pseudo-noise sequences allows to achieve good results of statistical tests, as well as a sequences obtained from the method with feedback have similar results, in that case these sequences can be successfully used as a cryptographic keys.

In Tab. 3 the results of linearity test [16] (after 20 tests) for linear as well as non-linear pseudo-noise sequences, and also for sequences generated with feedback method one presented. Results of this test confirm that LPN sequences are completely useless (all 20 samples failed test). On the other hand for non-linear pseudo-noise sequences as well as for sequences generated with feedback method the results of this tests were passes (sign (+) in a table).

7.   CONCLUSIONS

In this work the method of generating non-linear pseudo-noise sequences based on linear pseudo-noise sequences and quasigroups was presented. Additionally the method of generating sequences with feedback was shown. This method makes possible generating the infinite number of one-time keys, near simultaneous behaviour of good statistical parameters. The results of statistical tests as well as histograms of these sequences permit its suitable use as a safe cryptographical keys.

REFERENCES

[1] Dénes J., Keedwell A. D. 1974. 'Latin Squares and Their Applications'. *Akadémiai Kiadó*, Budapest.
[2] Gutmann P. 1998. 'Software Generation of Practically Strong Random Numbers.'. *Proceedings of the 7th USENIX Security Symposium.*

[3] Jackiewicz M., Kuriata E., Hebisz T. 2003. 'Safety of Key Generators'. *Proceedings of 1st International Conference on Computer Information Systems and Industrial Management Application CISIM'03.*, Elk

[4] Jacobson M. T., Matthews P. 1996. 'Generating Uniformly Distributed Random Latin Squares'. *Jornal of Combinatorial Designs*, 4(6): pp. 405–437

[5] Kościelny Cz. 1996. 'A Method of Constructing Quasigroup–Based Stream–Ciphers'. *Applied Mathematics and Computer Science*, vol. 6: pp. 109–121.

[6] Kościelny Cz. 1997. 'NLPN sequences over *GF*(*q*)'. *Applied Mathematics and Computer Science*, Quasigroup and Related Systems, vol. 4: pp. 89–102.

[7] Kuriata E. 2001. 'Teoria informacji i kodowania'. *Oficyna Wydawnicza Politechniki Zielonogórskiej*

[8] Kutyłowski M., Strothmann W. B. 1998. 'Kryptografia. Teoria i praktyka zabezpieczania systemów komputerowych'. *Oficyna Wydawnicza Read ME*, Warszawa.

[9] Lidl R., Niederreiter H. 1986. ,' Introduction to finite fields and their applications'. *Cambridhe University Press*

[10] McKay B. D., Rogoyski E. 1995. 'Latin Squares of Order 10'. *The Electronic Journal of Combinatorics*, vol. 2, no. 3: pp. 1–4,

[11] MacWilliams F. J., Sloane N. J. A. 1976. 'Pseudo–Random Sequences and Arrays'. *Proceedings of the IEEE*, vol. 64(12): pp. 1715–1729

[12] Marsaglia G. Statistical tests DIEHARD. http://stat.fsu.edu/~geo/diehard.html

[13] Menezes A. J., van Oorschot P. C. , Vanstone S.~A. 1996. 'Handbook of Applied Cryptography'. *CRC Press*

[14] Ritter T. Cryptography home page. http://www.ciphersbyritter.com

[15] Robling Denning D. E. 1983. 'Cryptography and Data Security'. *Addison–Wesley Publishing Company, Inc*

[16] Rukhin A. et al. 2001. 'A Statistical Test Suite for Random and Pseudorandom Number Generators for Crypographic Applications'. *National Institute of Standards and Technology Special Publication 800-22 (with revisions dated May 15, 2001)*

[17] Schneier B. 1994. 'Applied Cryptography. Protocols, Algorithms, and Source Code in C'. *John Wiley & Sons*

[18] Shannon C. E. 1949. 'Communication Theory of Secret Systems'. *Bell System Technical Journal*, 28(4): pp. 656–715.

[19] Stokłosa J., Bilski T., Pankowski T. 2001. 'Bezpieczeństwo danych w systemach informatycznych'. *Wydawnictwo Naukowe PWN*, Warszawa.

[20] Wieczorkowski R., Zieliński R. 1997. 'Komputerowe generatory liczb losowych'. *Wydawnictwa Naukowo–Techniczne*, Warszawa.

Tool support for detecting defects in object-oriented models

JANUSZ GÓRSKI, ALEKSANDER JARZĘBOWICZ,
RAFAŁ LESZCZYNA, JAKUB MILER, MARCIN OLSZEWSKI
Department of Software Engineering, Gdańsk University of Technology
Narutowicza 11/12, 80-952 Gdańsk
e-mail: {jango,olek,r.leszczyna,jakubm}@eti.pg.gda.pl, olszes@ds2.pg.gda.pl

Abstract: Object-oriented models are commonly used in software projects. They may be affected, however, by various defects introduced easily due to e.g. wrong understanding of modelled reality, making wrong assumptions or editorial mistakes. The defects should be identified and corrected as early as possible, preferably before the model is used as the basis for the subsequent representations of the system. To assure the effectiveness of the defect detection process we need both, better analysis methods and effective tool support. The paper introduces a new analytical method called UML-HAZOP and presents a tool supporting the application of this method.

Key words: UML, defect detection, inspection, object-oriented modelling

1.   INTRODUCTION

During a software development project multiple products are created including, apart from code, the documentation of the system and of the development process. This documentation takes different forms depending on the chosen development cycle model, the project management decisions, the supporting tools used etc. There are, however, a number of products that are common for most projects. First of all they include a (logical) sequence of subsequent representations of the system, starting from the requirements specification and ending at code. Among these are system models of different level of abstraction (business, analytical, design). It is a present tendency that such models are expressed in object-oriented terms.

Software products are not free from defects. A defect can be introduced during any phase of the development process and then it remains in the product of this phase. If the defect is not detected and removed at the end of the phase, it is passed to the products of the subsequent phases. A typical example of such propagation is a defect in the requirements. If goes undetected, it will affect all other representations, including the code. Experience shows that the cost of finding and removing a defect increases significantly if the defect goes undetected through a number of development phases. This causes a strong motivation to detect and remove defects as early as possible, preferably at the same phase where they were born. To fulfil this expectation we need adequate analytical methods, capable to detect defects in various software representations, including those that are created early in the development process.

Object-oriented models increase their popularity in the software development community. Such models are built early in the development process and therefore they are of particular interest from the defect detection standpoint. Partially formalized syntax of such models provides for more precise definition of the criteria and rules of analysis than it was possible with respect to the "raw" or partially structured text which is found in more "traditional" software project documents. The advent of the Unified *Modelling Language* (UML) which is becoming *de facto* standard for object-oriented modelling increases the motivation in researching towards new analytical methods of UML models because of their potential applicability to many software projects.

Defect detection in documentation usually takes a form of a review. Such reviews can take different forms depending on process definition, scope and level of formalisation. The reviews are supported by checklists that are used to store information about the most common defects. Such checklists can be developed in advance by systematic analysis of the language (UML) and the resulting modelling constructs.

In this paper we propose a new method of analysis called *UML-HAZOP*. Its brief description is presented in section 2 (a more thorough description can be found in [2]). The analysis of software models is an expensive process which requires the participation of humans and consumes significant resources. To decrease this effort, the application of the method should be automated, to as great extent as possible. The discussion of the scope of automation is presented in section 3. The conclusions from this discussion were used to design and implement a software tool supporting the application of UML-HAZOP. The paper presents the tool, its functionality and the support provided to particular activities of the method (section 4), as well as its architecture and technologies used in the implementation (section 5). We conclude by recalling some experiences with using the method and present plans for the future development.

2. UML-HAZOP METHOD

While building an object-oriented model, the most essential class of defects is related to incorrect representation of the modelled reality (resulting from e.g. wrong understanding of the modelled problem or making incorrect assumptions). Syntax errors are also possible, but their detection or prevention (e.g. by the mechanisms built into a CASE tool) is much easier, so we consider them as less interesting. We assume that the main focus of the analysis should be on the semantics of the model, not on its syntax. The essence of the modelling is to describe a part of reality using elements of a particular notation. By checking if a particular model element is used correctly (in the sense of proper representation of the reality being modelled) we can help in detecting defects that are present in the model. It is possible to systematically generate such checks and to store them in a form of checklists. The development of such checklists is not an easy task, however.

In the proposed approach we use HAZOP (*Hazard and Operability Study*) to support a systematic generation of checklists. HAZOP is an analytical method originally developed to detect hazards in safety critical systems. The method originated in the petrochemical industry and was adapted to software engineering in early nineties [3]. The method (in its original form) concentrates on systematic reviewing of the connections present in a system model. In the petrochemical domain, these connections are the pipes included in a chemical installation. In the software domain "connections" can be interpreted in different ways – it could be a physical communication channels but also a logical connection e.g. the relationship on a class diagram or the transition on a state diagram.

The idea of the method is very simple. For each reviewed connection, its attributes are first identified. An attribute is a well defined, atomic part or property of the connection. Then the method makes use of guidewords - a short phrases suggesting errors and deviations from the correct state of the connection e.g. NO, LESS, OTHER THAN, LATE. The application of the guidewords to the attributes results in the list of hypothetical deviations related to that connection.

UML-HAZOP method is an adaptation of HAZOP to the analysis of UML diagrams. At present, we have a complete set of checklists related to connections in class diagrams. The checklists for other UML diagrams are under elaboration. During the analysis of a class diagram the connections are e.g. the relationships between classes, in particular *Association* and *Generalization*. These relationships have a number of attributes e.g. *aggregation, name, multiplicity* etc. The guidewords form the set given in Table 1 are applied to the relationships and their attributes to suggest possible deviations. Not every suggestion gives a sensible result, but in many cases they refer to potential defects. The example interpretations related to the *aggregation* attribute are given in Table 2. All sensible interpretations (for the attributes included in the analysis) form so called *HAZOP table* for a given type of relationship e.g. *Association*. The analysis of an UML diagram is carried out by applying the HAZOP table (the checklist) to each relationship represented in the diagram.

Guideword	General interpretation
NO	The complete negation of the design intention. No part of the intention is achieved and nothing else happens.
MORE	A quantitative increase.
LESS	A quantitative decrease.
AS WELL AS	All the design intention is achieved together with additions.
PART OF	Only some of the design intention is achieved.
REVERSE	The logical opposite of the intention is achieved.
OTHER THAN	Complete substitution, where no part of the original intention is achieved but something quite different happens.
EARLY	Something happens earlier than expected relative to clock time.
LATE	Something happens later than expected relative to clock time.
BEFORE	Something happens before it is expected, relating to order or sequence.
AFTER	Something happens after it is expected, relating to order or sequence.

Tab.1. Generic HAZOP guidewords

Guideword	Interpretation
NO	The aggregation that should be present is not marked in the diagram.
AS WELL AS	The aggregation is wrong and should be removed.
OTHER THAN	Wrong aggregation type is marked i.e. strong instead of weak or inversely.
MORE	Too many classes are aggregated; some of them should not be included in this aggregation.
LESS	The aggregation does not include some classes (present in the diagram or not) that should be aggregated.

Tab. 2. Interpretations for *AssociationEnd.aggregation* attribute

The UML-HAZOP analysis is performed within a defined and managed process. The structure of this process is shown in Fig.1.

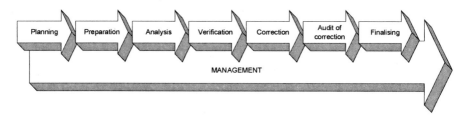

Fig. 1. Structure of UML-HAZOP analysis process

The process begins with the decision that a given UML model should be subjected to the UML-HAZOP analysis. Planning of the overall process is the first step and includes schedule preparation, assigning participants to tasks and selecting the checklists for all connections that are present in the model. The preparation phase consists of acquainting the analysts with the project documentation and with the method of analysis (if it is not already known). In the analysis phase, a systematic review of the model with use of checklists is performed and all detected defects are registered. Next, the list of defects is passed to the author of the model for verification (he/she accepts or denies their presence). The accepted defects are then corrected by the author during the correction phase. After that, an audit takes place to ensure that all defects have been removed. During the finalising step, the process is formally closed, the final product (the corrected model) is released and the process statistics (the number of detected defects, efficiency metrics etc.) are collected. To ensure its smooth realisation the process has to be managed by a person assigned to this task.

The detailed description of the method and its experimental results can be found in [2].

3.   SCOPE OF AUTOMATION

As UML-HAZOP heavily involves human judgement the extent of its potential automation is limited in scope. The decision, if a potential defect suggested by a checklist does really occur in the analysed diagram, often requires the use of additional knowledge, which is not directly expressed in the model and has to be derived and interpreted by the analyst. If the analysed models represent a single domain then such interpretations can be (partially) delegated to an "intelligent" tool as it was already proposed for chemical plants [4]. However, UML-HAZOP does not make any assumptions about the type of analysed systems nor the elements they are composed of. The method focuses on the features of UML – the language that can be used to model any system. Therefore, the decision, whether a suggested defect is present in the model or not, requires a human expert intervention.

The part of the UML-HAZOP analysis process in which a human can be replaced by a tool is the preparation of HAZOP tables. It is a laborious task that can result in many errors (e.g. if some connections are mistakenly omitted). Having a tool taking as the input an UML diagram (e.g. created by a CASE tool) and capable of generating HAZOP tables could save much time and effort. The tool could take care for the completeness and correctness of the generated tables as well. The application of a simple algorithm to eliminate redundant items from the HAZOP tables (those that suggest impossible defects for a particular connection) could be another advantage. For example, if in a given diagram, aggregation is not used with the *Association* relationship, it is pointless to consider the defect addressing "wrong type of aggregation" (strong instead of weak or inversely).

The tool could also support the analysis by providing a user friendly interface to collect and store the analysts' decisions and comments and by generating various kinds of statistics.

Another important issue is a support for teamwork. A network based tool could provide for communication and information exchange between the participants of the analysis process without the necessity of gathering all of them in one place.

4. FUNCTIONALITY OF THE TOOL

4.1 Scope of functionality

The tool supports the following phases of the UML-HAZOP process: planning, analysis, verification and management.

In the planning phase the tool allows to create a new project, to read in the data about diagrams to be analysed and to generate, for each diagram, the corresponding HAZOP tables. It also supports the assignment of the users to the project and to their roles within the project.

Analysis and verification are entirely performed with the use of the tool. All users' decisions concerning defects are registered and stored by the system.

Concerning the management of the analysis process, the tool supports users management (assigning to project, exclusion from project, change of roles), projects management and diagrams management.

4.2   Users and roles

The system is accessible only for registered users. A user has to enter his/her password before beginning his work. Creating and maintaining user accounts is the task of the administrator. It is in fact his only task – the administrator does not participate in the analysis process and does not have access to any other data.

Distinct participants of the analysis process usually have different duties; this is why the tool supports a number of predefined roles:

- **Manager** - a person responsible for the whole analysis of particular project documentation. He/she opens and closes the project and decides about granting to the other users the access rights to the project documents. The access rights can be read/write (in case of Analyst and Designer) or read-only (in case of Observer).

- **Analyst** – a user who performs the analysis and inserts the results to the HAZOP tables.

- **Designer** – the author of the UML diagram subjected to the analysis. His task is to verify the results of the analysis and, if necessary, to correct the diagram.

- **Observer** – a user who reviews the results of the analysis for e.g. training or verifying purposes, but does not directly participate in the analysis process. Observer does not enter any data to the system.

Within a project it is possible to assign more than one role to a user (e.g. Manager and Analyst) and to assign a given role to many users (Manager is an exception – there can be only one Manager per project). The assignment of roles is first done when opening a new project, but later it can be changed anytime by the Manager.

4.3   Managing projects and diagrams

The information stored in the system has been structured into multiple layers. Each autonomous analytical task is called a *project*. Each project has a Manager and other participants assigned. A project encompasses a number (usually many) UML *diagrams*. Each diagram has its Designer (the author of the diagram). With each diagram there is a set of associated *HAZOP tables* concerning its connections or other elements that are the subject of analysis. HAZOP tables are generated automatically and the results of analysis and verification are registered in them.

A new project is created by its Manager. The diagrams are imported in an electronic form from a CASE tool (e.g. Rational Rose) and the corresponding HAZOP tables are generated automatically (see section 4.4). Projects as well as diagrams can be deleted together with all their contents. It is also possible to close and reopen them many times. A closed diagram or project is still stored in the system and is visible to the users (but no changes are allowed) – this way it is possible to "freeze" the current state of work.

4.4   Importing data from a CASE tool

The import of UML diagrams from a CASE tool (*Rational Rose* in our case) is achieved by the upload of the file containing the diagram. It is necessary to specify the path to the MDL file in which *Rose* stores the complete information about the UML model of interest. After the file is read, the system interprets it and extracts the list of all diagrams contained in the model. For each diagram, the information about its name, type and package it belongs to is given to the user together with the possibility to choose for which diagrams HAZOP tables should be generated. The user can give a new name to the diagram, in other case the original names (sometimes ambiguous) extracted from the Rose document would be preserved.

The following tasks are performed in an entirely automatic way. First the system reads from the *Rose* document the contents of each chosen diagram (in particular the data of all connections present in the diagram). Then using the built-in list of potential defects, a separate HAZOP table for each connection is created. The redundant rows of tables representing impossible defects of a given connection are identified and removed, so the user is provided with a set of HAZOP tables ready to be analysed.

4.5 Analysis and verification of HAZOP tables

When a user selects a diagram for further analysis, he/she is given a list of HAZOP tables generated for this diagram. Each table represents one connection (a relationship in case of the class diagram) and is described by its name and names of associated elements (e.g. classes). It provides for traceability between the table and the diagram elements. The task of the Analyst is, for each row of HAZOP table, to decide about the credibility of the defect suggested by this row. Those decisions are reflected by changing the colour of the row on the user display. This allows to notice, in an easy way, all the defects detected by the Analyst. The inspected rows of the HAZOP table can be also extended with comments giving the rationale for the undertaken decision.

The Designer is in charge of verifying the analysis results. The comments given by the Analyst can be helpful in performing this task. Designer is the author of the analysed model and his task is to accept or deny the decisions of the Analyst. For each defect suggested by Analyst, Designer confirms or rejects its credibility. The tool again uses colours to distinguish the rows with confirmed defects and those defects that have been denied.

Apart from taking decision, the Designer can write an additional comment e.g. to explain Analyst's doubts. Comments of the Designer are presented together with the Analyst's ones making a record of discussion about the inspected diagram.

The Observer has a possibility to review the current state of HAZOP tables. His/her user interface is similar to that used by the other participants, with the read-only access.

5. ARCHITECTURE OF THE TOOL

UML-HAZOP tool is a client – server Internet application. The server side is responsible for receiving, processing and storing the data as well as for assuring the concurrent access to its services. The client side is responsible for the interaction with a user. An important feature of the system is the integration with a CASE tool which is the source UML models to be inspected. The current prototype version of our system interfaces with *Rational Rose*.

All what a user needs to work remotely with the UML-HAZOP tool is a workstation equipped with an Internet browser and connected to the Internet. No dedicated software is used on the client side. Input data required for the analysis are MDL files (*Rational Rose* format). A Rose document is uploaded to the server from the user workstation (optionally after being compressed to ZIP format). It is then processed on the server to extract the necessary information. Although the *Rose* tool is not directly used in the analysis, it is useful for reviewing and correcting the original diagrams. Fig. 2 shows the configuration of user's workstation.

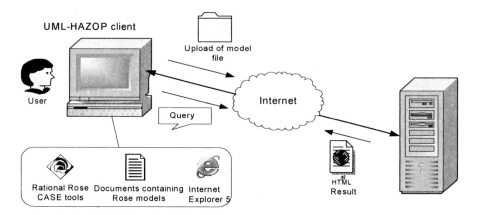

Fig. 2. Architecture of UML-HAZOP system from client perspective

The configuration of UML-HAZOP server is shown on Fig. 3. The main element of the system is a WWW server which processes users' queries. For security reasons, the communication is permitted only using HTTPS protocol. The WWW server works in a multi-threaded mode, so the concurrent access of many users is possible. The business logic of UML-HAZOP application is realised by *Active Server Pages* (ASP) in cooperation with *ActiveX* components and *Java* classes. The results of user's queries are returned by ASP scripts as HTML pages and sent by WWW server to client's workstation.

To ensure persistent and reliable data storage, a transactional DBMS system (SQL server) is used. The stored procedures encapsulate the internal data structure, making the use of defined interfaces the only way to get access to data.

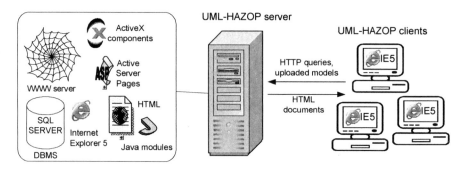

Fig. 3. Architecture of UML-HAZOP system from server perspective

Internal mechanisms of UML-HAZOP system are illustrated on Fig. 4. *Rational Rose* documents sent to the server by users contain data about UML models and diagrams expressed in a format used only by *Rational* products. To make integration of our system with other CASE tools possible, the introduction of an internal, intermediate data format was necessary. The purpose of this format is to form an interface between CASE tools using documents of different internal structure and UML-HAZOP tool data processing subsystems. We have decided to use XML language (and its standard interchange model – XMI), because it provides a complete representation of UML models and the processing of XML documents is supported by a number of Java packages available in the Internet. XML is also used in most of internal interfaces between UML-HAZOP tool subsystems.

The source data describing models to be analyzed is translated first to intermediate XMI format and then to the form of HAZOP tables, which are stored in the database. A user during the analysis process activities communicates with the WWW server and gets the visualization of current state of analysis as HTML pages. User's commands are received by the server as HTTP queries and translated by *Active Server Pages* scripts, which also update database contents if necessary.

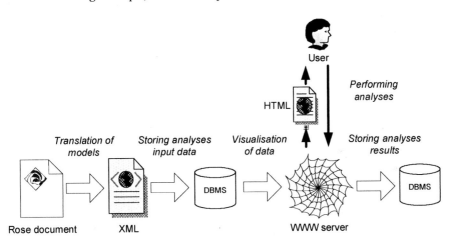

Fig. 4. Internal data processing of UML-HAZOP system

6. CONCLUSION

Development of UML-HAZOP and its supporting tool was a contribution to the EU 5th Framework Programme project DRIVE [1]. The project concerned the application of information technologies to support drugs distribution and application processes. UML-HAZOP method was applied to increase the assurance of software developed in DRIVE. It was used to analyze selected essential models e.g. the electronic patient record. The analysis results were included in the overall argumentation about the trustworthiness of the DRIVE solution (so called *trust case*) [6].

The tool served its purpose well. Its application resulted in the decrease of total effort related to the analysis process. The work spent on preparation of HAZOP tables was significantly reduced by the use of the tool. An improvement of the analysis and verification phases was also achieved due to the elimination of impossible defects from the HAZOP tables and the support provided by the user interface.

The client-server architecture and the use of Internet solutions provide for using the tool from remote locations. The possibility of cooperation and information exchange is especially important in distributed projects involving many partners. In our case, it resulted e.g. in performing analyses from Italy while some other analyses were performed at the same time from locations in Poland. The exchange of information between both sides was possible through the use of the tool.

The tool functionality is expected to expand with the progress of research on the UML-HAZOP method. The next step is to provide for analyzing the other types of UML diagrams. We will also experiment with other analytical criteria than those originally proposed by HAZOP (different selection of attributes and guidewords, different interpretations). Such criteria might originate from other methods derived from HAZOP (e.g. [5]). Various industrial case studies are being planned as well.

REFERENCES

[1] DRug In Virtual Enterprise, EU IST-DRIVE 1999-12040 research project, http://www.e-mathesis.it/Drive.
[2] Górski J., Jarzębowicz A., 'Detecting defects in object-oriented diagrams using UML-HAZOP', Foundations of Computing and Decision Sciences, vol. 27 (2002) no. 4.
[3] HAZOP Studies on Systems Containing Programmable Electronics, MoD Defence Standard 00-58, issue 2, 2000.
[4] Venkatasurbramanian V., Zhao J., Viswanathan S., 'Intelligent systems for HAZOP analysis of complex process plants', Computers and chemical engineering 24 (2000).
[5] Winther R., Johnsen O., Gran B., 'Security assessments of safety critical systems using HAZOPs', Proceedings of Computer Safety, Reliability and Security, 20th International Conference SAFECOMP 2001, Springer Lecture Notes in Computer Science 2187.
[6] Górski J., Jarzębowicz A., Leszczyna R., Miler J., Olszewski M. , 'An approach to trust case development', Proc. SAFECOMP 2003, Edinbourgh, UK, 2003

The Proposal of Protocol for Electronic Signature Creation in Public Environment

WŁODZIMIERZ CHOCIANOWICZ[1], JERZY PEJAŚ[1],
ANDRZEJ RUCIŃSKI[2]

[1] *Faculty of Computer Science & Information Systems, Technical University of Szczecin,
e-mail: filsys@unet.pl, jpejas@wi.ps.pl*
[2] *Unizeto Sp. o.o., Szczecin, Królowej Korony Polskiej 21, Poland,
e-mail: arucinski@unizeto.pl*

Abstract: Electronic signatures are introduced by more and more countries as legally binding means for signing electronic documents with the primary hope of boosting e-commerce and e-government. The security of an electronic signature creation process is the crucial issue especially in distributed environment where the frameworks (forms) of finally signed documents are delivered by the entity other than the Signing Entity (SE). Usually, after the completion of such a form with the data specific for SE, the final acceptance is performed via the encryption of completed data hash value with SE's private key. It is important to ensure the conditions when the whole document, including the form (template) delivered by the Application Provider (AP), could be trusted. It is quite different situation than the case of standing alone Secure Signature Creation Device (SSCD) separated from telecommunication channels during the signing procedure. The trust assigned to various APs can be limited so the participation of the commonly accepted Trusted Party (TP) operating on-line can be the solution of that problem.

The proposed cryptographic protocol is designed to fulfil the security requirements. It combines asymmetric and symmetric cryptographic means. SE after the completion of the form delivered by AP sends it back to AP for examination of formal correctness of the Data to Be Signed. The next steps of the protocol require the Signature Service Provider (SSP) confirmation of those data. That confirmation is transmitted directly to SE and after the mutual authentication of SSP and SE the secure channel is established and the secure electronic signature is created with the usage of the technical component (TC) being at SE's disposal. The final transfer of the signed document to AP depends on an individual SE's decision preceded by the verification of an obtained signature.

Key words: electronic signature, secure signature creation device, information security

1. INTRODUCTION

Secure signature-creation devices must, by appropriate technical and procedural means, ensure at least that (Annex III of 93/1999/EC [3]):
(a) the signature-creation-data used for signature generation can practically occur only once and their secrecy is reasonably assured;
(b) the signature-creation-data used for signature generation cannot, with reasonable assurance, be derived and the signature is protected against forgery using currently available technology;
(c) the signature-creation-data used for signature generation can be reliably protected by the legitimate signatory against the use of others.

Annex III further requires that secure signature-creation devices must not alter the data to be signed or prevent such data from being presented to the signatory prior to the signature process.

These requirements for secure signature-creation devices ensure the functionality of advanced electronic signatures. They do not cover the entire system environment in which such devices operate. There are no formal requirements in the Directive regarding the signature creation process and environment. However, a CEN Workshop Agreement (CWA 14170 [2]) supports the objectives of the EU directive by specifying security requirements for a signature creation environment (SCE), which allows the creation of qualified electronic signatures with the help of secure signature – creation devices and qualified certificates. The signature creation environment (SCE) contains a signer interacting with a signature creation system (SCS), which has embedded two components: a signature creation application (SCA) and a secure signature creation device (SSCD).

The Signature Creation System (SCS) working in a particular environment (public or non-public) should guarantee the security of a signing act for the signing entity. In practice no user is able to evaluate itself whether the system - which the signature is created in - is secure or not. Even an expert in electronic signature technology and IT security has to perform relevant investigations and tests to make such an evaluation.

Therefore the signer has to trust in somebody or something – firstly making the choice of SSCD type, then every time using that device to create an electronic signature. He or she has to be convinced that at the moment the signature is created the relevant signing software (SCA) and SSCD are the really secure SCS. The danger can occur the signature creation application (SCA) is not an original one but only imitates the software recommended by a certifying entity. *Software for electronic signatures must provide protection against malicious codes attacking the legally relevant signing process* (A. Spalka et al. [6]).

High level of security is guaranteed then and only then if SSCD blocks the usage of a private key before the successful mutual authentication of SCA and SSCD. In such a case an interoperability of SSCD is limited to the relevant dedicated software, e.g. the software of registered application provider (AP).

The user of SSCD can use it relatively freely in every environment treated as trusted by him or herself (even if it is not really trusted) or can select SSCD, which can be used in an environment stated as secure only.

Contemporary electronic signature schemes use strong cryptographic algorithms based on so called „hard computing problems", e.g. factoring of integer numbers, discrete logarithms calculation or finding some points on elliptic curves. On the other hand a widely accepted approach to electronic signature schemes forces the usage of smart cards for signing keys and signing function storage. Due to both above issues it is believed the forgery of electronic signatures by breaking the scheme or smart card security futures is nearly impossible. However it does not mean the forgery is impossible at all. The process of an electronic signature creation consists at least of four steps: a preparation of a source document to be signed, a transfer of it (completely, partly or a hash value only) from SCA to a smart card (or more precisely – to SSCD), a signature creation by a smart card operating system and sending it back to a user. It is obvious that the weak protection of transmitted data in every data exchange stated above results in doubts whether the data finally signed are really the proper input data. It is the reason why in practice the following extreme assumptions are made: (1) a user's computer or system has to be trusted, (2) a user's computer or system does not need to be trusted at all.

In further part of this paper, under the assumption that a user's computer or system is untrustworthy, the following proposals are made: a distributed signature creation environment and a functional model of signature creation applications, functions of model components and a secure protocol for advanced/qualified electronic signatures creation. The proponed system enables the user to create an electronic signature if, and only if SSCD being at his/her disposal recognizes an offered signature creation environment (SCE) as a secure one and ensuring the proper protection against malicious codes attempting to forge electronic signatures.

2. SOME PROPOSAL OF SIGNATURE CREATION SYSTEM AND RELATED SOLUTIONS

There is the only one known SCS in Poland fulfilling requirements of EU Directive and polish „Electronic Signature Act" (ESA). It is the system in which SSCD named „cryptoCertum" and SCA named „*Suscriptor Q*[1]" are combined (both produced and offered by Unizeto Co. Ltd). That system is intended for usage in non-public environment (under the signatory's control).

There are in Europe few other producers of similar devices enabling to create so called advanced electronic signatures (according to EU Directive [3] requirements; they can be identified with secure electronic signatures defined in polish ESA):

- *DigitalSign* offered by CompEd Software Design[2] – a software with SSCD, due to the producer declaration it enables advanced electronic signatures creation;

---

[1] The relevant software „proCertum SecureSignVer" compliant with it is used for signatures verification purposes.

[2] CompEd Software Design, Via delle Fabbriche 30E/14, 16158 Genova, ITALY, e-mail: info@comped.it, http://www.comped.it, fax +39 010 613.8118

- ***SafeGuard Sign & Crypt*** offered by Utimaco Safeware[3] AG – a software (also plug-ins for popular editors, browsers and e-mail tools) with SSCD and trusted viewer type modules;

- ***SecSigner*** offered by SecCommerce Informationssysteme GmbH – a software with SSCD, certified by BSI for accordance with ITSEC E2 high requirements;

- ***Trusted Pocket Signer*** offered by Fraunhofer-Institut Sichere Telekooperation (SIT)[4] – an independent device with a keyboard, a technical component and a display; a document to be signed is transmitted to a device, where it is browsed and signed.

Devices listed above belong to the group of integrated ones. It is assumed they are (physically) at exclusive disposal of a signing entity. There are also offered distributed solutions enabling to create electronic signatures with a signing server assistance. CoSign server offered by Algorithmic Research[5] is an example.

Systems like ***Trusted Pocket Signer*** are optimal solutions from EU Directive [3] requirements point of view: (a) a system for secure signature creation (including SSCD) is under an exclusive control of a signatory, (b) it can be used in private and in public environment as well, e.g. in banking area or e-government applications, and (c) it presents the user only this what he/she really wants to sign. However they are charged with one fundamental disadvantage – they are very expensive.

The solutions considered above are examples of three different approaches to facilitate the use of digital signatures in insecure environments. We refer to them as "secure hardware", "mental arithmetic", and "secure software" (A. Spalka, et al. [6]).

The other solution, proposed by authors of this paper and presented on Fig.1, includes a design and an implementation of a distributed system for electronic signatures creation. In our proposal the most expensive components and the ones requiring high protection and assurance level are under the full control of a signature service provider (SSP) and an application provider (AP); a signing entity has only SSCD at his/her disposal. Additionally a mobile operator can participate in signature creation process; its role is to provide end entity with additional information. The solution architecture has features of mental arithmetic electronic signature, because its integral parts are additional components increasing the trust without the necessity of additional computing performed by the user.

It is assumed a signer uses a computer with standard equipment (its own or available at some public place) connected to a network and equipped with a standard interface device (IFD) for communication with integrated circuit(s) cards (ICCs).

---

[3] Utimaco Safeware AG, Hohemarkstraße 22, DE-61440 Oberursel near Frankfurt a. M., phone +49 (61 71) 88-0, fax +49 (61 71) 88 -10 10, e-mail: info.de@Utimaco.de

[4] Fraunhofer-Institut Sichere Telekooperation – SIT[4], Rheinstrasse 75, D-64295 Darmstadt, http://www.sit.fraunhofer.de

[5] Algorithmic Research, US Headquarters: 5909 West Loop South, Suite 210, Bellaire, http://www.arx.com/ContactUs.htm

The role of SSCD can be played by ICC with crypto-processor SSCD[6]. It is also assumed an environment a signer acts in is wholly untrustworthy.

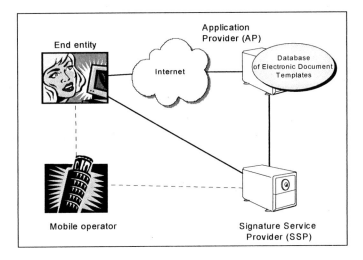

Fig. 1 Three corner functional scheme of distributed signature creation system

Three features of an optimal solution mentioned previously are achieved as follows:

- a device under an exclusive control of a signatory – the most important component of SSCD is at a signing entity exclusive disposal; moreover - a signing entity controls the whole signature creation process and can terminate it at any moment,

- private and public environment usage – the trust in a signing process is based on the trust in a process authenticating party (signature service provider); therefore it does not mean if a signature creation is performed in private or public environment,

- secure presentation of data to be signed (WYSIWYS – „What you see is what you sign" paradigm) – proprietary design of an information exchange protocol enables to detect any attempt for unauthorized modification of a document when a signature creation is pending.

One part of the system is a public database with electronic documents' forms (templates) (see Fig. 1). That base is provided by an application provider (AP). The signing entity (SE) has to get the proper one template from the base, to fill it with intended contents and then to transmit it in secure manner to the intended recipient (the last one can be an application provider or other entity whom application provider serves for). After the reception of completed document the recipient verifies its correctness (i.e. an accordance with the template) and requests the signature service provider for the secure signature creation process initiation (optionally it can be made by SE).

---

[6] Alternatively - SSCD can be a mobile phone with SIM card (card operating system should be able to establish trusted path and trusted channel)

3. SECURE SIGNATURE CREATION PROTOCOL FOR DISTRIBUTED ENVIRONMENT

Malicious programs can be the source of many threats during the signature creation process. Different types of exchanged data can be attacked: user's PIN digits; data transmitted to the application responsible for a preparation, signing and presentation before the final signature creation; and data transmitted to SSCD. All those threats can be eliminated when the following are guaranteed:

- data to be signed can be written once and read many times;
- it is not known *a priori* whether an intention of the user is only to create some document or to sign it as well;
- a signatory and verifiers see the same independently from an environment used (reliable presentation of data to be signed and signed data).

Stated above features of SCS are provided in an architecture shown on Fig.1 and in more detailed form on Fig.2. Firstly the user connects with Web Service established by AP. Using it he/she fills the relevant form (template) on and sends it back (without the signature) to AP's documents archive. Then the connection with AP is terminated. Signature creation requires for the establishment of the connection with signature service provider (SSP), the selection of relevant application provider (AP) and an identification of the document to be signed in AP's documents archive. That last action initiates an electronic signature creation process: AP sends the identified document (in graphic format specific for the system, e.g. JPEG format) to the user via SSP. SSP requests the confirmation of the signing intention and user's PIN (it could not be forgotten that PIN should get SSP in secure manner). PIN presentation enables to establish secure path and channel between SSP and SSCD, and finally the secure signature creation "inside" SSCD. The document signed by the end entity is then delivered to the intended recipient.

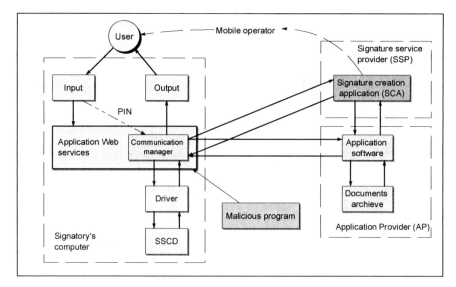

Fig.2 Detailed architecture of proposed secure signature system

Electronic documents used in proponed system are compliant with requirements defined in XML standards. Their structure enables to verify the template's integrity and to identify their issuers.

Any document – „naked" form (template) or document with the contents defined by SE - is signed in accordance with requirements of ETSI standard *XML Advanced Electronic Signature (XadES)* [4]. To ensure confidentiality (for the whole or the part of a document) W3C Recommendation XML Encryption Syntax and Processing [5] is applied.

3.1 Initiation Process

That process is performed every time SSP's server is started. It is assumed the following cryptographic keys, used for authentication purposes only, are installed in SAM/HSM module (S) of the Signature Service Provider (SSP): S''_{SSP}, P''_{SSP} – SAM module's private and public keys; S_a, P_a – application server's (software library) private and public keys (S_a is "dissipated" between an SSP application software/server (A) and SAM/HSM module – $S_a = f(S_{a1}, S_{a2})$).

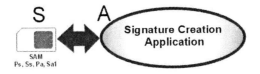

Fig. 3 Entities active in mutual authentication between an application and SAM/HSM module inside SSP environment

Protocol 1: Mutual authentication SSP's server-SAM/HSM
1. Server verifies P''_{SSP} certificate
2. Entity A reads out part S_{a1} of its private key from S
3. Entity A recovers $S_a = f(S_{a1}, S_{a2})$
4. Entity A requests for S random challenge
5. S → A: random challenge RND_s
6. A → S: $E_{Sa} (RND_a)$ (S's challenge is signed by the entity A and sent back)
7. Entity S verifies A's signature on RND_s
8. A → S: random challenge RND_a
9. S → A: $E_{S''SSP}(RND_a)$ (A's challenge is signed by S and sent back)
10. Entity A verifies S's signature on RND_a
11. Entity A and S complete mutual authentication

3.2 Signature creation process

Presented below, the signature creation process is intended to deliver a qualified electronic signature associated with a signer's document to the user or some other application process in a form specified by the user. Further goal of this process is to provide well define steps so that applying an electronic signature is as easy and error-free as applying a hand written signature.

A proposed qualified digital signature scheme is defined by the specification of the following steps:

1. The user (SE) logins to a client application (Web service application).
2. The Application Provider (AP) (using SSL strong authentication protocol) is authenticated by SE; the secure channel is established.
3. The user collects from AP required information concerning: obtainable forms (templates), signature policies and Signature Service Providers (SSPs) supporting secure signature creation:

$$AP \rightarrow SE: PreData_1.$$

4. The user takes off the relevant form (template):

$$AP \rightarrow SE: PreData_2$$

5. The user fills the form on, identifies SSP to use, selects transaction type, and all substantial data for future presentation in document authorization phase.
6. The user identifies the destiny of document authorization information (e-mail address, phone number).
7. The user states whether he/she wants to get back the signed document or not.
8. User's application prepares the final data to be signed (*Data*), including predefined transaction type (e.g. unique form identifier), calculates hash value on document data, defines its own transaction identifier $IDSE_{Trans}$, and identifies SSP (selecting $DNS_{SSPserver}$):

$$SE \rightarrow AP: Data, h(Data), DNS_{SSPserver}, IDSE_{Trans}, e\text{-}mail, phoneNumber, substantialData$$

9. The request is sent to AP server.
10. AP checks the correctness of *Data* structure and its integrity (comparing calculated *h(Data)* with *h(Data)* received from SE) and, if those are proper ones, confirms it with its signature $E_{S'AP}(h(Data'))$ using its private key for signing (S'_{AP}), where *Data'* include original *Data*, transaction identifier $IDAP_{Trans}$, and additional attributes optionally.
11. AP issues the token for non-repudiation of submission:

$$AP \rightarrow SE: h(Data), E_{S'AP}(h(Data)).$$

12. SSP and AP (using SSL strong authentication protocol) perform mutual authentication; the secure channel is established.
13. AP sends to SSP an original document *Data* with its hash value, a completed transaction identifier $ID_{Trans} = (IDSE_{Trans}, IDAP_{Trans})$ and signed *Data'*:

$$AP \rightarrow SSP: Data, h(Data), ID_{Trans}, Data', E_{S'AP}(h(Data')).$$

14. SSP server verifies the signature associated with received message.
15. SSP issues the token for non-repudiation of submission:

$$SSP \rightarrow AP: h(Data'), E_{S'SSP}(h(Data')).$$

16. SSP server signs *h(Data)* and creates a document image *DataIm*.
17. SSP server sends to SE document authorization data:

$$SSP \rightarrow SE: h(Data), IDTrans, DataIm, substantialData.$$

18. SE verifies data received from SSP, e.g. comparing received *h(Data)* value with an original *h(Data)* prepared in step 8, checking its part of ID_{Trans} and received *DataIm*.

19. SE application initiates SSL session with SSP, presents *h(Data)* and after SSP acceptance takes PIN from the user (SE); then the module directly communicating with SSP is used: PIN concatenated with ID_{Trans} and *h(Data)* is enciphered, for example, with P''_{SSP} key[7] and sent to SSP (other solution is discussed in chapter 5).
20. SSP initiates the communication between SE's technical component (TC) of SSCD and SSP's SAM/HSM.
21. During an authentication dialog between SAM/HSM and TC – a secure path and channel (secure messaging) are established (see Fig.4). The dialog has the form of Protocol 2.

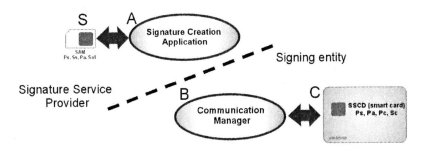

Fig.4. Model for secure messaging establishment (B is „communication manager" application; it manages data exchange between A and C)

Protocol 2: Mutual authentication SSP's – TC and key agreement
Summary. In TC the following cryptographic keys are installed: $Ps = P''_{SSP}$ – public key of SAM/HSM module, *Sc, Pc* – SE's private and public keys for authentication purposes, *Pa* – public key of SSP's software library, *Pc , Sc* – SE's private and public keys for signature creation purposes. 1. Entity A generates random challenge *RNDs2*. 2. A → C: *RNDs2*. 3. C → A: *Epa(Esc(K1, RNDs2, RNDc))* 4. Entity A deciphers response, verifies TC's signature and stores *K1*. 5. Entity A requests random challenge *RNDc1* from S. 6. C → A: *RNDc1*. 7. A → S: *RNDc1*. 8. S → A: *Epa (Ess(K2, RNDc1, RNDs3))=Epa (x)*. 9. Entity A deciphers response, verifies SAM's signature and stores K 10. A → C: *Epc (x)*. 11. Entity C deciphers „x" (in that way it authenticates S and A) and agrees session keys for transmitted data enciphering and MAC creation: *ksc=f1(K1, K2), ksi=f2(K1, K2)* 12. Both parties (SAM and TC) are mutually authenticated and session keys are agreed.

---

[7] Protection against replay attacks and PIN compromising.

22. TC creates signature using Protocol 3 and sends it back to SSP server (via secure channel).

Protocol 3: Signature creation protocol
Summary. SSP has got SE's PIN in step 19.   1. A → C: *Eksp, ksi(PIN)*.   2. Entity C verifies PIN   3. C → A: *Eksp,ksi(OK)* or C → A: *Eksp,ksi(Wrong PIN info)*   4. A → C: *Eksp,ksi(h(Data))*   5. Entity C enciphers *h(Data)* with *Sc*   6. C → A: *Eksp, ksi(Esc(h(Data))* = signature for Data)

23. SSP server links Data and received *Esc(h(Data)* completing the signed document.
24. The signed document is sent to AP server.
25. If SE wishes such a confirmation (see step 7) then the signed document is returned to a client's application (optionally with the token for non-repudiation of submission).

We believe that above signature creation process solves two main problems pointed out in literature (A. Spalka, et al. [6], A. Jøsang, et al. [7]): the problem of trusted presentation document to be signed and building a signature creation system that has a higher ease-of-use. Furthermore, if the user of our system accepts the presented data she or he sends a release command to the signature service provider (SSP) that involves the use of a hash value of the data to be signed.

4.   PROTOCOL SECURITY ANALYSIS

Four typical threats invoked by malicious programs have been analyzed:
(a) the capturing of PIN opening an access to a private signing key usage,
(b) data modification between a preparation of data to be signed and sending them to a signature creation application (SCA),
(c) the forgery of presented data before signing decision, and
(d) the forgery of data sent from SCA to SSCD (or more precisely – to TC, e.g. smart card).

Let us consider threat (a). The are two opportunities for PIN capturing: firstly during its input via the terminal keyboard, and then on communication line between SCA and SSCD. One countermeasure is mentioned in chapter 4 (step 19 of the main protocol). The other solution is to use PIN-pad link (maybe as the part of integrated Secure Smart Card Reader – SSCR) with independent secure channel established directly between SSP server and a signatory's computer.

Threats (b) and (c) can be considered jointly in systems where data to be signed are presented to SE before a final signature act (see also A. Spalka [6]). A malicious program should be able to modify not only data to be signed before their transmission to SCA, but to modify them at the moment of presentation as well. Here such a malicious action is hard (even impossible). Firstly – it is hard for a malicious program to trace which one from previously prepared documents will be signed (a communication session with AP is broken after every transmission of documents to AP's archive); on the other hand – after its deposit in AP's archive the document is accessible in "read only" mode. The document (its contents) is presented by SCA to SE in the JPEG format for example. If any maliciously modified document is deposited in AP archive then no malicious program can recover its original meaning.

The forgery of data sent from SCA to SSCD (threat (d)) is impossible because SCA establishes a secure path (the result of a end user authentication) and a secure channel before any transmission. Malicious program is not able to modify any data sent to SSCD without a knowledge concerning session keys used.

5. CONCLUSIONS

There are many more or less sophisticated attacks on signature creation systems (see also A. Jøsang [7]). It is the reason why in this paper the following assumption was taken into account: the trust should not be located in a signature creation system installed only on a client station (an end user terminal). The presented distributed signature creation system architecture (in authors opinion) could guarantee the high level of security.

Additionally the proposed solution ensures relatively high convenience and low costs for end users (SEs). A user having SSCD at his/her disposal (e.g. in the form of smart card) can create signatures on any station equipped with proper interface device (e.g. smart card reader). It is possible due to the usage of Web services provided by an application provider (AP) and a signature service provider (SSP).

A user can work only with trusted applications provided by APs and obligatory registered by SSP. Before that application registration the detailed assessment of its functionality and security has to be performed.

The proponed architecture and data exchange protocols can be generalized towards an environment with many signature service providers working independently. They could make available their services ("native" registered applications) for "alien" users. Such an idea is similar to roaming services offered by mobile service providers (see also ETSI TR 102 203 [8]).

REFERENCES

[1] CWA 14365 *Guide on the use of Electronic Signatures*, January 2003
[2] CWA 14170 *Security Requirements for Signature Creation Applications*, July 2001
[3] EU Directive 1999/93/EC of the European Parliament and the council of 13 December 1999 on a Community framework for electronic signatures
[4] ETSI TS 101 903 V1.1.1 *XML Advanced Electronic Signatures (XAdES)*.
[5] W3C Recommendation *XML-Encryption Syntax and Processing*, 10 December 2002

[6] A. Spalka, A.B. Cremers and H. Langweg *Trojan Horse Attacks on Software for Electronic Signatures*, Informatica **26** (2002) 191-203 pp.191-204

[7] A. Jøsang, D. Povey and A. Ho *What You See is Not Always What You Sign*, AUUG2002, Melbourne, 4-6 September 2002.

[8] ETSI TR 102 203 *Mobile Commerce (M-COMM) - Mobile Signatures - Business and Functional Requirements*, V1.1.1 (2003-05), Technical Report

On Arithmetic Subtraction Linear Approximation

KRZYSZTOF CHMIEL

Poznań University of Technology
pl. Skłodowskiej-Curie 5, 60-965 Poznań, Poland, e-mail:Chmiel@sk-kari.put.poznan.pl

Abstract: In the paper two methods of linear approximation of n-bit arithmetic subtraction function are considered. In the first method, called the model of approximation of a single S-box, approximations are calculated for arbitrary m consecutive bits, where $m \leq n$ is limited by the size of so-called table of pairs TP, used during calculation. In the second method, called the model of exact composition of approximations, the subtraction approximations are calculated as a composition of k approximations of m-bit subtraction cells, where $m \leq n$ is limited by the size of the same table of pairs TP. In the first method, the set of nonzero approximations is limited to approximations in the range of m consecutive bits while in the second method is not limited. For n-bit arithmetic subtraction function however, the approximation probability can be calculated with use of the methods in time $O(1)$ and $O(k)$, respectively.

Key words: Cryptanalysis, linear approximation, arithmetic subtraction function.

1. INTRODUCTION

Linear cryptanalysis [3,4,6-14] is besides differential cryptanalysis [1,2,5,11] the best known and most widely used general method of cryptanalysis. The basic concept of the method is the linear approximation, understood as a linear equation relating input bits to output bits of an algorithm, satisfied with some probability p for randomly chosen input and corresponding output. Approximations with nonzero value of the effectiveness measure $|\Delta p| = |p - 1/2|$, are said to be effective.

The most effective linear approximations of iterative block ciphers are obtained typically, in two main steps. First, the effective approximations of a single iteration are calculated, as a result of composition of approximations of component functions. One of the used component functions, for example in the algorithms RC5 and SAFER, is the considered in the paper arithmetic subtraction function. Next, the linear approximations of the entire algorithm are obtained, as a result of composition of approximations of consecutive iterations.

Linear cryptanalysis is essentially a known-plaintext attack. The most effective approximations of an algorithm, are used to find the key for sufficiently large family of known pairs: plaintext – ciphertext. To this end, various variants of cryptanalytic attack are applied [11,14]. Moreover, in the case of not random plaintexts, effective approximations with no plaintext bit may be found, that enable the only-ciphertext attack on a cipher algorithm [13].

2.   BASIC DEFINITIONS

In general, the *linear approximation* of function $Y = h(X)$: $\{0,1\}^n \rightarrow \{0,1\}^m$ is defined as an arbitrary equation of the form:

$$\underset{i \in Y'}{\oplus} y_i = \underset{j \in X'}{\oplus} x_j, \qquad\qquad (1)$$

satisfied with approximation probability $p = N(X',Y') / 2^n$, where $Y' \subseteq \{1,..,m\}$, $X' \subseteq \{1,..,n\}$ while $N(X',Y')$ denotes the number of pairs (X, Y) for which the equation holds. For simplicity the above equation is written in the following form:

$$Y[Y'] = X[X']. \qquad\qquad (2)$$

The sets of indexes X', Y' are called input and output *mask* respectively and the function $N(X',Y')$ is called the *counting function* of the approximation.

The linear approximation *characteristic* is defined as a sequence $(X', Y', \Delta p)$, where X', Y' are masks or sequences of input and output masks and p is the approximation probability. Among characteristics we distinguish the *zero-characteristic* $(\Phi, \Phi, 1/2)$, corresponding to the *zero linear approximation*, which probability is equal to 1 for arbitrary function h.

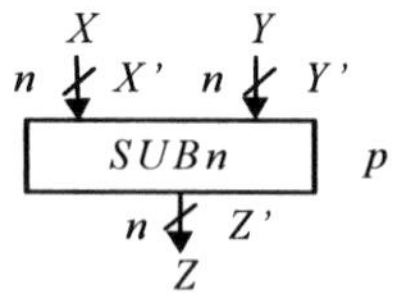

Fig. 1. Linear approximation of function *SUBn*

Composing linear approximations, it is necessary to formulate so-called *approximation conditions* that eliminate the bits of the internal variables from the resultant equation. The probability Δp of the composition of n approximations with probabilities Δp_i, is calculated as follows:

$$\Delta p = 2^{n-1} \prod_{i=1}^{n} \Delta p_i. \qquad\qquad (3)$$

The general form $Z[Z'] = X[X'] \oplus Y[Y']$ of the linear approximation of n-bit arithmetic subtraction function $Z = SUBn(X, Y) = (X - Y) \bmod 2^n$, is illustrated in figure 1.

Linear approximations of function *SUBn* can be described in the form of the *approximation table TASUBn*. The element $TASUBn[X', Y', Z']$ of the table, is defined as the number of triples (X, Y, Z) satisfying equation $Z[Z'] = X[X'] \oplus Y[Y']$, decreased by the half of all the triples. Thus, it can be calculated by the formula:

$$TASUBn[X', Y', Z'] = N(X', Y', Z') - 2^{2n-1}. \tag{4}$$

Approximation table *TASUBn* is obtained by examination, for each mask triple (X', Y', Z'), of all input triples (X, Y, Z) and contains the complete description of linear approximations of function *SUBn*. In other words, table *TASUBn* represents all the characteristics $(X', Y', Z', \Delta p)$ of function *SUBn*, where probability Δp can be calculated as follows:

$$\Delta p = TASUBn[X', Y', Z'] / 2^{2n}. \tag{5}$$

The approximation table of function *SUB2* is presented in figure 2. Besides the zero-approximation and the marked in the figure *one-approximation* with probability $\Delta p = 1/2$, there exist 8 effective approximations of the function with probability $|\Delta p| = 1/4$.

X', Y'	Z'			
	0	1	2	3
0 , 0	8	0	0	0
0 , 1	0	0	0	0
0 , 2	0	0	0	0
0 , 3	0	0	0	0
1 , 0	0	0	0	0
1 , 1	0	8	0	0
1 , 2	0	0	0	0
1 , 3	0	0	0	0
2 , 0	0	0	0	0
2 , 1	0	0	0	0
2 , 2	0	0	4	4
2 , 3	0	0	4	- 4
3 , 0	0	0	0	0
3 , 1	0	0	0	0
3 , 2	0	0	- 4	4
3 , 3	0	0	4	4

Fig. 2. Approximation table *TASUB2* of function *SUB2*

The size of the approximation table of function *SUBn* is $O(2^{3n})$ and based on the definition, calculation of a single entry of the table requires $O(2^{2n})$ operations. The presented in the paper methods, enable to calculate the values of *TASUBn* for arbitrary n, in at worst linear time with use of limited amount of computer memory needed for storage of so-called table of pairs *TP*.

3.   APPROXIMATION OF A SINGLE S-BOX

The idea of the approximation is illustrated in figure 3. Function *SUB16* is treated as a parallel composition of *independent* (i.e. without propagation of borrow) four S-boxes *SUB4ⱼ*. As a consequence, the S-boxes are statistically different and their *approximation tables* are different.

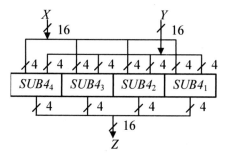

Fig. 3. Function *SUB16* as composition of four independent S-boxes

Similarly to S-boxes of algorithm DES, the greatest values of the approximation measure $|\Delta p|$ of such a parallel composition are obtained, apart from the zero-approximation of all S-boxes, in the case of nonzero approximation of a single S-box. The considered way of approximation of function *SUB16*, assuming nonzero approximation of one of the independent S-boxes, is called *the model of approximation of a single S-box*. The problem is to calculate the values of the approximation table of S-box *SUB4ⱼ*, for arbitrary *j*.

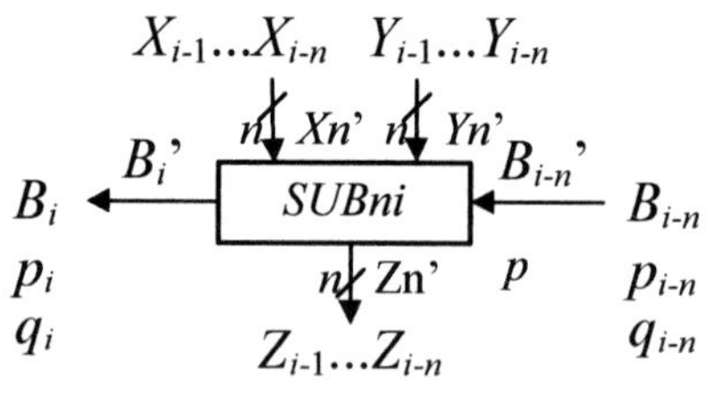

$$X_{i-1}...X_{i-n} \quad Y_{i-1}...Y_{i-n}$$

$$B_i \xleftarrow{B_i'} \boxed{\begin{array}{c} n\downarrow Xn' \ n\downarrow Yn' \\ SUBni \\ n\downarrow Zn' \end{array}} \xleftarrow{B_{i-n}'} B_{i-n}$$

$$\begin{array}{ccc} p_i & & p_{i-n} \\ q_i & Z_{i-1}...Z_{i-n} & q_{i-n} \end{array}$$

Fig. 4. Linear approximation of function *SUBni*

The generalisation of the above formulated problem is presented in figure 4. Function *SUBni* is the *n*-bit arithmetic subtraction function with input borrow B_{i-n} equal to 1 with probability p_{i-n} and to 0 with probability q_{i-n}, and with output borrow B_i equal to 1 and 0 with probabilities p_i and q_i, respectively. The probabilities of input and output borrow of function *SUBni*, are respectively equal to probabilities of borrow, generated by $(i-n)$-bit and i-bit arithmetic subtraction function. Probabilities p_i and q_i for $i \geq 0$, assuming $B_0 = 0$, can be calculated as follows:

$$p_i = 1/2 - 1/2^{i+1}, \qquad q_i = 1/2 + 1/2^{i+1}. \tag{6}$$

$B_{i-1}'X_{i-1}'Y_{i-1}'$			B_i' Z_{i-1}'		
			0 0	0 1	1 0	1 1
0	0	0	(4,4)	(2,2)	(3,1)	(3,3)
0	0	1	(2,2)	(2,2)	(3,3)	(1,3)
0	1	0	(2,2)	(2,2)	(1,1)	(3,1)
0	1	1	(2,2)	(4,0)	(3,1)	(3,3)
1	0	0	(4,0)	(2,2)	(3,3)	(3,1)
1	0	1	(2,2)	(2,2)	(3,1)	(1,1)
1	1	0	(2,2)	(2,2)	(1,3)	(3,3)
1	1	1	(2,2)	(4,4)	(3,3)	(3,1)

Fig. 5. Table *TP* of pairs ($N0$, $N1$) for function $SUB1i$ ($i \geq 1$)

An independent of i description of linear approximations of function $SUBni$ is the *table of pairs TP*, which elements ($N0$, $N1$) are values of the counting function N for B_{i-n} equal to 0 and to 1 respectively. Thus:

$$N0 = N(B_{i-n} = 0), \qquad N1 = N(B_{i-n} = 1). \tag{7}$$

The probability p for input masks B_{i-n}', X_n', Y_n' and output masks B_i', Z_n', can be calculated by the formula:

$$p = N0/2^{2n} \cdot q_{i-n} + N1/2^{2n} \cdot p_{i-n}. \tag{8}$$

The table of pairs *TP* and the table of probabilities p, for function $SUB1i$ are presented in figures 5 and 6, respectively.

$B_{i-1}'X_{i-1}'Y_{i-1}'$			B_i' Z_{i-1}'		
			0 0	0 1	1 0	1 1
0	0	0	1	1/2	q_i	3/4
0	0	1	1/2	1/2	3/4	p_i
0	1	0	1/2	1/2	1/4	q_i
0	1	1	1/2	q_{i-1}	q_i	3/4
1	0	0	q_{i-1}	1/2	3/4	q_i
1	0	1	1/2	1/2	q_i	1/4
1	1	0	1/2	1/2	p_i	3/4
1	1	1	1/2	1	3/4	q_i

Fig. 6. Table of probabilities p of function $SUB1i$ approximations ($i \geq 1$)

In general, the table of probabilities is dependent of i. There can be observed, however, *constant* (i.e. independent of i) values of p in the table, corresponding to so-called *constant approximations*. For a given pair ($N0$, $N1$), the probability p is constant if and only if $N0 = N1$. The values of p dependent of i, aim to the value 1/2 with the increase of i. Taking into account the existence of constant approximations of function $SUB1i$, the more instructive description than the approximation table is the table of probabilities Δp, presented in figure 7.

$B_{i-1}'X_{i-1}'Y_{i-1}'$	$B_i'\ Z_{i-1}'$			
	0 0	0 1	1 0	1 1
0 0 0	1/2	0	$1/2^{i+1}$	1/4
0 0 1	0	0	1/4	$-1/2^{i+1}$
0 1 0	0	0	$-1/4$	$1/2^{i+1}$
0 1 1	0	$1/2^i$	$1/2^{i+1}$	1/4
1 0 0	$1/2^i$	0	1/4	$1/2^{i+1}$
1 0 1	0	0	$1/2^{i+1}$	$-1/4$
1 1 0	0	0	$-1/2^{i+1}$	1/4
1 1 1	0	1/2	1/4	$1/2^{i+1}$

Fig. 7. Table of probabilities Δp of function $SUB1i$ approximations ($i \geq 1$)

In the considered model of approximation of a single S-box, the masks of input and output borrow must be equal to 0. Therefore in the model, the upper left quarters of the tables from figures 5-7 are important, defined by $B_{i-1}' = B_i' = 0$. For function $SUB2i$, the table of probabilities Δp for $B_{i-2}' = B_i' = 0$, is presented in figure 8. The table for $i = 2$, corresponds to the approximation table $TASUB2$ from figure 2.

$X2'Y2'$	$Z2'$			
	0	1	2	3
0 0	1/2	0	0	0
0 1	0	0	0	0
0 2	0	0	0	0
0 3	0	0	0	0
1 0	0	0	0	0
1 1	0	$1/2^{i-1}$	0	0
1 2	0	0	0	0
1 3	0	0	0	0
2 0	0	0	0	0
2 1	0	0	0	0
2 2	0	0	$1/2^i$	1/4
2 3	0	0	1/4	$-1/2^i$
3 0	0	0	0	0
3 1	0	0	0	0
3 2	0	0	$-1/4$	$1/2^i$
3 3	0	0	$1/2^i$	1/4

Fig. 8. Table of Δp of function $SUB2i$ approximations for $B_{i-2}' = B_i' = 0$ ($i \geq 2$)

In figure 9 are presented the constant approximations of function $SUB2i$. Besides the zero-approximation, there are four nonzero approximations with probability $|\Delta p| = 1/4$, independent of the value of $i \geq 2$.

X2'	Y2'	Z2'	Δp
0	0	0	1/2
2	2	3	1/4
2	3	2	1/4
3	2	2	-1/4
3	3	3	1/4

Fig. 9. Constant approximations of function *SUB2i* ($i \geq 2$)

An algorithm to compute values of the approximation table *TA* of function *SUBni*, is presented in figure 10. For a given *i*, the values of *TA* are calculated on the base of independent of *i*, table of pairs *TP*, for $B_{i-n}' = B_i' = 0$. The complexity of the algorithm is O(1).

TA-SUBni(*TP*, *X'*, *Y'*, *Z'*, *n*, *i*)
1. $(N0, N1) \leftarrow TP[0, X', Y', 0, Z']$
2. $p_{i-n} \leftarrow 1/2 - 1/2^{i-n+1}$
3. $q_{i-n} \leftarrow 1/2 + 1/2^{i-n+1}$
4. $p \leftarrow N0 / 2^{2n} \cdot q_{i-n} + N1 / 2^{2n} \cdot p_{i-n}$
5. **return** $(p - 1/2) \cdot 2^{2i}$

Fig. 10. Algorithm computing values of *TA* of function *SUBni* ($i \geq n$)

For S-box *SUB4ⱼ* from figure 3, the value of the approximation table can be calculated as follows: TA-SUBni(*TP*, *X4'*, *Y4'*, *Z4'*, 4, 4·*j*), where *TP* is the table of pairs for function *SUB4i* and *X4'*, *Y4'*, *Z4'* are masks of the S-box.

4. COMPOSITION OF APPROXIMATIONS

The idea of the approximation is illustrated in figure 11. Function *SUB16* is treated as a composition of *dependent* (i.e. with propagation of borrow) four S-boxes *SUB4*.

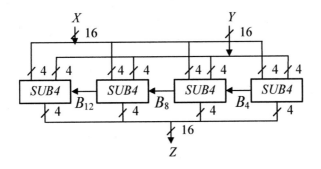

Fig. 11. Function *SUB16* as composition of four dependent S-boxes

As a consequence, the S-boxes are identical and their approximation tables are the same. The presented way of approximation of function *SUB16* is called *the model of exact composition of approximations*. The problem is to calculate the values of the approximation table of function *SUB16*, on the base of the approximation table of S-box *SUB4*.

The solution to the above formulated problem requires in general the method for calculation of the approximation table values of the *extended* function *SUBn* from figure 12. The function is an *n*-bit arithmetic subtraction function with input borrow B_0 and output borrow B_n. It can be treated as function *SUBni* from figure 4, for $i = n$.

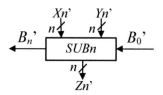

Fig. 12. Linear approximation of extended function *SUBn*

In figure 13 is presented an algorithm computing the values of the approximation table of the extended function *SUBn*. The values of the table are calculated on the base of the table of pairs *TP*.

TA-SUBn(*TP*, B_0', *Xn*', *Yn*', B_n', *Zn*', *n*)
1. $(N0, N1) \leftarrow TP[B_0', Xn', Yn', B_n', Zn']$
2. $p \leftarrow (N0 + N1) / 2^{2n+1}$
3. **return** $(p - 1/2) \cdot 2^{2n+1}$

Fig. 13. Algorithm computing values of *TA* of extended function *SUBn*

An algorithm to compute values of the approximation table *TA* of composition of *k* extended functions *SUBn*, is presented in figure 14. The correctness of the algorithm is based on the following argumentation.

The probability Δp of composition of *k* extended functions *SUBn*, is equal to:

$$\Delta p = 2^{k-1} \prod_{i=1}^{k} \Delta p_i. \tag{9}$$

Denoting by w_i the value of *TA* for the *i*-th extended function *SUBn*, from the above formula we obtain:

$$\Delta p = 2^{k-1} \cdot \prod_{i=1}^{k} (w_i / 2^{2n+1}) = 1 / 2^{2kn+1} \cdot \prod_{i=1}^{k} w_i. \tag{10}$$

Let *w* denote the value of the approximation table of composition of *k* extended functions *SUBn*. For *w* we obtain the following equation:

$$w = \Delta p \cdot 2^{2kn} = 1/2 \cdot \prod_{i=1}^{k} w_i. \tag{11}$$

Thus, the value of the approximation table of the composition is equal to the product of the values of approximation tables of component extended functions *SUBn*, divided by 2.

For a given i, the variable $w_i 01$ denotes the value of approximation table *TA* of the i-th extended function *SUBn* for the mask of input borrow $B_{0i}' = 0$ and the mask of output borrow $B_{ni}' = 1$. Similar meaning have the variables $w_i 00$, $w_i 10$ and $w_i 11$.

Variable $w20$ denotes the value of *TA* of composition of i extended functions *SUBn* for the mask of output borrow $B_{ni}' = 0$ and the variable $w21$ for the mask $B_{ni}' = 1$. Similar meaning but with respect to composition of i-1 extended functions *SUBn*, have the variables $w10$ and $w11$.

The way of calculation of values $w20$ and $w21$ in steps 8 and 9 of the algorithm follows from consideration of the values 0 and 1 of the input borrow mask B_{0i}'. The complexity of the algorithm is $O(k)$.

TA-kSUBn(TP, X', Y', Z', n, k)
1. $w20 \leftarrow 1$, $w21 \leftarrow 1$
2. **for** $i \leftarrow 1$ **to** k **do**
3. $\quad w10 \leftarrow w20$, $w11 \leftarrow w21$
4. $\quad w_i 00 \leftarrow$ TA-SUBn(TP,0,Xn_i',Yn_i',0,Zn_i',n)
5. $\quad w_i 01 \leftarrow$ TA-SUBn(TP,0,Xn_i',Yn_i',1,Zn_i',n)
6. $\quad w_i 10 \leftarrow$ TA-SUBn(TP,1,Xn_i',Yn_i',0,Zn_i',n)
7. $\quad w_i 11 \leftarrow$ TA-SUBn(TP,1,Xn_i',Yn_i',1,Zn_i',n)
8. $\quad w20 \leftarrow w10 \cdot w_i 00 + w11 \cdot w_i 10$
9. $\quad w21 \leftarrow w10 \cdot w_i 01 + w11 \cdot w_i 11$
10. **return** $w20 / 2$

Fig. 14. Algorithm computing values of *TA* of composition of k extended functions *SUBn*

5. CONCLUSION

The based on definition, calculation of a value of the approximation table *TASUBn* of n-bit arithmetic subtraction function *SUBn*, requires $O(2^{2n})$ operations. The presented in the paper methods – the model of approximation of a single S-box and the model of exact composition of approximations – enable to calculate the values of *TASUBn* in time respectively $O(1)$ and $O(k)$, where $k \leq n$. In the first method the calculation is restricted to approximations in the range of $m \leq n$ consecutive bits, while in the second method is not limited. Both methods can be exploited to solve specific generation problems, typical for calculation of multilevel characteristics of iterative block ciphers.

REFERENCES

[1] Biham E., Shamir A. 1993. 'Differential Cryptanalysis of the Data Encryption Standard'. *Springer-Verlag*, New York.

[2] Chmiel K. 1998. 'Principles of Differential Cryptanalysis through the Example of the *DES* Algorithm'. (In Polish). *Technical Report No. 461*. Poznań University of Technology, Chair of Control, Robotics and Computer Science, Poznań (Oct.).

[3] Chmiel K. 1999. 'Principles of Linear Cryptanalysis through the Example of the *DES* Algorithm'. (In Polish). *Technical Report No. 471*. Poznań University of Technology, Chair of Control, Robotics and Computer Science, Poznań (Oct.).

[4] Chmiel K. 2000. 'Linear Cryptanalysis of the Reduced *DES* Algorithms'. *Proceedings of the Regional Conference on Military Communication and Information Systems'2000* (Zegrze , Oct. 4-6) WIŁ, Zegrze, vol. 1, pp. 111-118.

[5] Chmiel K. 2000. 'Differential Cryptanalysis of the Reduced *DES* Algorithms'. (In Polish). *Studia z Automatyki i Informatyki*, vol. 25, pp. 127-146.

[6] Chmiel K. 2000. 'Linear Approximation of S-box Functions'. (In Polish). *Technical Report No. 471*. Poznań University of Technology, Chair of Control, Robotics and Computer Science, Poznań (Oct.).

[7] Chmiel K. 2001. 'Linear Approximation of some S-box Functions'. *Proceedings of the Regional Conference on Military Communication and Information Systems 2001* (Zegrze, Oct. 10-12) WIŁ, Zegrze, vol. 1, pp. 211-218.

[8] Chmiel K. 2001. 'Linear Approximation of Arithmetic Sum'. (In Polish). *Technical Report No. 481*. Poznań University of Technology, Chair of Control, Robotics and Computer Science, Poznań (Oct.).

[9] Chmiel K. 2002. 'On Some Models of Arithmetic Sum Function Linear Approximation'. *Proceedings of NATO Regional Conference on Military Communications and Information Systems 2002* (Zegrze, Oct. 9-11) WIŁ, Zegrze, vol. 2, pp. 199-204.

[10] Chmiel K. 2002. 'Linear Approximation of Arithmetic Sum Function'. *Proceedings of the 9-th International Conference on Advanced Computer Systems ACS'2002* (Międzyzdroje, Oct. 23-25), Szczecin, vol. 2, pp. 19-28.

[11] Górska A., Górski K., Kotulski Z., Paszkiewicz A., Szczepański J. 2001. 'New Experimental Results in Differential – Linear Cryptanalysis of Reduced Variants of DES'. *Proceedings of the 8-th International Conference on Advanced Computer Systems ACS'2001*, Mielno, vol. 1, pp. 333-346.

[12] Matsui M. 1993. 'Linear Cryptanalysis Method for DES Cipher'. *Advances in Cryptology Eurocrypt'93*.

[13] Matsui M. 1998. 'Linear Cryptanalysis Method for DES Cipher'. *Springer-Verlag*, New York.

[14] Zugaj A., Górski K., Kotulski Z., Szczepański J., Paszkiewicz A. 1999. 'Extending Linear Cryptanalysis - Theory and Experiments'. *Proceedings of the Regional Conference on Military Communication and Information Systems'99* (Zegrze , Oct. 6-8) WIŁ, Zegrze, vol. 2, pp.77-84.

Secure Data Transmission via Modulation of the Chaotic Sequence Parameters

S. BERCZYŃSKI[1)], YY.A. KRAVTSOV[2)],
J. PEJAS[1)], E. D. SUROVYATKINA[3)]

[1)] *Technical University of Szczecin, Poland. E-mail: Stefan.Berczynski@ps.pl*
[2)] *Maritime University of Szczecin, Poland. E-mail: kravtsov@wsm.szczecin.pl*
[3)] *Space research Institute, Russ.Acad.Sci., Moscow, Russia. E-mail: selena@iki.rssi.ru*

Abstract: The method for secure information transmission via chaotic sequences with modulated parameters is studied. Information decoding in this method implies solution of the inverse problem of chaotic dynamics, as suggested by Anishchenko et al (1998, 1999). Algorithms for reconstruction of information parameters in single-channel and multiple-channel schemes of data transmission are discussed and requirements for map, generating chaotic sequence are formulated. The method under consideration impedes unauthorized access to the information transmitted and may serve as flexible instrument for multipurpose cryptographic applications.

Key words: chaotic signals and sequence; secure data transmission; chaotic cryptosystems, cryptography.

1. INTRODUCTION

The methods for secure data transmission on the basis of chaotic signals are widely discussed in the literature (see publications [1-17] and references therein). One of the prospective approaches is data transmission via chaotic signals and sequences with modulated parameters. The most important element of this method is reconstruction of the hidden information from received chaotic signals.

Algorithm for information parameter reconstruction might be considerably simplified when the prior information on the structure of a chaotic system and on the values of all its parameters except one is available [15,16]. In this case all variations in the chaotic signal can be imparted to a single information parameter that is yet unknown. V.S. Anishchenko et al [15,16] spectacularly have demonstrated advantages of this approach by the example of the image transmission. In this paper data transmission via chaotic sequences with modulated parameters is considered in details with emphasis on cryptographic aspects.

2. PROPERTIES OF SEQUENCES, GENERATED BY NONLINEAR MAP

Let the map

$$x_{n+1} = F(x_n; \mathbf{a}) \tag{1}$$

generates the sequence $\{x_n, x_{n+1},...\}$, depending on a set of parameters $\mathbf{a} = \{a_0, a_1,..., a_k,..., a_K\}$. The trajectories on $\{x_n, x_{n+1}\}$ plane belong to one of the following three types. First of all, there exist trajectories, tending to the stable points of a map (1), which satisfies the equation $\overline{x} = F(\overline{x}; \mathbf{a})$. Secondly, some trajectories approach to the periodic orbits, what is characteristic, for instance, for period doubling bifurcations. At last in definite areas of parameter $\{a_k\}$ space the nonlinear map (1) generates chaotic sequences $\{x_n\}$ chaotic, which look quite similar to random sequences and are of primarily interest for secure data transmission.

By the way of example Fig.1 presents the values xn, generated by the sinusoidal map

$$x_{n+1} = a \sin x_n. \tag{2}$$

This map demonstrates stable states in the interval $1<a<2.2$, periodic orbits in the interval $2.2<a<2.8$ and chaotic behaviour in few intervals, say, in the interval $3.7<a<4.5$ of length $\Delta a \approx 0.8$.

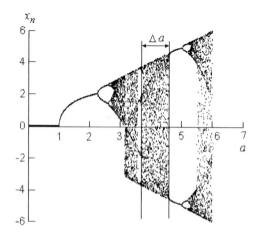

Fig.1. Stable points (s), periodic orbits (p) and chaotic trajectories (c), generated by nonlinear map (2).

3. DATA TRANSMISSION VIA CHAOTIC SEQUENCES

In principle, all the parameters $\mathbf{a} = \{a_0, a_1, ..., a_k, ..., a_K\}$ of a map (1) may serve as information carriers. Data transmission on the basis of parameters $\{a_k\}$ modulation reminds conventional data transmission by modulation of amplitude A, frequency ω and phase φ of the sinusoidal signal $u(t) = A\sin(\omega t + \varphi)$. The basic problem is how *to extract the information parameters* $\{a_k\}$ from the observed chaotic sequences. Chaotic nature of signals is doubtlessly a factor, which is greatly conducive for secure data transmission.

4. SINGLE-CHANNEL DATA TRANSMISSION

The maps $F(x; \mathbf{a})$, which *linearly* depend on all the parameters $\mathbf{a} = (a_0, ..., a_K)$, are of special interest for hidden information transmission because of simplicity of the reconstruction algorithm. In this case Eq. (1) takes a form

$$x_{n+1} = F(x_n; \mathbf{a}) = \sum_{k=1}^{K} a_k f_k(x_n). \tag{3}$$

Here $\{f_k\}$ is a specified set of smooth functions, e.g., a set of power functions $f_k(x) = x^k$, trigonometric functions $f_k(x) = \sin kx$, some orthogonal polynomials etc. The variable x is supposed to be normalized in such a way, that x is of order of a unity: $x \propto 1$.

Assume also, that all parameters a_k in the map (3) are known except a single "information" value a_p, which is subjected modulation. This modulation scheme will be treated as *single channel* data transmission.

Separating in Eq. (3) the term, containing information parameter $a_p(n)$, one can rewrite this equation in the form

$$x_{n+1} = \widetilde{F}(x_n) + a_p(n) f(x_n), \tag{4}$$

where

$$\widetilde{F}(x) \equiv F(x; \mathbf{a}) - a_p f_p(x) = \sum_{k=1}^{p-1} a_k f_k(x_n) + \sum_{k=p+1}^{K} a_k f_k(x_n) \tag{5}$$

is a map $F(x;\mathbf{a})$ without the information term $a_p f_p(x)$. By virtue of (4), parameter $a_p(n)$ can be expressed in terms of measured values x_{n+1} and x_n:

$$a_p(n) = \frac{x_{n+1} - \widetilde{F}(x_n)}{f_p(x_n)}.$$ (6)

As examples, one can consider a quadratic map

$$F[x, a_0, a_2] = a_0 + a_2 x^2.$$ (7)

In this case

$$a_0(n) = x_{n+1} - a_2 x_n^2,$$ (8)

if the information parameter is $a_0(n)$, and

$$a_2(n) = (x_{n+1} - a_0)/x_n^2,$$ (9)

if information is transmitted by modulation of parameter $a_2(n)$.

In a particular case of the logistic map $F(x) = \lambda x(1 - x)$, which has a single information parameter $\lambda(n)$, information might be reconstructed by the formula

$$\lambda(n) = \frac{x_{n+1}}{x_n(1 - x_n)}.$$

Similar formula $a_1(n) = \dfrac{x_{n+1}}{\sin x_n}$ takes place in the case of the sinusoidal

mapping $F(x) = a_1 \sin \pi x$.

According to (6), two sample elements x_{n+1} and x_n allow to determine single parameter $a_p(n)$. Respectively, three sample elements x_n, x_{n+1} and x_{n+2} yield two values, $a_p(n)$ and $a_p(n+1)$; $K+1$ sample elements x_n, $x_{n+1},...,x_{n+K}$ yield K values of the parameter $a_p(n)$, $a_p(n+1),...,$ $a_p(n+K-1)$. In other words, we can retrieve K values of the information parameter $a_p(n)$ from $K+1$ sample elements x_n, $x_{n+1},...,x_{n+K}$.

5. PROCEDURES FOR INFORMATION TRANSMISSION AND RECONSTRUCTION

Practical realization of the single channel transmission on a sender side involves the following steps.

(i) Presentation of the primary message as a sequence of symbols s_j (letters, numbers, special symbols); total number of symbols is typically $J=50$.

(ii) Choice of the map with sufficiently wide interval of chaotical behavior $\Delta a_p^{chaotic}$. Interval $|a_p^j - a_p^{j+1}|$, corresponding to distance between neighbouring symbol s_j and s_{j+1} is of order

$$|a_p^j - a_p^{j+1}| \approx \frac{\Delta a_p^{chaotic}}{J} \approx 0.001 - 0.01. \tag{10}$$

(iii) Conversion of the symbols s_j into values of control parameters a_p^j.

(iv) Generation of the chaotic signal

$$x_{n+1} = F(x_n, a_p^j) = a_p^j f(x_n) + \widetilde{F}(x_n),$$

carrying information in parameter a_p^j.

(v) Digital-to-binary conversion of the signal x_{n+1}.

(vi) Transmission of the binary signal to recipient, using conventional (amplitude, frequency, pulse-code and so on) communication lines.

Corresponding operations on a recipient side are as follows.

(i) Binary-to-digital conversion of the received signal x_n.

(ii) Reconstruction of the control parameters a_p^j from the received sequence y_n on the basis of algorithm (6).

(iii) Conversion of the extracted parameters a_p^j into symbols s_j.

(iv) Reconstruction of the total message from the set of s_j symbols.

These operations are rather simple for practical realization. In the same time they provide sufficiently high barrier for unauthorized access.

6. MULTICHANNEL DATA TRANSMISSION

Message transmission by modulation of two or more parameters in the map (3) might be treated as *multichannel transmission* [15,16]. In this Section we would intend to illustrate characteristic features of multichannel transmission by the example of two modulated parameters (double channel transmission).

Let only two parameters, $a_p(n)$ and $a_q(n)$, be modulated within two successive steps $n+1$ and $n+2$, whereas all the other parameters remain constant. Supposing that parameters $a_p(n)$ and $a_q(n)$ preserve their values during these two steps, $a_p(n+1) = a_p(n)$ and $a_q(n+1) = a_q(n)$, the expressions for two successive sample values x_{n+1} and x_{n+2} can be presented in the form:

$$
\begin{aligned}
x_{n+1} &= \widetilde{F}_{(p,q)}(x_n) + a_p(n)f_p(x_n) + a_q(n)f_q(x_n), \\
x_{n+2} &= \widetilde{F}_{(p,q)}(x_{n+1}) + a_p(n)f_p(x_{n+1}) + a_q(n)f_q(x_{n+1}),
\end{aligned}
\tag{11}
$$

where $\widetilde{F}_{(p,q)}(x_n)$ is a map (2) without the p-th and q-th information terms.

It follows from (11), that

$$
\begin{aligned}
a_p &= \frac{1}{D}\left[X_{n+1}f_q(x_{n+1}) - X_{n+2}f_q(x_n)\right], \\
a_q &= \frac{1}{D}\left[X_{n+1}f_p(x_{n+1}) - X_{n+2}f_p(x_n)\right]
\end{aligned}
\tag{12}
$$

where

$$
\begin{aligned}
D &= f_p(x_n)f_q(x_{n+1}) - f_p(x_{n+1})f_q(x_n), \\
X_{n+1} &= x_{n+1} - \widetilde{F}_{(p,q)}(x_n), \\
X_{n+2} &= x_{n+2} - \widetilde{F}_{(p,q)}(x_{n+1}).
\end{aligned}
$$

Thus, three sample values x_n, x_{n+1} and x_{n+2} allow to reconstruct two parameters a_p and a_q in frame of two-tact scheme. Analogously $2K+1$ sample elements $x_n, x_{n+1}, \dots, x_{n+2K}$ generate K pairs of parameters a_p and a_q, which can be reconstructed by algorithm like (12). Reconstruction of three, four and more information parameters may be performed in a similar way.

7.   SENSITIVITY OF THE RECONSTRUCTION ALGORITHM TO SMALL CHANGES IN THE MAP

Correct reconstruction of the information parameters a_p^j and thereby all the symbols s_j as well as the total message is possible, if deviations of the reconstructed parameters Δa_p^j are small as compared to typical distance (10) between values a_p^j and a_p^{j+1}, corresponding to neighbouring symbols s_j and s_{j+1}.

Admissible variations ΔF of the key function $F(x_n; \mathbf{a})$ should satisfy the inequality

$$\Delta F_{admissible} << \frac{\Delta a_{chaotic}}{J} \approx 0.001 - 0.01 \cdot \tag{13}$$

This inequality should be satisfied for any chaotic values xn within interval $x_n < \max|x_n|$ and for all allowable idle coefficients a_k.

8. CRYPTOGRAPHIC ASPECTS

The single-channel cryptographic scheme under discussion implies in fact two kinds of ciphering: (i) conversion of symbols s_j into information parameter values a_p^j and (ii) conversion of the coefficients a_p^j into chaotic sequence x_n. The key-information in the second kind of the ciphering is contained in the set of basic functions $f_k(x)$ and in the idle parameters, which don't carry specific information, but impede unauthorized access to data transmitted. In principle, all the basic functions $f_k(x)$ and idle parameters could be divided in two groups, corresponding to public and private keys.

Additional barrier for unauthorized access to transmitted data might be introduced by simultaneous modulation of several control parameters (multi-channel data transmission, Sect.6) or by using multidimensional (matrix) maps.

9. CONCLUSION

The algorithm described is sufficiently simple for practical realization, seriously impedes an unauthorized access to the information transmitted and looks prospective for a number of applications. As for the digital domain, where noise does not come in as a factor, we can use it as a general purpose encryption algorithm and apply these algorithms to provide a safe and secure channel over unsafe links such as the Internet. The big problem of proposed chaotic cryptosystem is the lack of security proof. But this is not the problem of this cryptosystem only. Due to the difficulty of cryptanalysis, the security of the chaotic cryptosystem cannot be readily quantified, and hence the level of security is as yet not very well characterized. This is opposed to conventional cryptosystems, for example the RSA algorithm, which security is based on the intractability of the integer factorisation [19].

Our chaotic cryptosystem is waiting for the cryptoanalytic works to measure its security exactly. The authors would indebt to everybody who will point out explicit and hidden shortcomings of the method under discussion.

REFERENCES

[1] Kocarev L., Halle K.S., Eikert K. et al. Int. J. Bifurcation Chaos, 1992, 2(3), 703.

[2] Cuomo K.M., Oppenheim A.V. Phys. Rev. Lett., 1993, 71(1), 65.

[3] Didien H., Kennedy M.P., Hasler M. Analog-digital signal processing. IEEE Trans. Circuits Syst.,1993, 40(10), 634.

[4] Anosov O.L., Butkovskii O.Ya., Kravtsov Yu.A. et.al. Dynamic equation reconstruction from the observed 1D time series. In: Dynamical Systems and Chaos (Y.Aizawa, S.Saito, K.Shiraiwa, Eds.). World Scientific: Singapore, 1994, Vol. 2, pp.378-380.

[5] Anosov O.L., Butkovskii O.Ya. A discriminant procedure for the solution of inverse problems for non-stationary systems. In: Predictability of Complex Dynamical Systems (Yu.A.Kravtsov, J.B.Kadtke, Eds.). Springer Verlag: Berlin, Heidelberg, 1996, pp.67-78.

[6] Kolumban G., Vizvari B., Schwarz P., Abel A. Differential chaos shift keying: a robust coding for chaos communication. Proc. Int. Workshop NDES'96, Seville, Spain, 1996, pp.87-92.

[7] Hasler M. Synchronization of chaotic systems and transmission of information. Int. J. Bifurcation Chaos, 1998, 8(4), 213.

[8] Kuleshov V.N., Udalov N.N. Nonlinear filtering of modulated chaotic oscillations. Proc. Int. Workshop NDES'97, Moscow, Russia, pp. 537-542.

[9] Kolumban G., Kennedy M.P., Kis G. Multilevel Differential Chaos Shift Keying. Proc. Int. Workshop NDES'97, Moscow, Russia, 1997, pp. 191-196.

[10] Kapranov M.V., Morozov A.G. Application of chaotic modulation for hidden data transmission. Proc. Int. Workshop NDES'97, Moscow, Russia, pp. 223-228.

[11] V.N.Kuleshov, M.V.Larionova, N.N.Udalov. Information transmission system with chaotic carrier: demands to the accuracy of symbols generation. Proc. 1998 Int. Symp. "On Acoustoelectronics, Frequency Control and Signal Generation", St.-Petersburg, Russia, 1998, pp. 192-199.

[12] Dmitriev A.S., Starkov S.O. Uspehi sovremennoi radioelektroniki (Advances in Modern Radio Electronics, Moscow), 1998, no.11, p. 4.

[13] Tratas Yu.G. Application of statistical communication theory to the problems of chaotic signal transmission. Uspehi sovremennoi radioelektroniki (Advances in Modern Radio Electronics, Moscow), 1998, no.11, pp. 57-80.

[14] Kennedy M. P. Three steps to chaotic communications: coherent, non-coherent, and differentially coherent approaches. Proc. Int. Symp. NOLTA'98, Crans-Montana, Switzerland, 1998, pp. 63-68.

[15] Anishchenko V.S., Pavlov A.N. Global reconstruction in application to multichannel communication. Phys. Rev. E, 1998, 57(2), 2455.

[16] Anishchenko V.S., Vadivasova T.E., Astakhov V.V. Nonlinear Dynamics of Chaotic and Stochastic Systems (in Russian). Saratov: Saratov Univ., 1999, 368 pp.

[17] Kapranov M.V., Kuleshov V.N., Larionova M.V., Morozov A.G., Udalov H.H. Properties of information transmission systems on the basis of parameters and initial data manipulation in generators of chaotic oscillations. Uspehi sovremennoi radioelektroniki (Advances in Modern Radio Electronics, Moscow), 2000, no.11, pp.48-62.

[18] Bilchinskaya S.G., Butkovskii O.Ya., Kapranov M.V., Kravtsov Yu.A., Morozov A.G., Surovyatkina E.D. Signal reconstruction errors in data transmission on the basis of modulation of the parameters of chaotic sequences. J. Comm. Technol. Electron., 2003, 48 (3), 284-292.

[19] A. Menezes, P. van Oorschot and S. Vanstone Handbook of Applied Cryptography, London, CRC Press 1997.

Chapter 2

Biometric Systems

Some Advances and Challenges in Live Biometrics, Personnel Management, and Other "Human Being" Applications

LEONID KOMPANETS

Czestochowa University of Technology, Institute of Computer & Information Sciences,
Center for Intelligent Multimedia Techniques
Dabrowskiego Street, 73, 42-200 Czestochowa, Poland
e-mail: leonid.kompanets@icis.pcz.pl

Abstract: In the paper, the results of transdisciplinary scientific-technical analysis of current state-of-the-art in "human being" fields, and some author's insights and specific studies are presented.

It is shown that transdisciplinary development direction in „human being" fields is the qualitative broadening of knowledge about human, especially about his cognition-personality features. For example, in disciplines concerning human - quite a current issue is the change (shift) of the actual paradigm in the direction of the novel understanding of reality, existence, and human nature; in management - solving of the basic problem of the evaluation of mental workers (personnel) effectiveness and the creation of synergic work teams; in net communication – providing a higher level of security than with PKI (Public Key Infrastructure) by the creation of live biometrics techniques; in computer aided human work – urgent development of artificial intelligence methods; in smart environments creation – the study of the technologies of interpretation of human behavior and interactions coordination.

Selected systemic problems are also discussed: biometric myths and an inevitability of different kind identification errors; fusion of biometrics; abilities of modern cognitive vision; emergence of novel direction in biometrics – "asymmetry" live biometrics.

As new studies, there are presented some ideas, sketches and opportunities, namely: 1) ophthalmogeometric biometric technique, 2) face asymmetry biometric technique, 3) Czestochowa's model of an asymmetric face, 4) S. Dellinger's geometric typology of personality and T. Valchuk's mental one. A. Anuashvili's typology, which bases on the objective parameter measurement of brain hemispheres functioning, are discussed. Simultaneously, new instruments (pseudo-information criteria, algorithms of biometric feature measurement, and holistic manner of results interpretation) are discussed.

Key words: Live biometrics, Artificial intelligence, Personnel management, Personnel typologies, Ophthalmogeometry, Face asymmetry, Brain asymmetry, Information theoretic measure.

1) The main issue of this book is to outline the urge of western scientific studies to approach the change of the paradigm of dimensions till now invisible, owing to which our idea of reality and human nature shall change. This change will finally raise a conceptual bridge to link the ancient wisdom with modern science reconciling eastern spirituality and western pragmatics. ...The probability of the fact that human consciousness developed from chemical or primeval ocean, only owing to random sequence of mechanical processes, has lately been very accurately compared to the probability of a hurricane that passes through the gigantic refuse dump to randomly compose „Boeing 747" [11].   ***Grof** Stanislav*

2) The foundation of modern society , economics and human relations is a managed organization as a social institute, the aim of which is to achieve a result. ...The only valuable assets of any XX century company were the productive equipment. The only valuable asserts of any XXI century company will be knoweledge workers and their productivity. ...the future flourishing or even self-existence of the developed countries will depend exactly on the productivity of this group of workers. ...In the year 2000 the studies on the rising of knowledge worker productivity are approximately at the level of the work state in 1900 after the rise of physical worker productivity. ...Knoweledge workers possess their productive capital, which is the knowledge preserved in their minds. It is fully "portable" and of extreme capacity as a kind of main capital. The primary necessary achievement of management in XXI century concerns with the increase in knowledge worker productivity [3].   ***Drucker** Peter F.*

3) If you give a fish to a man, you will feed him for a day. If you give him a fishing rod, you will feed him for life. We can go one step further: If we can provide him with the knowledge and the know-how for making that fishing rod, we can feed the whole village (and for life).]   The great Chinese philosopher *Kuang-Tzu* [1]

4) Through SCI2003 conferences, we are trying to relate the **analytic** thinking required in **focused** conference sessions, to the **synthetic** thinking, required for analogies generation, which calls for **multi-focus** domain and **divergent** thinking. We are trying to promote a **synergic relation** between analytically and synthetically oriented minds, as it is found between left and right brain hemispheres, by means of the corpus callosum. Then, SCI 2003 might be perceived as a ***research corpus callosum,*** trying to bridge analytically with synthetically oriented efforts, convergent with divergent thinkers and focused specialists with non-focused or

multi-focused generalists.

Metaphor of Intern. Multi-Conference
on Systemics, Cybernetics, Informatics
(Site of *The IIIS*, http://www.iiis.org/sci2003, [39])

TRANSDYSCIPLINARY BACKGROUND OF "HUMAN BEING" STUDY

To define the transdisciplinary contents of the invited paper, above, there have been cited four quotations that belong to scientists distinguished in their fields and prominent publishers.

The basic philosophical scientific issue has always been, and will remain, the acceptance of fundamental principle determining the priority of matter or spirit. The first quotation and works [*11, 12*, 13, 20, 21, 9] not groundlessly tell about the predominance of psyche (spirit) priority and forecast the approaching change (shift) of scientific paradigm. This change is in the first place significant in the fields of psychology, sociology, philosophy and religion. It will also have a striking influence on information-communicational studies, especially on the work on artificial intelligence/life. It is known that in artificial intelligence the Computational Model of the Mind has been accepted [*6*, 4, 5, 7] and intelligent artifacts simulate without crossing line boundaries of the mentioned model. However, the principles and structures of a live being [8, 9, 18, 19] and the artificial [4-7] are diametrically opposed.

By means of the second quotation the main scientific and practical challenges of the XXI century are differentiated: the cognition of the mechanisms of mental work effectiveness and realization of transition from the managers principle to synergism one in future organization management. The third quotation stresses the fact that knowledge processing, not data processing, becomes the basic cognition-personality feature of a modern man, especially of a mental worker. The forth quotation illustrates modern, till of low effectiveness, direction of the realization of enumerated challenges.

In computer science the notions of *hardware* and *software* are used. By means of soft- and hardware algorithmic (formalized) tasks of computer functioning are fulfilled only. The problems of intelligent information computer systems functioning are solved by means of heuristics and other advanced means, which we shall call *brainwave*. The analysis of the state of development of studies on natural intelligence provides the basis for drawing a conclusion that the main challenge is to reveal the mystery of brain functioning and psychological and social human behavior formation. Analogically to computer science we shall define the problem as a „*brainware*" problem.

1. STRUCTURED "HUMAN BEING" STUDY AREA

In Table 1, the division of "human being" area of our study is presented and relevant challenges, advantages, and concrete interesting problems to be solved in separated directions are differentiated.

Some system nuances and the advances that are numbered (bold) in Table 1 are the subject to be discussed in this invited paper.

Table 1. Scientific and technological advances and challenges for selected informatics/communications fields

Sub area	Challenge	Traditional field	Advance (having some author's subjectivity)
"Human being" sciences	1.Change/shift of the scientific paradigm	-	[11, 3, 9, 12, 20, 21, 40, 41, 1]
Manage-ment	2. Creation of a knowledge worker productiveness theory 3. Change/shift of the managerism approach in a synergism one	Personnel manage-ment Theory of manage-ment, and theory of intelligent system	**9. Personnel typologies** based on human cognition and personality abilities [14, 15, 16, 17, 20, 21, 34, 38, 39, 46] 10. Attempts of trans- and inter-disciplinary know-ledge and thin-king method interchanging [The IIIS [40], 11, 6, 12, 20, 35, 41] 11. Creation of **mental ty-pology of personnel** [38, 35, 41]
Networks informatics and commu-nications	4. New types of authentication/ide n-tification user tech-nologies creation 5. Live biometrics techniques creation and fusion them with PIN, cryptography, hiding, other ones	Networks security te-chnologies (Live) biometrics technolo-gies	12. Creation of physiolo-gical and behavioral tech-niques of **live biometrics** [43, 44, 28, 23, 24, 25, 33] 13. Creation **ophthalmo-geometry** and **face asym-metry** live biometrics techniques [46, 41] 14. Creation of **Czestocho-wa's precise model** of a face [46]
Artificial intelligence	6. New pattern recognition methods creation 7. Creation of cognitive multime-dia system theory and technologies	Cognitive vision system [45]	15. Creation and widening of **pseudo-information theory** to evaluate a similarity of multimedia information objects in holistic manner [29, 30, 36, 37, 39, 42, 48]
Information environment	8. Theory and technologies of smart (intelligent, virtual, wearable computing, ubiquitous) environment creation	"Looking at people" technology Interaction in smart environ-ment with-out detai-led instru-ctions	[2, 45]

2.   ON SOME SYSTEMIC NUANCES

▪ **Biometric myths and errors of different kinds.** In connection with rapid development in the field [44] and newly-created companies that use specialized analytics of medial qualifications, „mythical" considerations can be met. For example, the possibility of person identification with the probability of *1* for human fellowship on Earth, has been discussed. In commercials concerning iris system it can be heard that probability of two same iris being met give precisely the same monochromatic record in *IrisCode*, equals 1 to 10^{78}. Here, it is probably worth mentioning the fact that the number 10^{-78} (or 10^{78}) is the so called A. Kolmogorov's great number (that is, out-earth and transcomputable – non-calculable). There happen some considerations that do not rely to the principles of Shannon's information theory and possibilities of lossless compression signal theory.

The main sources of such myths, according to the author, are the facts:
1)   Thesis on the theoretical persistence of biometrics individuality not proved in any science about man (refer, for example, materials concerning fingerprints individuality [22]).
2)   The boundaries of technical systems have to be realistically understood [46].
3)   The potential possibilities of making a decision provided in scheme in Fig. 1 have to be understood.

The basic set of biometric system characteristics are: FRR (false rejection rate) error, FAR (acceptation) error, CER - cross error rate, time of enrollment, and authentication time [44]. In Fig.1, the rule of statistical decision making is illustrated for a non-trivial case. Information about states of system (D_1 – working state, D_2 – non-working state), conditional probability density function of states ($f(x/D_1)$ and $f(x/D_2)$). The choice of optimal parameter value x_0 is realized by the next decision rule

$$\text{for } x<x_0\, x\in D_1 ; \quad \text{for } x>x_0\ x\in D_2$$

in terms: H_{11} i H_{22} – correct decisions; H_{21} - false alarm (FRR); H_{12} – FAR error.

The example of curve FRR and FAR is shown in Fig.2. Error values for modern biometric systems is given in Table 2. It is worth drawing attention to the fact that the existence of error is *a crucial issue*, the relation of FRR to FAR depends on x_0 parameter value.

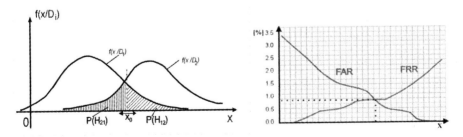

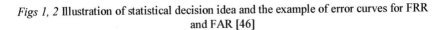

Figs 1, 2 Illustration of statistical decision idea and the example of error curves for FRR and FAR [46]

Table 2 Decision error values for some modern biometric system types

Biometric	FRR [%]	FAR [%]
Voice	1	0,1
Voice via telephone	2,95	0,44
Fingerprints	0,5	0,001
Iris pattern	2,8	0
Signature	0,2	< 0,6
Palm geometry	0,15	0,15

▪ **On fusion of biometrics.** The biometrics (and methods) fusion problem is a complicated theoretical problem, and also the art of their usage. However, it is worth to remind the effect of more reliable systems synthesis (Fig. 5) from less reliable elements (Fig.3).

To be precise, it is worth to define the process of biometrics fusion as a process of parallel joint of s elements, for example, arithmetic automates that increase the input number n to $(n+1)$.

Let every automat s function with probability p_i of working state (reliability). A system consisting of two parallel joined elements has the probability of system working state $P''_\Sigma = 1-(1-p_i)^2$. A series joint of two s elements gives the system probability $P_\Sigma^{++} = p_i^2$. If, for example, the probabilities p_i take values 0,5; 0,8; 0,95, then the corresponding values for system reality probability are:

$$P''_\Sigma = 0,75 \ (\mathbf{+0,25}); \ 0,96 \ (\mathbf{+0,16}); \ 0,9975 \ (\mathbf{+0,0475}), \ (\ + \rightarrow \mathbf{1} \ );$$
$$P_\Sigma^{++} = 0,25 \ (\mathbf{-0,25}); \ 0,64 \ (\mathbf{-0,16}); \ 0,9025 \ (\mathbf{-0,0475}), \ (\ - \leftarrow \mathbf{1} \ ).$$

In practice, the fusion procedure is much more complicated and has intelligent traits. However, the example a) illustrates quantitative fusion dependencies and b) proves the absurdity of fully reliable system presence (P''_Σ goes for, but never achieves 1).

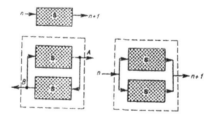

Figs 3, 4, 5. Illustration of system of reliability improving (in our interpretation – the improving of decision quality by means of fusion biometrics (Fig. 5)) and the emergence of new properties – emergence, synergy [47] (Fig. 4)

4. ABILITIES OF MODERN COGNITIVE VISION

To evaluate the difficulty of the challenge 7, which is a part of the challenge 8 (Table 1), set of modern cognitive vision models is presented. Among scientists, who make projects of systems for learning and understanding dynamic scene activity, according to Buxton Hilary [45], the following parametric models for signal processing (Table 3) are used.

Table 3 Cognitive model relationship

Initial	Ixtention	Final
Gaussian	Mixture	VQ
Gaussian	Reduce dimension	PCA
VQ	Dynamic.	HMM
PCA	Independence	ICA
HMM	Coupling	CHMM
HMM	Variable length	VLMM
ICA	Hierarchy	BBN
BBN	Dynamic	DBN
DBN	Utility	DDN

The table objects signify: Principal Component Analysis (PCA); Gaussian mixture or Vector Quantization (VQ); Hidden Markov Model (HMM); Bayesian Belief Network (BBN); Coupled HMM (CHMM); Variable Length Markov Model (VLMM); Independent Component Analysis (ICA); Dynamic Bayesian Network (DBN); Dynamic Decision Networks (DDN).

As seen, there is nothing unknown and intelligent in such an advanced field as computer vision. Only some new secondary possibilities of description of cognitive behavior are present by means of the possibility of description of temporal and/or dynamic statistical dependences between hidden states or models (see CHMM, VLMM). Also, more meaningful mechanisms incremented in BBN, DBN, DDN. BBN models, by means of which one can evaluate these statistical independence properties plus a possible hierarchy of dependences between the hidden model variables.

This means that the possibilities of modern cognitive systems in comparison with natural intelligence are in the primary state.

5. CREATION OF MENTAL TYPOLOGY

Among different psychological typologies [15, 14, 13, 20], there is no typology, by means of which the cognitive style and potential abilities (as knowledge processing transformation) of a person may be evaluated. In order to create mental typology [34, 38, 41] some students' groups (about 150 persons) were subjected to the test named as "*Test_Kotelnikov-Shannon_Theorem*". The test was aimed at the synthesis of the scale of the personality cognitive types consisting of five types. It is constructed by analogy to A. Turing's well known test.

Sampling theorem: „If an continuous function $s(t)$ •) exists on the interval -$\infty < t > \infty$, ••) has Fourier transformation $S(f)$, and •••) its spectrum differs from zero outside an interval -F, F, then this function may be represented as a set of samples at discrete time moments, distant from one another on $\Delta t = 1/2\ F$, where F – upper frequency of the continuous spectrum; amplitudes of samples $s(k\Delta t)$ correspond to the formula

$$s(t) = \sum_{k=-\infty}^{\infty} s(k\Delta t) \frac{\sin 2\pi F(t - k\Delta t)}{2\pi F(t - \Delta t)}$$

where $s(k\ \Delta t)$ – the continuous function values in time moments $t = k\ \Delta t$".

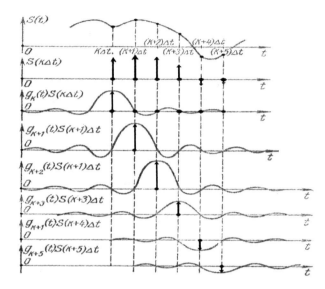

Fig. 6 Illustration of Kotelnikov-Shannon theorem.
[$(g_k(t),\ k=\pm\infty)$ – full set of orthogonal SINCus-functions; s(t)- an input signal]

The theorem geometric interpretation is given in Fig. 6. This theorem describes the simple and inverse information transformations between continuous and digital notation of a signal. The students of the communicational studies and of the computer studies are taught the theorem in a modern multimedia representation. The unit of an autonomous, special knowledge concerning the understanding of the theorem included the scientific, applied and systemic knowledge in a full scope. During the test, a person processes the complex information (knowledge). S/he must fill out a questionnaire included a set of special questions. The questions concern a wide range of knowledge (from simple professional activity to systems analysis and perspectives). In the results, expert(s) have possibility to estimate a person's manners and potential abilities to transform a special knowledge.

The input and output information for the test and the questionnaire are represented below.

IN: 1) A knowledge unit (paper) on an continuous signal digitalization and invertible transformation without an information loss must be written in student's native language, and must be available to multiple reading. 2) The paper must include an autonomic integral knowledge unit, and must be written by a high rank academic specialist. 3) An educational level of the paper must correspond to an according knowledge level of the computer science and communication studies of university.

OUT: The answer on the questionnaire must be presented in strict, relevant manner and modern multimedia form (more then 50% knowledge must be represented as figures, algorithms, formulas, tables, and so on) . The student's answers must be done in unaided manner.

Questionnaire:

1. Point out formal object, field of knowledge, and aspect of research
2. Formalize scientific/technical problem, and goal of research
3. Identify object formalism (mathematical model, algorithm, and so on), its components, interactions between components
4. Discuss specific events "What will it be, if ..." regarding to 3
5. Point out lack/irrelevant parts of knowledge
6. List noise/disinformation thoughts
7. Estimate scientific/technical, multimedia, cultural level
8. Reveal problem-solve properties
9. Define modern internal/external directions of problem development of the unit
10. Write an abstract
11. (Estimate your answers 1-10 in scale from 1 to 10.)

Questions 1-10 include the following knowledge levels: special professional one, problem solving, common educational, cultural, and so on.

The result of the test has confirmed the idea. It has given a possibility to construct the scale of person's mental types (*person's manners and potential abilities of a knowledge processing*).

There emerged five cognitive types of the person: IGN - *Ignoramus* (A superficial); PRG - *Pragmatist* (A satisfactory); RPR - *Reproducer* (A versatile); CNC - *Conceptologist* (A theoretical) and/or CRT - *Creator* (A creative).

Because of mental abilities, person's methodology of knowledge processing (cognitive style), educational particularities, and other facts, a person is able in the case of: ICN $\rightarrow$ to absorb and manipulate some fragments of special knowledge only; PRG $\rightarrow$ to solve not complicated tasks concerned with usage of special professional knowledge; RPR $\rightarrow$ to absorb and manipulate full special professional knowledge and to understand, more or less, tasks of near fields; CNC $\rightarrow$ to understand paradigm contradictions of own special knowledge field and to have some skill of problem solving; CRT $\rightarrow$ to create new conceptions and paradigms.

6.   CZESTOCHOWA'S PRECISE MODEL OF A FACE AND "ASYMMETRY" BIOMETRICS

In modern biometrics the symmetry principle (for face, silhouette and other parts of human body) is used as default. Actually, this is not true. In the paper [48], included in this proceedings, Czestochowa's precise model of a face is described. The model is treated in terms of brain hemispheres functional asymmetry phenomenon. Apart from two new biometrics (ophthalmogeometric pattern, face asymmetry) model contains new algorithmic and information mechanisms to compare concrete face asymmetric performances and their chosen sets.

In [48, 41], the effectiveness of face asymmetric model usage was proved. Moreover, the model can constitute an example for the new biometrics approach creation, which may be called "precise" or "asymmetry" live biometrics.

REFERENCES

[1] Reddy Ray: The Challenge of Artificial Intelligence. *Computer*, October 1996, 86-98

[2] Pentland, Alex: Looking at People: Sensing for Ubiquitous and Wearable Computing. *Pattern Recognition and Machine Analysis (PAMI)*, vol. 22, No 1, January 2000, 107-119

[3] Peter F. Drucker: *Management Challenges for the 21st Century*. Butterworth-Heinemann, London, 1999, ISBN 0-7506-4456-7

[4] Shapiro Stuart: Artificial Intelligence, *Encyclopedia of Artificial Intelligence (EoAI)*, Stuart C. Shapiro – Editor-in-chief, Sec. Ed., vol.1, 54-57

[5] Ackerman Phillip: Intelligence, Human. *EoAI*, vol. 1, 706-715

[6] Van Gulick: Philosophical Questions. *EoAI,*. vol.2, 1137-1147

[7] Holyoak K.: Cognitive Psychology, *EoAI*, vol. 1, 181-186

[8] Ingber Donald: The Architecture of Life. Life's Architecture: Cells Grow with "Tensegrity", *Scientific American*, January 1998, .30-39

[9] De Kerckhove Derrick: *The Skin of Culture*. Somerville House Books Ltd., Toronto, Canada, 1995

[10] Ebel Robert: *Measuring Educational Achievement*. Prentice-Hall, Inc, Englewood Cliffs, New Jersey, 1965

[11] Grof Stanislav: *Beyond the Brain: Birth, Death and Transcendence in Psychotherapy*. State University of New York Press, 1985.

[12] Penrose Roger: *The Emperor's New Mind Concerning Computer, Minds, and the Laws of Physics*. Oxford University Press, 1989

[13] Hall Calvin S., Lindzey Gardner: *Theories of Personality*. Sec. Ed., John Willey & Sons, 1970

[14] Myers I. B., McCaulley M. H.: *Manuel: A Guide to the Development and Use of the Myers-Briggs Type Indicator*. Palo Alto, CA: Consult. Psychol. Press, 1985

[15] Anastasi, Anna, Urbina, Susan: *Psychological Testing*. Prentice-Hall, Inc., 1997

[16] Dellinger Susan E.: *Communicating Beyond Our Differences: Introducing the Psycho-Geometrics^{TM} System*. (Prentice-Hall, 1989 / Jade Ink, 1996)

[17] *Psycho-Geomertics^{tm}*. Dr Susan Dellinger Home Page. Available at http://www.drsusan.net

[18] Carter Rita: *Mapping the Mind*. California, 1998

[19] Gazzaniga Michael: The Split Brain Revisited, *Scientific American*, July 1998, 34-39

[20] Anuashvili Avtandil: *Fundamentals of Psychology: Scientific, Philosophic and Spiritual Fundamentals of Psychology*. The Institute for Control Problems Press, Moscow, 2001 (In Russian).

[21] Muldashev, Ernst R.: *Whom did we descend from?*, OLMA-PRESS, Moscow 2002 (In Russian)

[22] Pankanti Sharath, Prabhakar Salil, Jain Anil K.: On the Individuality of Fingerprints. *PAMI*, Vol. 24, No 8, August 2002, 1010-1025

[23] Face Modeling. Microsoft Current Research. Available at http://research.microsoft.com/research/projects/

[24] Research Videos. Available at http://seeingmachines.com/videos/research

[25] Kukharev Georgy, Kuzminski Adam: *Biometric Techniques. Part 1: Methods of Face Recognition*. Technical Univ. of Szczecin Press, Szczecin, 2003 (In Polish)

[26] Pantic Maja, Rothkrantz Leon J. M.: „Automatic Analysis of Facial Expressions: the State of the Art", PAMI, vol. 22, No 12, December 2000, 1424-1445

[27] Lam Kim-Man, Yan Hong: An Analytic-to-Holistic Approach for Face Recognition Based on a Single Frontal View, *PAMI*, vol. 20, No 7, July 1998, 673-686

[28] Brain Fingerprinting Laboratories Inc. Home Page. Available at http://www.brainwavescience.com

[29] Kompanets Leonid: Introduction to the Pseudo-Entropical Quantitative Theory of Information Transformation and/or Technologies. Proc. 3rd Intern. Symposium on *Methods and Models in Automation and Robotics – MMAR'96*, 10-13 Sept. 1996, Miedzyzdroje, Poland, vol.2, 665-670

[30] Kompanets Leonid, Piech Henryk, Pilarz Andrzej: Pseudo-Entropy and Beyond. Proc. 2nd Intern. Conf. on *Parallel Processing and Applied Mathematics – PPAM'97*, 2-5 Sept. 1997, Zakopane, Poland, 564-578

[31] Goksay Erhan, Principe Jose C.: Information Theoretic Clustering. *PAMI*, vol. 24, No 2, February. 2002, 158-171

[32] Santini Simine, Jain Ramesh: "Similarity Measures," PAMI, vol. 21, No 9, ," Sept. 1999, 871-883

[33] Liu Y., Weaver R. L., Schmidt K., Serban N., Cohn J.: Facial Asymmetry: A New Biometric. *The Robotic Institute of Carnegie Melon Univ.*, 2001. Available at . http://www.ri.cmu.edu/projects/project_437.html

[34] Kompanets Leonid, Valchuk Tetiana: Biometric Methods for Natural Intelligence Testing: S. Dellinger's Geometrical Approach, and T. Valchuk's Mental One, Proc. Intern. Conf. *IT.FORUM, SECURE 2002*, Warsaw, 6-7 November 2002, NASK and MULTICOPY Press, vol. 1, 87-95

[35] Kompanets Leonid, Valchuk Tetiana: Identification/Authentication of Person Cognitive Characteristics. The IEEE *AutoID'02* Proc. 3rd Workshop on *Automatic Identification Advanced Technologies*, 14-15 March 2002, Tarrytown, New York, USA, 12-16

[36] Kompanets Leonid: Pseudo-Entropy Measure *JeK* of Similarity for Biometric Applications. The IEEE *AutoID'02* Proc. 3rd Workshop on *Automatic Identification Advanced Technologies*, 142-146

[37] Kompanets Leonid, Bobulski Janusz, Wyrzykowski Roman: Pseudo-Entropy Similarity for Human Biometrics, Post-ECCV'02 Workshop on *Biometric Authentication*. 1st June, 2002, Copenhagen, Denmark. In: *LNCS # 2359*, Springer, 2002, 68-77

[38] Valchuk Tetiana, Wyrzykowski Roman, Kompanets Leonid: Mental Characteristics of Person as Basic Biometrics. Post-ECCV'02 Workshop on *Biometric Authentication*. *LNCS # 2359*, 78-90

[39] Kompanets Leonid, et al.: Based on Pseudo-Information Evaluation, Face Asymmetry and Ophthalmogeometry Techniques for Human-Computer Interaction, Person Psyche Type Identification, and Other Applications". Proc. 7th *World Multi-Conference on Systemics, Cybernetics, and Informatics – SCI 2003. Vol. XII, Information systems, Technologies and Applications II, 235-240*. The International Institute of Informatics and Systemics (*The IIIS*), Orlando, Florida, USA, 27-30 July 2003. Available at http://www.iiis.org/sci2003

[40] Kompanets Leonid: Counter-Terrorism Oriented Psychology and Biometrics Techniques: Part 1/2. Terrorism problem and modern person typologies; proposed research trend. Pre-proceedings of Symposium on *The Role of Academy in the War on Terrorism*. Eds: Callaos Nagib, Kompanets Leonid, Takeno Junichi, Wei Huaqiang, July 29, 2003,

11-17. *7th World Multi-Conference on Systemics, Cybernetics, and Informatics.* The IIIS, Orlando, Florida, USA, 27-30 July 2003. Available at http://www.iiis.org/sci2003

[41] Kompanets Leonid: Counter-Terrorism Oriented Psychology and Biometrics Techniques: Part 2/2. Based on Brain Asymmetry, Eyes Fingerprints, Face Asymmetry, and Person Psyche Type Identification Information Techniques. Pre-proceedings of Symposium on *The Role of Academy in the War on Terrorism.* Eds: Callaos Nagib, Kompanets Leonid, Takeno Junichi, Wei Huaqiang, July 29, 2003, 18-21. *7th World Multi-Conference on Systemics, Cybernetics, and Informatics.* The IIIS, Orlando, Florida, USA, 27-30 July 2003. Available at http://www.iiis.org/sci2003

[42] Kompanets Leonid, Valchuk Tatiana, Wyrzykowski Roman: Pseudo-Information and Pseudo-Information Similarity. Proc. Intern. Conference on *Computer, Communication and Control Technologies – CCCT 2003* and 9th Intern. Conference on *Information Systems Analysis and Synthesis – ISAS 2003. Vol. II, Communication systems, Technologies and Applications.* Orlando, Florida, USA, July 31 – August 2, 2003, 17-22. Available at http://www.iiis.org/ccct2003

[43] Bowman Erik: Everything You Need to Know About Biometrics. Available at http://www.ibia.org/EverythingAboutBiometrics.PDF

[44] First International Conference on Biometric Authentication: ICBA'04. 15-17 July 2004, Hong Kong. Available at http://www4.comp.polyu.edu.hk/~icba/

[45] Buxton Hilary: Generative Models for Learning and Understanding Dynamic Scene Activity. Proc. 1st Intern. Workshop on *Generative-Model-based Vision: GMBV 2002* in conjunction with ECCV 2002, 71-82. Technical Report DIKU-TR-2002/01, ISSN: 0107-8283. 2 June 2002, Copenhagen, Denmark

[46] Liu Simon, Silverman Mark: A Practical Guide to Biometric Security Technology. *IT Pro,* January/February 2001, 27-32

[47] *The Oxford Dictionary of Current English. Over 120,000 words, phrases, and definitions.* 3rd Edition, Major New Edition, 2001

[48] Kompanets Leonid, Kubanek Mariusz, Rydzek Szymon: Czestochowa's Precise Model of a Face Based on the Facial Asymmetry, Ophthalmogeometry, and Brain Asymmetry Phenomena: the Idea and Algorithm Sketch. (In *this proceedings*). Available at http://acs.wi.ps.pl

An environment for recognition systems modeling

GEORGY KUKHAREV, ADAM KUŹMIŃSKI
Technical University of Szczecin
Faculty of Computer Science & Information Systems (Poland)
e-mail: akuzminski@wi.ps.pl

Abstract: In this paper we present possibilities of the FaReS-Mod environment, which is assigned for design and examine face recognition systems. The FaReS-Mod allows to: analyse gotten results of a recognition process and select optimum parameters for a model. Described environment considerable accelerates design of a recognition system due to use set of function blocks and intuitive interface. The FaReS-Mod uses the most popular methods of feature space reduction (PCA, LDA) and preliminary processing.

Key words: FaReS-Mod environment, recognition system, PCA, LDA

1.   INTRODUCTION

Presented approach allows to design a new system, which realizes recognition tasks and uses for this purpose the most popular methods of feature space reduction (PCA, LDA) [1] and preliminary processing, and permits on analysis of efficiency of model. Due to it is possible to analyse different configurations and choose the most effective system. For presentation the course of a project design and a recognition process there are used different manner of visualization: structures of systems and databases, tables of results, mapping-diagrams of clasterization, sets of images and results of processing for each stage.

The environment has been designed for modelling and analysing a face recognition system, however, nothing stands on barrier, in order to use the FaReS-Mod for modelling a recognition system, which will take advantage of an other image type (e.g. aircrafts, fingerprints).

The FaReS-Mod allows to [2]:
- quickly build a recognition system with all essential procedures of processing;
- check the result of a project design on a chosen collection of data;
- analyse results in a chosen place of a designed system;

- modify a model in any point of processing;
- prepare a report based on the results of the test of the entire process applied;
- compare variants of systems for assigned image database;
- research efficiency of designed system: recognition rates, stability of recognition process, analysis time, feature decomposition;
- examine the influence of an individual parameter on recognizing:
  R = f({K, L, Q}, {M, N}, {q}, {PCA/LDA}, {Δ}, ...), where:
  - K, L, Q – parameters of database;
  - M, N – image size;
  - q – image quality;
  - PCA/LDA – choice of methods;
  - Δ – metrics used to comparison.

The environment has been tested on standard databases (e.g. Olivetti face database) and specialized. Within the confines of the environment many recognition systems were designed, which were used from 3 to 250 classes of images and from 5 to 30 images per a class.

The application has been designed with the help of the C++ and works under the Microsoft Windows operating system. The module structure of the program enables simple extension that permits on continuous extending possibilities.

2.   THE STRUCTURE AND BASIC BLOCKS OF THE ENVIRONMENT

It is possible to extract three main elements in the structure of the FaReS-Mod environment: database, project module and module of analysis [3].

The database contains sets of images (fig. 1), which are used in a process of recognizing and a system analysis. It has hierarchic structure: images belonging to one object (e.g. person) create a class, all classes, which use similar preprocessing transformations, are organized into a group. It is possible to divide images depending from realized function on: test – allows to verify an efficiency of the researched recognition system; base – uses to build a mathematical model; not active – not used in a recognition process.

Fig. 1. Sample databases

The project module is a graphic environment, which allows to design a new system with utilization of sets of function blocks. This module is a platform between two remaining parts: source data becomes from the image database, and results are transferred to the module of analysis. This intuitive tool enabling fast and simple elaboration of recognition systems. Projecting of a new system relies on choice of proper function blocks, its right connection and selection of parameters.

Function blocks are a graphic representation of suitable techniques and methods used in assignments of recognition systems. An user can use several blocks: group, crop, FFT (fast Fourier transform), filter, histogram, mask, median, scale, LDA, PCA, PCArc, PCA Plus, Multi Pattern, and Analysis.

The last module allows to analyse the modelled system. Simple interpretation of gotten results is possible due to different manners of presentations of results, it is possible to select optimal parameters of the examined system by that faster.

3. SYSTEM DESIGN

Thanks to use the visual environment, the process of a new systems modelling is fast and simple – the designer defines only the base of images, chooses function blocks, from of which has to consist a model of the system, connects it to proper structure and selects parameters for individual methods. This way, the system of identifying emerges, which is ready to analyse and optimise, in order to get best results for the chosen database. The process of design of the system is presented on the figure 2.

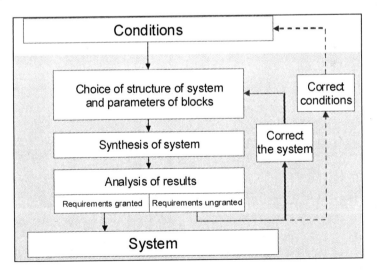

Fig. 2. The process of a system designing

In current version of the FaReS-Mod an user has to select initial structure of the system and parameters of each block. These parameters can be static or dynamic. Static parameters do not change during the process of the system analysis while dynamic parameters change within the limits defined by the user (fig. 3).

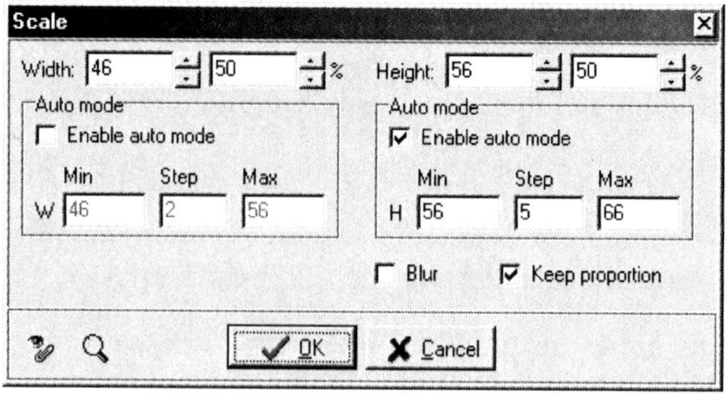

Scale ✕

Width: [46] ÷ [50] ÷ %   Height: [56] ÷ [50] ÷ %

┌─ Auto mode ─────────────────┐   ┌─ Auto mode ─────────────────┐
☐ Enable auto mode   ☑ Enable auto mode

Min   Step   Max   Min   Step   Max

W [46]   [2]   [56]   H [56]   [5]   [66]

☐ Blur   ☑ Keep proportion

✎ Q   [✓ OK]   ✗ Cancel

Fig. 3. Sample of use of static (left side) and dynamic (right side) parameters

On the fig. 3, for example, the parameter width of an image will be constant during the analysis (46 pixels), whereas the height of an image will accept values: 56, 61 and 66 pixels. It allows to analyse the influence of different parameters on the efficiency of modelled system.

Generally, the system modelling begins from defining a database, which should contains at least one test image in order to make possible analyse the modelled system. The more test images the gotten results are more reliable. However, the amount of test images should not be greater than the amount of base images [4].

Next step is designing a model of the system. At the beginning the designer should place the "Group" block in the project area, which will be the link between the database and the model of the system. After this it is possible to add other function blocks. For example, when the designer want to stretch a histogram, then resize an image, and finally use the PCA method, he should chooses proper blocks from the container, places in the project area, connects together and sets parameters of the each block (fig. 4).

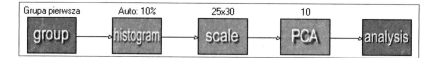

Fig. 4. Sample structure of a recognition system

Now the system is ready to analysis. In case, when the user needs to use more groups in the system, he can adds suitable amount of "Group" blocks, and defines individual set of transformations for all of them. It belongs to remember, that output images should have same size after transformations for each groups, besides, it is not possible to use for the each group individual set of feature extraction blocks. After the system preparation the analysis is performed.

4. MODEL ANALYSIS

The module of analysis contains two pages. The first page contains options can be used to analyse the system in the standard mode with use of static parameters (fig. 5). When the user selects a test image then the environment shows closest images from the database (no more than 5), the table with distances to all base images and the diagram with feature distribution. The second page allows use dynamic parameters. The user can analyse the influence of certain parameters on the recognition rate, by means of use the configurable diagram. This page contains also the table, which shows obtained results for all possible combinations of value of parameters, it makes possible simple selection of an optimal variant.

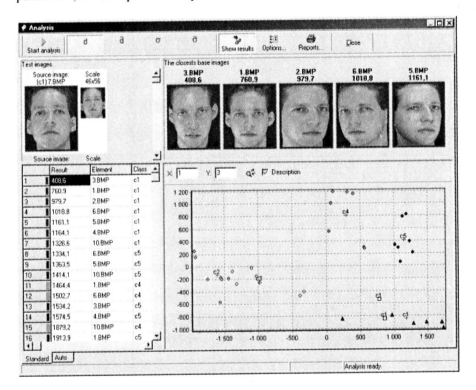

Fig. 5. The analysis window

For example, the database of the system presented on the fig. 5 contains 5 classes (persons). It is easy to notice, that closest images belong to the same person, besides the table, which contains distances between the chosen test image and all base images, shows, that next closest images belong to the same class. It means, that the system correctly identified the tested person. By analysing distribution of features, it is possible to remark that all classes are well-separated and individual elements are concentrated around centre of a class. These are determinants of well designed structure of the system and proper selected parameters of function blocks.

Calculation of the recognition rate usually relies on verification if a base image, for which the Euclidean distance to a test image is smallest, belongs to the same class as the test image. If both images belong to the same class, then the application assumes that the given person has been recognized correctly. The environment calculates several variants of ratios depending on a chosen criterion of recognition. Results of analyses are also available in some function blocks, first of all, in blocks of reduction of feature (like PCA), where diagrams with eigenvalues of covariance matrix are updated after each analysis.

5.   EXPERIMENTS

First we will try to find which feature is responsible for a face rotation. The database parameters are: 15 classes, 2 images in each class (1 base and 1 test image). All faces are rotated from 0° to 180° around the axis Y. Few of faces are showed on the fig. 6, which presents the structure of the system and the database.

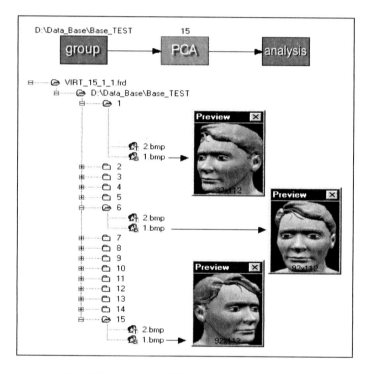

Fig. 6. The structure of the system and the database

This recognition system does not require preliminary image resizing, does not use two-stage feature reduction and use the PCA method with smart method of calculation of a covariance matrix. The analysis window of described system is presented on the fig. 7.

By analyzing the distribution of the feature space, it is possible to notice, that one of a feature is responsible for turn of head, because distribution looks like a semicircle, which answers to angle of a head rotation.

In the second example we will try to check the influence of preliminary image resizing (fig. 8) and the number of features after reduction (fig. 9) on the recognition rate. The database parameters are: 5 classes, 10 images in the each class (7 base and 3 test images), size of each image is: 92x112 pixels.

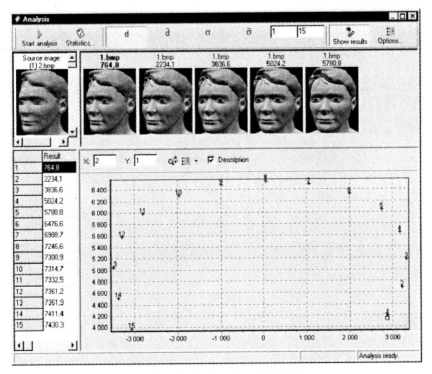

Fig. 7. The distribution of two first feature

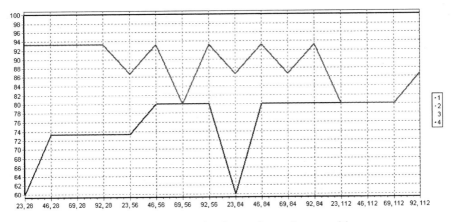

Fig. 8. The influence of an image size on the recognition

We use the system, which consists of four blocks: group, scale, PCA and analysis. Both parameters of the scale block are dynamic, the width accepts values: 23, 46, 69 and 92, while the height: 28, 56, 84 and 112. The parameter in the PCA block (number of items in the feature vector) accepts values from 1 to 4. So there are 64 (4x4x4) different variants.

The diagram on the fig. 8 presents relation between an image size and the recognition result. It seems that size of images use in this example, does not have influence on the result. Next diagram shows relation between the number of features and the recognition rate. It is possible to notice, that the more features the better results are obtained, although 3 features are enough to receive the maximum result. By analysing these diagrams the designer is possible to select optimal parameters for the system, e.g. relatively small size of an image 23x28 to speed up further calculations and high level of feature reduction (3 features) to compute distances between images quickly.

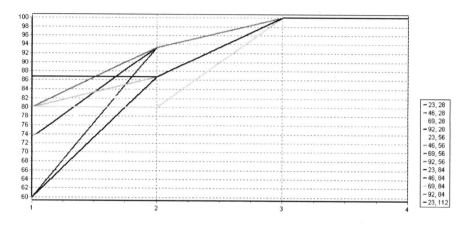

Fig. 9. Relationships between number of features and the recognition rate

6.   SUMMARY

The FaReS-Mod environment allows to analyse of gotten results, select optimum parameters of recognition process and considerable accelerate design of the recognition system. It has practical and educational value. Designers and students can use this environment to model, test and compare various of recognition systems. Besides it helps to apprehend phenomena in the course of recognition process and influence on it. Additional advantage is possibility of use of various databases, e.g. with faces, signatures, aircrafts, ships.

REFERENCES

[1] Swets D.L., Weng J. 1996. 'Using Discriminant Eigenfeatures for Image Retrieval'. *IEEE Trans. PAMI, vol. 18, no. 8.*

[2] Kukharev G., Kuzminski A. 2003. 'Techniki Biometryczne Część 1 – Metody Rozpoznawania Twarzy'. *Politechnika Szczecińska Wydział Informatyki.*

[3] Kuźmiński A. 2001. 'Opracowanie systemu do analizy zadań rozpoznawania twarzy'. *Politechnika Szczecińska Wydział Informatyki.*

[4] Tsapatsoulis N., Alexopoulos V., Kollias S. A. 1998. 'Vector Based Approximation of KLT and Its Application to Face Recognition'. *Proceedings of the IX European Signal Processing Conference EUSIPCO-98, Greece, vol.III*, pp.1581-1584.

Modified Gradient Method for Face Localization

GEORGI KUKHAREV, PAWEŁ MASICZ, PIOTR MASICZ
Technical Uuniversity of Szczecin
Żołnierska 49, 71-210 Szczecin, Poland, e-mail: georgi.kucharev@wi.ps.pl, gmasicz@wi.ps.pl

Abstract: In this paper we present our research and its results in face localization in color images. We use modified gradient method with oval object detection. This method gives very good speed results and our improvement gives better accuracy than it was in original gradient methods. Our system works well in different lighting condition and without any manual interactions. We will show how the system works with various pictures delivered from digital cameras, camcorders and television and with multiple faces localization. The differences in head size, lighting and background are considerable. We achieved very good results in detection rate - more than 93% in poor conditions and reach 99% in good. Our system is implemented in C++ and works well and fast.

Key words: localization, face, gradient method

1.   INTRODUCTION

In latest few years it was very rapidly research progress in digital face processing problems. It bases on assume that person's identity information, his behavior, could be extracted from images and in dependence on that computer could response. Most of recognition or tracking systems basis of dependence that localization of face in image is well known. But if system may works in fully automated version, face must be localized in source image. Face localization and detection in images is not easy because face could have various size, orientation, pose and position [1,2,7]. Other problem is classification – "face/nonface" [5,6]. There are many approaches in face detection and localization problems. Most of them depends on Principal Components Analysis (PCA) [3,4], neural network, machine learning, Hough transform, movement extraction and color analysis. All of them have weak points, for example solutions which based at neural network requires lots of testing images [7] (faces and nonfaces) and in most cases are built to detect faces in front position in grayscale image. Usually, group of methods which based at holistic representation works better than other, when faces on images are small and when image quality is rather poor. Other methods, which based on geometrical features, have better results for rotated faces. When system uses face's color information there is a problem with poor resistance on various lighting condition and specific background. Our algorithms use color analysis for preprocessing. After that it uses Gradient method with oval object detection which is one of feature invariant methods [8]. In chapter 2, we introduce the original Gradient method. In chapter 3, we describe our proposition to improve this method. Results and summary are in chapter 4 and 5.

2. GRADIENT METHOD WITH OVAL OBJECT DETECTION

There are many types of gradient methods. All of them have one shared feature which depends on examination of local luminance value changing in images. To compute the matrix of gradients, in most cases, it is used grayscale images because color information is not necessary. Data which are achieved from this computation could be applied to work in many problems, for example to edges and shapes detection – including oval object [9].

First step in original gradient method with oval object detection is rescaling source image to size 120x90. Next it is applied disproportionate rescaling in way that face shape became an oval from elliptic. This step strongly decreases amount of calculations. Experiment proves that width of face is close to 75% of its height which is showed on figure 6. Next step is normalization (*fig. 6b*) which standardize characteristic of pixels from source images. To do this there are applied histogram equalization and filters. Next, there are computed two matrixes – Gx i Gy (*fig. 1a, 1b*) which contain information about local luminance changeability in two planes – vertical and horizontal [9]:

$$Gx_{y,x} = \frac{1}{2}\left(P_{y,x+1} - P_{y,x-1}\right), \; Gy_{y,x} = \frac{1}{2}\left(P_{y+1,x} - P_{y-1,x}\right), \quad (1)$$

where:

$P_{y,x}$ - value of color in point [y,x],
$Gx_{y,x}$ - value of horizontal gradient in point $P_{y,x}$,
$Gy_{y,x}$ - value of vertical gradient in point $P_{y,x}$.

For each pixel of image length of gradient's vector is computed using simply equation:

$$G_{y,x} = \sqrt{(Gx_{y,x})^2 + (Gy_{y,x})^2}, \quad (2)$$

where: $G_{y,x}$ - gradient's vector length in point [x,y].

If length of vector G is known, all points where gradients have too small value are automatically eliminated from next calculation. This step allows us to decrease amount of calculations and improve accuracy of method because points where value of gradient are too small doesn't contain information about human face shape.

The procedure, which allows us to find centre of human face in source image, depends on three parameters: value of horizontal gradient Gx, value of vertical gradient Gy and radius R. All points in image are computed (except points which are eliminated in previous step) in way that is presented below (*fig. 2*).

a)   b)   c)

Fig. 1. Source image (a) and matrixes of gradient – Gx (b) and Gy (c)

Symbols used in figure 2:

$S_{y,x}$ - centre of face (probable),
R - radius of face (expected),
$Gx'_{y,x}$ - horizontal component of vector R,
$Gy'_{y,x}$ - verticalal component of vector R.

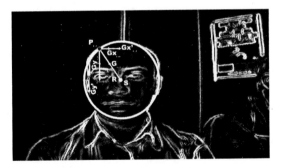

Fig. 2 Illustration of way to achieve $Gx'_{y,x}$ i $Gy'_{y,x}$ basis of value of gradients and radius R

The "hit" points we calculate using equations which are easy to derive basis of figure 2:

$$R^2 = (Gx'_{y,x})^2 + (Gy'_{y,x})^2, \; G_{y,x}^{\;2} = (Gx_{y,x})^2 + (Gy_{y,x})^2, \quad (3)$$

$$\frac{Gx_{y,x}}{G_{y,x}} = \frac{Gx'_{y,x}}{R}, \; \frac{Gy_{y,x}}{G_{y,x}} = \frac{Gy'_{y,x}}{R}. \quad (4)$$

After transformations we received:

$$Gx'_{y,x} = \frac{R \cdot Gx_{y,x}}{\sqrt{Gx_{y,x}^2 + Gy_{y,x}^2}} , \quad Gy'_{y,x} = \frac{R \cdot Gy_{y,x}}{\sqrt{Gx_{y,x}^2 + Gy_{y,x}^2}} .(5)$$

The centre of face coordinates:

$$S_{y,x} = (x + Gx'_{y,x}, y + Gy'_{y,x}), \tag{6}$$

where:
  x - x coordinate for computed point,
  y - y coordinate for computed point.

Computation for each pixel using conditions mentioned above return coordinates where in high probability is centre of finding face. To store achieved results it is created special matrix called "matrix of hits" (all their values at start are 0). Each S, which is returned from algorithms described above, increase values of pixel in "matrix of hits" using dependence visible in figure 3 (coordinates for point contained value +3 is identical with coordinates for point S).

	+1	+2	+1	
	+2	+3	+2	
	+1	+2	+1	

Fig. 3 The way to fill up "matrix of hits"

After above analysis for all pixels we receive a matrix which contains information about hits for radius R.

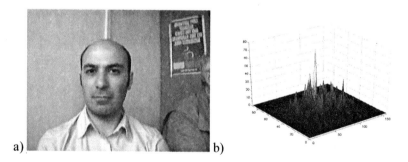

Fig. 4 Source image – 320x240 (a), „matrix of hits" (b) for radius equal 22

In figure 4b it is clearly visible that in neighborhood of centre of face is largest cluster of pixels contained high value in opposition to rest. There is also the pixel with highest value. In high probability it is the centre of finding face. It is necessary to add information that in original gradient method face must have identical or very close radius to searching radius R because only then received "matrix of hits" and results could be correct. To solve this problem, pyramids of images are used (fig. 5). This solution is very time-consuming, but it allows us to execute original algorithms with one, constant radius R. Source image is rescaled to different resolutions and then face have different size. The assumption, that in one of this rescaled images radius of face is equal to searching radius R, is logically.

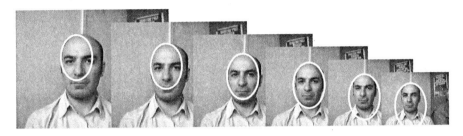

Fig. 5 Pyramids of images with results of computation for constant R

Illustration of gradient method with oval object detection, which is described in this chapter, is showed below (*fig. 6*).

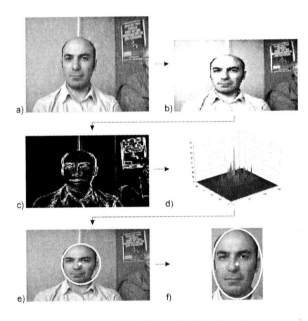

Fig. 6 Work scheme for gradient method with oval object detection: source image (a), after normalized and disproportionate rescaled (b), matrix of gradient (c), "matrix of hits" (d), results of findings (e), extracted face (f)

There are pictures showed below (*fig. 7*) which illustrate correct results of gradient method with oval object detection. We can see that gradient method is very resistant in various lighting condition. Unfortunately, when radius of face doesn't equal to searching radius R results achieved from algorithm are wrong (*fig. 8b,c*). Other objects which have oval shape could also generate wrong results (*fig. 8c*).

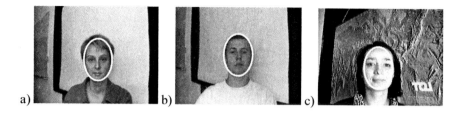

Fig. 7 Examples of correct working

Fig. 8 Examples of wrong working

3.   EXTENDED GRADIENT METHOD WITH OVAL OBJECT DETECTION

The method described above has one undeniable advantage – speed. This advantage makes it very interesting to implement it in real-time systems. But it has also few weak points: only grayscale images are possible to compute (color information is omit), constant radius R (face must have right, known size), accuracy (not very high). Our improvements minimize those weak points.

First step is proportionate rescaling source image (320x240) to resolution 60x45 and then disproportionate rescaling to 80x45 (*fig. 9a*). The ratio between 60 and 80 is equal to 75% which is equal to ratio between head's height and width. As we can see on figure 9a after rescaling face shape is very close to oval in opposition to elliptical which was before. This solution gives one additional advantage – improves speed, because amount of calculation is much smaller when we find oval shapes. Other improvement are using I2 component (*pic. 9b*) from modified I1I2I3 color space [9]:

$$I2 = R - G ,$$ (7)

where:

    R, G   - components from RGB color space.

Color information is not lost when we use component I2. We use one additional normalize step which depend on cutting and histogram equalizing (*fig. 9c*). Figure 9c shows us, that using component I2 in opposition to grayscale makes possible to narrow down area where we search a face. It reduces amount of calculation and improves accuracy because objects which haven't color similar to typical face disappeared (*fig. 9c*).

a)   b)   c)

Fig. 9 Rescaled source image in RGB color space (a), in I2 color space (b), in I2 color space with normalize step c)

Image prepared in way described above is passed to module which calculates gradient matrixes (*fig. 10*). To improve accuracy of gradient method we calculate two additional gradient matrixes – G45 and G135 (*fig. 11*):

$$G45_{y,x} = \frac{1}{2}\left(P_{y+1,x+1} - P_{y-1,x-1}\right), \ G135_{y,x} = \frac{1}{2}\left(P_{y+1,x-1} - P_{y-1,x+1}\right),$$

where:

$P_{y,x}$ - value of color in point [y,x],
$G45_{y,x}$ - value of gradient (45 degree) in point [y,x],
$G135_{y,x}$- value of gradient (135 degree) in point [y,x].

a)   b)   c)

Fig. 10 Illustration of matrixes of gradient Gx (a), Gy (b) and their sum (c)

a)   b)   c)

Fig. 11 Illustration of matrixes of gradient G45 (a), G135 (b) and their sum (c)

We decided to use two additional matrixes (G45 and G135) because original gradient method process data only in two directions – vertical and horizontal and omit information in diagonal. In our algorithm this two additional matrixes is computed in the same way that Gx and Gy and results from next calculations are wrote to the same "matrix of hits". We decided to modify original algorithm depend on pyramids of images because image rescaling is very time-consuming. Our new approach uses variable searching radius R in opposition to constant in original method. The R radius is contained in 15-50% compartment of height rescaled image (results of algorithm's work are visible in figure 12). We also decided to use one collective "matrix of hits" which includes maximums from all "matrixes of hits" (because for every radius R new "matrix of hits" is computed). This approach makes possible to extract many faces from image.

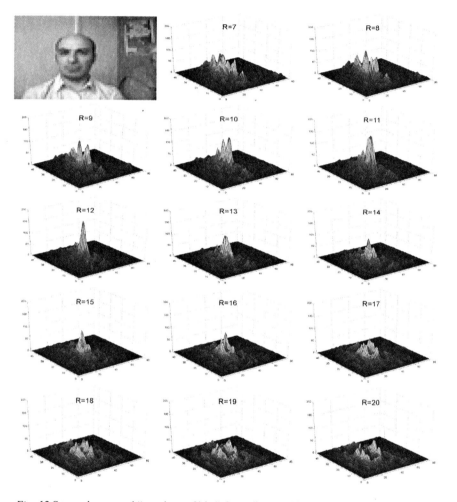

Fig. 12 Source image and "matrixes of hits" for radius R which values is contained in 7-20 pixels (the best result is also shown by black frame)

4. RESEARCH RESULTS

We tested our algorithms using many face databases. Unfortunately, most of them are designed rather for image recognition systems than for detection. Those databases often contain grayscale images where faces are in centre and where background is not very vary. Even special databases, which were created to solve detection problem, have only grayscale images (for example Carnegie Mellon University (CMU), BioID Database or FERET Database). That is why we created our own databases. First of them contains 179 pictures delivered from digital cameras, web-cams and Internet (*fig. 13*). Most of those pictures have 320x240 resolutions in 24-bits color depth (JPG and BMP). Second one contains image sequence (1693 pictures) delivered from TV video stream (*fig. 14*). Parameters: resolution – 320x240, color depth – 24-bits.

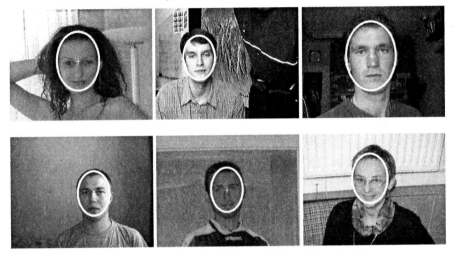

Fig. 13 Few results of face detection in image delivered from digital cameras, web-cams and Internet (database 1)

Fig. 14 Few results of face detection in image delivered from TV video stream (database 2)

To achieve high diversity of data we choose images in which faces have various size, color and pose. Lighting conditions are also different. Among examples in both our databases (*fig. 13*) there are faces located in background which has very similar color to face's color. In that case systems depend of color segmentation have very hard problem to achieve correct results. We tested our algorithms to locate multiple faces (*fig. 15*) and results are very good. Faces could encounter themselves and could be covered (no more than 50%). We successfully located even 10 faces on single image (resolution - 320x240). Our algorithms have one special advantage –

locating multiple faces doesn't enlarge time-consuming and amount only 1% more for each additional face.

Fig. 15 Examples of multiple face detection

There are results of our research in table 1. We studied effectiveness of our system depending on size of gradient matrix. We also tested it when two additional matrixes (for angle 45 and 135) is used and not used. We tested our gradient algorithm using our own databases.

Images source	Matrix of gradient size			
	60x45	100x75	200x150	320x240
Gradient method + 45/135 gradients				
Digital camera	174/179 97,2%	172/179 96,1%	188/179 93,8%	185/179 92,2%
TV video stream	1596/1693 94,2%	1518/1693 89,6%	1351/1693 79,8%	1164/1693 68,7%
Det. Time	13 +/- 5 ms	53 +/- 12 ms	308 +/- 59 ms	1,23 +/- 0,53s
Gradient method				
Digital camera	168/179 93,8%	167/179 93,3%	165/179 92,2%	158/179 88,3%
TV video stream	1509/1693 89,1%	1298/1693 76,7%	1128/1693 66,6%	1011/1693 59,7%
Det. Time	10 +/- 5 ms	34 +/- 11 ms	252 +/- 52 ms	1,01 +/- 0,42s

Tab. 1 Illustration of effectiveness and detection time of our method
depending on size of matrix of gradient

As we can see methods, which are proposed by us, are very useful in practice. We also proved that two additional matrixes (for angle 45 and 135) improve accuracy of gradient method, especially when source data is from poor quality video stream. In that case we noticed 10-15% improvement of accuracy. During our experiments we also noticed that smaller size of matrix of gradient is better to use than larger. This is because source image rescaling is some kind of normalization step (wrong data from picture are eliminated). Fortunately, smaller size of matrix of gradient improves speed of our method. We also tested our algorithm on images where face is in bad lighting condition (*fig. 18*) and different size (*fig. 17*).

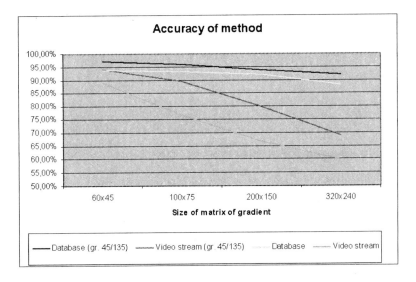

Fig. 16 Results from table 1 in graphical version

Fig.17 Samples of face extraction with various face dimensions

Fig.18 Algorithm's result with various lighting conditions

5. CONCLUSION

Our experiments proved that our method have possibility to locate even 10 faces in single image and works well in unfavorable condition like changing lighting condition, various background, when face is partially covered. Especially this last advantage makes our method very special distinct from other detection method. We see possibility to next improvements, for example using other color space (HSV, YCrCb) and make from them better source to gradient method. It is also necessary to implement effective „face/nonface" algorithms.

REFERENCES

[1] D. Chai, K. N. Ngan „Locating facial region of a head-and-shoulder color image", *International Conference of Face and Gesture Recognition*, (1998), 124-129.

[2] B. Fasel „Fast multi-scale face detection", *IDIAP-COM 4*, (1998).

[3] G. Kukharev, A. Tujaka „Pattern recognition methods for visitor identification and access control", *Pattern Recognition and Information Processing*, (2001), 19-34.

[4] G. Kukharev, A. Kuźmiński „Techniki Biometryczne, Część I: Metody rozpoznawania twarzy", Szczecin 2003.

[5] S. McKeena, S. Gong, Y. Raja „Face recognition in dynamic scenes", *British Machine Vision Conference*, (1997).

[6] H. A. Rowley „Neural network-based face detection", *PHD thesis, Carnegie Mellon University, Pitsburgh*, (1999).

[7] H. Rowley, S. Baluja, T. Kanade „Neural Network-Based Face Detection", *IEEE Trans. Pattern Analysis and Machine Intelligence, vol. 20, no. 1* (1998) 23-38.

[8] Q. B. Sun, W. M. Huang, J. K. Wu „Face detection based on color and local symetry information", *International Conference of Face and Gesture Recognition*, (1998), 130-135.

[9] Georgi Kuchariew, Paweł Masicz, Piotr Masicz „Real-time face detection using modified gradient method", *Pattern Recognition and Information Processing*, (2003), vol. 2, 195-200

Three stage face recognition algorithm for visitor identification system

ADAM NOWOSIELSKI

Technical University of Szczecin Faculty of Computer Science and Information Technology
Ul. Żołnierska 49, 71-210 Szczecin, e-mail: anowosielski@wi.ps.pl

Abstract: In this paper a three stage face recognition algorithm is proposed. It utilizes well known recognition methods connected in a sequential mode. Some modifications to original methods are presented. The aim was to build a visitor identification system which would be able to operate in mode with a camera and present results on-line. The emphasis on speed and accuracy was stressed.

Key words: Face recognition, visitor identification, face detection, real-time

1.   INTRODUCTION

The visitor identification system belongs to class of face recognition systems. This particular system addresses problems connected with real-life: guests (visitors) identification. The camera (which is a part of the security system) registers the entrance of the building and takes pictures of the scene. In the next step, face detection is performed and for every face detected, the face recognition algorithm is executed.

The main features of the system are [e.g. 3, 4, 5, 8]: the ability to operate nearly in real-time and the ability to recognize people from frontal face images. The adaptation to new conditions is also required as the face addition and deletion from database are frequent.

The visitor identification system might be used to recognize a frequent buyer in the shop [e.g. 5] or as a security guard [9]. In the last case, visitors entering buildings are usually screened by guards. Over time, guards learn to connect visitors and lodgers, and can inform the hosts of their guests' arrival. The guards' work might be taken over in such a case by the visitor identification system.

In the article a visitor identification system is presented. It utilizes three stage face recognition algorithm which is proposed. It is based on recognition methods: L_0 metric, correlation and cosine transform. These methods are connected in a sequential order.

The system built upon presented scheme operates in MS Windows environment with a colour camera. Its scope of application is wide and include: identification of people entering the possessions or office premises, recognition of frequent buyer in a shop, guests in different kind of institutions, and also portal visitors in Internet (after adequate installation and adaptation).

The remainder of the paper is structured as follows. Section 2 outlines the rules of the visitor identification system. In section 3 face detection methods are presented and in section 4 three stage face recognition algorithm is presented. Some modifications to original methods are presented too. The article ends with summary where conclusions are presented.

2.   VISITOR IDENTIFICATION SYSTEM

Visitor identification system consists of two main subsystems namely face detection and face recognition (Fig. 1.). The first one solves the task of face detection and its output is a collection of image regions which contain faces. These regions constitute input of the second subsystem. There follow the process of features extraction and matching process of every face with face from reference database. The result of recognition – the list of peoples' names from the input image – is the output of the system.

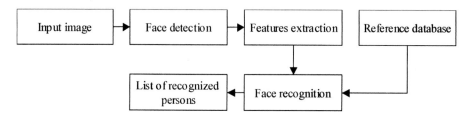

Fig. 1. General scheme of the visitor identification system

The visitor identification system performs its work in real-world conditions. It is expected to work in a stable and reliable fashion. It should operate fast. Face detection and recognition are time restricted. Slow algorithms are therefore useless in spite of their high accuracy.

The face database cannot be specified once as new faces are frequently added and old removed. The system should be easily adapted. It is clear that with such conditions methods which require training on the full face database are very difficult to implement.

The proper verification of face recognition is required. It should ensure that a person who does not have his or her image in the database is rejected. In specific installation of the system it is possible that people who appear in the scene are not known and only few of them were registered in the database. But if such a person walks through the door, the system should properly identified him or her.

When elaborating the visitor identification system one should take into consideration some characteristic situations. People, when enter a building, usually look straight ahead. It allows to constrain face detection system only to frontal faces with small deflections in the pose. Face recognition from such pictures is easier too. The head scale in the image is not known. As a person approaches the entrance (with a camera) the face becomes bigger. Face size cannot be therefore restricted. Moreover, the analysed scene might contain more than one walker. Frequently people walk in groups. In case the camera is installed in front of an office building, there are times of particular intensity (work beginning at set hours).

For the visitor identification system it is characteristic that cost of incorrect identification is not high. Face recognition is performed under conditions when security requirements are not strict. People are identified only to inform others that guests arrived or to collect information how often specified person visit controlled place. But the higher recognition accuracy the better.

3. FACE DETECTION

Any system of face detection can generate two types of errors [10]. One is when it does not detect a face and second - when it erroneously classifies as a face a region without a face. By adjusting parameters of one approach one can achieve reduction of the first kind of errors but in the same way increase the second types of errors. Such a solution is favourable in the visitor identification system. The regions which were incorrectly detected can be verified in following stages. Eventually, the image which does not contain a face will not be similar to any image from the database of recognition subsystem. In this way very high detection level is assured.

Presented visitor identification system uses the face detection subsystem already described in [7]. Face detection is based on skin colour approach (features invariant approaches [10]) and mask analysis (knowledge – based methods [10]). A verification process of so called face candidates is generally performed as the last stage of face detection. In that case, face recognition subsystem receives only images with faces. It is proposed here to transfer the verification process in presented scheme to next level (to higher subsystem). It is performed in the first step of face recognition.

4. FACE RECOGNITION

Face recognition in the proposed scheme consists of three stages. In the first step the recognition process is based on L_0 metric and face images of reduced resolution (16x16). This solution is similar as in systems described in [3] and [8].

The L_0 metric between two images (described as vectors $\vec{x}$ and $\vec{y}$) is defined as [8]:

$$L_0(\vec{x} - \vec{y}) \equiv \sum_{|x_i - y_i| > \delta} 1 \qquad (1)$$

where δ is the threshold.

In practice it is more convenient to use normalized value, which can be defined as:

$$L_0^{(n)}(\vec{x} - \vec{y}) \equiv 1 - \frac{L_0}{m} \tag{2}$$

where m is the length of vectors $\vec{x}$ and $\vec{y}$.

If the absolute difference between the intensity value of two corresponding pixels is smaller then the threshold, then it is assumed that these pixels are similar. In practice, when the threshold is too high, errors occurs. On the other hand, if the threshold is too low, similar faces might not be matched. Such situations may appear when considerable differences between images exist (lighting conditions, viewing angle). The threshold in presented system was set at a value equal 25. The decision about similarity of the given face and database faces is made by minimizing the L_0 distance or maximizing the $L_0^{(n)}$. In the remainder part of the article normalized $L_0^{(n)}$ measure is considered (1 for the highest similarity, 0 for lack of similarity).

In case of erroneous face detection some of the regions might not contain faces. They will be characterized by low similarity coefficient with any face from the database. When this coefficient is smaller than 0.6, then region which is being tested is discarded as not face-like or as the depicted person is not similar to any from the database. If the coefficient is greater then 0.6, then analysis of a given face is continued. Proposed solution thus realizes two tasks. Firstly, it performs face detection. Secondly, it prepares face database for further (more precise) examination.

In the second step of the face recognition process the method of correlation is employed [1]:

$$C(X,Y) = \frac{\overline{X \circ Y} - \overline{X}\,\overline{Y}}{\delta(X)\,\delta(Y)} \tag{3}$$

where $\circ$ is the pixel-by-pixel product, and δ is the standard deviation.

For the correlation coefficient the threshold was set to 0.7. Experiments suggest that this value cannot be lower. For a safety reasons it should be set at 0.8. If the maximum correlation coefficient between given face and any face from the database is lower than 0.7, then it is assumed that face which is being examined does not belong to known person. Otherwise, from classes with the highest similarity the winner is chosen. The winner is a class with the highest similarity measure between vectors resulting from cosine transform of examined images. Such a solution significantly reduces the processing time. In the third step the time-consuming operations are performed only if the face which is being examined is similar to any face from the database (determined in two preceding stages) and comparisons are carried out on a small subset of record from the original database.

The discrete cosine transform (DCT) is used as the extraction method of the most significant facial features. The main advantage of this transform is its high compression rate (exploited for example in the JPEG standard). In presented system the DCT is performed on the full face image. It is similar to solution described in [2] but owing to proposed scheme it is faster. Comparisons on the last stage do not include full database.

For a face image X of dimension MxN the coefficients of the cosine transform are calculated and only small subset of them (low and middle frequencies) is saved as a feature vector. They have the greatest variance. There again, to accelerate the process it is sufficient to calculate only the coefficients which are needed. That is for $p, q = 0..7$, according to equations [6]:

$$\begin{cases} C(p,q) = \alpha_p \alpha_q \sum_{m=0}^{M-1} \sum_{n=0}^{N-1} X(m,n) \cos \frac{(2m+1)\pi p}{2M} \cos \frac{(2n+1)\pi q}{2N} \\ \alpha_p = \begin{cases} 1/\sqrt{M} & \text{if } p = 0 \\ \sqrt{2/M} & \text{if } 1 \le p \le M-1 \end{cases} ; \alpha_q = \begin{cases} 1/\sqrt{N} & \text{if } q = 0 \\ \sqrt{2/N} & \text{if } 1 \le p \le N-1 \end{cases} \end{cases} \quad (4)$$

Obtained 8x8 matrix is transformed into a vector and the Euclidean distant classifier is used to compare the given face ($\vec{a}$) with a database face ($\vec{b}$):

$$E = \sqrt{\sum_{i=0}^{63} (a_i - b_i)^2} \quad (5)$$

The winner is the class whose member has the lowest distance with the examined face. Moreover, the threshold value equal to 2025 was set here, to ensure correct classifications and rejections.

The scheme which is proposed has two main advantages. It reduces total amount of calculations. It utilizes the discrete cosine transform which is characterised by high accuracy. Presented visitor identification system works therefore nearly in real-time and performs its job reliable. ᵃᵈ

To test the proposed solution The ORL Database of Faces (10 pictures of 40 person each) was used. First, the database was sorted (like in [5]) in a way that faces with the highest variance were assigned the smallest indexes. This way the database is representative. Database of known individuals was built from the first 30 classes (8 images were used). The remaining 60 images (2 faces, 30 classes) were used to test recognition accuracy. The remaining 10 classes (100 images) were used to test the false acceptance rate. The results are 96.67% for recognition accuracy (RA) and 5% for FAR.

4.1 Virtual database

The eyes location allow precisely determine face boundary. As the most stable facial features they are used to normalize face size. Knowing their position and distance between them it is possible to extract a face. Adequate equations were proposed earlier in [7]. However, problems occur when the locations are slightly shifted (Fig. 2.) (inward to the centre of the face or outward) which is generally caused by shadows and glasses. In that case, the distance between the eyes might be greater or smaller causing face boundary appear too big or too small. Sometimes, the distance might be correct but locations might be shifted in the same direction –

slightly left or right. Experiments demonstrated that eyes locations might also be shifted a little up or down. These situations might occur in combination. To overcome this problem it is proposed to shift the eyes locations according to a pattern and for each case extract and write new face image to the database.

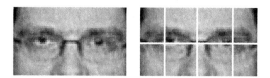

Fig. 2. An example of erroneous eyes localization

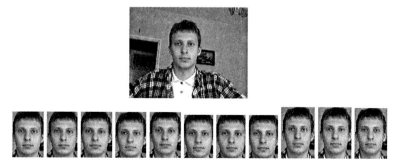

Fig. 3. An example of virtual faces created from a single face image

Figure 3 shows an example of virtual faces (bottom row). They are formed from a single scene (top image). The first image in the bottom row is the original image (1). Then both eyes locations are moved left (2), right (3), up (4) and down (5) by turns. For new locations face is extracted separately. The scale of that shift is set to 10% of the distance. Then zooming in is considered. Eyes locations are shifted inwards to make the distance 5% smaller than original distance (6). With smaller distance movement to right (7) and left (8) is also performed. Similarly, the zooming out is considered, giving three face images: zoomed out (9), zoomed out and shifted to the right (10) and zoomed out and shifted to the left (11). When the initial eyes locations are incorrect it is possible by proposed procedure to find better approximation of their location. Eventually, from a single face 11 faces are extracted and saved in the database. When input image to the system is considered and it contains a face incorrectly extracted (due to inaccurate eyes locations) it is possible to properly recognize a given person because the database contains also shifted and zoomed images. They are called virtual images and hence the name of the database: "virtual database".

5.   CONCLUSIONS AND COMMENTS

The visitor identification system built upon described algorithm might be used to identify people entering buildings, in stores or to recognize frequent visitors in different kind of institutions. To make system work efficiently and reliably some conditions must be fulfilled.

In proposed solution there are no methods that eliminate any kind of directional light. When such an illumination exists in the scene, shadows might occur on the face. It significantly complicate the process of face detection and recognition. Algorithms that solve above problem are slow and usually do not cope with it satisfactorily. To add such an algorithm would render the proposed scheme slow. It is much cheaper to install suitable illumination and a cover in front of the door which would limit the influence of the sun.

However, the best solution would be to implement and algorithm that analyse the scene whether or not directional light exist. If the answer to above question would be positive then additional light would be turned on or system would try to reduce its negative influence. For now, it is future task.

Visitor identification system, built on the base of proposed algorithm, operates approximately in real-time. The processes of detection and recognition takes 0.11 second (it is average time for images of dimensions 320x240 and 99 faces database) achieving 9 images per second. It is a good result especially when taking into consideration computer speed of 900 MHz on which the tests were performed. Figure 4 shows the main window of the visitor identification system. On the right hand side of the window there is an input from the camera. In the centre there is the database image of the best recognized person from the scene. On the left hand side there is a list of all recognized persons from the image.

Fig. 4. Visitor identification system built upon proposed scheme

Contemporary recognition systems reached very high recognition rate (nearly 100% [e.g. 5]). In comparison with the human recognition ability they still have to be improved. A human takes into consideration a lot of visual factors like way of walking, clothes, etc. In a computer security system, however, face might be utilized as an additional factor which might increase the credibility. On the other hand, when the safety requirements are not high computer systems might fully substitute a human.

The visitor identification system solves the task of guests identification. The combination of methods proposed in the article might be used in another face recognition system. Presented scheme might be used after adaptation and threshold adjustment to solve other tasks. It might be used as an independent component in an access control system. In might be used to solve the task of authentication. Some of presented task might be used in current version of realized system but only in the manual mode.

REFERENCES

[1] R. Brunelli, T. Poggio, *Face Recognition: Features versus Templates*, „IEEE Transactions on Pattern analysis and machine intelligence", October 1993, 15(10).

[2] Z. M. Hafed, M. D. Levine, *face Recognition Using the Discrete Transform*, International Journal of Computer Vision 43(3), 2001.

[3] G. Kuchariew, A. Tujaka, *Real – time face recognition system for visitor identification*, „Proceedings of Sixth International Conference: Advanced Computer Systems" (ACS '99), Technical University of Szczecin, Poland, November 1999.

[4] G. Kuchariew, A Tujaka, *Pattern Recognition Methods for Visitor Identification and Access Control*, „Pattern Recognition and Information Processing", Proceedings of Sixth International Conference PRIP '2001, Minsk, Republic of Belarus, 18-20 May 2001.

[5] G. Kukharev, A. Kuźmiński, *Techniki Biometryczne Część 1 Metody Rozpoznawania Twarzy"*, Wydział Informatyki Politechnika Szczecińska, 2003.

[6] MATLAB, *Image Processing Toolbox User's Guide*, version 2.

[7] A. Nowosielski "Realizacja uniwersalnego modułu detekcji twarzy", *Materiały VII Sesji Naukowej Informatyki*, Technical University of Szczecin, Poland, Informa 2002 .

[8] T. Sim, R. Sukthankar, M. Mullin, S. Baluja, *High-Performance Memory-based Face Recognition for Visitor Identification*, Technical Report JPRC-TR-1999-01, JustSystems Pittsburgh Research Center, vol. 1.

[9] R. Sukthankar, R. Stockton, *ARGUS: An Automated Multi-Agent Visitor Identification System*, „Proceedings of AAAI-99", July 1999.

[10] M. Yang, D. Kriegman, N. Ahuja, *Detecting Faces in Images: A Survey*, „IEEE Transactions on pattern analysis and machine intelligence", vol. 24, No. 1, January 2002.

A New Approach for Hand-Palm Recognition

KHALID SAEED[1], MARCIN WERDONI[2]
Faculty of Computer Science, Bialystok University of Technology,
Wiejska 45A, 15 – 351 Bialystok, Poland,
http://aragorn.pb.bialystok.pl/~zspinfo/
e-mail: [1]*aidabt@ii.pb.bialystok.pl* [2]*mwerd@tlen.pl*

Abstract: A new algorithm for human recognition by hand-palm images is presented in this paper. The suggested approach is based on characteristics of the minimal eigenvalues obtained from Toeplitz matrices for image description. The recognition steps in the algorithm use both classical and new approaches. The achieved results are promising although of not very high rate of classification. The effectiveness of the recognition has achieved 100% in small classes and about 70% in large classes using the new trend of minimal eigenvalues. It reaches, however, a 100% rate of classification following the classical methods of comparison and classification for even bigger classes.

Key words: Hand-Geometry, Human Identification, Classification, Toeplitz, Biometrics

1. INTRODUCTION

Methods and algorithms for different biometric identification techniques have their own advantages and disadvantages. Among these techniques, hand geometry possesses the least disadvantages from the authors' point of view [1].

The general systems for hand geometry identification work in two phases: an enrollment phase and a comparative one. In the enrollment phase, several photographs are taken of the user. These photographs are then preprocessed to enter the feature extraction block, where a set of measurements is performed. With the features extracted, the user's pattern is computed and stored in a database. In the verification phase, a single photograph is taken, preprocessed, and entered in the feature extraction block. This single set of features is compared with the template previously stored, obtaining a ratio of likeliness to determine who the user is whose hand had been photographed.

The comparative block was configured as a classifier, where the extracted features are compared with all of the users' templates to determine which the examined person's palm is.

All the different blocks of the designed hand-geometry identification system are given throughout the following minimal-eigenvalue-based algorithm. The algorithm is introduced in two stages, feature extract and classification.

2.   FEATURE EXTRACT

The aim of this first block is to capture a sample of the user's hand geometry from palm side, process it extracting a set of feature points. To achieve this, three tasks are performed.

2.1   Image Capturing

The sample signal is obtained with a HP 4400c scanner. The hand is placed onto a platform (Fig.1a) designed to properly formulate the hand-palm geometry and location. This platform has been modified (Fig.1b) to allow more flexibility of feature capturing. The platform works as the data acquisition device for the hand-palm identifying system.

Fig. 1. The used-in-work platform, the original (a) and the modified one (b).

The hand-palm is scanned in grayscale with resolution of 72 dpi to BMP format. The image is captured and saved for data acquisition and processing.

2.2   Preprocessing

After the image is captured, preprocessing is performed. The first step in the preprocessing block is to transform the grayscale image into a black and white one.

The simplest segmentation process is the gray level thresholding [2]. The algorithm searches all the pixels of the image. An image element at the segmented image is an object pixel, if $f(x,y) \geq T$, and is a background pixel otherwise. x and y are the coordinates of the pixels, T is the captured image threshold.

In the next step the algorithm separates the object pixels from the background ones. In this way the feature points are selected and registered. The following section shows the way this is done according to the method used in this work for image input data necessary to work with in the proposed analysis method.

2.3 Characteristic Features

After preprocessing, the image is analyzed and the feature points are selected (Fig.2). The selection of these points is based on the choice of points describing the palm parameters [3], that is, finger width and length, palm width and length, and so forth as shown in Fig.2b. Thirteen different characteristic points are selected for the sake of classification.

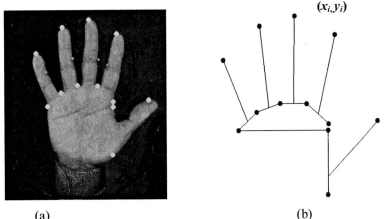

(x_i, y_i)

(a)   (b)

Fig. 2. Feature points localization.

3. CLASSIFICATION

Here, in the classification stage, the image of Fig.2b is put on the x-y plane to determine the coordinates of the feature points extracted from the captured image. These points are the input data to the classifying algorithm and its adjacent recognizing system both described in details in [4]. Instead of matching the hand image points one-to-one to a reference image, this work proposes to use an algorithm based on the minimal eigenvalues of Toeplitz matrices. These matrices are evaluated from the transfer function whose coefficients are determined from the characteristic points of the hand geometry. The algorithm proceeds in a similar manner of the classification used in some previous work of the first author [5,6]. For convenience the classifying criterion is given below.

Read the values of x_i and y_i coordinates of all n points (x_i, y_i), $i = 0,1, 2, ..., n$, from Fig. 2b.

Form the following rational function:

$$H(z) = \frac{P(z)}{Q(z)} = \frac{x_0 + x_1 z + x_2 z^2 + ... + x_n z^n}{y_0 + y_1 z + y_2 z^2 + ... + y_n z^n} \tag{1}$$

in which the coefficients in the polynomials $P(z)$ and $Q(z)$ are respectively the x and y co-ordinates of the points (x_i, y_i), $i=0, 1, 2, ..., n$.

For the rational function of $H(z)$ in $Eq.(1)$ find Taylor series:

$$T(z) = c_0 + c_1 z + c_2 z^2 + ... + c_n z^n + ... \tag{2}$$

The coefficients c_i, $i = 0, 1, 2, ... n$, are expressed by the coordinates of x_i and y_i of the points as follows:

$$c_0 = \frac{x_0}{y_0}, \ c_1 = \frac{1}{y_0^2}\begin{vmatrix} x_1 & y_1 \\ x_0 & y_0 \end{vmatrix}, \ c_2 = \frac{1}{y_0^3}\begin{vmatrix} x_2 & y_1 & y_2 \\ x_1 & y_0 & y_1 \\ x_0 & 0 & y_0 \end{vmatrix}, \ ... \tag{3}$$

From these coefficients the determinants of Toeplitz matrices are evaluated as follows:

$$D_0 = c_0 = \frac{x_0}{y_0}, \ D_1 = \begin{vmatrix} c_0 & c_1 \\ c_1 & c_0 \end{vmatrix}, \ D_2 = \begin{vmatrix} c_0 & c_1 & c_2 \\ c_1 & c_0 & c_1 \\ c_2 & c_1 & c_0 \end{vmatrix}, \ ... \tag{4}$$

Once the determinants have been calculated, determine their eigenvalues and evaluate the lowest (minimal) eigenvalue for each determinant. For the ith determinant D_i, the lowest eigenvalue is λ_{min_i}, designated simply by λ_i:

$$\lambda_{min}\{D_i\} = \lambda_{min_i} = \lambda_i, \ i = 0, ..., n. \tag{5}$$

The successive eigenvalues λ_i for $i = 0, 1, 2, ..., n$ form a monotonically nonincreasing series, i.e.,

$$\lambda_0 \geq ... \geq \lambda_i \geq ... \geq \lambda_n, \ i = 1, ..., n\text{-}1 \tag{6}$$

The final result given in $Eq.(6)$ is used as the main tool for describing and classifying input and output data. The series of minimal eigenvalues of each image is then saved, sketched and compared with the data base images. The method used for this purpose is the absolute deviation [4] in testing for the minimal difference between the unknown image Ψ and the reference one Φ:

$$g(a,b) = \sum_{i=1}^{n} |\Psi - \Phi| \tag{7}$$

with $\Psi = y_i$ and $\Phi = ax_i + b$, the approximating line. After similarity process has been done, the output is given either as a graph representation of the image or as a written output on the screen.

4. EXPERIMENTS AND RESULTS

Now, to show how this theory works, consider the following experiments. The experiments start with the creation of hand-palm database of a number of people to compare with the under identification person. The under-test database has been changed several times for better checking of the system. The most recent data is composed of 45 scanned images taken from 15 people, 3 from each person.

The experiments were conducted applying *Eq.*(1) as the reference for data collection. Also, some modifications were applied to enter the *x-y* values of the numerator and denominator as polar coordinates, but this is not within the topics of this paper and is left for future work and applications. The number of input elements as system input data, that is the number of minimal eigenvalues considered in our experiments, was varying from a minimum of 10 to a maximum of 60 showing a large difference in the rate recognition. Therefore, the optimal number for better recognizing rate for the under testing class was 60 minimal eigenvalues as shown in Table 1. Thus, considering larger number of eigenvalues would increase the effectiveness rate to more than 90% definitely, but of course increasing the computation size to a double or triple one of that in the original algorithm. Notice that the results are worse than those in [1] but still the classical application is approaching almost 100% following the data extract method given above and the classical method in comparison for similarity. It is this result that makes us continue modifying the method of eigenvalues to replace the classical approach for the same preprocessing and describing data. Table 1, however, shows the low effectiveness of using the algorithm for both description and recognition. Although the system of minimal eigenvalues has proved its success in image description [3,4] for both small and large classes of images, it still needs more modification to use similarity comparison.

The results of classification experiments are given in Fig.3, 4, 5 and 6. The hand-palms of Iza, Marcin and Radek are scanned three times each, described and classified for recognition. Figures 3, 4 and 5 show the graphs of the minimal eigenvalues series obtained for their images with Fig.6 to show them together for comparison. Although the graphs furnish similar shapes for the individual examined hands (Fig.3, 4, 5), they show quite different behavior when put on the same plane with the same scale assuring that they are identified as graph representing images of different sources.

Number of Minimal Eigenvalues	Algorithm of Effectiveness
10	40 %
20	60 %
30	53.3 %
40	53.3 %
50	53.3 %
60	**66.7 %**

Tab. 1. Results of recognition rate experiments.

The three lines of Iza's hand in Fig.3, for example, are similar to one another (with about 99% recognition rate). From classifying and comparison point of view this comes from the fact that all the lines of the three graphs furnish similar behavior. This, in turn, means that the series of the minimal eigenvalues are of the same values. Hence, the points yielding them through Taylor series represent the same reference in the data base giving the indication that they belong to the same hand-palm image.

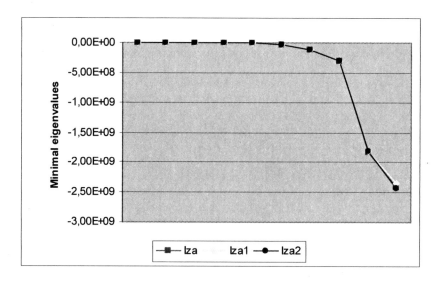

Fig. 3. The graph of minimal eigenvalues for Iza

The same discussion holds for Marcin's hand in Fig.4. Here the rate of recognition is a bit lower as the series of minimal eigenvalues, which the images yield, diverge when approaching their limits to show different values. This affects the values of the input data to both *Eqs* (6) and (7) leading to less efficiency of the algorithm. However, Marcin's hand was still identified as *his* in more than 85%. This point is considered as one of the important conclusions that have been reached. Simply, if the limit of the series is taken into consideration as an additional element in classification and hence description, the results of comparison may seem more reasonable. This leads to a higher rate of identification and recognition.

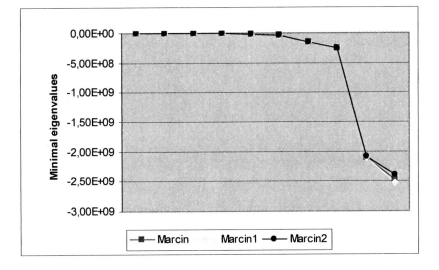

Fig. 4. The graph of minimal eigenvalues for Marcin

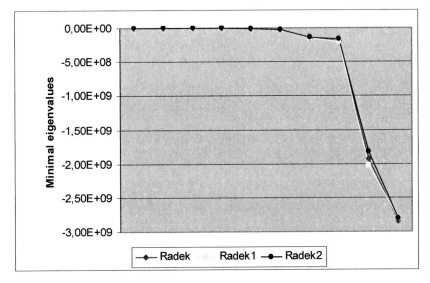

Fig. 5. The graph of minimal eigenvalues for Radek

Radek's hand processing results with rather another different behavior (Fig.5). The lines do not approach the limit of the series fast. They tend to follow different routes. However, the most important thing here is that they go through parallel paths and again showing almost the same character. They, therefore, belong to the same person, to Radek and differ from those of Iza's and Marcin's.

Fig. 6, however, shows the three hand-image average-graphs of Iza, Marcin and Radek all in one figure. As can easily be noticed they are different from each other showing that they belong to different hand-images.

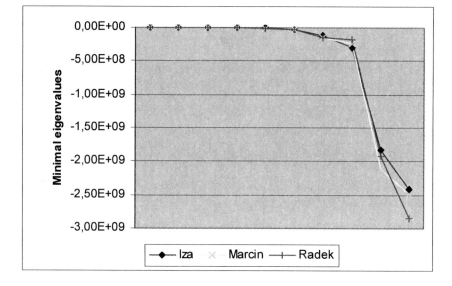

Fig. 6. The graph of minimal eigenvalues for Iza, Marcin and Radek

5.   CONCLUSIONS AND FUTURE ASPECTS

The achieved results are encouraging. The recognition rate can approach 90% in the case of increasing the size of Toeplitz matrices. The time of recognition is about 1.5 second per image, working on processor Intel Celeron 633MHz. These results, therefore, show that the approach given in this work is developing. However, as the increasing in the rate of recognition associates with the increasing of the computing size, then the method so far used is costly for ideal results. It demands that the data matrix size becomes much larger than that made used of in classical methods. This is impractical. The classical methods of feature-to-feature comparison, from the other side, have shown almost ideal results of about 100% of correct recognition in most cases. Therefore, the best expected results would be obtained when decreasing the size of the equivalent to the Toeplitz ones and then considering eigenvalues-to-eigenvalue comparison instead of making the tedious feature-to-feature comparison. Obviously, the number of the computed minimal eigenvalues should be much less than the number of the extracted features in order to be able to speak about better system of classification and recognition.

The use of Toeplitz matrices theory has proved the possibility of applying the worked out previously algorithm on other biometric fields [5, 6, 7, 11, 12, 13], to this topic of human identification.

The current and future work will concern a number of other aspects. This would include the increasing of the database size and creating a hybrid system to identify a person by hand geometry recognition in parallel with another biometric technique, for example the recognition of person fingerprints, his iris or signature. Moreover, we are following some studies to consider the limit of the minimal eigenvalues series as a useful tool, too. This adds an additional element to better classification and would certainly result in more precise comparison and may give more precise decision leading to a higher rate of identification and recognition. This means that a two-feature-vector system is then used $U = (V, W)$ where V is the vector whose elements are those obtained from eigenvalues series while W would carry the properties of the sequence limit. Moreover, the data extracted from the hand-palm would not be limited to the fingers and their dimensions and characteristics. The thickness of fingers, the palm-print and all other possible parameters that may increase the information data and hence decreasing the number of calculations more eigenvalues for more precise results, as the usual taking place situation.

The scanning platform used as data acquisition device is also of special importance and its improvement has really increased the effectiveness of the approach in both the classical and the eigenvalues methods raising the efficiency of the algorithm and increasing the rate of recognition.

ACKNOWLEDGEMENT

This work is supported by the Rector of Bialystok University of Technology (grant number W/II/3/01).

REFERENCES

[1] Saeed K., Werdoni M., " An Experimental Algorithm for Human Identification by Hand-Palm Geometry," 10th International Conference on Advanced Computer Systems - ACS'03, October 22-24, Miedzyzdroje 2003.

[2] Gonzales R. C., Woods R.E., *"Digital Image Processing"*, Prentice-Hall, New Jersey 2002.

[3] Werdoni M., *"An Experimental Algorithm for Person Identification by Recognizing Geometrical Parameters of His Hand"*, M.Sc. Thesis, Bialystok University of Technology, 2003.

[4] Saeed K., *"Computer Graphics Analysis: A Criterion for Image Feature Extraction and Recognition,"* MGV - International Journal on Machine Graphics and Vision, Institute of Computer Science, Polish Academy of Sciences, Volume 10, Issue 2, Warsaw 2001, pp. 185-194.

[5] Saeed K., *"Object Classification and Recognition Using Toeplitz Matrices,"* Artificial Intelligence and Security in Computing Systems, edited by Jerzy Sołdek and Leszek Drobiazgiewicz, The Kluwer International Series in Engineering and Computer Science, Volume 752, September 2003.

[6] Saeed K., Tabędzki M., Adamski M., *"A New Approach for Object-Feature Extract and Recognition,"* The 9th International Conference ACS (Advanced Computer Systems), pp. 389-397, 23-25 October, Międzyzdroje 2002.

[7] Kuchariew G. A., *"Biometric Systems – Methods and Approaches of Human Personality Identification,"* Politechnic Press (in Russian), Petersburg 2001.

[8] Sanchez-Reillo R., Sanchez-Avila C., Gonzalez-Marcos A.: *"Biometric Identification through Hand Geometry Measurements,"* IEEE Transactions on Pattern Analysis and Machine Intelligence, Vol. 22, No. 10, October 2000, pp. 1168-1171.

[9] Lindeburg L., "*Scale-Space Theory in Computer Vision*," Kluwer Academic Publishers, Boston 1994.

[10] Rao A. R., Jain R. C., "*Computerized Flow Field Analysis: Oriented Texture-Fields*," IEEE Trans. Pattern Analysis, and Machine Intelligence, vol. 14, no. 7, pp. 693-709, July 1992.

[11] Saeed K., Kozłowski M., "*An Image-Based System for Spoken-Letter Recognition*," Lecture Notes in Computer Science, Springer-Verlag, pp. 494-502, 10th CAIP Int. Conference on Computer Analysis of Images and Patterns, August 25-27, Groningen, The Netherlands 2003.

[12] Saeed K., "*Efficient Method for On-Line Signature Verification*," Proc. ICCVG Int. Conf. on Computer Vision and Graphics, Zakopane, Poland, pp. 635-640.

[13] Saeed K., "*A New Approach in Image Classification*," Proc. 5th International Conference on Digital Signal Processing and its Applications - DSPA'03, Vol. 1, pp. 49-52, Moscow 2003.

An Experimental Criterion for Face Classification

KHALID SAEED[1] PIOTR CHARKIEWICZ[2]
Faculty of Computer Science, Bialystok University of Technology
Wiejska 45A, 15-351 Bialystok, Poland
http://aragorn.pb.bialystok.pl/~zspinfo/
e-mail: [1] aidabt@ii.pb.bialystok.pl,
[2] piotr.charkiewicz@gazeta.pl

Abstract: In this work a new algorithm for automatic human face recognition from computer images, is presented. The proposed approach is based on minimal eigenvalues obtained from Toeplitz matrices. The promising results and their relatively high recognition percentage encourage making further studies and modifications to reach more general effective and faster methods for face identification.

Key words: Face Feature Extract; Face Identification and Recognition.

1. INTRODUCTION

The automatic face identification and recognition is very interesting issue both in social and industrial environments. However, this task is one of the most difficult problems in pattern recognition. This is because lighting conditions change, which change the characteristics of the given face. Facial expressions and pose variations also change with environmental conditions. These and other factors affect every algorithm worked out for the sake of human face identification and recognition. Human faces, beside speech and writing make up one of the most important Medias of communication between people as they carry and transfer the huge quantity of information. Recently, a number of works have been published in this area. These achievements have found their various applications. At present however, the main direction of development is to aid security systems. Machines equipped with image register would be able to detect an individual face in crowd, then to identify it and then to take the appropriate decision or facilitate undertaking adequate decision to us. Full automation of such a process, without the man's interference is extremely difficult to realize, because the scene is very complicated and image analysis causes many problems. The characteristics of a human face have a large individuality.

However, on logging several images of the same face (in different moments) it is hard to obtain the similar conditions (the differences in head position, the background and lighting). Identification system has to separate the face from the scene and identify it by making the basic comparison with pictures aggregated in the database [1].

2.   FACE RECOGNITION ALGORITHMS

The face recognition has become the subject of many research groups. However, only considerable number of them [2,3,4,5] has shown results of particular importance to the solution of the problem of finding an easy-to-implement fast and cheap system. The methods presented in research reviews and journals depend on different techniques. The known face recognition systems can generally be divided, depending on the way they identify the face, into two main categories:
1. Analytic systems [6] where the anatomical face features are considered. Such methods are either of mathematical   character, or approaches based on artificial intelligence (neural network).
2. Systems based on global approaches [2,4,7], where the image of the face is treated as a whole. Here, the recognition basis is either of one-pattern character, or of many patterns one.

Of course, such category classification is conventional, as there are some hybrid systems, which combine techniques coming from different groups [8,9]. The work introduced in this paper is of experimental basis and uses minimal eigenvalues of Toeplitz matrices in a way partly based on existing solutions [10,11,12].

3.   THE SUGGESTED BY AUTHORS' CRITERION

The following assumptions were through in the suggested criterion:
*   input image has 255 grey levels,
*   input image width is equal to 200 pixels,
*   the input face-image is frontal,
*   no objects shade the face.

The selection of the characteristic points $p_j \left(x_j, y_j \right)$ of a given face forms the input image-data to the system, $j = 0,1,2, \ldots, 10$. Fig.1 shows an example of a human face with the characteristic points on it.

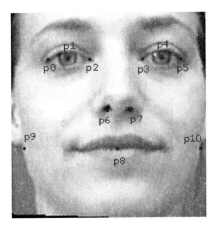

Fig.1 Selected characteristic points

Fig.2, however, shows the block diagram construction of the classifying system. The system consists of preprocessing - preparation of image to next stages, segmentation - the initial areas localization: eyes, mouths and nostrils, edge detection, feature extraction - the precise location of characteristic points and the classification on the basis of characteristic points' co-ordinates forming the elements of the Toeplitz matrices whose minimal eigenvalues are the main classifying tools.

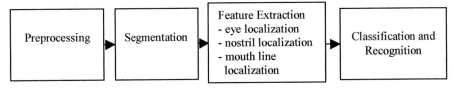

Fig.2 Classifying system block diagram

3.1 Preprocessing

The image preprocessing allow to get rid of input image noise like undesired background, change in hair-style, beard appearance, eyeglasses or ear-rings existence, change in lighting, image rotation and dislocation, and so forth. It can be realized in many ways, in dependence from effect, what we want to get. One of the important preprocessing parameters is the brightness improvement as it has direct influence on next stages performance.

3.2 Segmentation

Segmentation here splits the image into separate areas. As a result we get image fragments characterized with specific attributes (e.g.: eyes, mouths, nostrils), marked off from background, that is areas which are not a subject of analysis. The main known methods of image segmentation are Thresholding, Region Growing, Region splitting and Edge Detection methods. In our work we have used the first one.

3.2.1 THRESHOLDING, FILTERING and EDGE DETECTION

Generally, the thresholding method of segmentation, which is also called binarization, depends on determination of a threshold value T (in scale of image brightness), which divides the image points into two groups - points for which $I(x, y) > T$, and points of $I(x, y) < T$. In our algorithm T has been fixed experimentally to have the value 100. Unfortunately, binarization has also defects, namely, after thresholding the output image may possess unwanted groups of pixels (noise), which could cause problems while precisely locating desirable areas. In order to get rid of that noise median filter has been used. This filter is described in details in [13]. For edge detection, however, there exist a number of good detectors [1,13,14]. Canny's algorithm [13] has proved to be very optimal in edge detection.

3.3   Feature Extraction

Now, after data preparation from input data in Fig.1, the feature extract starts. The feature extracting consists of four stages:

• eyes detection - the points from p_0 to p_5 in Fig.1,

• nostril detection - the points p_6 and p_7,

• mouth line detection - the point p_8 ,

• face width detection on plane of mouth line - the points p_9 and p_{10}.

Biometrics properties show that the frontal face image can be divided into the sections shown in Fig.3.

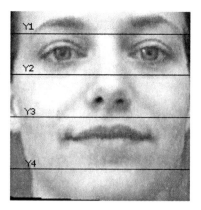

Fig.3 Face image divided into sections

In the shown sections, the eyes are in $[Y_1, Y_2]$, the nostril in $[Y_2, Y_3]$ and the mouth is in $[Y_3, Y_4]$.

On the basis of these sections and the biometrical features, now it is easy to situate those characteristic points p_j existing in each of the sections.

3.3.1 EYE LOCALIZATION

As it is the essential and most important step, the eyes localization is considered carefully. The approach most often used here is the gradient brightness analysis. For more accurate eye location, a hybrid system of eyes detection that makes use of two known methods, Image Gradient [7] and Variance Projection Function [15], has been worked out. The details of these methods are given in [7,15].

3.3.2 NOSTRILS DETECTION

*   The nostrils detection process is much simpler than eyes detection. It is mainly based on the results obtained in the segmentation process. Having specified the image section $[Y_2, Y_3]$, then the largest two pixel concentrations in black color are the nostrils. However, sometimes it does not go as easy as that way. In such a case some simple techniques can be used to help detect them. The intensity function $H(y)$ of image gradient G_h in the horizontal direction in section $[Y_2, Y_3]$ helps to localize the nostrils line. Simply, the maximum value of the function $H(y)$ is found in the section $[Y_2, Y_3]$.

3.3.3 MOUTH LINE DETECTION

The mouth line detection is a very similar process to nostrils detection. It can also be fixed the maximum value of the intensity function $H(y)$ of image gradient G_h in horizontal direction in $[Y_3, Y_4]$ section

3.4   Classification and Recognition

Evaluating the points $p_j(x_j, y_j)$, the algorithm of minimal eigenvalues of Toeplitz matrices [10,12] can now be used. Simply, the characteristic points p_j form the numerator and denominator of a transfer function, from which the coefficients of Taylor series are calculated. These coefficients will develop the determinant forms of Toeplitz matrices. The minimal eigenvalues λ_i, $i = 1, 2, ..., m$, where m is the size of the feature vector, are then computed. The minimal eigenvalues form a specific feature vector $x = [\lambda_0, \lambda_2, ..., \lambda_n]$. The elements of this vector form a nonincreasing series to carry the characteristics of each section or the whole face. Each series has its own behavior and shape distinguishing it from others. Not all examples have shown satisfying results of recognition when using minimal eigenvalues approach in classification. We still are working on its modification as it has some drawbacks especially when the number of the considered points is very large. The higher the number of minimal eigenvalues is, the longer is the time of computing. From the other side, when considering less number of eigenvalues, then the recognition rate is low. That is why another feature vector was used along with that of minimal eigenvalues. Its elements are the x-y coordinates of the points p_j. This hybrid classification system makes it easy to follow any of the recognition methods.

The recognition procedure, however, is of more interest. It follows the Absolute Deviation [12] in testing for the minimal difference between the unknown face image elements X_{Ψ_i} and the reference one X_{Φ_i} for all elements of the feature vectors:

$$E = \sum_{i=0}^{m} \left| x_{\Psi i} - x_{\Phi i} \right|,$$

where E is the error to be minimum for better recognition.

4. RESULTS

The system behavior was checked at various lighting conditions on 60 images of 20 persons, in which 40 being in database and remaining 20 were to recognize. All images come from generally accessible base [16], including 1521 faces of 23 persons. They have quite diverse size and belong to both sexes, different age groups. Among them are images including faces rotated about small angle as well as persons with eyeglasses, or closed eyes. The percentage of correct detection of characteristic points is introduced in Table 1.

Characteristic Points	Successful Detection Rate
$p_0 - p_5$	60 %
$p_6 - p_7$	90 %
$p_8 - p_{10}$	85 %

Table 1. Detection rate of characteristic points in particular sections

The effectiveness of point detection $p_0 - p_5$ is dependent to a large degree on the Image gradient method used. Depending on the conditions, under which the samples were taken. For example, the horizontal eye line detection was in most cases 100% while the detection of the vertical line passing through the pupil was of 70% effectiveness in the tested cases. This in turn has its influence on the correct results of the classifying algorithm. Bad specified location of characteristic points causes, that minimal eigenvalues sequence λ_i doesn't converge to the same limit as the series of the original image. In effect, this leads to the fact that minimal eigenvalues of different persons begin to overlap and cover each other. This, of course, decreases the percentage of recognition which sometimes falls too much.

The time lasted in each stage of the authors' algorithm is given in Table 2. The average time of image processing is short - about 0.7 second. The most time-consuming is the calculation of minimal eigenvalues.

Stage	Average operation time
Preprocessing	10 ms
Segmentation	50 ms
Edge Detection	60 ms
Feature Extraction	0.6 s
Classification	6.7 s

Table 2. Average Time for particular stages in authors' Algorithm

5. CONCLUSIONS AND FUTURE PLANS

The work introduced in this paper shows our contribution to the solution of the face classification problem. It shows an attempt to work out an experimental algorithm to identify and recognize a human face in a cheap and rather fast way. The suggested algorithm is partly based on existing solutions [10,12]. The innovation and the main conception of the system is to use the algorithm of minimal eigenvalues obtained from Toeplitz matrices. Minimal eigenvalues algorithm was successfully put-upon in different biometrics fields, and this is a trial to add the face recognition as a new possibility. As a part of the worked out system the digital image processing module was implemented, in which are the operations of image brightness improvement, segmentation, edge detection, particular characteristic points' location. The conducted tests of sensibility demonstrated that the system is comparatively resistant to changes connected with lighting conditions and contrast. The future work on this algorithm is related to the modification of Toeplitz matrices application. This gives less number of calculations to compute their minimal eigenvalues and hence allowing the criterion to consider more characteristic points. In fact, this is the main drawback of the system. It simply limits the extension of the algorithm as it increases the size of computation. Higher number of minimal eigenvalues gives longer time of computing. But, when considering less number of eigenvalues, then the recognition rate is low and the efficiency of the system is low, too.

ACKNOWLEDGEMENT

This work was supported by the Rector of Bialystok University of Technology (grant number W/II/3/01).

REFERENCES

[1] Charkiewicz P., *"An Experimental Algorithm for Human Face Recognition,"* M.Sc. Thesis, Bialystok University of Technology, 2003.

[2] Skarbek W., Pietrowcew A., *"Lokalna Analiza Składowych Głównych Drugiego Rzędu w Rozpoznawaniu Twarzy,"* Elektronizacja – Podzespoły i Zastosowania Elektroniki, 4/2003.

[3] Kukharev G., Kuzminski A., *"Biometric Systems – Methods and Approaches of Human Personality Identification,"* Politechnic Press (in Russian), Petersburg 2001.

[4] Yongsheng G., Maylor K.H. Leung, *"Face recognition using line edge map,"* IEEE Transactions on Pattern Analysis and Machine Intelligence, Vol.24, no.6, 2002.

[5] Kukharev G., *"Biometric Techniques – Face Recognition Methods,"* Technical University of Szczecin Press (in Polish), 2003.

[6] Ranganath S., Krishnamurthy A., *"Face Recognition Using Transform Features and Neural Networks,"* Pattern Recognition, Vol. 20. No. 10, 1997.

[7] Baback M., *"Principal Manifolds and Probabilistic Subspaces for Visual Recognition",* IEEE Transactions on Pattern Analysis and Machine Intelligence, Vol.24, no.6, 2002.

[8] Hyun-Chul K., Daijin K., Sung Yang B., *"Face Recognition Using the Mixture-of-Eigenfaces Method",* Pattern Rcognition Letters, 2002.

[9] Tistarelli M., Grosso E., *"Active Face Recognition with a Hybrid Approach,"* Pattern Recognition Letters, 1997.

[10] Saeed K., *"Computer Graphics Analysis: A Criterion for Image Feature Extraction and Recognition,"* Vol.10, Issue 2, 2001, pp. 185-194, MGV - International Journal on Machine Graphics and Vision, Institute of Computer Science, Polish Academy of Sciences, Warsaw.

[11] Saeed K., *"Efficient Method for On-Line Signature Verification,"* Proceedings of the International Conference on Computer Vision and Graphics - ICCVG'02, Vol. 2, 25-29 September, Zakopane, 2002.

[12] Saeed K., *"A New Approach in Image Classification,"* Proc. 5th International Conference on Digital Signal Processing and its Applications - DSPA'03, Vol. 1, pp. 49-52, Moscow 2003.

[13] Wróbel Z., Goprowski R., *"Przetwarzanie Obrazu w Programie MATLAB",* University of Slazk Press (in Polish), 2001.

[14] K. Saeed, M. Rybnik, M. Tabędzki, "More Results and Applications about the Algorithm of Thinning Images to One-Pixel-width," 9th CAIP Int. Conference on Computer Analysis of Images and Patterns, Sept. 5-7, 2001, pp. 601-609, Springer-Verlag, Warsaw 2001.

[15] Feng G.C., Yuen P.C., "Variance Projection Function and its Application to Eye Detection for Human Face Recognition," Pattern Recognition, 1998.

[16] Takacs B., *"Comparing Face Images Using the Modified Hausdorff Distance,"* Pattern Recognition, Vol.31, pp. 1873-1881, 1998.

Contour Objects Recognition Based On UNL-Fourier Descriptors

DARIUSZ FREJLICHOWSKI
Faculty of Computer Science and Information Systems, Technical University of Szczecin
Żołnierska Street 49, 71-210 Szczecin, Poland, e-mail: dfrejlichowski@wi.ps.pl

Abstract: The shape is one of the most popular representations of an object. Algorithms of extracting object's shape are well known and widely used. Furthermore, there are many descriptors based on information about silhouette. However, there are some problems to overcome, for example noise, occlusion, distortion caused by affine transformations. This paper presents experimental results of applying the UNL-Fourier Descriptors to contour objects. The approach utilizes the transformation from Cartesian to polar coordinates system (it is close to so-called "signatures") ith normalization, and subsequently, Fourier transform, which can be used to feature reduction. It is worth to note, that the UNL-Fourier Descriptor belongs to larger class of affine invariants.

Key words: Pattern recognition, contour objects, affine invariants, UNL-Fourier transformation

1. INTRODUCTION

There are two main ways of representing an object in recognition tasks. They are different from each other in many aspects and usually involve employing different algorithms. The first one rely on pictorial representation of an object, for example colour or grayscale pictures, infra-red images. The second one uses binary information – silhouettes extracted from pictorial images. The main problems to overcome in both representations are briefly depicted in [1]. Let us enumerate here only the connected with contour representation ones: noise, occlusion, modification of a silhouette (caused for example by additional subparts), influence of affine transformations, change of point of view, direction of tracing and starting point selection, amount of points ([1], see Fig.1).

The two fundamental issues, examined in this paper, are affine transforms and noise. Both of them strongly influence the silhouette. The former deformates the shape as a whole, the latter changes the location of individual points. The affine transforms, namely rotation, scaling and translation, make recognition of an object difficult, because they lead to its considerable deformations in comparison with the instance stored in database.

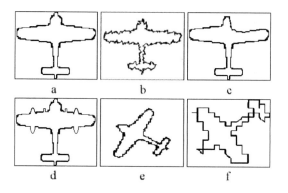

Fig. 1. Some problems to overcome in contour representation: a) orginal object, b) noise, c) occlusion, d) alternate warload, e) different point of view, f) small amount of points.

The noise is a very commonly occuring problem in recognition and can be caused by lots of reasons: the nature of a device capturing the image, the weather conditions, clutter related to the transfering process, discrete nature of an image, transforming one representation of an object into another (e.g. grayscale image to binary silhouette) and many more.

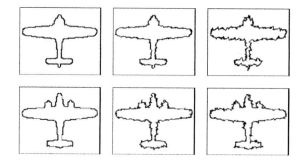

Fig. 2. Examples of different amount of noise corrupting the shape. First column includes original silhouettes.

The remainder of this paper is organized as follows: Section 2 describes briefly the UNL-Fourier descriptors and the UNL transform itself, Section 3 presents some experimental results and Section 4 includes conclusions and future plans.

2. THE UNL-FOURIER DESCRIPTORS

One of the methods of avoiding problems mentioned in the former section is the application of affine invariants ([3]). The connection of these shape descriptors with deformation of a silhouette caused by affine transforms is obvious, but some algorithms can manage the noise quite efficiently, as well. An example is the UNL-Fourier descriptor, proposed by Rauber ([2]). It consists of two stages (as indicates the name): UNL transform and succeeding Fourier transform. The former one is invariant to scaling (due to normalization) and translation. The rotation becomes a cyclic shifting and can be overcame by the latter transform.

The UNL transform converts Cartesian into normalized polar coordinates, using the parametric curves. As the output it gives the binary image containing the transformed silhouette. The exhaustive formulation of the method can be found in [2] and [4]. Here, only the basis of the algorithm will be presented.

Initially, the Cartesian coordinates of each point are extracted and written as parametric complex curves ([2]):

$$z_i(t) = x_i(t) + jy_i(t) \qquad\qquad t \in (0,1) \qquad\qquad (1)$$

Then, the centroid of the object is derived - the mean of all pattern coordinates. It becomes the origin of the transformed polar coordinates. We choose the maximum Euclidean distance M from centroid to all curve points.

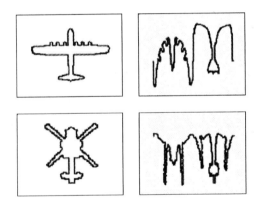

Fig. 3. Examples of objects and its corresponding UNL – descriptors.

The UNL-transform for single parametroic curve can be now written as ([2]):

$$U(z(t)) = R(t) + j \times \theta(t) = \frac{\|z(t) - O\|}{M} + j \times \mathrm{atan}(\frac{y(t) - O_y}{x(t) - O_x}) \qquad (2)$$

where:

$O = (O_x, O_y)$ – the centroid

$z(t) = x(t) + jy(t)$ – single parametric curve, represented as a complex number.

Received parametric curves are inserted into image, which is transformed using Fast Fourier Transform. Obtained spectrum is the output of the UNL-Fourier transform ([2]). We can apply the reduction stage - by selecting the most significant elements from the Fourier spectrum.

3.   THE UNL-FOURIER DESCRIPTORS

The aim of the study was to investigate the behaviour and effectiveness of the UNL-Fourier descriptors in two distinct cases – when recognizing similar and unsimilar contour objects. Further, the effectiveness of the method in the presence of reduction was explored. The way of feature reduction was simply the selection of the most significant part of the Fourier spectrum. Recognition rate with decreasing size of the reduced spectrum was tested.

All shapes used are the same as in [1]. Precisely, in the first case, when unsimilar shapes were examined, it was used 5 silhouettes: aircraft, catr, helicopter, outline of an airfield and building. In the second case, where objects were expected to have similar shape, we have used outilnes of 10 different airlpanes. The imagery of the tested objects is presented in [1].

The testing rule was as follows. An object was rotated in the image plane. The range of rotation was 10 to 360 degrees, with the step of 10 degrees. That gave 36 instances of an object. Every instance was transformed separately to achieve its UNL-Fourier invariant. Each of them was matched then invariants derived for original untransformed objects, using correlation as a classification method. The maximum value of correlation indicated the recognized object. The percentage of correct matching gave the recognition rate for an object.

The first test we performed had to examine recognition rate for UNL-Fourier invariant, without spectrum reduction. The average value of correct classification was 95,6% for unsimilar and 94,6% for similar shapes. The results for each class are presented in Table 1 and Table 2. As we can see, the worst values are equal to 80,6% and 69,4%, for unsimilar and similar objects, respectively.

Aircraft	Car	Helicopter	Airfield	Building
100 %	100 %	80.556 %	97.22 %	100 %

Tab. 1. Average recognition rate for unsimilar objects.

Object	1	2	3	4	5	6	7	8	9	10
Recognition	100%	97 %	100%	69 %	100%	100%	100%	97 %	97 %	86 %

Tab. 2. Average recognition rate for similar patterns (airplanes).

It is clear, that the recognition effects have to be associated with angles of rotation, which influence the object's shape. To illustrate this, we present the dependence of the false recognition rate on the angle (that is, the average false classification rate for particular angles) for the case of airplanes. As we can see, the problems occur in three main ranges: 40-70, 120-140 and 210-250 degrees. It means, that rotation within theese ranges mostly deformates the object's silhouette.

Applying the Fourier transform makes the feature reduction possible. It is clear, because the most significant features are placed in corners of the spectrum matrix. The rejection of low frequencies can in some cases even increase the recognition rate, because we reject mainly small contour's perturbations caused by noise, discretization and other deforming actions.

The latter test explored the recognition rate when decreasing the square of frequencies taken into consideration. Figures 5 and 6 show the average recognition rate for unsimilar and similar shapes, respectively, using reduced spectrum matrix of size from 2x2 to 50x50. As we can see, in the first case, the best result is already achieved with square of size 3x3. In the latter instance the appropriate size if from 5x5 to 7x7.

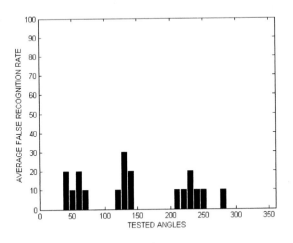

Fig. 4. Average false recognition rate for airplanes depending on tested angles.

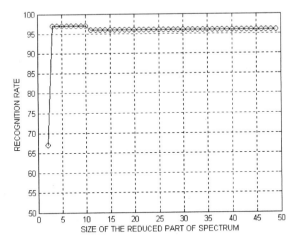

Fig. 5. Average recognition rate for unsimilar objects using reduced UNL-Fourier descriptors.

4. CONCLUSIONS AND FUTURE WORK

Recognition rate achieved using UNL-Fourier decsriptor indicates, that this method is a quite effective tool in recognizing contour objects. Values – 97 and 96 percent, for unsimilar and similar shapes, respectively, provide an impetus to further work with this feature descriptor. There is however necessity of additional shape's deformation, for instance by allowing for randomly generated noise or discontinuities in solhouette. Small rotation in 3 dimmensions can be examined, as well.

During the analysis of results presented in former section, some interesting characteristics can be observed. It turned out, that some rotation angles are more affecting the shape's disturbance than another. In performed tests such a property was especially apparent in: 40-70, 120-140 and 210-250 degrees. It is obviously connected with the noise caused by digital character of the image.

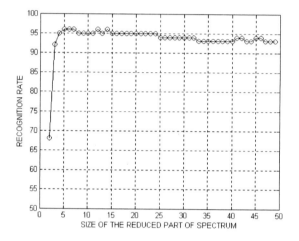

Fig. 6. Average recognition rate for similar objects using reduced UNL-Fourier descriptors.

REFERENCES

[1] Frejlichowski D 2002. 'Brief review of aircraft recognition methods'. *Proceedings of the 9th International Conference on Advanced Computer Systems, Szczecin, Poland,* pp. 353–364.
[2] Rauber T.W. and Steiger-Garcao A.S. 1992. '2-D form descriptors based on a normalized parametric polar transform (UNL transform)'. *Proc MVA'92 IAPR Workshop on Machine Vision Applications, 1992.*
[3] Wood J. 1996. 'Invariant pattern recognition: a review'. *Pattern Recognition v. 29 no. 1,* pp. 1–17.
[4] Frejlichowski D. 2003. 'The UNL-transform applied to contour objects'. *Proc of International Conference on Computer Information Systems and Industrial Management Applications, Ełk, Poland, 2003.*

Sonar Image Simulation by Means of Ray Tracing and Image Processing

MARIUSZ BORAWSKI, PAWEŁ FORCZMAŃSKI
Technical University of Szczecin, Faculty of Computer Science and Information Systems
71-210 Szczecin, Zolnierska Str. 49, e-mail: mborawski@wi.ps.pl, pforczmanski@wi.ps.pl

Abstract: A problem of simulating sonar images in order to build better and more efficient sonar image recognition systems is still unsolved. The authors present an approach to this simulation by means of simplified ray tracing and image processing techniques. The process is divided into few stages: creating models, image synthesis and distortion simulation.

Key words: Sonar image, ray tracing, image processing, simulation

1.   INTRODUCTION

The sonar system, which is a very complicated device, can be useful in many offshore applications. In many cases, there is a need of simulating it, which is associated with different scientific and practical tasks. The main stream of applications is related to naval navigation, which is strongly dependent on global positioning systems like GPS or GLONASS. These systems can be noised or arbitrary switched off what can lead to collisions and other dangerous sea accidents. Therefore it is so important to develop other alternative ways of navigation which does not relay on information form outside systems. One of the most promising alternatives is navigation by means of sea-bottom observation. It should be pointed out that - in this case - a complicated problem of underwater object recognition is to be solved. These objects – observed by sonar - can be divided into several classes, and not all of them are useful for navigation (for example natural structures).

Successful recognition requires the presence of many templates [5]. It is so important, because objects presented in sonar images change their appearance with the change of ship's course. The process of collecting templates by scanning sea-bottom with sonar is time-consuming and expensive, which causes it to be unpractical. To reduce time and financial cost, it is possible to replace real sonar system with a simulated one to generate synthetic images used in recognition.

2.   OBJECTS IN SONAR IMAGES

The sea-bottom contains different types of objects and structures. Most of them are of natural origin, but nowadays more and more are placed there as a consequence of human activity. Therefore, we can divide all objects placed on sea-bottom (which can be seen by sonar) into 3 groups:
1.   geological;
2.   biological;
3.   technical (artificial) – left there as a result of the offshore human activity.

Geological objects have - in most cases – big dimensions, without any specific constant shape, which can change it time. One of geological form which is not easy to describe is a sand dune, therefore it is suitable to recognize it by means of texture or surface quality, rather than shape. This problem requires a different approach to recognition and will not be further discussed.

The second group contains biological objects that means: sea creatures and plants living in water environment and on sea-bottom. In most cases this objects have small dimensions and are often not visible for sonar. It is possible only to locate their large clusters, for example drifting plankton.

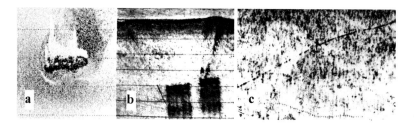

Fig. 1. Technical objects: a) ship (courtesy of Autocomp Electronics, Szczecin, Poland), b) traces of sea platform [1], c) underwater cable [1]

The human activity associated with sea (transport means, exploration of natural resources) leaves, purposely or not, various traces, namely miscellaneous artificial objects (fig. 1). The character of these objects varies. Not all of them can be treat the same [6]. Therefore it is so important to divide them into classes related to different recognition methods they need:
1.   objects of finite and possible to evaluate contour (fig. 1 a, b);
2.   long objects – with specified width and practically infinite length. (lines, pipes – fig. 1c);
3.   small objects that are represented in sonar image by only several pixels (mines, torpedoes).

The third group (technical objects) is the easiest to identify and therefore the most useful for navigational purposes. It should be stressed out that small objects represented by few pixel groups are rather useless because they can be covered by sand or moved by stream

For objects that lay on sea-bottom and are not covered by sand, it is possible to observe – besides the image of objects itself – their acoustic shadows. The acoustic

shadow can be described as a zone, which is behind an object and is not reached by sonar beam. Therefore, we can divide objects in sonar images using another criterion, namely the presence of an acoustic shadow – into two classes:
- objects with an acoustic shadow,
- objects without one.

The acoustic shadow gives useful information about object's geometry, which is not included in object's image itself. That is why it is a very important component used for recognition. On the other hand, its shape is strongly dependent on the distance between sonar antenna and sea-bottom and on the ship's course. In the first case, the proportions of width and height of the shadow change. In the second case, which is more significant, the shape of the shadow changes, which can make recognition more complicated (or even impossible). These distortions are caused by complicated acoustic shadow creation process – the projection, which is a combination of perspective and parallel one (fig. 2).

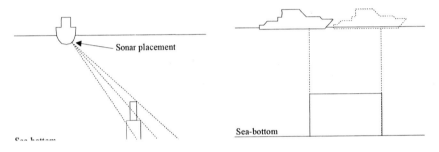

Fig. 2. Acoustic shadow creating by means of projection of object on sea-bottom.

3. SIMULATING THE SONAR IMAGE

Simulated sonar image have to be distorted in a way that real sonar image is. That is why the simulation process consists of several steps, which are presented in fig. 3.

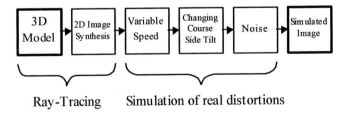

Fig. 3. Process of simulating the sonar image

The first step is to make three-dimensional models of objects placed on a sea-bottom. Sample 3D scene is presented in fig. 4. It should be pointed out that the bottom should neither be planar nor uniform because we want to simulate local changes of surface type (and color). This effect can be obtained by certain bump-mapped texture applied to bottom surface.

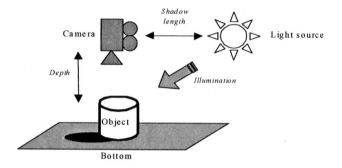

Fig. 4. The rules of building three-dimensional scene

On the background we place different objects (3D models of real objects: ships-wrecks, infrastructure, etc. – see fig. 5.). A camera, which observes these objects is placed vertically above the surface. The distance between the camera and the surface is related to the required observation depth. On this same height, but not in the same position as the camera, we place a light source that illuminates the scene. The distance between the light source and the camera simulates the vertical distance between the ship and observed objects.

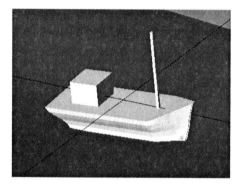

Fig. 5. Sample 3D model of a ship

All these conditions are necessary to create close-to-reality image (similar approach, which is presented in [2-4] does not implement distortions specific to these kind of sensing, for example the distortions associated with variable ship's speed, changing course and side tilt). In our approach imaging conditions are simulated by:
1. Local stretching and narrowing of the image along perpendicular to the line connecting the camera and the light source – it simulates variable speed of the ship (fig. 6).

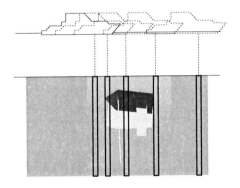

Fig. 6. Variable speed simulation

2. Image scanning along some curve. The image created from three-dimensional model (fig. 5) is scanned along straight lines perpendicular to some curve, which simulates changing ship's course. (fig. 7).

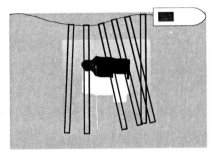

Fig. 7. Changing course simulation

3. Moving each line of the image by some offset, which simulates side tilt (fig. 8).

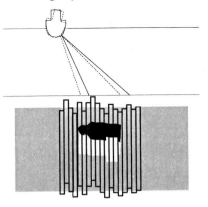

Fig. 8. Side tilt simulation

The last stage involves noise addition, which simulates noise received by a sonar [7].

As an effect of operations presented above, we get an image with distortions which are close to real conditions of sonar sensing. Intermediary images and a result of simulation are presented in fig. 9.

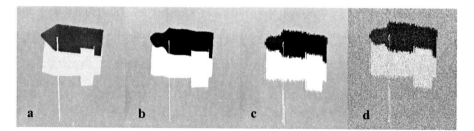

Fig. 9. Complete process of simulating the sonar image: a) an image obtained by ray-tracing, c) simulating the changing speed of a ship, d) simulating the changing course and side tilt, d) resulting image with noise added

4.   SUMMARY

The method presented in this paper gives a possibility of simulating sonar image together with all distortions, that are characteristic for sonar imaging technology. We should be aware of limitations that are common for this and all simplified method. It does not consider specific physic-based conditions of sound wave in water environment. Therefore it is not suitable for building recognition systems that use reflection factors. However it is still enough for systems that use only image information for recognition.

REFERENCES

[1] Belderson R.H., Kenyon N. H., Stride A.H., Stubs A.R., 'Sonographs of the sea floor', Amsterdam, London, New York, 1972
[2] Bell J. M., Linnett L. M. 'Simulation and Analysis of Synthetic Sidescan Sonar Images', *IEE Proceedings - Radar, Sonar and Navigation,* 144(4), p. 219-226, Aug. 1997
[3] Bell J. M., 'Application of optical ray tracing techniques to the simulation of sonar images', *Optical Engineering,* 36(6), pp. 1806-1813, June 1997
[4] Russell G.T., Bell J.M., Linnett L.M., 'Computer Model Creates Synthetic Sidescan Sonar Images', *Offshore Research Focus,* No. 115, December 1996
[5] Kuchariew G., 'Przetwarzanie i analiza obrazów cyfrowych', Szczecin 1998
[6] Mignotte M., Collet C., Perez P., 'Markov random field and fuzzy logic modeling in sonar imagery: application to the classification of underwater floor', *Computer Vision and Image Understanding,* July 2000
[7] Pratt W. K., 'Digital image processing', Wiley-Interscience, New York, 1991

The PCA Reconstruction Based Approach for Extending Facial Image Databases for Face Recognition Systems

LIMING CHEN[1], GEORGY KUKHAREV[2], TOMASZ PONIKOWSKI[2]

[1]*Departement MI, Ecole Centrale de Lyon, laboratoire ICTT, BP 163, 36 avenue Guy de Collongue, 69131 Ecully Cedex, France ph: (+33 4) 72186583, fax: (+33 4) 72181615, e-mail: liming.chen@ec-lyon.fr*
[2]*Computer Science and Information Systems Department, Technical University of Szczecin, ul. Żołnierska 49, 71-210 Szczecin, ph: (+48 91) 48 764 85, fax: (+48 91) 48 764 39, e-mail: gkoukharev@wi.ps.pl, tponikowski@wi.ps.pl*

Abstract: The one of most problematic subject in face recognition system is to make them immune from variance of pose under which face image is taken. The solution this could be generation of additional images for face recognition system database. a In this paper PCA based approach is presented. It allows to generate subimages to supplement images taken from camera.

Key words: PCA, feature, eigenface, eigenvalue, feature space reduction

1. INTRODUCTION

The successful face recognition system should be able to compensate changeable data acquisition conditions. In the case of image registration some kinds of image distortions could be met. The face image distortion could be divided into groups presented below:
1. distortions caused by environment (changeable illumination conditions)
2. distortions caused by registration hardware and optics (barrel distortion, pincushion distortion, vignetting, CCD noise etc.)
3. distortions caused by photographed person behavior (face images with different orientations and sizes, changeable clothing elements, make-up, etc.)

Changes caused by personal age influence are taken out of consideration. The paper area of interest is placed in third kind of distortions. Exactly the face image orientation variance compensation methods are discussed and the PCA based approach is presented in detail.

2. IMAGE SYNTHESIS APPROACH

2.1 Methods brief review

The main assumption of image synthesis approaches is based on information about taken image depth map. If we have image taken and have an information about depth of every pixel in it, we could easily generate derivative images basing on image synthesis methods (e.g. IBR – Image Based Rendering methods).

The image synthesis methods looks great for ideal depth maps (for example synthetically generated), but they have serious limitations connected with real depth map calculation inaccuracy .

There are some methods which allow to get an image depth map. The image depth map extraction methods could work with the single image or with the sequence of images.

The depth map extraction methods breakdown:

1. photoclinometry methods ("shape/depth from shading") – the photographed surface depth is determined basing on information about surface type, illumination distribution etc. with use of single image or sequence of images taken in the different illumination conditions – there is a lot of known shape from shading solutions (to see review of photoclinometry methods please see [9]]),

2. "shape/depth from focus/defocus" – the photographed surface depth is determined basing on set of taken images analysis; characteristic for images used in this approach is that the focus is hold on different objects in scene under constant registration device optical parameters (focal length and aperture value which determines image depth of field); if this approach is used, the one very important condition should be fulfilled – the position of photographed objects must be the same in each image from the sequence (it could be hard to provide this in the case of live person photographing); depth map with use of "shape/depth from focus/defocus" approach could be for example obtained with use of specially prepared set of filters [13],

3. methods based on stereovision – information about image depth is calculated basing on two (stereo-pair) or more images (stereo sequence) taken with registration device shift in the plane perpendicular to view axis, with use of epipolar geometry; the stereovision methods are similar to human vision mechanism (two eyes, focusing shifted images); the main disadvantage of these methods is connected with necessity of localization corresponding pixels (objects) in each image of used set, to determine shift; there are a lot of scientific papers connected with this subject, but most important and very helpful in the case of real application of stereovision is the taxonomy of two-frame stereovision methods written by D. Scharstein and R. Szeliski [17],

4. methods based on image morphing algorithms (the basics of image morphing are described in [20]) – novel images are generated with use of a set of images with different head position (2 or more) with selected characteristic points in each of them; the morphing transform allows to obtain transitional images between key frames (images from original face recognition system database).

2.2 Conclusions

Image synthesis (e.g. IBR) is a good way to generate novel facial images only if we have complete, not distorted information about image depth and its texture. Image depth map calculation process is very complex and its inaccuracy is significant for quality of finally generated image. The process of extracting image depth map is rather complex and uses advanced mathematical and physical formulas. The methods based on morphing techniques are successful only in the case of properly selected characteristic points used to interpolate transitional images (ideal solution should be based on robust automatic selection of characteristic interpolation points in key frames).

3. PCA BASED RECONSTRUCTION APPROACH

3.1 Introduction to PCA

The PCA (principal component analysis) method is widely known method for data dimensionality reduction [4]. The PCA reduction is performed with use of Karhunen-Loeve transform. The main idea of PCA use for face recognition is to obtain and describe changes in face image sequence (input database of face recognition system) with use of a linear combination of few eigenvectors (eigenfaces) – the face recognition system which uses PCA method is described in [2]. Orthogonal transformation over eigenvector base (Karhunen-Loeve transform) allows to transform input data (input features space) to new feature space with significantly reduced dimensionality . Described process is known as feature space dimensionality reduction. The PCA method and its applications for face recognition systems are described in detail in [1].

3.2 Virtual Face Images Generation

Lets consider a sequence of facial images taken in a way which allows to determine its rotation around vertical axis (it could be a set of images rotated around any axis). For proper description of algorithm lets assume some values to describe set of input images:

$K = 1$ – number of classes (number of image types – in case of face recognition – number of photographed persons)
$L=15$ – class quantity (images per class)
$M=40$ – image height
$N=38$ – image width

The set of images is presented in fig. 1.

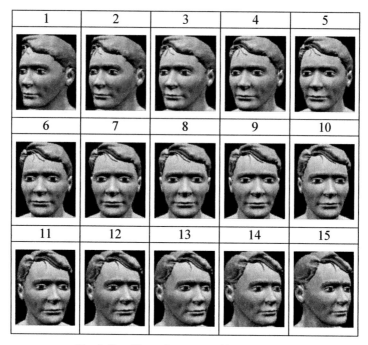

Fig. 1. Set of input images used in experiment.

The images are synthetically generated, to avoid distortion caused by environmental conditions. In this paper we will try to answer questions presented below:

- which features are responsible for rotation around Y axis
- how looks eigenfaces for selected image set,
- it is possible to design parametric face model for around Y axis rotation

At the beginning, some values needed for Karhunen-Love transform should be calculated:

$$DIM = MN = 40 \times 38 = 1520; \; KL = 15. \tag{1}$$

The DIM>>KL, so we should use following procedure for calculating eigenvectors and eigenvalues [1]:

$$R = D^{T}D; \; \Lambda = W^{T}RW; \; V = DW, \tag{2}$$

where:
D – matrix containing selected features of input data (size: DIMxKL)
R – covariance matrix with rank KL
Λ, W – matrices containing eigenvalues and eigenvectors of covariance matrix
V – matrix (DIMxKL) of eigenvectors used in Karhunen-Loeve transform (KL columnar eigenvectors)

In accordance with PCA method, Karhunen-Loeve transform for whole input data is performed:

$$Y_{p \times KL} = F_{p \times DIM} D \qquad (3)$$

where:

$F_{p \times DIM}$ – matrix of Karhunen-Loeve transform composed of p rows of matrix $[V]^T$ corresponding to largest eigenvalues (from Λ)
Y – matrix with facial images in reduced features space:

$$Y_{p \times KL} = \left[Y^{(1)} \ Y^{(2)} \ \ldots \ Y^{(KL)} \right] \qquad (4)$$

Matrix Y contain KL vectors with $p \times 1$ size. Each vector in matrix Y is a spectrum of Karhunen-Loeve transform for input image and is interpreted as principal components of input image. The set of first six principal components for all fifteen images is presented in fig. 2 (X axis – image number, Y axis - component).

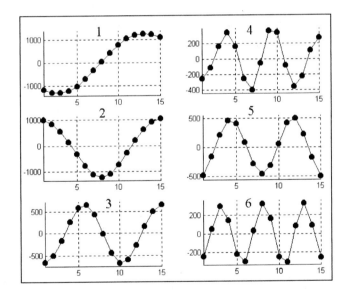

Fig . 2. First six principal components values

In the fig. 2 we could observe, that first component values oscillates by sinus function. In the point with X coordinate equal to eight, value of component is equal to zero. Additionally, values of second component are symmetrical with respect to the same point.

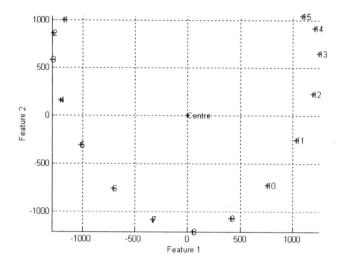

Fig. 3. Mapping of feature 1 and 2 on the plane.

It seems to be most probable, that first component is responsible for face rotation around Y axis, and the second is responsible for average value of face image (it is proportional to face area in the image – first and fifteenth image have the largest face area, and eighth image have the smallest). Mapping of the first two components onto plane is depicted in the fig. 3 (the same mapping, but with the adequate facial images placed in mapping points is presented in fig. 4).

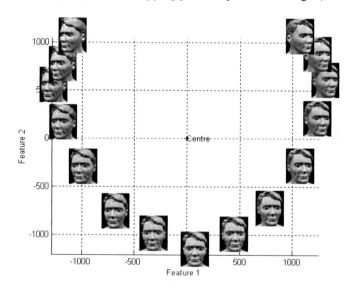

Fig. 4 Mapping of feature 1 and 2 on the plane with images placed in mapping points.

In the reduced features space, number of principal component is the number of the feature. It implies, that in reduced features space responsible for Y axis facial image rotation is feature with number 1. The remaining features are not being analyzed.

We have decided about feature responsible for Y axis rotation, and now we could try to reconstruct the facial images from feature set.

The matrix V of eigenvectors is sized with DIM = MxN, where M, and N are the input images dimensions. If every row of matrix V we arrange in the form of matrix sized with MxN, and treat these matrices as digital image, we will obtain the images with shapes similar to the faces. The described form of eigenvectors is called eigenfaces. The set of fifteen eigenfaces calculated for images presented in fig. 1 is presented in fig. 5.

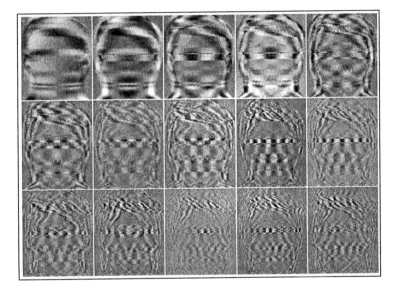

Fig. 5. Eigenfaces calculated for images from fig. 1

The input image reconstruction is performed with inverse Karhunen-Loeve transform. This transform uses given spectrum and eigenfaces to obtain new images, which could be interpreted as a result of input images approximation. The quality of approximation depends from number of components used in inverse Karhunen-Loeve transform (total number of components is equal to DIM, the approximation uses only $p << DIM$ number of components). The new images, which are transitional for database images could be obtained by changing spectrum values. In this way virtual (not really taken by camera) facial images could be generated.

The reconstruction process is illustrated in figures presented below:

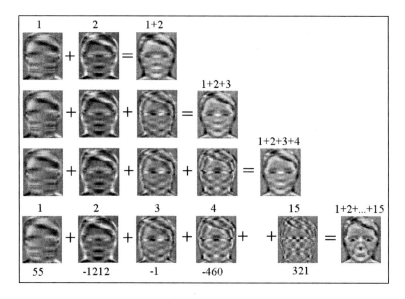

Fig. 6. Reconstruction of virtual face images with use of inverse Karhunen-Loeve transform ("en-face" image reconstructed).

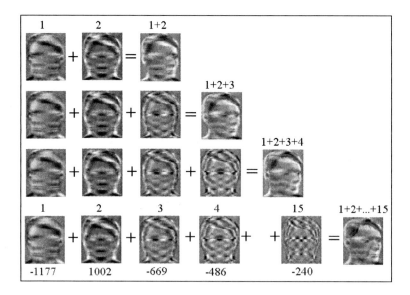

Fig. 7. Reconstruction of virtual face images with use of inverse Karhunen-Loeve transform (rotated left image reconstructed).

The coefficients depicted at the bottom of fig. 6 and fig. 7 are the approximation coefficients used to generate virtual face image, basing on eigenfaces (coefficients determines share held by each eigenface in approximated image). The approximation is performed with use of coefficients and eigenfaces,, with use of formula:

$$img = \sum_{i=1}^{p} \alpha_i f_i,\tag{5}$$

where:

img – reconstructed image; f_i – it-h eigenface image; α_i – i-th approximation coefficient; p – number of used eigenfaces and approximation coefficients for novel image reconstruction;

3.3   Results of Experiments

In this chapter results for real images taken from digital camera are described. In figures presented below, it is characteristic, that some images are placed in nearly the same position (for example, please see 3rd and 4th image in fig. 8 and theirs 1st and 2nd feature value in fig. 10). Similarity of image representation place (fig. 11) in reduced features space is caused by not really significant differences in series of images taken from camera during short period of time.

The presented results implies that methods based on PCA reconstruction approach, could be the accurate solution for expanding recognition systems databases in the case of avoiding influence of geometrical distortions of images on recognition process.

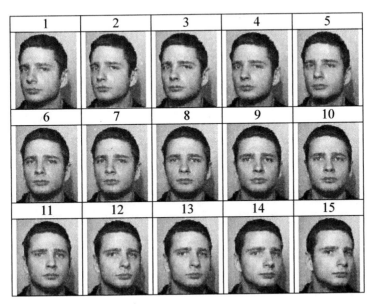

Fig. 8. Set of input images used in experiment.

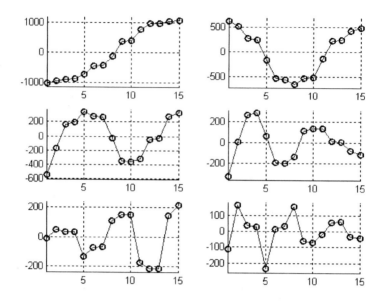

Fig . 9. First six principal components values

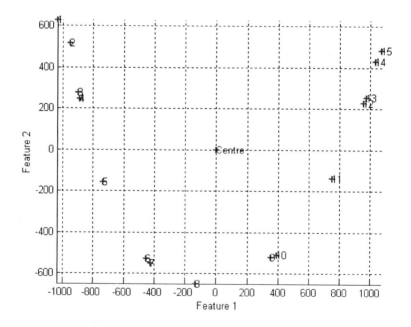

Fig. 10. Mapping of feature 1 and 2 onto the plane

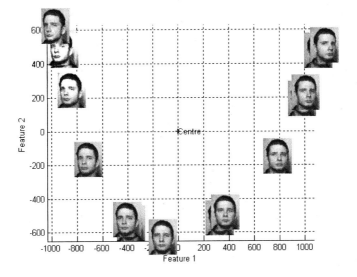

Fig. 11 Mapping of feature 1 and 2 on the plane with images placed in mapping points

In the fig. 12 reconstruction results with use of different number of features (up to 9) are presented. For experiments set of synthetically generated images (with rotation around Y axis with range –45 to +45 degrees) was used. It is clearly visible , that image quality is quite good for not really big amount of features used in reconstruction process. The reconstructed image looks similar to original in the case of use only few features (5 could be treated as a minimal value needed to obtain accurate reconstruction results).

4. CONCLUSIONS

The presented analysis results show possibility of generation subsamples for expanding face recognition system database by use of the feature values interpolation between node points (feature values calculated for database). To obtain images with sufficient quality to recognition tasks, only set of a few features could be used (9-10 seems to be enough as it is depicted in fig. 12). The images used in experiments contains man's head rotated around vertical axis. Presented solution could be used for images with face in orientation different from presented in this article – only database with input images should be changed.

In the future works authors will perform analysis for complex transformations (e.g. rotation around more then one axis and scale), and for images with complex background and different illumination conditions (in current work backgrounds are uniform and images are taken in constant illumination conditions to avoid distortion of feature dependence on image rotation).

Number of features	Reconstruction results (angles range: -45..45 degrees)
1	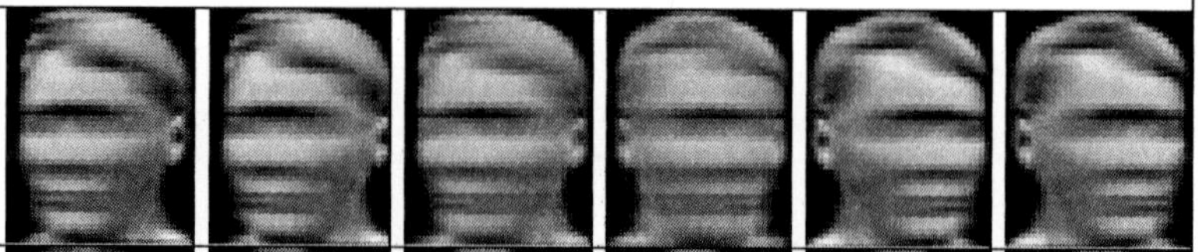
3	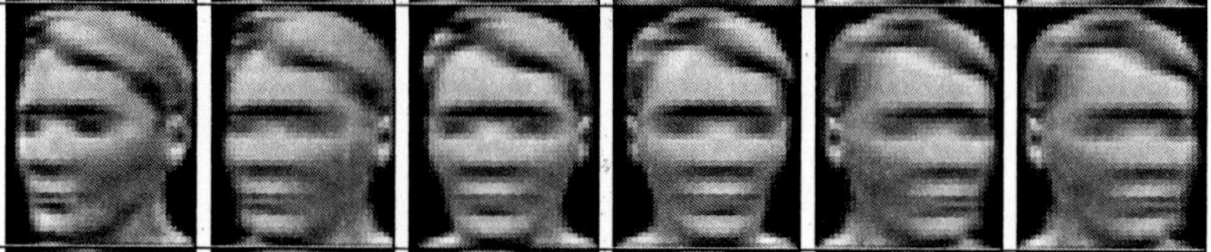
5	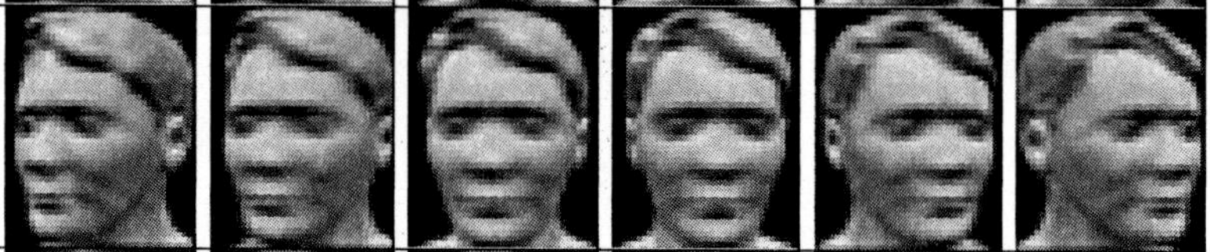
7	
9	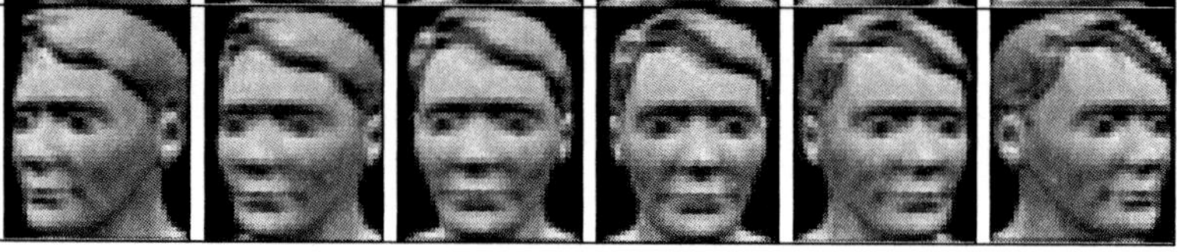

Fig. 12. Reconstruction results with use of different number of features.

REFERENCES

[1] G. Koukharev, A. Kuźmiński: *Biometric techniques part I – methods for face recognition,* *(currently in polish only)* – Faculty of Computer Science & Information Systems, Technical University of Szczecin, Szczecin, Poland, 2003

[2] G. Koukharev, A. Tujaka: *Pattern Recognition Methods for Visitor Identification and Access Control* – Proceedings of Sixth International Conference Pattern Recognition and Information Processing (PRIP '2001), May 2001, Minsk, Republic of Belarus, pp. 19-34

[3] G. Koukharev, P. Forczmański, P. Kraszewski, T. Bryłka, T. Ponikowski: *Realtime face recognition system for personal identification*; Proceedings of Advanced Computer Systems '99, Faculty of Computer Science & Information Systems, Technical University of Szczecin, Szszecin, Poland, November 1999

[4] W. Zhao, A. Krishnaswamy, R. Chellappa, D. L. Swets, J. Weng: *Discriminant analysis of principal components for face recognition*; Proceedings of the NATO Advanced Study Institute to Applications, Stirling, Scotland, UK, 1997

[5] G. L. Marcialis, F. Roli: *Fusion of LDA and PCA for face recognition*; Roli LNCS 2359, p. 30

[6] F. De la Torre, M. J. Black: *Robust principal component analysis for computer vision*; ICCV 2001: p. 362-369

[7] A. Pentland, B. Moghaddam, T. Starner: *View-based and modular eigenspaces for face recognition*; IEEE Conf. on Computer Vision & Pattern Recognition, Seattle, WA, July 1994

[8] L. Zhao, Y. Yang: On illumination effects in PCA-based vision system; June 23, 1997. (to appear in *Pattern Recognition*).

[9] R. Zhang, P. Tsai, J. Cryer, M. Shah: *Shape from shading: A survey*; IEEE Transactions on Pattern Analysis and Machine Intelligence, Volume 21, Number 08, August, 1999, pp 690-706

[10] Berthold K.P. Horn: *Height and gradient from shading*, International Journal of Computer Vision, Vol. 5, No. 1, pp. 37-75, August 1990

[11] M. Shah, P. Tsai: *A fast linear shape from shading*; CVPR92(734-736). IEEE Site Version

[12]W. Y. Zhao, R. Chellappa: *SFS based view synthesis for robust face recognition*; 4th IEEE Conference on Automatic Face and Gesture Recognition, Grenoble, France, 2000, pp. 285-292

[13] M. Watanebe, S. K. Nayar: *Rational filters for passive depth from defocus*; International Journal of Computer Vision, Vol. 27, No. 3, p. 203-225, 1998

[14] P. Favaro: *Shape from focus/defocus*; Washington University 2000

[15] A. Mennucci, S. Soatto: *On observing shapes from defocused images*; Proc. of the IEEE. Conf. on Image Analysis and Processing, 1999

[16] S. Baker, R. Szeliski, P. Anandan: *A layered approach to stereo reconstruction*; Conference on Computer Vision and Pattern Recognition, Santa Barbara, CA, June 1998.

[17] D. Scharstein, R. Szeliski: *A taxonomy and evaluation of dense two-frame stereo correspondence algorithms*; IJCV, 2002

[18] D. Scharstein: *Stereo vision for view synthesis*; IEEE CVPR' 96, pp.852-858

[19] G. Wolberg: *Image morphing – a survey;* The Visual Computer (1998) 14:360-372 , Springer-Verlag 1998

[20] J. Gomes, T. Beier, B. Costa, L. Darsa, L. Velho: *Warping and morphing of graphical objects*; Course notes – SIGGRAPH 1997

[21] Stephen J. McKenna, Shaogang Gong: *Realtime face pose estimation;* Department of Applied Computing, University of Dundee, Dundee DD1 4HN, Scotland; Department of Computer Science, Queen Mary and westfield College, London, England

[22] S.J. McKenna: *View-based estimation of head pose;* Tech. Rep. IA377656, BR, Advanced perception, BT Labs., Martlesham Heath, England, 1996

[23] M.Turk. A. Pentland: *Eigenfaces for recognition; J.of cognitive neuroscience, Vol. 3, No. 1, 1991*

[24] D.J. Beymer: *Face recognition under varying pose;* AI Memo 1491, MIT, Cambridge Massachussettes, 1993

[25] Rein-Lein Hsu, Anil K. Jain: *Face modeling for recognition;* Dept. of Computer Science and Engineering, Michigan State University, MI 48824

Investigation of fingerprint verification algorithm based on local centers method

EDWARD PÓŁROLNICZAK

Technical University of Szczecin, Faculty of Computer Science
e-mail: epolrolniczak@wi.ps.pl

Abstract: There is a lot of fingerprint verification methods proposed in scientific articles. They consist of many stages. One of them is pattern matching. Usually matching needs high computing power, and it is highly complex. In this article method of minutia patterns matching using local centers is investigated. Some results and conclusions are presented.

Key words: fingerprints, matching, minutiae, verification

1. REVIEW FINGERPRINT VERIFICATION ALGORITHMS

Many of fingerprint verification algorithms have been proposed in the literature. Fingerprint can be treated as the pattern of ridges on the surface of fingertip. This structure is formed in the fetal period and is not changing during human life.

There are several well-known properties of fingerprints:
- structure of ridges have different characteristic for different fingerprints,
- configuration of details is an individual characteristic,
- configurations of ridges and details are permanent and don't change with time except of scratches, scarring and injury.

The uniqueness of fingerprints is determined by local ridge characteristic - minutiaes. There are many minutiae details identified in ridges lines characteristic. Such characteristics can be for example the ridge endings and the ridge bifurcations. There are available a few standards of verification depending on those features. The American National Standards Institute uses for types of minutiaes: ridge ending, bifurcation, trifurcation and undetermined [4]. The Federal National Bureau of Investigation uses only two features: endings and bifurcations [3], but that model is the most popular in fingerprint verification systems.

To detect minutiaes many approaches have been proposed. Usually these approaches consist of a series of processing operations. There can be specified main following steps:
−   preprocessing of fingerprint image,
−   extraction of features,
−   matching step.

In preprocessing step very important is to clarify visibility of ridge lines − then extraction of features will be more precise and number of extracted false features will be minimized. To achieve this goal many filtration methods have been proposed:
−   bandpass filtration,
−   contextual/directional filter,
−   directional Fourier transform filter [8],
−   Gabor filters [7], and other approaches.

Extraction of features can be then done. Also to extract minutiaes can be use different approaches. There are two main ways to extract minutiaes I have found in literature:
−   first called by me "multi-step" minutiaes extraction, and
−   second which I called "all-in-one-step" minutiaes extraction.
−   First type of extraction of features consists of series steps. These are mainly:
−   binarization done on filtrated fingerprint image, and then
−   thinning, which produces image of one-pixel-wide ridge lines.
−   Usually on such prepared image it is easy to find minutiaes, which are simply points where lines of ridges connects or ends.

The second method of features extraction depends on fact that in "multi-step" method usually different calculations are performed separately still on the same set of pixels (one pixel is taken into account few times). In "all-in-one-step" method different calculations connected into one operation are performed for each pixel of fingerprint image [1].

In this place I want to stress that in both methods there is present very important filtration step. Without this step results may strongly vary depending on finger and environment conditions.

After minutiaes are extracted matching can be performed. Also there are many matching algorithms. Matching algorithms usually consists in few steps. The most important is to find reverse transformation. After the transformation parameters are found patterns can be simply aligned and common minutiaes can be counted.

Describing these methods is beyond the scope of this section and can be found in referenced literature.

2. METHODOLOGY OF MINUTIA PATTERN MATCHING ALGORITHM INVESTIGATION

In the previous part it's been told that fingerprint recognition methods consists of several elements. In some approaches the main stages are operations aimed at minutiae extraction (with stages: quality enhancement, thresholding, thinning, searching for minutiae), minutiae pattern matching.

It is important, to choose methods of matching minutiae patterns, that can be efficient in distorted images. The distortions are caused by many factors:

— poor quality of fingerprint scanner,
— bad condition of fingertip,
— negligent process of image acquisition,
— wrong chosen algorithms of image enhancement effecting in introducing false minutiae despite image quality improvement.

The goal of the procedure described in this part is to determine conditions of generating synthetic series of minutiae patterns with controlled distortions reflecting the real ones. The patterns generated automatically allow testing in simple way algorithms of minutiae patterns matching and defining their ability of functioning in noised conditions. The procedure would allow defining typical rates of recognition, like FAR and FRR, but also conditions (level of distortions) in which given parameters will be obtained. It will also allow specifying how the speed of increasing distortions increases error recognition rate. It will allow to find algorithm resistance to distortions.

In the following part of the article the method of generating synthetic minutiae pattern will be described. Next the algorithm of minutia pattern matching and the procedure of testing of minutia pattern matching algorithm will be presented. Finally the results of the investigation will be put forward.

3.   GENERATING OF DISTORTED TEST MINUTIAE PATTERNS

Synthetic generated patterns have to undergo the same modifications as in real fingerprint images. The following are the most important of them:

— rotations of the whole patterns (global rotations),
— translations of the patterns,
— small changes of global scale (don't have to be taken into account),
— local shift groups of points (in order to simplify the model they will not be taken into account – they will be included in local shifts of particular minutiae),
— shifts of single minutia by random number of pixels,
— rotations of minutiae by random angle,
— a change of minutiae type,
— hiding of minutia (minutiae may vanish – they may not be localised),
— appearance of new minutiae (called false minutiae, in natural conditions introduced in stage before minutia pattern extraction.

Each of the minutiae patterns will be characterised by following variables:

— GROT – global rotation of pattern according to orientation of original pattern,
— GTRNS – global shift of pattern,
— GSCALE – change of scale according to original pattern.

- Each minutia from pattern is described as following:
- LFI – local minutiae orientation,
- LX – co-ordinate X of minutia,
- LY – co-ordinate Y of minutia,
- LTYPE – minutia type: "1" means ridge ending, "2" means ridge bifurcation.

Some of those modifications resulting in appearing and disappearing of minutiae on space of minutiae pattern. During generating of synthetic patterns coefficients regulating level of distortions will be set up. Those coefficients will make possibly to check influence of distortions on Recognition Rate of tested matching algorithm:

- random chosen tolerance of magnitude of global rotation - GROTTOL – it will simulate rotation of real finger during acquisition,
- tolerance of global shift – GTRNSTOL – it will simulate shift of real finger according to scanner, random chosen quantity from specified range,
- tolerance of global scale – GSCALETOL – simulating shift of real finger according to scanner, random chosen quantity from specified range,
- magnitude of local rotation – LROTTOL – simulating distortions of detected orientation of minutia, random chosen quantity from specified range,
- tolerance of magnitude of local shift – LTRNSTOL – simulating distortions of detected location of minutia, random chosen quantity from specified range,
- value LCHANGE specifying in percents how many minutiae should be of other type that the real one (present in reference pattern),
- value LDISAPPEAR specifying in percents how many real minutiae should be lost (disappear) proportionally to reference pattern,
- value LFALSE specifying in percents how many false minutiae should appear proportionally to reference pattern.

Which minutiae should disappear, change their type or where false minutiae should appear is also random chosen.

All simulations will be carried out in Matlab environment – making an assumption that time of execution could be neglected at this stage. Each one of generated patterns will be saved at separate file, it means every file will contain description of reference pattern and patterns originating from it. Files will form series of patterns reflecting modifications of the same file.

In classic fingerprint pattern number of minutiae range from dozen to over hundred. Number of minutiae detected by system depends on several factors:

- what minutiae are searched by system – only basic or complex too,
- what area is covered by searching (ultrasound scanners cover the widest area),
- what algorithms have been used to improve quality and expose minutiae (some algorithms introduce false minutiae and other cause disappearing of real ones),
- what has been condition of finger before acquisition,
- what are the individual features of finger's owner.

However systems assume automatically that there is a minimal number of minutiae in pattern requisite for identification – usually about dozen.

In the presented system minutiae are generated so that number of them in generated pattern average 100.

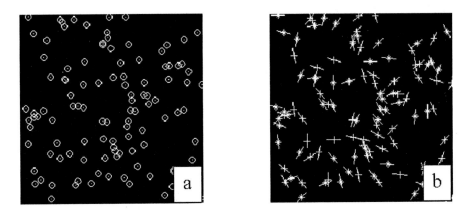

Fig.1. Generated minutiae pattern (a) and its features (b)

The figure above shows an example of generated set of data. In the left picture position of minutiae are shown (points inclosed in circles), in the right picture there are shown all parameters characterising minutia: position, orientation and type.

Minutiae generated in this way don't meet one assumption present in real patterns – changes of minutiae orientation are limited in their surroundings. However because it seems that algorithms operating at this model all the more will operate at less restricted real model the fact of limited orientation changes in local surroundings will be neglected.

4. REVIEW OF MINUTIAE PATTERN MATCHING METHODS

Samples of data generated according to the criteria presented before will serve for the purpose of comparing efficiency of various minutiae pattern-matching methods.

Analysis of minutiae pattern matching methods leads to a conclusion that these standard patterns are initially treated globally to find global transformations (rotations, shifts and scale changes). Just in the next step when global transformations are known the operation of patterns alignment is executed and the assessment of fingerprints resemblance is made at this moment. In the simplest way it's investigated for tested fingerprint if there exist a minutia with orientation and type like for reference fingerprint (stored in base) in given location (with a certain tolerance) [2]. The given tolerance serves the purpose of FAR (False Acceptance Rate) and RR (Recognition Rate) adjusting. Increasing tolerance ratio causes decrease in algorithm restriction what's connected with FAR increasing but also enables considerable RR increase and FRR (False Reject Rate) decrease. The FRR sense is that in case of its high value system is difficult in use requiring from a user repeated attempts of fingerprint scanning. In the consequence at given allowable number of failures user might be rejected by system and treated like an intruder.

An attempt of reducing tolerance ratio influence is applying additional techniques at minutiae patterns matching. One of the most known techniques is DP (Dynamic Programming) [4] which enables reduce influence of local distortions. Specifying cost of distortions leading to optimal solution makes assessment of resemblance in this case. Obviously the parameter describing cost of distortion serves estimating similarity level and its value exceeding established threshold will effect in rejection of tested fingerprint as the one that doesn't match.

Another issue, not described in this paper, is necessity of pattern alignment before matching. Hough Transform for example is used for this purpose [4]. This method based on maximal value in so-called accumulator permits determination of approximate value of global transformations. Another approach uses set of fingerprint formations for example delta, arc and loop for pattern alignment. Unfortunately its localisation is not always possible.

In present paper results of minutiae patterns matching investigation based on concept of local centres will be presented.

5. LOCAL CENTRES METHOD

This method has been constructed basing on approach presented in article [3]. Presented results lead to the conclusion that it's fairly promising method. Differing from methods discussed before the method stands a good chance to become irrespective of distortion influence caused for example by uneven press of finger. It's based on fact that every minutia with its surroundings should retain most of interrelations of minutiae in vicinity. Minutiae situated in the centre of examined vicinity are called central minutiae and minutiae placed in surroundings of given radius are called neighbour minutiae. Every central minutia needs to have some given number of neighbours.

Examples of relations connecting both central minutiae and the neighbours (Fig. 2) are:
- distance between neighbours and the centre (in figure 2 indicated with c letter: $c=$ sqrt(a^2+2^2))[3],
- difference between orientation of central minutia and orientation of its neighbours ($\tilde{\alpha}\beta$),
- with some tolerance the types of minutiae in vicinity should be compatible [3],
- difference between θ and α ($\theta-\alpha$), where θ is an angle of line connecting central minutia with its neighbour, α is orientation of central minutia [3], the difference with the distance allow establish the location of minutia in surroundings: ($\theta=$atan(b/a)),
- number of minutiae in vicinity,
- number of fingerprint lines separating minutiae in surroundings and central minutiae.

Resemblance of minutia patterns establishing is executed in accordance with the following procedure.

Orientation of central minutia being the direction of a tangent to ridge line at which the minutia is located will be the element allowing alignment of surroundings from compared arrangements. It needs to be notified that 100% accuracy can't be expected because calculated directions can be distorted, but it's probable that there will be found minutiae which angle will be calculated relatively precisely. The next step after alignment is an attempt of finding neighbour minutia in vicinity from tested pattern in the distances the same as the ones memorised in vicinity from reference pattern of neighbour minutiae. Establishing of existence of minutiae runs clockwise and is combined with neighbour minutia orientation matching. Extent of resemblance above specified threshold in percentage terms is the base of acceptance of the local centre as identified. The next matching local centre is searched in the given distance, which is the multiple of maximal radius of the previously found local neighbour. Distances between identified local centres need to be similar in tested and reference pattern. After the next matching centre is found succeeding distances between identified local centres are matched. The process goes on until the specified number of identified local centres is found.

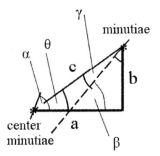

Fig.2. Relations connecting neighbour-minutiae and central-minutiae.

6. RESULTS OF CHOSEN METHOD INVESTIGATION

There are presented partial results below.

At the first I tried to investigate if I can compare two minutiae patterns simply by searching in patterns for similar minutiae neighbourhoods.

As it can be seen (and it isn't unusual) sometimes for one neighbourhood it can be found more than one similar neighbourhoods. But anyway as we can see it seems that we can compare minutiae patterns by counting similar neighbourhoods.

Similarity of patterns from one "synthetic fingerprint" is much bigger than similarity between two patterns, which belongs to different "synthetic fingerprints". At the end of the tables there is value called "Mean of PMVS", which describing similarity of extraneous patterns to tested patterns. It depends on number of features we will use to compare neighbourhoods. As we can suppose better results we can achieve using more features. In this case using 4 features (distance, type of minutia, angle of neighbour, relative angle of neighbour) I've received similarity of extraneous neighborhoods at level 0,06413 (1 means maximum similarity). Using 3 features I've received level of similarity of extraneous neighborhoods equal 0,26399 (Table.1). Using 1 feature I've obtained similarity level equal 0,796538 (Table.2), so one feature can't be used for minutiae pattern comparing (Table.3).

	1_0	2_0	3_0	4_0	5_0
1_0	1,06	0,0238	0	0,0638	0,12
...					
1_5	0,72	0,0476	0	0,0213	0,08
2_0	0,0476	1,4048	0,0714	0,2128	0,119
...					
2_5	0,0698	1,3488	0,0233	0,1277	0,2326
3_0	0	0,0714	1	0,0426	0
3_1	0,04	0,0238	0,5833	0	0
3_2	0,04	0,0476	0,9167	0,0213	0
3_3	0	0,0476	0,7692	0,0213	0,0417
3_4	0,04	0,0476	0,8462	0	0
3_5	0	0,0238	0,8182	0,0213	0
4_0	0,0638	0,1915	0,0426	1,2979	0,0638
...					
4_5	0,0444	0,2	0,0222	1,0851	0
5_0	0,12	0,119	0	0,0638	1,125
...					
5_5	0,04	0,1429	0	0,1277	0,8333
Mean value of similarity minutiae patterns from one simulated fingerprint (MVOS1)	0,735133	1,40735	0,822267	1,183433	0,94635
Mean value of similarity minutiae pattern according to others minutiae patterns (MVOS2)	0,057142	0,102796	0,020533	0,075371	0,076863
Percentage MVS1 in MVS2 (PMVS)	0,07773	0,073042	0,024972	0,063688	0,08122
Mean of PMVS	0,06413				

Table 1. Partial results of comparing of centres using 4 features
(columns: reference patterns, rows: tested patterns)

Mean value of similarity minutiae patterns from one simulated fingerprint (MVOS1)	0,9341	1,987617	0,844517	1,968833	1,133767
Mean value of similarity minutiae pattern according to others minutiae patterns (MVOS2)	0,264371	0,576913	0,147425	0,495563	0,363263
Percentage MVS1 in MVS2 (PMVS)	0,283022	0,290253	0,174567	0,251704	0,320403
Mean of PMVS	0,26399				

Table 2. Partial results of comparing of centres using 3 features

Mean value of similarity minutiae patterns from one simulated fingerprint (MVOS1)	10,4623	14,12523	4,7605	18,59287	10,65197
Mean value of similarity minutiae pattern according to others minutiae patterns (MVOS2)	8,734867	10,72716	4,676821	10,51684	8,950929
Percentage MVS1 in MVS2 (PMVS)	0,83489	0,759433	0,982422	0,565638	0,840308
Mean of PMVS	0,796538				

Table 3. Partial results of comparing of centres using 1 feature

7. CONLUSIONS AND FUTURE INVESTIGATIONS

Results show that use of very simple method enables fast and efficient minutia patterns matching. It's easy to see that efficiency depends on number of features taken into account. The method doesn't need high computing power and is very simple. Anyway that method should be extended using suggestions mentioned below.

In the future replacing of the distance between neighbour and the centre with number of lines separating these minutiae is planned. For this purpose change of the way of patterns for investigation generating or usage of programs for synthetic fingerprints generation and applying previous stage of features extraction will be necessary. In the next stage comparing of other minutiae patterns matching methods is planned with the purpose of determining possible improvement and applications of prepared algorithm. It's planned to create complete fingerprints matching system based on computably undemanding and efficient algorithms – to elaborate universal and effective system.

REFERENCES

[1] American National Standard Institute, Fingerprint Identification – Data Format for Information Interchange, New York, 1986

[2] Dario Maio, Davide Moltoni, Direct Gray-Scale Minutiae Detection in Fingerprints, IEEE Transactions On Pattern Analysis and Machine Intelligence, vol. 19, no. 1, January 1997

[3] Zsolt Miklos Kovacs-Vajna, A Fingerprint Verification System Based On Triangular Matching and Dynamic Time Warping, IEEE Transactions On Pattern Analysis and Machine Intelligence, vol. 22, no. 11, November 2000

[4] Anil K. Jain, Salil Prabhakar, Shaoyun Chen, Combining Multiple Matchers for a High Security Fingerprint Verification System, Pattern Recognition Letters, no. 20, 1999

Czestochowa's Precise Model of a Face Based on the Facial Asymmetry, Ophthalmogeometry, and Brain Asymmetry Phenomena: the Idea and Algorithm Sketch

LEONID KOMPANETS[1], MARIUSZ KUBANEK[2], SZYMON RYDZEK[3]
Technical University of Czestochowa, Institute of Computer & Information Sciences,
Dabrowskiego Street, 73, 42-200 Czestochowa, Poland
[1]*leonid.kompanets@icis.pcz.pl*
[2] *mariusz.kubanek@icis.pcz.pl*
[3]*szymon.rydzek@icis.pcz.pl*

Abstract: We have presented a precise model of a face, based on the latest knowledge of face asymmetry, ophthalmogeometry, brain hemispheres functioning asymmetry phenomena, and, in a sense, suited to the specification of the problem of the creation of modern and prospect person's authentication/identification information techniques in live biometrics and/or human-computer interaction, identification of cognition-psyche type of personality in human resource management, education, and so on.

The result of the creation and new ideas of development are presented: 1) a procedure of 2D normalization of a single 2D frontal view of a face image using a unit called the *Muld*, 2) an algorithm of person's ophthalmologic pattern visualization, 3) an algorithm of the synthesis of special pictures (composites) for face asymmetry characteristics evaluation, 4) a criterion and algorithm of precise mapping and evaluating the pseudo-informational similarity of compared objects in a holistic manner, 5) some theses concerning the cognition-psyche and interdisciplinary interpretation of gained information parameters. The above mentioned type of a face representation has been called *Czestochowa's face*. The model is aimed at being used in different modern areas: human-computer interactions, person live biometric authentication/ identification, person cognition-psyche type identification for human resource management and education, smart environment design, and other similar cutting-edge information technology applications.

Key words: Precise 2D model of human face, Face asymmetry, Ophthalmogeometry, Brain asymmetry, Information theoretic measure, Human-computer interaction, Live biometrics, Person's cognition-psyche type identification.

1.   GENERALIZED PROBLEM

In this paper, the result of initial development of a precise model of a human (asymmetrical) face taking into consideration the ophthalmogeometry, face asymmetry, and brain asymmetry phenomena are presented. The model development is concerned with the processing and interpretation of face and eyes part of facial image features as information resources in algorithmic manner.

However, there exist a few inter- and/or transdisciplinary „bottlenecks", which quantitatively hold back the development in a particular direction. 1) Informational objects, which are beginning to be dealt with, are „non-mathematical" and/or having intelligent behavior (Fig.1-4, 5-7) [12-18]. 2) The known models of face and head [1-3] built on the basis of the thesis of their geometric symmetry. (Having the author's evaluation done, the error of parameters measurement is raised by about 5-8% in comparison with the potential accurateness boarder.) 3) In the modern fields [7-12, 18] an interesting aspect is the cognition-psyche interpretation of the cognition information gained by means of traditional algorithmic methods.

During the creation of the model and its approval on the basis of pictures of about 100 people, the described problems were successfully solved to some extent. Below in the form of a sketch the result of the study is presented. The lack of space allows only to focus on the graphic and algorithmic means of contents transmission.

2.   "NON-MATHEMATICAL" AND/OR INTELLIGENT INFORMATION OBJECTS

Advanced modern problems, for instance for our examples, have produced some new scientific issues that cannot be solved by means of known classical mathematic and information methods.

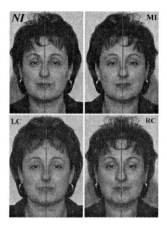

Fig. 1-2, 3-4 Results of calculating "truthful" vertical facial axis *Y* of asymmetrical face and synthesizing *NI*-, MI-, LC-, RC-images (natural and mirrored images; left/left and right/right composites)

(Manhattan, New York City, 2002,   Copenhagen)

Fig.5-7 Examples of "non mathematical", intelligent, and metaphorical information objects

The objects have been called by me "non- mathematical" and/or "having intelligent behaviour". Examples of the objects are face, voice, human silhouette, and others that are observed in the context of emotional, behavioural, psychological, communicational, metaphorical peculiarities. Features of such objects characterize principal non-traditional changeability of their forms and colours, elasticity, *n*-dimensionality, natural intelligent behaviour. The mentioned specific character is the reason why some scientists are particularly changing an existing scientific paradigm [7-9, 12, 18]. Indicators of such a change are, for example, usage of analytic-to-holistic approach in reception applications [3], organization of transdisciplinary meeting [18].

3. NOTION OF PSEUDO-INFORMATION SIMILA-RITY OF OBJECTS IN HOLISTIC MANNER

Main procedure of any communication-information technique is the measuring of meaningful similarity of two information objects. Traditional mathematical measures of nearness are not adequate to any psycho-physiologic or cognition measures that are used by human being. The fundamental reason for the existence of such situation is connected with the phenomenon that the well-known Weber-Fechner law describes. A human being perceives images into psycho-physiological space, but not physical one, and in a holistic manner, but not in an algorithmic one.

In [15], it was proved that the pseudo-information measure (1) is an effective tool for a holistic similarity evaluation and the measure advantages were presented. The functional for the new measure (1), which is used in the paper presents below.

$$\pm JeK^{(Z)} \left[PDF(\sum_{z=1}^{Z} F_i^{(Z)}); PDF(\sum_{z=1}^{Z} L_i^{(Z)}) \right] = \frac{\sum_{i,z} [f_i^{(z)} - l_i^{(z)}] \log_2 [f_i^{(z)} / l_i^{(z)}]}{-\sum_{i,z} f_i^{(z)} \log_2 f_i^{(z)} - \sum_{i,z} l_i^{(z)} \log_2 l_i^{(z)}} 100 \qquad (1)$$

where: $F_i = f\{f_1,...,f_I\}$, $L_i = \{l_1,...,l_I\}$ – basic (*F*) and comparing (*L*) functions (for example, sample sequences or images, correlation or other functions, *pdf*s (a probability density function), etc.) that answer requirements of *pdf*; *I*, $i=1,...,I$ – grid, on which values of the functions *F, L* are formed; *Z, z=1,...,Z* – a number of comparing objects components (five components in Fig.25); ±*JeK* – the sign that identifies a situation, when a default basic function is *F* – (+), and, on the contrary - (-).

In the numerators, the functionals for G. Jeffrey's divergences are placed. Shannon's entropies of suitable functions *F* and *L* are used in the denominators. Peculiarities of the measures are described in [15]. In an area of little deviations, the *JeK* values may be described by a linearized function and interpreted as cybernetic similarity of complex information objects. The usage of the logarithmic function conforms psycho-physiological properties of human reception (Weber-Fechner law).

To generalize the content of statistical information notions such as entropy, information, divergence to non-probabilistic cases, the two compared functions *F(.)* and *L(.)*, which may have any nature, must possess formal properties of a traditional *pdf*. This means that the functions *F(.)* and *L(.)* must be normalized under the mentioned demands (marked as *PDF[F], PDF[L]*). Contents of statistical information notions are preserved and common interpretation may be expanded to any nature functions. Furthermore, mathematical and rich in content complications may be avoided.

An advantage of the measure (1) is the fact that *PDF[.]*-function can describe the whole object or set of its components. In (1), the mentioned *PDF*-function vectors have been combined by *Z* suitable vector components. If the vector components are independent, then an additive property of the measure is guaranteed by using the logarithmic function. By means of the (1), it is possible to evaluate cybernetic similarity of two objects of any nature that are considered both monolith objects, and objects consisting of its components (Fig.25). G. Jeffrey's divergence is used in constructions of (1) as the basic element. The areas of usage, content, context and properties of the divergence are expanded and improved essentially.

The main problem of an application of (1) concerns the art of content-related and exact *F* and *L* vectors extraction.

4. ON THE NOVEL TYPE OF BIOMETRICS AND ON COGNITION-PSYCHE CONSTRUCT

In the fields of live biometrics, psychological personality type testing, mental abilities testing, objective diagnostics of feelings and sensations or psychological/somatic diseases, and identification nationality study, the only subject is a human being. That is why the inter- and/or transdisciplinary approach is required.

In modern biometrics, only physiological and behavioral biometrics are used, to state it vividly, human „traces". Such characteristics can be measured. In psychological testing the so called psychological constructs are observed [10, 9, 13], instrumental measurement of which is, in traditional sense, impossible, or contently complicated. Principally, the extension of biometrics set can be realized in the following directions: 1) extension of „traces" (physiological and behavioral) to new „traces" biometrics, 2) extension with cognitive-psychological biometrics, in which the notion of psychological construct is used, 3) interdisciplinary fusion of physiological-behavioral and cognitive-psychological characteristics. The present work as well as [12-18] attempts at realization of the listed directions.

5. PERSON OPHTHALMOLOGIC PATTERN AND SKETCH OF ITS VISUALIZING ALGORITHM

The ophthalmogeometry phenomenon was invented by Ernst Muldashev just recently [8]. In Fig.8 (fragment *e*), the object of the first study is presented. The object is a set of peculiarities of a person's ophthalmogeometric pattern. The paper is aimed at working out an algorithm of pattern's precise visualization and interpretation in the above enumerated fields. According to [8], person's psychological and other states are described with 22 parameters of an eyes part of face. We use information that is included in some planar figures, which are produced with tangents of four eye corners, appropriate eye silhouettes, wrinkles over eyes, and other facial elements. The *only constant of a human being organism* after 4-5 years old is his/her cornea (iris) diameter, which is equaled $10\pm0,56$ mm [8, p.14].

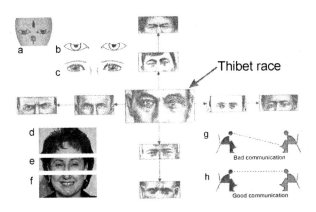

Fig. 8. Illustration of a preliminary idea of the ophthalmogeometry phenomenon [8]. (The Tibet human race has statistic average ophthalmo-geometric parameters; 35 races traced back to Tibet race migrated in four directions. *c* – The scheme of a modern human's eyes, *e* – an ophthalmogeometric part of a face, *h* – crucial communicative information contained in the eye *e*-sphere of the facer.)

An example of an ophthalmogeometric pattern is given in Fig.9-10. The sequence of calculating steps is as follows.

IN: 2D single frontal view facial image.

OUT: Person's ophthalmogeometric pattern.

Step **1.** Find the placement of circles described around the eyes cornea (iris) and measure the amount of pixels that constitutes 1 *Muld* (Fig.9).

Step **2.** Build a coordinate system $Y^*-O^*-X^*$ (Fig.9) and the figure $1^*,2^*,3^*,4^*$. If points 1* and 3* are placed on the Y-line, ***then***

Step **3.** Measure the *Base 1* and memorize in *Muld*s the primary ophthalmologic pattern.

Step **4.** Build the external figures 1,2,3,4 and internal – 5,6,7,8, the triangles $5,8,8^*$ and $5,6,6^*$, 3,14,15, the angle 10,9,12 (Fig.10).

Step **5.** Find point 9 which corresponds to *O1*.

Step **6.** Find the system $Y-O1-X1-O2-X2$ (Fig.9). Distance between points O1 and O2 equals **4,75 *Muld*s.**).

Step **7**. Fit the ophthalmogeometric coordinate system Y^*-O^*-X^* and face asymmetry system Y-$O1$-$X1$-$O2$-$X2$.

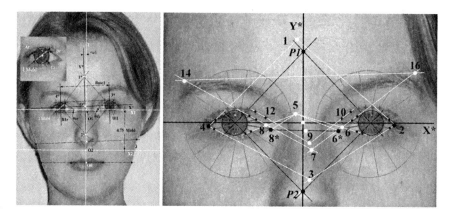

Fig.9-10 Illustration of the preparatory and content-related stages of an ophthalmogeometrical pattern visualization

6.   EXAMPLES AND PROPERTIES OF THE OPHTHALMOGEOMETRIC PATTERN

Below, the examples of patterns for a person observed in different emotional states, as well as for their relatives and person's age are presented.

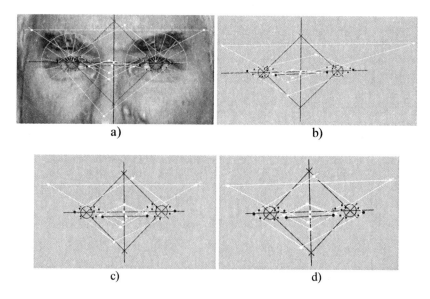

Fig. 11-12, 13-14 Example of an ophthalmogeometric pattern for different emotional facial states of the same person: a) –neutral, b) – smiling, c) – surprised, d) – angry

The results of the preliminary experience of the ophthalmogeometric idea allow to state that: 1) an ophthalmogeometric pattern is individual and contains original information about a person (Fig.18-21), 2) the ophthalmologic method can be effectively realized algorithmically, 3) the new type of face image normalization has many advantages, 4) an ophthalmogeometric pattern of a person does not change its topological features (Fig.11-14), 5) it not depends on family relations (Fig.15-17).

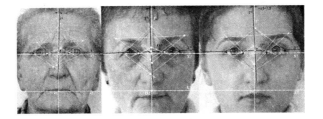

Fig.15-17 Example of the normalized ophthalmologic patterns for grandmother (84), mother (54), and daughter (24)

(5 years old) ←The person's images→ (25 years old)

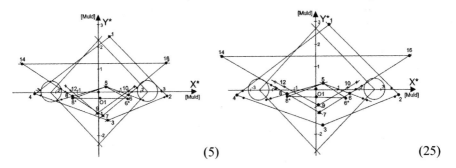

Fig.18 19, 20-21 Example of an ophthalmogeometric pattern for the same person having 5 and 25 years old

7.   ON FACE ASYMMETRY AND ON BRAIN
ASYMMETRY PHENOMENA

The serious research of thinking mechanisms and psyche may be done only on the basis of usage and transdisciplinary interpretation of information (knowledge) metabolism principle. As proved in practice, the cognitive approach of C. Jung [10, 9] for creating typology of personality, based on a person perception and decision procedures properties, has been a most productive one (above 17000 scientific works on this theme; well-known I. Myers-Briggs's person typology). However, then (C. Jung's time) the phenomenon of brain asymmetry was not yet known. Now, the knowledge of asymmetry of the functions of brain hemispheres [4, 5, 10, 11] is practically not used. Many scientists use the term „left-, and right-hemisphere thinker" or „left-, right-brained thinker" [11] on the non-formal level. Nonetheless, a more productive, synergic and effective thinking or research team may be synthesized in the manner that the SCI-Conference metaphor [18].

Face asymmetry phenomenon was known long ago and researched by painters, psychologists and other specialists of this kind. In live biometrics, psychological testing, human resources management, the phenomenon is not widely used. At the moment, the interesting interpretation of facial asymmetry is based on the technical and/or psychological formalization of the brain hemispheres asymmetry phenomenon, being dealt with in [9].

The idea of face asymmetry phenomenon usage as biometrics came to the first author's mind while getting familiarized with [13] in New York in March 2002. It's first presentation with the slide session was realized by the author during the oral presentations [17]. The materials [6, 9] were found in the Internet later on. In this article the connected model, algorithmic and some developmental procedures concerning both techniques are presented.

At the moment, two *quantitative* approaches to the face asymmetry phenomenon usage has been presented: 1) the direction [6] that is based on the traditional biometric methods, and 2) A. Anuashvili's oryginal hypothesis and method [9] that is based on the original model of the brain hemispheres asymmetry functioning and some new hypotheses. According to [9] interpretation, a man possesses two bases: 1) spirit, intuition (I) - principles of life (things obtained by man from nature – from God and from his ancestors, and 2) mind, logic (L) - personal manifestations in real life at a certain moment. To fulfill the purpose of life that consists of a creative spirit and vital energy for the future, it is necessary to achieve harmony (H) between these two bases. If the harmony of the spirit and mind is disturbed (D), there appears dissoluteness either in mind or spirit. If the harmony of the spirit and mind is not disturbed, a man is in a stable (S) state. The concrete type is identified by a set of parameters in coordinates {I-L, S-D}. There are 49 established types.

The model has been constructed as a model of a dynamic system, in which two coherent harmonic processes exist. These can simulate a cooperative work of two hemispheres. A difference (ΔA) of the two harmonic process amplitudes and a coefficient of coherence (C) are the outputs of the model. A coefficient harmony (H) of a personality is calculated. Two hemispheres accomplish quite different functions: the right hemisphere is responsible for intuition (spirit), while the left one is responsible for logic (mind). Anuashvili has ascertained that the cerebral asymmetry is displayed on a person's face in quite a definite manner). On this base, two new images - person's face composites, may be synthesized. The first image – *spiritual* portrait - reveals spirit, intuition, principles of life (i.e. things given to the human beings by nature). The second image – *life* portrait – reveals the mind, logic, and personal manifestation in real life at the moment. On the basis of information which is included in the portraits Anuashvili's type of personality is identified by means of an original (!?) algorithm. Main advantage of Anuashvili's method is that it is one of the primary instrumental psychological methods concerning the examination of brain asymmetry phenomena and face asymmetry in various applications. Besides, some examples of personality type identification by means of [9] will be used in our work to verify the results gained on the basis of images processing taking into consideration the face asymmetry information and the ophthalmogeometric pattern (for example, a thesis about using the point 3 as an indicator of the prevailing hemisphere).

8. PRINCIPLES OF *MULD*-NORMALIZATION AND FACIAL IMAGES SIMILARITY EVALUATION

Following thesis that the results of brain hemispheres functioning are displayed on a face in a complicated manner, there is much sense in executing the experience of the face asymmetry effect. The basic and necessary element of such examination is the synthesis of precise model for mapping (asymmetric) face and evaluating the informational properties of a face or set of facial components in a holistic manner.

The object of examination is anthropological peculiarities of person's facial asymmetry phenomenon. The paper aim is to work out the *Muld*-normalization procedure and an algorithm for facial images similarity evaluation as well as interpretation of these results in terms of person's authentication/identification in live biometric applications and person's cognition-psyche type identification.

During problem solving process several new ideas were used:

1) 2D facial image *Muld*-normalization, which is based on the 1 *Muld* unit usage.
2) Determining the „truthful" vertical axis Y of a face.
3) Synthesis of the coordinate system $Y\text{-}O1\text{-}X1\text{-}O2\text{-}X2$ that retains an accurate mapping of the compared faces and/or their component sets, and the virtual ophthalmogeometric coordinate system $Y^*\text{-}O^*\text{-}X^*$.
4) Face composites synthesis.
5) Creation of a map for face/components features and state-of-the-art vectors F and L forming (see (1)).
6) The choice or creation of a measure for holistic evaluation of faces similarity in respect of the human psycho-physiological reception properties.
7) The examination of informational marginal and joint properties of the ophthalmogeometry, face asymmetry, and brain asymmetry phenomena
8) Development of the algorithmic procedure of evaluation and interpretation of human testing characteristics in respect of cognition-psyche context.
9) Developmental problems.

The sequences of calculating and interpretation steps may be understudied from paper's illustrations.

9. EXAMPLES OF THE CZESTOCHOWA-FACES

The woman's and man's facial images in Fig.22-23 have been represented in a form called *Czestochowa-face images*, that is:

1. After carrying out the special normalization in the *Muld* scale (the value of cornea diameter is the only known constant of human body after 4-5 years old).

2. Taking into consideration the discoveries of the ophthalmogeometry, brain asymmetry phenomena and problem of their interpretation in live biometrics and psychological testing.

3. Presenting the possibility of exact facial image mapping and/or its proper component sets in the *uniformed absolute* measure values scale.

4. Enabling the algorithmic (automatic) execution of comparing procedures.

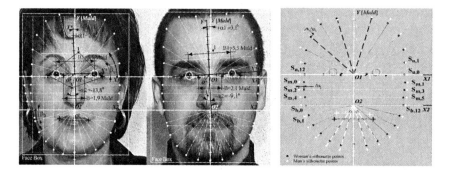

Fig.22-23 and *24* Example of the *Czestochowa-faces* (an illustration of the *Muld*-normalization procedure and an operation of a *Face_Box* area determining) as well as mapping procedure for these Czestochowa-faces silhouettes similarity evaluation

In Fig.24, the result of the *Muld*-normalization and mapping two facial images for *F* -, *L*-vector extraction and similarity evaluation (see (1)) of the facial silhouettes is given. Dashed lines are used to indicate not visible silhouette points. Woman's and man's facial images are mapped, *F*-, *L*-vector extracted, and pseudo-information similarity evaluation of facial silhouettes done. According to (1), *JeK* (*F, L*) = **- 0,0927**.

10. EXAMPLES OF FACE SIMILARITY EVALUATION

Values of pseudo-information similarity for the pairs of *NI*-face and MI-face, LC-face and RC-face silhouettes (Fig.1-4) are given in Table 1.

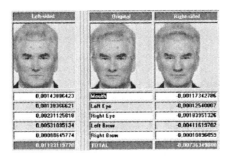

Fig.25 Result of the pseudo-information similarity evaluation of original (natural) and left/left and right/right composites for a case of facial components *Z*=5. (The values must be multiplied by 100, see (1))

11. MAIN STUDY RESULT

On the base of the study, the following *theses* have been accepted:

1. An existing range of experience into live biometrics, in which the *only* physiologic and behavioral human being characteristics are used, must be expanded to natural range, that is some cognition-psyche constructs must necessarily be used.

2. Face asymmetry and eyes part of face characteristics can be used as live biometrics. The characteristics are sources of unique ("poor") signals for psychoanalysis, management, and other techniques.

3. The known face models in artificial intelligence, virtual reality, biometrics, are based on the idea of symmetry of both face and head. In traditional applications, it is the cause of geometric errors of about 5-8%.

4. The novel pseudo-information technique for measuring similarity of a pair of complex objects (asymmetrical faces, face emotional states) is effective and understandable for any engineer, especially in communication/multimedia apps.

In the paper, the *result* of an initial development of the theses is presented.

A. The novel 2D 9asymmetrical) face model, based on a single frontal view, has been created. Two main problems of the creation are: *a1)* finding the "truthful" vertical axis on person's face image, *a2)* creating the combined coordinate system *Y-O1-X1-O2-X2* for the *Muld-normalization* of two any sets of facial components.

B. Basic markers, points, facial elements and their combinations that are representative from anthropological/psychological point of view and can be found in automated modes have been defined. The main novelty is the introduction of a unit called 1 *Muld* for 2D facial image normalization.

C. The novel pseudo-information criterion $\pm JeK^{\Sigma}[.]$ have been constructed to measure a similarity value of a pair of compared "non-mathematical" and/or intelligence information objects in holistic manner.

D. The algorithms of measuring pseudo-information similarity of asymmetrical faces and visualizing of ophthalmogeometric pattern have been created and approbated.

E. During examination of the ophthalmogeometry and face asymmetry phenomena properties, interesting hypotheses appeared. For example, we can suspect that the ophthalmogeometric point 3 is an indicator of the „left- or right-sided" thinker.

F. The interesting peculiarities of the facial asymmetry and ophthalmogeometry phenomena have been noticed: uniqueness of the face asymmetry and ophthalmogeometry characteristics; topologic non-changeability of person's ophthalmogeometric pattern; using point 3 as an indicator of the dominant brain hemisphere; uniqueness of face image normalization using the *Muld*-scale.

12. CONCLUSION

A novel 2D face model and algorithm for precise mapping and facial images comparing have been devised from the basics for the needs of modern and far-reaching techniques in the fields of live biometrics, artificial intelligence, psychological testing, personality types identification, and so on.

The face images, called *Czestochowa-faces* were presented in this form in analogy to the existing types of Fisher-, Eigen-. Chernoff-, Wavelet-faces. In respect to the fact that this model regards the modern knowledge about face asymmetry phenomena, brain asymmetry and ophthalmogeometry, as well as having the new possibility of precise and scaled in the *Mulds* asymmetric faces mapping, this model can be classified as an interdisciplinary facial model of a new generation.

ACKNOWLEDGEMENTS

This work is sponsored by Polish State Committee for Scientific Research under Grant No. 4T11C 00325.

REFERENCES

[1] Pentland Alex: "Looking at People: Sensing for Ubiquitous and Wearable Computing". Pattern Recognition and Machine Analysis (*PAMI*), vol. 22, No 1, Jan. 2000, 107-119
[2] "Research Videos". Avail.at http://seeingmachines.com/videos/research
[3] Lam Kim-Man, Yan Hong: "An Analytic-to-Holistic Approach for Face Recognition Based on a Single Frontal View", *PAMI*, vol. 20, No 7, July 1998, 673-686
[4] Carter Rita: Mapping the Mind. California, 1998
[5] Gazzaniga Michael: „The Split Brain Revisited", *Scientific American*, July 1998, 34-39
[6] Liu Y., Weaver R. L., et al.: „Facial Asymmetry: A New Biometric". CMU, 2001. Avail. at http://www.ri.cmu.edu/projects/project_437.html

[7] Grof Stanislav: *Beyond the Brain: Birth, Death and Transcendence in Psychotherapy.* State University of New York Press, 1985

[8] Muldashev E.: *Whom did we descend from?*, OLMA, Moscow 2002 (In Russian)

[9] Anuashvili A.: *Fundamentals of Psychology. Scientific, Philosophic and Spiritual Fundamentals of Psychology.* The Institute for Control Problems, Moscow 2001 (In Russian)

[10] Anastasi Anna, Urbina Susan: *Psychological Testing.* Prentice-Hall, Inc., 1997

[11] "Psycho-Geomertics[tm]". Dr Susan Dellinger Home Page. Avail. at http://www.drsusan.net

[12] Kompanets Leonid, Valchuk Tetiana: "Biometric Methods for Natural Intelligence Testing: S. Dellinger's Geometrical Approach, and T. Valchuk's Mental One", Proc. Intern. Conf. IT FORUM. SECURE 2002, Warsaw, 6-7 November 2002, *NASK and MULTICOPY Press*, vol. 1, 87-95

[13] Kompanets Leonid, Valchuk Tetiana: "Identification/Authentication of Person Cognitive Characteristics." The IEEE *AutoID'02* Proc. 3rd Workshop on *Automatic Identification Advanced Technologies*, 14-15 March 2002, Tarrytown, New York, USA, 12-16

[15] Kompanets Leonid: "Pseudo-Entropy Measure *JeK* of Similarity for Biometric Applications." The IEEE AutoID'02 Proc. 3rd Workshop on *Automatic Identification Advanced Technologies*, 142-146

[17] Valchuk Tetiana, Wyrzykowski Roman, Kompanets Leonid: "Mental Characteristics of Person as Basic Biometrics." Post-ECCV'02 Workshop on *Biometric Authentication. LNCS # 2359*, 78-90

[18] Kompanets Leonid, et al. "Based on Pseudo-Information Evaluation, Face Asymmetry and Ophthalmogeometry Techniques for Human-Computer Interaction, Person Psyche Type Identification, and Other Applications". IEEE Proc. 7th World Multi-Conference on *Systemics, Cybernetics, and Informatics* – SCI 2003. Orlando, Florida, USA, 27-30 July 2003, Vol. XII, 235-240

Chapter 3

Methods of Artificial Intelligence and Intelligent Agents

A fuzzy expert approach for comparing alternative end uses for requalification of contaminated sites

GISELLA FACCHINETTI[1], ILDA MANNINO[2],
GIOVANNI MASTROLEO[1], STEFANO SORIANI[2]
[1] University of Modena & Reggio Emilia, Italy,
[2] University of Venice, Italy.
facchinetti@unimo.it,, mannino@unive.it, mastroleo@unimo.it, soriani@unive.it

Abstract: An important aspect in the issue of contaminated sites is their use after remediation. The choice of a certain use has got necessarily socio-economic implications that make it more or less suitable for that site. For this reason it is important to insert socio-economic analysis within the studies on contaminated site remediation and to implement approaches that calibrate extent and modality of the remediation on the basis of potential uses of the site after it. In particular it is important to provide decision-makers with tools that offer them the possibility to consider also this aspect, in order to support their decisions.

The specific aim of the socio-economic module is providing the decision makers with a tool that makes possible to compare the different use destinations, outlining possible scenarios linked to alternative uses of the considered site, on the basis of socio-economic considerations (often founded on theories and methods of the spatial analysis) and of local characteristics. Comparing these scenarios it aims at giving indications on which use is more suitable and why. The final objective is just to establish which is the "best" use for that site. The term "best" indicates that it is possible to rank the whole different use destinations. This is a typical multicriteria decision making problem: there is not a natural order in a multidimensional space, so it is necessary to find a device to do it. A method to rank them is to define a function from the attribute space in the real line and so obtain a total order induced by the real number one. The scientific literature is reach of several ways to approach this problem. Here we propose a method typical of Artificial Intelligence: a Fuzzy Expert Systems (FES). The final product is a software prototype for the remediation of contaminated sites: DESYRE (DEcision Support sYstem for the REqualification of contaminated sites, www.r3environmental.co.uk/dstdemo/), that represents a useful tool for decision-makers. Entering data, relative to the considered site, the software is able to elaborate them to give back one numerical index for each possible use destination (UD). These indexes represent synthetic and comparable expressions of the socio-economic implications deriving from each UD. In this way the decision-makers can compare the opportunities coming from the different uses and have a synthetic indicator, without losing the whole information. The software works in a very transparent way, so that it is possible to highlight which factors determine the high or low index value.

Key words: Environmental analysis, contaminate sites, socio-economic variables. fuzzy expert systems.

1.   INTRODUCTION

The choice of the post-remediation use of contaminated sites is crucial for assessing the rehabilitation strategy. The latter requires socio-economic analysis to provide stakeholders with decision tools including all significant issues. It is the case of the decision support system DESYRE (Decision Support sYstem for the Requalification of contaminated sites), a software prototype for the remediation of contaminated sites.

The specific aim of the socio-economic module included in the software is to provide the decision makers with a tool capable of comparing alternative end uses of the considered site. The selection of the end uses is the result of general socio-economic considerations and local characteristics; moreover the module design is assisted by spatial analysis' approaches. The final objective is to establish which is the "best" use for that site, on the basis of the socio-economic constraints and opportunities. The term "best" indicates that it is possible to rank the whole different end uses on the basis of a set of criteria. This is a typical multicriteria decision making problem: as there is not a natural order in a multidimensional space, it is necessary to find a device to do it. A method is to choose a function from the attribute space to the real line and so obtain a total order induced by the real number one, for every fixed use destination (UD). The scientific literature is rich of several ways to approach this problem. The new researches in Artificial Intelligence propose three different types of methods: the first group is formed by Expert Systems (ES), Fuzzy Expert Systems (FES), Hierarchical methods (AHP), the second one is formed by Data-Mining methods (Neural Networks, Genetic Algorithms, etc.), the third are hybrid methods (Neurofuzzy systems, Neurogenetic systems...).

The first group includes methods that do not use the past data and live on a real contact with the experts that may allow into the study all the experience matured in years of work. The second group includes methods that are called "knowledge-discovery in data base" and are based only on data. The third is based on hybrid methods that mix experts information and data information. The problem is that they need a great number of data to be efficient. When the data are insufficient we have to use the first type.

We have decided to use Fuzzy Expert System for its efficiency and capacity to approximate the complicate function that describes the problem as we have only one data, the ones relative to Porto Marghera area. Porto Marghera (Municipality of Venice, Italy) is one of the most important port and industrial area in Mediterranean Europe. It has developed since the first decades of the last century. The chief industries were coal distillation, pesticide manufacture, shipbuilding, oil refining and petrochemical activities. With an extension of about 2000 hectares it reached a peak employment level of 35000 in 1965. As many other port and industrial areas in the most developed countries, it got into crisis during the 1970s and 1980s. Since then, several hundreds of industrial land has become redundant. One of the main problem is that of attracting new investments in the area, but this in turn calls for the environmental reclamation of many sites (Soriani, 1996).

The software we propose is the result of a complex study as the choice of the DU's and the input variables are not only typical of the Porto Marghera area but they are "exportable" in other contaminated sites.

2.   THE MODEL

The specific aim of the socio-economic module included in the software of the Decision Support System DESYRE (Decision Support sYstem for the Requalification of contaminated sites) is to provide the decision makers with a tool capable of comparing alternative end uses of the considered site. The final objective is to give indications about which choice can be the best for the site after remediation, on the basis of the socio-economic constraints and opportunities.

The model designed for this purpose is composed of three steps:
−   Selection of the end uses
−   Selection of the variables
−   Construction of the tree structures

At the first step the possible alternative uses are selected; in fact, depending on the framework where the site is situated in, different uses can be hypothesized as consistent ones. The socio-economic experts collaborating to this project tried to identify the main possible end uses for a generic site, in order to make the model applicable to the general case and so exportable to different sites.

The selection has indicated six alternative end uses, as described in the table below.

End uses	Description
1. Residential	residential area
2. Recreational	green areas, with or without facilities, to satisfy population's recreational needs
3. Industrial	industrial area with small factories and handicrafts activities
4. Tourist	tourist areas (hotels, restaurants, etc.)
5. Population services	principally the large-scale retail trade (hypermarket, mega store, etc.)
6. Services for business and firms	activities of the tertiary sector, answering the needs of firms (consulting firms, haulage contractors, retail trade)

Table 1 End uses selected and their description

In order to achieve the final aim of the model it is necessary to compare the socio-economic scenarios corresponding to each end use selected. To do this it is necessary to identify the variables that outline how the site answers to socio-economic constraints and opportunities linked to each alternatives.

The experts identified four socio-economic dimensions as the key ones to outline the scenarios. These macro-indexes are in common with the several DU:

–   the demand for that use at a local level,
–   the attraction of alternative sites for the same use,
–   the attraction of that site
–   the consistency of that use with the surrounding context (vocation index).

Following in the specialization of the variables every macro-index has been split into other variables, which depends on DU. The choice of them depends on the availability of data for the site considered, but also in this case the socio-economic experts tried to identify variables for which the values should be collected quite easily.

In the table below the variables chosen and their description are reported.

Aspect	Variable	Description	End use
Demand for the use	Number of factories	number of factories in the municipality	3, 6
	Born/death factories	ratio of born factories to death factories	6
	Population density	number of inhabitants in the municipality	2, 3, 5
	Population age 25-40	number of inhabitants in the municipality at the age of 25-40	1
	variation of the population density	difference in number of inhabitants between two years	1
	saturation of the hotels	level of saturation reached by the existing facilities	4
	mega stores already working	sm. occupied by mega stores already working in the surrounding	5
Attraction of alternative sites	land value	land value in €/sm in alternative sites with the same use	1, 3, 4, 5, 6
	mq alternative sites	sm. available for the same use elsewhere in the surrounding	1, 3, 4, 5, 6
	mq ricreative elsewhere	sm. of ricreative areas present in the surrounding	2
Site attraction	Isochrones 30 min.	people that can be reached from the site in 30 minutes by car	1, 2, 3, 5, 6
	land value after remediation	land value of the site in €/sm after its remediation	1, 3, 4, 5, 6
	distances from doors	Sum of the distances of the site from motorway, airport, harbour, rail station	3, 4, 5, 6

Context index	Local priorities	Sum of the scores assigned by experts to the local priorities, identified as the consensus of the local community towards that use, trade-union consensus coming from the increase of employments, improvement of the quality of life, improvement of the area competitiveness, absolute improvement of the environment quality	1, 2, 3, 4, 5, 6
	Impacts on traffic	increase of car number due to the end use	3, 5, 6

Table 2 Variables chosen to draw the socio-economic scenario for each end use and their description

3. THE FUZZY MODEL : A FUZZY EXPERT SYSTEM

An expert system is an intelligent machine that uses knowledge and inference procedures to solve problems that are difficult enough to require significant human expertise for their solutions. The knowledge of an expert system consists of facts and heuristics. The facts usually constitute a body of information that is widely shared, publicly available, and generally agreed upon by experts in the field. Heuristics concerns mostly private information and rules of good judgment that characterize expert-level decision making in the field. A fuzzy expert system is an expert system that utilizes fuzzy sets and fuzzy logic to overcome some of the problems that occur when the data provided by the user are vague or incomplete. The power of fuzzy set theory comes from the ability to describe linguistically a particular phenomenon or process, and then to represent that description with a small number of very flexible rules. In a fuzzy system, the knowledge is contained both in its rules and in fuzzy sets, which hold general description of the properties of the phenomenon under consideration. One of the major differences between a fuzzy expert system and another expert system is that the first can infer multiple conclusions. In fact it provides all possible solutions whose truth is above a certain threshold, and the user or the application program can then choose the appropriate solution depending on the particular situation. This fact adds flexibility to the system and makes it more powerful. Fuzzy expert systems use fuzzy data, fuzzy rules, and fuzzy inference, in addition to the standard ones implemented in the ordinary expert systems.

Functionally a fuzzy system can be described as a function approximator. More specifically it aims at performing an approximate implementation of an unknown mapping $\varphi : A \subset R^n \to R^m$ where A is a compact of R^n. By means of variable knowledge relevant to the unknown mapping [Kosko, 1992] and [Wang, 1992] independently proved that fuzzy systems are dense in the space of continuous functions on a compact domain and therefore can approximate arbitrarily well any continuous function on a compact domain. The following are the main phases of a fuzzy system design:

- Identification of the problem and choice of the type of fuzzy system which best suits the problem requirement. A modular system can be designed consisting of several fuzzy modules linked together. A modular approach, if applicable, may greatly simplify the design of the whole system, dramatically reducing its complexity and making it more comprehensible.
- Definition of input and output variables, their linguistic attributes (fuzzy values) and their membership function (fuzzification of input and output).
- Definition of the set of heuristic fuzzy rules. (IF-THEN rules).
- Choice of the fuzzy inference method (selection of aggregation operators for precondition and conclusion).
- Translation of the fuzzy output in a crisp value (defuzzification methods).
- Test of the fuzzy system prototype, drawing of the goal function between input and output fuzzy variables, change of membership functions and fuzzy rules if necessary, tuning of the fuzzy system, validation of results.

The fuzzification and the construction of rule-blocks are obtained through interviews with the experts of the problem. In this case we have not sufficient data to propose data mining methods, we have only the data relative to Marghera area.

But even in this framework we have decided to produce a software able to work also in other contaminated sites. Our main goals are:

- constructing a general framework able to handle many cases of social-economics opportunities;
- verifying the theoretical soundness and robustness of the model through sensitivity analysis, in order to assure that actual applicability is not biased;
- showing the decision rules in a indisputable way.

For example we present two of the six expert systems we have built. The "industrial system" (Fig.1) and the "recreational system" (Fig.2). Of the first, we present the input drawing pictures for two variables (Fig. 3: Attraction of alternative sites; Fig. 4: Municipal inhabitants), from which is possible to focus on the ranges, and one of the rule blocks. For both we present the final indexes we have obtained using the inputs value estimated by the experts.

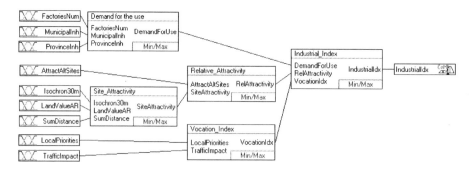

Figure 1 Tree structure for the end use "Industrial"

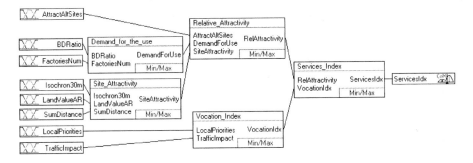

Figure 2 Tree structure for the end use "Services for business and firms"

Abbreviations list of input, intermediate and output variables of Industrial system

AttractAltSites	Attraction of alternative sites
FactoriesNum	Number of factories
Isochron30m	isochrones 30 min.
LandValueAR	land value
LocalPriorities	Local priorities
MunicipalInh	Population density
ProvinceInh	Population density
SumDistance	Sum of the distances from doors
TrafficImpact	Impacts on traffic
Industrial	Final index for industrial
DemandForUse	DemandForUse
RelAttraction	Relative Attraction
SiteAttraction	Site Attraction
VocationIdx	Vocation Index

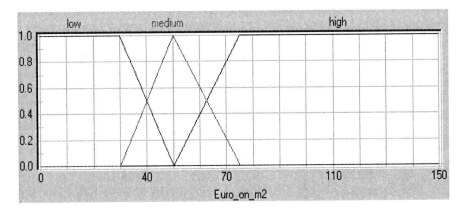

Figure 3: MBF of "AttractAltSites"

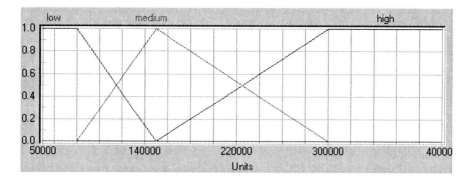

Figure 4: MBF of "MunicipalInh"

#	FactoriesNum	MunicipalInh	ProvinceInh	DemandForUse
1	low	low v medium	low	very_low
2	low	low	medium	very_low
3	low v medium	low	high	low
4	low v medium	medium	medium	low
5	low	medium	high	low
6	low	high	low v medium	low
7	low v medium	high	high	medium
8	medium v high	low	low	low
9	medium	low	medium	low
10	medium	medium	low	low
11	medium	medium	high	medium
12	medium v high	high	low	medium
13	medium	high	medium	medium
14	high	low v medium	medium	medium
15	high	low	high	medium
16	high	medium	low	medium
17	high	medium v high	high	high
18	high	high	medium	high

Figure 5: Rule Block "Demand_For_Use"

The table below shows that there are three blocks of values. The first block is due to the input variables the experts have decide to be correct for the Porto Marghera area. In the second block we find the defuzzified Intermediate Variables value and in the third we have two macro-indexes we try to find.

The defuzzified intermediate variables permit to understand in a explicit way what the experts have done. All these partial information are useful in a tuning opportunity of all the system.

	Industrial	Services for business and firms
Attractivity of alternative sites (land value in €/mq)	37,88	37,88
Impacts on traffic	14333	12286
Isochrones 30 min.	81000	81000
Ratio of born factories to death factories		1,23
Number of factories	86192	86192
Number of inhabitants in the municipality	270639	
Number of inhabitants in the province	814581	
Local priorities	6	6
Sum of the distances from doors (Km.)	24,7	12,5
Alternative sites with the same use (land value in €/mq)	51,65	51,65
Site Attractivity (intermediate score)	1,00	1,00
Relative Attractivity (intermediate score)	0,75	0,86
DemandForUse (intermediate score)	1,00	0,82
Vocation Index (intermediate score)	0,90	0,95
Final index	0,95	0,88

Table 4 Result of the comparison between the industrial and the recreational uses.

On the basis of the results, the site can be considered more attractive for the industrial use than for the recreational one, since the final valuation index is closer to the value 1 in the first case than in the second one.

4. CONCLUSIONS AND FINAL REMARKS

The model considered provides methodological support for the assessment of the attractiveness of a site to be reclaimed as regards a range of different uses; it allows to rank these uses expressing a final rating for each of them between 0 and 1. Attractiveness is assessed on the basis of both spatial and socio-economic logic: the characteristics of the "surroundings" (identified in the Municipality and/or Province) and the position related to the area to be reclaimed (in terms of distance or proximity) have been searched for, in order to assess demand and the suitability of the local territory. The model also provides intermediate scores for the different uses; this can help to evaluate which are the strength and weakness points for each use.

At this stage, some crucial aspects are worth pointing out.

1. The model has been tested for an area to be reclaimed at Porto Marghera. The results confirms the direction provided by the planning system, which in fact envisages that the area is to be used for industrial purposes. In this sense the model is "conservative", since it favours continuity with the past history of the area. It clearly depends on the past evolution of Porto Marghera area (in particular from the infrastructural point of view), which still makes it attractive for industrial activities, even if they are new ones (in the sense of "light industry").

2. The model does not consider all the socio-economic aspects related to environmental reclamation: for example the model does not consider the cumulative effects of the selection of any given use. If we refer, for example, to use "industry", the model considers some significant variables (for example the

presence of companies, area demand, market values of the areas included in "surrounding" industrial activity areas) to assess the attractiveness of the site with regard to this use; on the other hand, it does not consider the possible effects of the choice (namely that of using the site for industry after it has been reclaimed) on the market of redundant sites.

3. The model presents a high level of abstraction and handles questions that may either be too detailed in their logic (one example is the fact that environmental legislation may also put different uses together, such as industry and services, or residence and tourism, in a single "use destination") or may be "overruled" by political or planning decisions that obey political logic that is far more complex than that of the model.

4. The model proposed ranks possible uses. In practice, mainly in the case of megasites, and also for reasons connected with financial risk to investors, re-utilisation projects often propose a mix of different uses (multi-functional re-utilisation project). Nevertheless, it is the very complexity of the picture that characterises megasites that makes it helpful to have a model that assesses the "quality" of possible uses considered in themselves.

5. Data collection is an extremely delicate phase, as the data are almost always the results of other surveys or estimates.

6. The way the "experts" interact with the model is a crucial factor for two reasons. Firstly, the application of the model requires profound knowledge of the area at local level; the selection of data and the definition of the ranges of variability (definition of the intervals to define whether the value of a variable is classified as low, medium or high) is in fact a delicate operation, on whose adequacy the final results inevitably depend. Secondly, the role of "experts" is important in various phases: (a) the definition of variability ranges; (b) the construction of trees; (c) the definition of the sets of rules – the different "weight" the variables have in influencing the final result; (d) the definition of local priorities. These are extremely delicate phases; however, what must be stressed is that while scientific literature and experience in the field can be helpful in phases (a), (b) and (c), for phase (d) the situation is much more complex: in fact, the definition of local priorities (e.g. to reduce unemployment, or to search for consensus from trade-unions, or to improve environmental conditions, or to attract investments in the most dynamic sectors in the global economy, etc.) implies that experts are asked to express "value judgments". Nevertheless, this aspect may at the same time be considered one of the model's strong points, since it requires the experts to make these values explicit.

To conclude, the model helps to evaluate and decide, to translate the complexity of relations between variables into possible choices, but does not take the place of the experts and the local community (or the regional or national community, etc.) in attributing merit or value; nor does it provide results that can be considered "neutral". In this sense the model seems useful because it makes the positions of the experts explicit, thus helping the local community (and other experts as well) to confront with them.

REFERENCES

[1] Bandermer H., Gottwald S. (1996) Fuzzy sets, fuzzy logic fuzzy methods. John Wiley &Sons New York.

[2] Desfor G. e Keil R., Contested and Polluted Terrain, in Local Environment, vol. 4, n. 3, 1999.

[3] Facchinetti G.: (2001). "Fuzzy Expert Systems: Economic and Financial Applications" In Advanced Computer System J. Soldek and J Pejas eds, 3-26. Kluwer Academic Publishers.

[4] Facchinetti G.-Mastroleo G.-Paba S.: (2000) "A fuzzy approach to the geography of industrial districts"; "Proceedings of the 2000 ACM Symposium on Applied Computing" Carrol J., Damiani E., Haddam H., Oppenheim D. Editors. ISBN: 1-58113-239-5, Vol.1 514-518.

[5] Facchinetti G.-Bordoni S.-Mastroleo G.: (2000) "Bank Creditworthiness using Fuzzy Systems: A Comparison with a Classical Analysis Technique" Risk Assesment and Management in Technology, Environment and Finance. Da Ruan, Fedrizzi M. e Kacprzyk J. Editors. Springer Verlag Press. Pubblicato nella sezione Fuzzy Applications and Library del sito web http:/www.fuzzytech.com.

[6] Facchinetti G.- Magni C.- Mastroleo M- Vignola V. " Valuing strategic investment with a fuzzy expert system: an italian case" on proceedings of International Fuzzy System Association Fuzzyness And Soft Computing In The New Millenium (IFSA 2001), July 25-28 Vancouver Canada.

[7] Kasabov N.K. (1996) Foundations of Neural Networks, Fuzzy Systems, and Knowledge Engineering. MIT Press.

[8] Kosko, B., 1992. Fuzzy Systems as Universal Approximators. Proc. IEEE Int. Conf. On Fuzzy Systems, 1153-1162.

[9] Meyer P.B., Williams R.H. e Yount K.R., Contaminated Land: reclamation, redevelopment and reuse in USA and EU, Aldershot, Gower, 1995.

[10] Soriani S. (1996) "The Venice Port and Industrial Area in a Context of Regional Change", in Cityports, Coastal Zones and Regional Change, B.S. Hoyle ed., Chichester, Wiley, pp. 235-248.

[11] von Altrock C. (1997). "Fuzzy Logic and neurofuzzy applications in business and finance." Prentice Hall.

[12] Wang, L., 1992. Fuzzy systems are universal approximators. Proc. Of Int. Conf. On Fuzzy Systems.

Training assisting program with hybrid decision supporting system

PAWEŁ BANAŚ

Faculty of Computer Science & Information Systems, Technical University of Szczecin, ul. Żołnierska 49, 71-210 Szczecin, Poland, e-mail: pbanas@wi.ps.pl

Abstract: Use of simulation the computer aided training systems make possibility of teaching dynamic systems' operators in situations when training process with use of real object could be dangerous or impossible. It is also much cheaper than classical training when real object is in use. But use of computer gives also possibility to make a program which have some instructor's abilities. Such program gives advices to trainee and estimates his skills what allows instructor to focus on other aspects of training process. It is necessary the teaching program must adapt to trainee skills, trained situation and other aspects of training. To meet this requirement the program should use artificial intelligence. This article presents a training assisting program based on cooperation of predicate logic (main method) supplemented by fuzzy logic and neural network. Presented system is designed to train civil aviation pilots but it is possible to adapt them to train operators of any dynamic object (ex. car drivers, production line operators, etc.).

Key words: artificial intelligence, training system, hybrid system

1. INTRODUCTION

Computer based training with use of dynamic object simulation may be very effective form of teaching [5, 6, 7]. However this method still needs instructor's inspection. But there are situations when some functions of instructor could be done by proper program. Relieved instructor can pay his attention on other aspects of training.

There are several problems to solve: the "Artificial Instructor" should react on trainee actions, the system must adapt to trainee – his skills, the faults he make and frequency of these faults. To meet this requirements, use of artificial intelligence is essential. This article presents an idea of "Artificial Instructor" with abilities to support trainee during teaching process and some elements of trainee's evaluation.

The support is realized by advices given to a trainee. Evaluation is based on differences between scores achieved by trainee and reference values proper to training conditions.

2. STRUCTURE OF TUTORING SYSTEM

2.1 General structure

The possible variant of general scheme of tutoring system is presented on fig. 1. The basic functional links are shown by solid lines and optional links by dashed line. Basic interacting components of a system are: trainee, instructor, system of simulation and teaching machine.

The simplest version of system contains trainee, simulator and teaching module. Trainee can communicate to simulator only. Information from teaching module is transferred through a simulator. More complicated versions contains instructor and provides direct information transfer between elements of the training system.

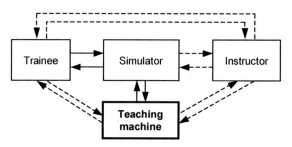

Fig. 1. General scheme of tutoring system

The simulator may be realized as full-flight, fixed-base, simplified or personal computer based (PC-based) simulator. Presented system is designed to cooperate with PC-based simulator such like that one designed in ASIMIL Project [10], but only small changes are needed to achieve possibility of cooperation with any other type of simulator.

2.2 Teaching machine

Teaching machine is a set of cooperating elements: two step of decision units based on two kinds of logic and neural network which is used to recognize state of simulation. The scheme of connections between them is presented on figure 2.

The base method used in teaching module is predicate logic build into 1-st step decision block as logical rules. This method was chosen because of notation manner of procedures designed to train pilots. Using data from simulator 1-st step block evaluate if trainee's action is proper. When this actions were recognized as wrong, initial data and result of 1-st step go to 2-nd step, fuzzy logic based decision block. The final decision depends on value of deviation and conditions of its appearance.

The third element with build-in artificial intelligence is module of flight state recognition. It contains neural network used to recognize a state of flight. This data is used to find in data bases of rules a proper ones which are used by decision blocks.

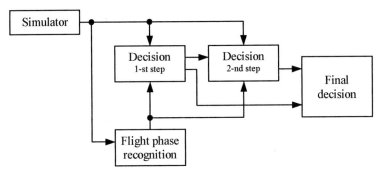

Fig. 2. Elements of hybrid decision supporting system

2.3 1-st step of decision – predicate logic

This block is a base of training system – it evaluates trainee's actions in ordinary situations described by training procedures in Pilot's Book. It has built-in logic rules educed from these procedures. Structure of this block is shown on figure 3.

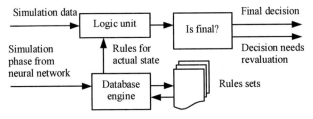

Fig. 3. Structure of decision block with rule based logic

Logic rules are stored in knowledge base as sets – one set for every flight phase allowed by Pilot's Book. The neural network recognize current phase and transmit this information to database engine. The database engine gets proper set of rules and transfer it to logic unit. The logic unit executes these rules for data gotten from simulator. Result of execution says if the aircraft state is proper or not. The are may be two types of logic rules. Final rules gives final decision. Results of rules other than final may be revaluated by 2-nd step decision unit.

The mechanism of extracting logic rules from training procedures was described in previous publications [8, 9].

2.4 2-nd step of decision – fuzzy logic

2-nd step decision block gives the system possibility to evaluate some trainee's actions when a little fault appears but too large to meet requirements of classical predicate logic used in 1-st step decision block. This solution also gives possibility to adapt some parameters to actual state of flight and unpredictable influences, ex. whether changes.

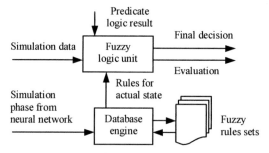

Fig. 4. Structure of decision block with fuzzy logic

Base structure of this block, shown on figure 4., is very similar to previous block where predicate logic was used. The main difference is use of fuzzy rules instead classic logic rules. Also decision made by this block is final – there is no third evaluator in this system. The fuzzy logic unit has additional job – it gives a mark to trainee. This mark depends on deviations between standard flight parameters and these gotten from simulator.

The basis to set-up fuzzy rules is interview with expert – instructor and pilot. This interview is supplemented by data from aircraft producer – allowed flight parameters. Final rules are written to the fuzzy knowledge base as membership functions used by fuzzy logic unit.

2.5   Flight phase recognition – neural network

Every flight is different to other. But there is possible to find some finite number of flight states. Every flight can be splitting to these states. There is possible to pass from one state to another, but between some phases there is no direct path. An example net of flight states is shown on figure 5.

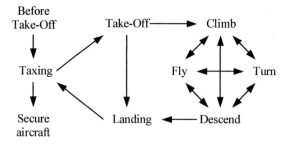

Fig. 5. Example of possible flight states network

The last method of artificial intelligence used in this system is neural network. Function of this module is to find in which phase is simulated aircraft. This is necessary to set proper rules to both logic modules – different sets of parameters are needed during take-off, landing, turning and other possible phases of flight.

Structure of neural network depends on number of flight states – more states, more neurons are needed in layers of network. Exact structure and neurons' number will be found during researches.

3. USED SOFTWARE

All teaching system elements' prototypes arise in MATLAB package with Simulink extension. Use of this environment gives possibility of very simple develop of logic rules, fuzzy rules and neural network – the mechanisms are build-in into package or are provided by additional toolboxes. Also use of MATLAB/Simulink package gives also possibility for very fast building of application interface, what very simplifies prototypes debugging.

A part of system is translated to JAVA programming language. In future, when all procedures and functions will be ready, whole system will be rewritten in JAVA. There is also possibility to transfer system's code to C++ language, what induce speed-up of whole system but reduce software migration between hardware/software platforms. Use of MATLAB/Simulink or JAVA reduces speed but system can work on very different computers under different operating systems.

4. SYSTEM DEVELOPMENT

4.1 Current state

At this moment the working prototype of predicate logic subsystem for mechanics is generally ready. Some elements of it was used in ASIMIL project. Current work focuses now on debugging the prototype, developing rules' sets for flight tasks and on fuzzy logic subsystem. In near future, neural network will be developed. This system is a part of author's Ph.D. dissertation.

4.2 Future work

The future development of system in presented field goes to debugging present elements and adding new flight procedures and additional logical and fuzzy rules for flight in normal and emergency conditions. It is possibility of minor changes of system's structure.

It is also possible to use this system in another fields of use – ex. to train car drivers, production line operators, and to many other specific trainings. Of course there will be necessary to change rules and all databases, but the structure of a system will not need complicated changes – almost all of them will be done in databases.

5. CONLUSIONS

Pilots training includes wide range of procedures which each pilot has to know before receiving of Pilot license. Some part of training may be automated by use a specific expert system as "Artificial Instructor". This article presents a project of teaching system which base on predicate logic supported by fuzzy logic and neural network. This connection makes the system work in many different conditions, even not predictable by training procedures. Future work will focus on development this system in aeronautical field but also in another fields where a dynamic object simulation is used to train people. Structure of this system gives also possibility to use it in real objects, ex. as supporting system for pilots during flight in very difficult conditions.

REFERENCES

[1] Mulawka J. J. 1997. 'Systemy ekspertowe'. Warszawa, WNT (in Polish).
[2] Białko M. 2000 'Podstawowe właściwości sieci neuronowych i hybrydowych systemów ekspertowych'. Koszalin, Wydawnictwo Uczelniane Politechniki Koszalińskiej (in Polish).
[3] Goonatilake S., Khebbal S. 1995. 'Intelligent Hybrid Systems', Chichester, John Wiley & Sons.
[4] Edmunds R. A.1998. 'The Prentice Hall guide to the expert systems'. Englewood Cliffs, Prentice Hall.
[5] Cerri S.A., Gouarderes G. 2002 Paragacu F., 'Intelligent Tutoring Systems', Springer-Verlag, Berlin Heidelberg.
[6] Popov O., Lalanne R., Gouarderes G., Minko A., Tretyakov A. 2001. 'The structure of multi-agent learning system and its application in aeronautical training', Proceedings of the 10- th International Conference on System Modeling Control SMC'2001, Zakopane, Poland.
[7] Popov O., Lalanne R., Gouarderes G., Minko A., Tretyakov A. 2001. 'Some Tasks of Intelligent Tutoring Systems Design for Civil Aviation Pilots', Proceedings of the 8-th International Conference Advanced Computer Systems ACS'2001, Szczecin, Poland, ISBN 83-87362-38-7.
[8] Tretyakov A., Banaś P., Hochard G. 2002. 'Structure of the expert system and example of realization of training's tasks in the computer tutoring system for aircrew of civil aviation'. *ITS 2002* Biarritz, France, San Sebastian, Spain.
[9] Tretyakov A., Banaś P. 2002. 'Expert System Components in the Pilots' Training System', Proceedings of the 9-th International Conference Advanced Computer Systems ACS'2002, Szczecin, Poland, ISBN 83-87362-47-6.
[10] Popov O. Barcz A. Piela P. Sobczak T. 2002. 'Practical realization of modelling an airplane for an intelligent tutoring system', Proceedings of the 9-th International Conference Advanced Computer Systems ACS'2002, Szczecin, Poland, ISBN 83-87362-47-6.

Numerical problems with evaluating the fractal dimension of real data

ADAM SZUSTALEWICZ
Institute of Computer Science, Wrocław University,
Przesmyckiego 20, 51-151 Wrocław, e-mail: asz@ii.uni.wroc.pl

Abstract: A new program *RIVER* for evaluating the fractal dimension of real data sets was written. Its performance was compared with two programs *HarFA* – demo version and *CoastLine*, available in Internet. The three programs were tested on about 50 data sets. The program *RIVER* yielded the maximal errors less than 3 percentages for all tested data sets, while the other tested programs gave more than 10 percentage errors.

Key words: Dimension, Fractals, Fractal dimension, Box-counting, Structure complexity

1. INTRODUCTION

Historically, Felix Hausdorff in 1919 introduced *fractal dimension*, meaning dimension being a noninteger number (Section 3). Benoit Mandelbrot [12] used then this term in his definition of fractals.

In the paper, for better understanding of all used notations, we firstly recall the rather known classical concepts of dimension like Euclidean and topological dimensions (Section 2). Next we introduce in more details the definition of the fractal dimension (Section 3). Then we show a practical method for evaluation of fractal dimension for complex sets, namely – the *box-counting method* (Section 4).

There exist many fractals that are artificial and self-similar structures (self-similar means that some part of the object is similar to the whole structure). They can be easily created using recurrence definitions (Section 3).

Benoit Mandelbrot investigated the relationship between fractals and nature. He noticed in 1977 that fractals could be used to characterizing and modelling complex objects in natural or artificial systems [12]. In the future we would like to use the fractal dimension in measuring the complexity of river shapes. We will need methods good enough both for fractals and for smooth figures.

Sections 5, 6 and 7 describe respectively the used test structures, tested programs and obtained results.

2. CLASSICAL CONCEPTS: EUCLIDEAN AND TOPOLOGICAL DIMENSIONS

2.1 The Euclidean Dimension

Generally, *a set* S *is* n *-dimensional if we use* n *independent variables to describe a neighbourhood of any point of* S . $\square$

A line is one-dimensional because only one number is needed to uniquely define any point of it. The number can be the distance from the fixed point called zero.

A plane is two-dimensional, a cube is three-dimensional, and a sphere in R^n is a two-dimensional object too.

From the conceptual point of view, description of the dimension is connected with the dependence how the whole volume of an object behaves when its linear size (diameter, side-length) changes:
- if we enlarge the linear size of a line segment three times, then the segment's volume (length) enlarges three times too – the segment's dimension equals one,
- if we enlarge the linear size of a rectangle three times, then its area (triangle's olume) enlarges nine times: $9 = 3^2$. The rectangle's dimension equals two.

The relationship between the scaling factor m that changes the linear size of an object and the resulting factor M of the object's volume change takes the form

$$M = m^d \qquad or \qquad d = \frac{\log M}{\log m} \tag{1}$$

2.2 The Topological Dimension

It relays on the following intuitively obvious observations:
- we need at least a point to split a curve into two parts,
- we need at least a curve to split a surface into two parts,
- we need at least a surface to split a volume into two parts.

Henri Poincare gave an inductive definition of the *Topological Dimension*:
Define the dimension of a point equal to zero, and the dimension of a connected set to be equal to 1 plus the dimension of the least set needed to split it into two parts. For a disconnected set define the dimension of the set to be the maximum of the dimensions of the connected components. $\square$

A sphere can be split into two parts by a smooth curve. It remains a two-dimensional object again as it was in the previous section. A river and a coastline are one-dimensional objects both in the meaning of the Euclidean and the topological dimension.

There exists another, equivalent definition of topological dimension, which is called the *Covering Dimension*. The concept of a *covering* plays an important role in definitions of both topological and fractal dimension. We say [3, 14]:

A covering of a set S *(in a topological space* X *) is a collection* C *of open subsets in* X *whose sum contains all points of* S .

Then, we say: the Covering Dimension of S *is equal to* n *if there exists such a covering* C *that every point of* S *belongs to at most* $n+1$ *subsets from* C *and* n *is the smallest such integer.* □

3. WHAT IS MEANT BY A FRACTAL

To introduce the concept of fractal we need the concept of a measure. We say that *measure is a function of sets which permits to compare their size.*

Felix Hausdorff published in 1919 a paper in which he introduced a function $H^p(S)$ permitting to measure the sets S from a metric space X . This function considers sets from X and is additionally characterized by a real parameter $p \geq 0$. The function $H^p(S)$ is known today as the *Hausdorff p-dimensional measure* and is described by the formula:

$$H^p(S) = \liminf_{\varepsilon \to 0 \ A_\varepsilon} \sum_{A \in A_\varepsilon} (diam(A))^p$$

where A_ε denotes any ε-cover of the set S . (A_ε *is an* ε *-cover of* S means that every point of S belongs to some sets $A \in A_\varepsilon$ and $diam(A) < \varepsilon$.)

If one considers the metric space R^n with the usual metric, then the Hausdorff measure $H^p(S)$ with $p = n$ is equal to the *n*-dimensional Lebesgue measure and $H^n(S)$ equals to the ordinary *n*-dimensional volume of the set S [2].

It is true that for every given set S there exists a unique real number d such that

$$\begin{cases} \text{if } p < d \text{ then } H^p(S) = \infty, \\ \text{if } p > d \text{ then } H^p(S) = 0. \end{cases}$$

This number d is called the *fractal dimension* or the *Hausdorff dimension of* S . □
In other way we can write

$$d = \inf\{p : H^p(S) = 0\} = \sup\{p : H^p(S) = \infty\}.$$

Since the Hausdorff's paper in 1919 practically all sets that could be assigned such noninteger fractal dimension are called *fractals*. Mandelbrot [12] introduced in 1977 a more strict definition:
Fractal is a set whose Hausdorff dimension differs from its topological dimension. □

Hausdorff's definition of the fractal dimension – shown above – usually is easy to calculate only for some artificial self-similar structures [2]. The definition of *self-similarity* (or *affine-self-similarity*) is as follows:
A set S is self-similar if there exists a subset of S that can be linearly transformed onto the whole S. □

Hausdorff dimension is difficult to evaluate for real data sets. Therefore several other definitions of fractional dimension have been introduced like the 'box-counting dimension', the 'similar dimension', the 'capacity dimension', the 'correlation dimension', etc., which are much easier applicable to real data.
In the next sections we show two examples of fractals and we will show how to evaluate for them their fractal dimensions using the intuitively clear formula (1).

3.1   The Koch-Curve

This structure is constructed recursively. We begin with one line segment. Then, at each stage of the construction we divide each line segment into three equal parts and replace the middle one with two segments of the same length, in the form ∧ of the vertex of the equilateral triangle:

Fig. 1. Construction of the Koch-Curve

The limiting structure – *Koch-Curve* is a self-similar structure. It has the topological dimension equal to one. We can cover it with discs of arbitrary small radius in such a way, that each point of this figure belongs mostly to two discs only. But Koch-Curve is not a curve. The length of it between any two different points is equal to infinity. We can easily check it observing that in every step of the construction the length of the structure grows larger $4/3$ times. Thus, we could say that Koch-Curve is too big to be thought of as of a one-dimensional object, and too thin to be a two-dimensional one. Federik Stromberg [15] has shown that the Hausdorff dimension of the Koch-Curve is equal to $\ln(4)/\ln(3) \approx 1.2618595$.

There is an easy way to obtain the fractal dimension d of the constructed self-similar structure analogously to the formula (1). Let us transform linearly the given Koch-Curve enlarging it three times in all directions – we say that its linear size enlarges three times, or that the scaling factor m equals three. As we see in *Fig. 2*, the resulting structure is the sum of four originals composed in the form $\_\wedge\_$. It means that the volume's enlarging factor M equals four. From the equality $4 = 3^d$ (formula (1)) the fractal dimension d of the Koch-Curve can be calculated as

$$d_{Koch-Curve} = \frac{\log 4}{\log 3} \approx 1.2618595 \ .$$

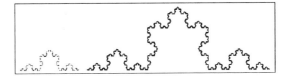

Fig. 2. The structure in the right is the result of a triple linear enlarging (scaling) of the original in the left. The result is the sum of four originals in the form $\_\wedge\_$

3.2 The Sierpiński-Triangle

The Sierpiński-Triangle can be recursively constructed too. Let us start with a solid equilateral triangle and remove the inner triangle formed by the midpoints of its three sides. There are three smaller triangles. Continuing the process by removing their inner triangles we obtain the limiting figure, a strictly self-similar structure – the *Sierpiński-Triangle*.

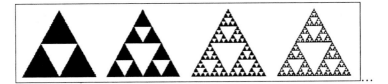

Fig. 3. Construction of the Sierpiński-Triangle

At each stage of the construction the area of the remaining parts of the triangle grows smaller and smaller. In every step the area grows less $3/4$ times. How should we describe the dimension of the limiting structure? Intuitively we feel that in the limit the dimension should be less than two.

The dimension of this structure, evaluated by the Hausdorff method can be found in [2], but we will do it here the same way as for the Koch-Curve. Let us enlarge twice the Sierpiński-Triangle in all directions (we double its linear size).

The obtained structure (see *Fig. 4*) equals the sum of three originals and the formula (1) says that the equality $3 = 2^d$ holds or equivalently, the dimension d of the Sierpiński-Triangle can be calculated as

$$d_{Sierpinski-Triangle} = \frac{\log 3}{\log 2} \approx 1.5849625 \ .$$

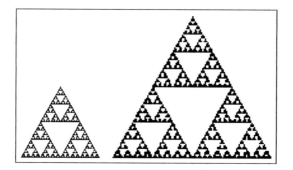

Fig. 4. The linear size of a self-similar Sierpiński-Triangle in the left is enlarged two times. The structure obtained this way (in the right) is the sum of three originals

4. A MORE PRACTICAL DEFINITION: THE BOX-COUNTING DIMENSION

The fractal dimension can be defined in several ways. We report one of possible definitions which introduces so-called *Box-Counting Dimension* denoted by d again. This definition was firstly introduced by Kolmogorov [9].

Let S be a structure in R^n and let for any $\varepsilon > 0$, $N(\varepsilon, S)$ be the minimum number of *n*-dimensional cubes in diameter or side-length at most ε, needed to cover S.

If there exists a number d such, that for some positive const the equality

$$\lim_{\varepsilon \to 0} \frac{N(\varepsilon, S)}{1/\varepsilon^d} = const$$

holds, then d is called the Box-Counting Dimension of S. ☐

We can take the logarithm of both sides and obtain the equivalent formula

$$d = \lim_{\varepsilon \to 0} \frac{\log N(\varepsilon, S)}{\log(1/\varepsilon)} \ . \tag{2}$$

In many papers and Internet publications with computer results the value d of box-counting dimension is approximated by the slope of the best-fit straight line for the set of k points

$$\{(\log(1/\varepsilon_i), \log(N(\varepsilon_i, S)))\}, \qquad (i = 1, ..., k) \qquad (3)$$

obtained for a sequence of somehow chosen $\varepsilon_1, ..., \varepsilon_k$. This sequence may be chosen in many ways. Each choice of a sequence of ε's results in another algorithm of evaluating the value d. All these methods, let us denote them *Box-Counting Methods* (*BCM*) are the most popular methods applied in practice to approximate the fractal dimension d of considered structure.

5. APPLYING THE BOX-COUNTING METHODS (BCM) USING TEST DATA

In practice, considering some maps or pictures with given structures, we use data sets that have a form of a bounded binary image. The image is stored as a rectangular data matrix. All pixels representing the investigated structure S are stored as 1 and pixels from the structure's background are stored as 0.

There are two problems:

– we state, looking at the Kolmogorov's definition where $\varepsilon \to 0$, that BCM must be limited by the image resolution, and

– it is possible that the recorded binary representation of more complicated structure can contain some graphical errors or damages (see *Fig. 5*).

So, we had some doubts if BCM applied to data of different sorts provide results close enough to the accurate values of the dimensions of considered data sets. Therefore we decided to test some of accessible in Internet procedures or programs realizing BCM on some chosen test data with known fractal dimensions. We have written also the new program *RIVER* to test on the same data different variants of constructing the sequences $\{\varepsilon_1, ..., \varepsilon_k\}$ used in BCM. In the next sections we describe these data and applied programs.

5.1 Data

We use some images accessible in Internet and some others prepared by ourselves. Each of them contains a structure with known fractal dimension.

In the first place we use images prepared by Gonzato [4, 5, 7] who considers three images, each of size 2048×2048 pixels. His first image – denoted *LINE256* – contains a horizontal line represented by a sequence of 256 following pixels. From the *LINE256* we have cut off a part of the image of size 565×450 pixels containing the line. The smaller image will be denoted *LINE256a*.

The other Gonzato's images, denoted *KC2048* and *ST2048* contain two big fractals: the *Koch-Curve* and the *Sierpiński-Triangle*, both with 2048 pixels in their horizontal length. An enlarged piece of ST2048 is shown in *Fig. 5*. We can notice some graphical errors in it.

In the second place we use structures prepared by Kraft [10, 11]. He considers 30 images of size 512x512 pixels, each of them contains one object only, but shifted to different points of the image. We used 10 images containing differently shifted circle (*Circles*), 10 images containing differently shifted quadrat (*Quadrats*), and 10 images containing differently shifted Sierpiński-Triangle (*Striangles*).

From these images we cut off three smallest pieces of these images, containing the structures and denoted: *Circle_cut*, *Quadrat_cut* and *STriangle_cut*.

From Kraft's data sets we chose yet the image – denoted *ST682* – of size 688x612 pixels containing the Sierpiński-Triangle with 682 and 612 pixels in its side and height lengths respectively. By *ST682_cut* we denote the smallest piece of the image that has been cut from the whole image and contains *ST682*.

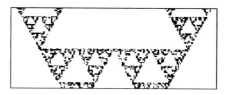

Fig. 5. An enlarged piece of the large Sierpiński-Triangle.
One can notice some graphical errors on it

In the third place we use the two Koch-Curves in horizontal positions drawn by ourselves in small images: *KC345* – with 345 pixels in its horizontal length, and *KC299* with 299 pixels in length.

Without introducing additional graphical damages into the test structures we can rotate them three times over a right angle, obtaining this way four images with the same, only rotated structure Let us denote such data sets by *rotated structures*.

The considered data sets can be treated in the sense of computer graphics as
–   *Structures without errors* – the curves are thin and smooth like *Line256*, *Line256a*, *Circles* and *Quadrats*.
–   *Structures with errors* – where some graphical errors appeared (see *Fig. 5*). There are two sources of errors: a non-optimal algorithm of the structure's construction or too small images containing the structures.

6.   PROGRAMS USED

We have found in Internet two interesting programs realizing BCM.

The first is the demo version of the program *HarFA* [6, 1] programmed by the team from the Institute of Physical and Applied Chemistry Faculty of Chemistry in the Brno University of Technology. The program performs image analysis via the Box-Counting Dimension, but we got only a free downloaded demo version.

The second is the Matlab procedure *CoastLine* included into the very interesting *Course Materials E240* about fractals, prepared by Tadeusz Patzek [13] from the University of California Berkeley. Professor Patzek was so kind and sent us for tests also the procedure *CountinBoxes* called inside of *CoastLine*.

The third is the program *RIVER* – a new one, prepared by ourselves in Matlab.

6.1 HarFA

The free downloaded *HarFA.exe* is a demo version of the main program and realizes the box-counting method in two variants:

– *Discrete* – it applies (in default version) 30 different square side-lengths uniformly distributed in the segment $[2, N_{max}]$, where N_{max} is close to the one third of the shorter side-length of the image containing the structure.

– *Continuous* – it applies all possible lengths from the segment $[2, N_{max}]$.

HarFA realizes a modification [1] of traditional BCM using the covering of the image by a square grid.

The program analyzes separately squares that are completely black, completely white, and separately squares that contain black and white pixels. The investigated structure can be the whole object drawn black or drawn white, or it can be only the border between the both objects.

By this modification program obtains not one, but three approximations DB, DW, DBW of fractal dimensions and the user decides which results to choose. The sum DB+DBW can be a good value of the fractal dimension calculated for the thick object drawn black.

The data images *Line256*, *KC2048* and *ST2048* were too big and could not be dealt by the demo version of *HarFA*.

6.2 Procedure CoastLine

Professor Tadeusz Patzek [13] from the University of California Berkeley describes results of BCM applied to some binary images of coastlines prepared in the BAR LLAN University and accessible in Internet [8]. The Matlab procedure CoastLine, included into his didactic materials, relays on the best least squares fit to five points in the form (3). The shorter side-length of the image containing the considered structure is divided into 4, 8, 16, 32 and 64 parts and these five numbers (lengths) are the values of used $\{\varepsilon_i\}$.

6.3 Program RIVER – our realization of BCM

There are many possibilities in constructing the sequence of $\varepsilon_1,...,\varepsilon_k$ (see Section 4). The size k of the sequence depends mostly on the data. Apart from this, the values of the ε's may be generated in computer realizations according to 16×12 rules. Each run of the program with specifically generated ε's will be called a *variant of calculations*. We wanted to check if there exist such variants in practical realization of BCM that give small enough errors for all test structures: smooth curves and complex fractals.

Thus, we had written the Matlab program *RIVER* that contains the possibilities of generating the sequences $\varepsilon_1,...,\varepsilon_k$ in 16×12 ways. On each of the data structures described in Section 5 we run the program using all the variants of generating the ε's. We have retained only these variants that gave the smallest errors for **all** tested sets of data – i.e. smooth curves and fractals. There were **four variants of calculations only** for which the errors were less than 3 percentages for all tested data sets.

There is no space to describe that all now, it will be done in a separate paper.

7.   RESULTS

In the *Table 1* we present the percentage errors of the results obtained by the three used programs: *HarFA*, *CoastLine* and *RIVER* for structures contained in used images.

TABLE 1. The percentage errors of the results obtained for the contained structures by the three used programs: *HarFA, CoastLine* and *RIVER*

Images	HarFA			CoastLine	RIVER
	modif.	discrete	continous		
Circles	BW	[-4.0 , 2.6]	[-3.7 , 9.0]	[-9.4 , 5.5]	-0.7 ; -0.6
Circle_cut	BW	9.5	13.4	-0.2	-0.7 ; -0.6
Squares	BW	[-2.0 , 8.0]	[-2.5 , 1.1]	[-9.0 , 4.6]	1.4 ; 1.5
Square_cut	BW	4.7	10.7	6.7	1.4 ; 1.5
Line256 rotated		-	-	20	0
Line256a rotated	BW	[-6.4 , -4.3]	[-6.2 , -5.6]	[-9.8 , -8.2]	0
KC2048		-	-	1.0	-2.8 ; -2.6
KC345 rotated	BW W+BW	[1.4 , 2.7] [3.3 , 4.3]	[2.7 , 3.3] [4.3 , 4.7]	[-6.8 , 15.3]	0.1
KC299 rotated	BW W+BW	[-5.7 , -0.5] [-5.4 , -3.0]	[-4.8 , 1.3] [-4.7 , 1.4]	[6.2 , 7.5]	-2.9
ST2048		-	-	2.6	-1.4
ST682 rotated	BW B+BW	[0.0 , 0.9] [1.6 , 2.0]	[2.3 , 2.8] [2.8 , 3.5]	[2.3 , 5.9]	-0.9 ; 0.1
ST682_cut rotated	BW B+BW	[0.2 , 0.5] [1.9 , 2.1]	[2.3 , 3.0] [3.0 , 3.6]	[2.7 , 6.1]	-0.9 ; 0.1
STriangles	BW W+BW	[-8.6 , -2.9] [-7.2 , -1.6]	[-12.5 , -1.9] [-11.9 , -1.3]	[-12.0 , -2.2]	0.9
STtriangle_cut rotated	BW W+BW	[0.3 , 0.9] [2.0 , 2.1]	[1.9 , 2.7] [2.8 , 3.7]	[1.1 , 6.4]	0.9

Our algorithm is not optimal yet. This is connected with the part of the algorithm that constructs the minimal covering of the investigated structure. But our variants give results with error less than three percents both for one-dimensional simple curves and for fractals.

The other tested programs give more than ten percentage errors for tested data.

Our next considerations will be connected with further testing and improving other methods of calculating fractal dimensions. In the future we would like to use the fractal dimension in measuring the complexity of river shapes. We will need methods good enough both for complex structures and for smooth figures.

REFERENCES

[1] Buchnicek M., Nezadal M., Zmeskal O. 2000. '*Numeric calculation of fractal dimension*'. Nostradamus 2000. Prediction Conference.

[2] Edgar G. 1990. 'Measures, Topology and Fractal Geometry'. Springer-Verlag, New York.

[3] Falconer K.J. 1985. 'The Geometry of Fractal Sets'. Cambridge University Press. Cambridge.

[4] Gonzato G., Mulargia F., Ciccotti M. 2000. 'Measuring the fractal dimensions of ideal and actual objects: implications for application in geology and geophysics'. Geophys. J. Int. 142, 108-116.

[5] Gonzato G., Mulargia F., Marzochi W. 1998. 'Practical application of fractal analysis: problems and solutions'. Geophys. J. Int. 132, 275-282.

[6] HarFA - Zmeskal O., Nezadal M., Buchnicek M. 2000. '*Harmonic and Fractal Image Analyzer*'. http://www.fch.vutbr.cz/lectures/imagesci/harfa.htm. Brno.

[7] http://www.iamg.org/CGEditor/cg1998.htm. (look for Gonzato).

[8] http://polymer.bu.edu/ogaf/html/chp21lab2.htm. Simulab 2: Covering a coastline.

[9] Kolmogorov A. 1958. 'Sur les proprietes des functions de concentrations de M.P. Levy'. Ann. Inst. H. Poincare. 16, 27-34.

[10] Kraft R. 1995. 'Fractals and Dimensions'. HTTP-Protocol at www.weihenstephan.de. http://www.weihenstephan.de/ane/dimensions/dimensions.html .

[11] Kraft R. 'Test Images'. http://www.weihenstephan.de/dvs/idolon/idolonhtml/testimg.html

[12] Mandelbrot B.B. 1977. 'The fractal geometry of nature'. W.H.Freeman and Co., San Francisco.

[13] Patzek Tad.W. 2003. E240 Lecture 3: 'The Fractal Dimension'. 27 pp. http://patzek.berkeley.edu/indexold.html. main page. http://petroleum.berkeley.edu/patzek/e240/Lecture04Materials.htm. Coastline.

[14] Peitgen H.O., Jurgens H., Saupe D. 1992. 'Chaos and Fractals. New Frontiers of Science'. Springer-Verlag. New York.

[15] Stromberg F. 'Iterated function systems, the chaos game and invariant measures'. Uppsala Universitet. http://www.math.uu.se/staff/pages/?uname=fredrik.

Multi-stage ship control in a fuzzy environment

ZBIGNIEW PIETRZYKOWSKI
Maritime University of Szczecin, Department of Communication and Sea Cybernetics,
ul. Wały Chrobrego 1/2, PL-70500 Szczecin, Poland, e-mail: zbip@wsm.szczecin.pl

Abstract: Serious consequences of marine accidents necessitate the development and implementation of systems enhancing the level of navigational safety. The analysis of navigational situations and preparation of collision avoiding manoeuvres call for particular attention. These issues are connected with the determination of a ship's optimal and, first of all, safe trajectory. Ship control is connected with decisions made in the conditions of uncertainty, which results from difficulties in describing control goals and constraints. The problem of ship control as a task of multi-stage control in a fuzzy environment is presented. Simulation research of ship encounter situations in an open area has been carried out. The results have been discussed.

Key words: multi-stage control, fuzzy environment, ship movement control

1.   INTRODUCTION

The planning of a ship's safe trajectory is required for safe and optimal carriage of cargo and people – execution of a sea passage. Navigational decisions refer to various time ranges. The decisions include weather planning of a voyage and ship control (collision prevention and avoidance). The former is executed by dedicated land-based centres and the decisions made are strategic ones. Ship control aiming at the prevention and avoidance of collisions rests solely on the navigator handling the ship. These are operating decisions.

An increasing volume of available information and growing complexity of shipboard technical systems make the information management and decision making on this basis more difficult. Especially in the case of complicated navigation situations, e.g. damage, making the right decision can go beyond the capabilities of the decision-maker, that is the navigator. One way of finding solutions to this problem is the development of decision support systems. Such systems are implemented on the basis of analyses of decision processes taking place while handling a ship.

Methods and tools of knowledge engineering offer increasingly wider ranges of application. They make it possible to acquire, represent and utilize the knowledge and experience of experts in decision making processes. This is particularly important when a decision is to be made in the conditions of uncertainty. Such conditions occur when a sea-going vessel is steered. Inaccuracy and imprecision characterize, *inter alia*, an assessment of a navigational situation, the moment of starting a collision avoiding manoeuvre, the type and range of a manoeuvre (e.g. alteration of the course, scope of the alteration) and manoeuvre execution. In this connection, the problem of safe ship control can be treated as a multi-stage decision making process in a fuzzy environment.

2. DECISION-MAKING PROCESS OF SHIP MOVEMENT CONTROL

The decision making process can be divided into stages that have to be properly executed for the decision to be the right one and for the action taken to be effective (Figure 1).

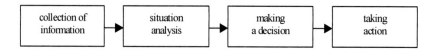

Fig. 1. Stages of the decision making process

The correctness of a decision depends on such factors as the scope and quality of information, knowledge, experience and skills of the decision maker and his / her acquaintance of the problem (task) to be solved. The following are of importance: the navigational situation model used, the methods of navigational situation analysis and assessment as well as the kind and scope of decision the navigator has considered as acceptable (Figure 2).

There are a number of factors affecting a decision that is made. These include properties and parameters of the ship and of the area, traffic conditions, hydrological and meteorological conditions etc. The criteria of choice (decision maker's criteria) are essential. In the case of decision making, the information describing the problem may differ in character: deterministic, probabilistic, uncertainty, fuzziness.

Two major approaches in decision process modelling are presented in [5]:

– descriptive approach; not based on the knowledge of a model defining the output (effect) as the function of input (cause); however, it is based on the knowledge of input values that are required to obtain desired output values.

– prescriptive approach; it is based on the knowledge of a model defining the output (effect) as the function of input (cause); a certain algorithm is used for the optimal process control (conventional non-fuzzy optimizing algorithm).

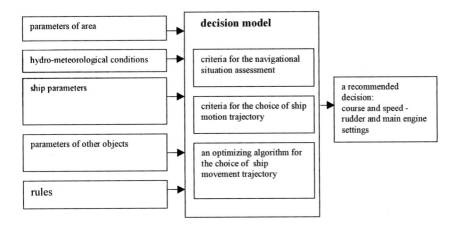

Fig. 2. A model of a navigational situation

In the case of a sea-going ship the controlled process is that of ship movement along a determined trajectory. The input x may be the ship's present position, its course, speed, rudder or engine settings, while the control may refer to, respectively, the choice of ship's course, rudder setting or main engine setting. When two ships meet each other out at sea, the control process may consist in setting the own ship's course so that the passing of the target ship takes place at the preset CPA_L. In both cases the control can be performed with the use of classical or fuzzy controllers. The prescriptive control has been herein considered, in which methods of multi-stage fuzzy control have been used for optimal control.

3. CRITERIA FOR SITUATION ASSESSMENT

The analysis and assessment of a navigational situation based on the selected criteria are of utmost importance in the decision making process. From the information on the current navigational situation – the type of area, its specific properties, encounter situation (ship, stationary objects, obstructions to navigation, land- and seamarks) – the regulations applicable in a given situation are selected and prioritised. Thus, the decision whether action is to be taken or not is based on the regulations in force and appropriate criteria of the navigational situation assessment. When certain measures have to be taken, the kind and scope of actions is specified. The following criteria for a navigational situation assessment can be distinguished:

- criteria directly imposed by the regulations,
- closest point of approach,
- safety level,
- ship domain,
- fuzzy closest point of approach,
- ship fuzzy domain.

This widely used criterion for navigational situation assessment is applied in the automatic radar plotting aid (ARPA). It is assumed that the navigator will determine the minimum (limit) distance at which other objects will be passed (CPA_L). An additional criterion is the time to closest point of approach ($TCPA$) – its minimum value $TCPA_L$ is also defined by the navigator. There are also criteria taking into account both CPA_L and $TCPA_L$ at the same time.

The navigator intuitively tends to maintain a certain area around the ship clear of other navigational objects - ship domain [4]. Any entry into the ship domain is interpreted as a hazard to navigational safety. Two- and three-dimensional domains are proposed. The shapes of two-dimensional domains can be circular, rectangular, elliptical, polygon, or more complex figures. The domain shape and size depend on a number of factors, which makes the determination of the domain difficult. The human factor, naturally, plays an important role in the determination of a ship's domain.

The value of the closest point of approach CPA_L set by the navigator defines a safe distance at which two ships will pass each other. If the ships pass each other at a 'slightly larger' distance, the safety level will be higher. It is possible to 'lower slightly' the value of CPA_L ($CPA < CPA_L$). Then the ships passing will not lead to a collision and is acceptable. Thus, a certain interval of tolerance can exist $\langle CPA_{Lmin}, CPA_{Lmax} \rangle$.

The term 'ship fuzzy domain' [9, 10] means an area around the ship which should be maintained free from other craft and objects by the navigator (Fig. 3); its shape and size depend on the preset level of navigational safety, understood as the degree of membership of a navigational situation to the fuzzy set "dangerous navigation".

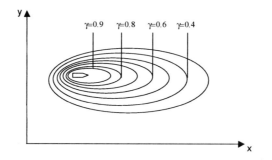

Fig. 3. Fuzzy domain; its boundaries for various values of navigational safety level γ
($\gamma \in \langle 0,1 \rangle$); $\gamma=0$ – very safe situation; $\gamma=1$ – very dangerous situation

4.   DECISION MAKING IN A FUZZY ENVIRONMENT

The work [1] defines the term of fuzzy environment as the ordered four

$$\langle G, C, D, U \rangle \tag{1}$$

where: G – fuzzy goal
C – fuzzy constraints

   D – fuzzy decision
   U – set of decisions

The fuzzy goal is defined as a fuzzy set $G \subseteq U$ whose membership function μ_G:

$$\mu_G : X \times U \rightarrow [0, 1] \in R \tag{2}$$

whilst the fuzzy constraint is defined as the fuzzy set $C \subseteq U$ with the membership function μ_C:

$$\mu_C : X \times U \rightarrow [0, 1] \in R \tag{3}$$

   When a decision is to be made in a fuzzy environment, i.e. with the goal G and constraint C, described by respective membership functions $\mu_G(x)$ and $\mu_C(x)$, the fuzzy decision D is determined from this relationship:

$$\mu_D(x) = \mu_G(x) * \mu_C(x) \tag{4}$$

where $(*)$ is an aggregation (e.g. of the minimum or product type). It is assumed that an optimal decision is a maximizing decision, i.e.

$$\mu_D(x^*) = \max_{x \in X}(\mu_D(x)) \tag{5}$$

   This also refers to a situation where many (n) goals and many (m) constraints exist. Then the fuzzy decision is defined as:

$$\mu_D(x) = \mu_{G1}(x) * \mu_{G2}(x) * \dots * \mu_{Gn}(x) * \\ * \mu_{C1}(x) * \mu_{C2}(x) * \dots * \mu_{Cm}(x) \tag{6}$$

   where: n – number of goals,
            m – number of constraints.

   One example in this context is the determination of a safe distance of passing another ship (goal G) with the minimum possible deviation from the original trajectory (constraint C). To do this, we have to identify fuzzy conditions (the function) of goal and constraints, described by the adequate functions of membership to relevant fuzzy sets (Figure 4)
   Then, the decision (D) has this form:

$$D = G * C \tag{7}$$

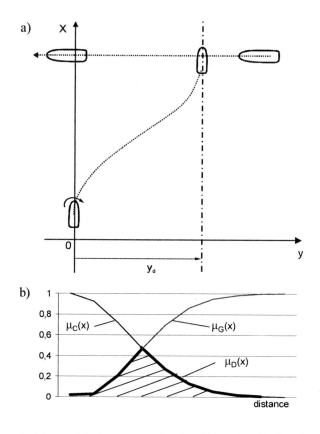

Fig. 4. Fuzzy decision model: a) encounter situation; b) membership functions to the sets of goal (G), constraint (C) and decision (D)

The passing of another ship at a safe distance (goal), depending on the assumed criterion, features a fuzzy closest point of approach or a fuzzy domain. For crisp (non-fuzzy) goals and constraints these would be, respectively, the closest point of approach CPA_L or a ship domain D_S.

The fuzzy closest point of approach CPA_{LF} and the fuzzy domain D_{SF} are described by the membership functions $\mu_{CPALF}(CPA)$ and $\mu_{DSF\angle Ki}(d_{Ki})$:

$$\mu_{CPALF}(CPA) = \begin{cases} 0 & for\ CPA < CPA_{L\min} \\ \dfrac{CPA - CPA_{L\min}}{CPA_{L\max} - CPA_{L\min}} & for\ CPA_{L\min} \le CPA \le CPA_{L\max} \\ 1 & for\ CPA > CPA_{L\max} \end{cases} \tag{8}$$

$$\mu_{DSF\_\angle Ki}(d_{Ki}) = \begin{cases} 0 & for\ d_{Ki} < D_{S\min}(\angle K_i) \\ \dfrac{d_{Ki} - D_{S\min}(\angle K_i)}{D_{S\max}(\angle K_i) - D_{S\min}(\angle K_i)} & for\ D_{S\min}(\angle K_i) \le d_{Ki} \le D_{S\max}(\angle K_i) \\ 1 & for\ d_{Ki} > D_{S\max}(\angle K_i) \end{cases} \tag{9}$$

where:

CPA	– value of the closest point of approach,
CPA_{Lmin}, CPA_{Lmax}	– minimum and maximum closest points of approach, respectively,
$\angle K_i$	– heading angle on the target ship; $i = 0, 1,...,180$ [°],
d_{Ki}	– distance to the target ship on the heading angle $\angle K_i$,
$\mu_{DSF\_\angle Ki}(d_{Ki})$	– membership function of distance on the heading angle $\angle K_i$ of the ship's fuzzy domain,
D_{Smin}, D_{Smax}	– boundaries of the fuzzy domain, respectively, for the navigational safety level: $\gamma = 1$ (very dangerous situation) and $\gamma = 0$ (very safe situation),
$D_{Smin}(\angle K_i)$	– distance from the boundary of domain D_{Smin} on the heading angle $\angle K_i$,
$D_{Smax}(\angle K_i)$	– distance from the boundary of domain D_{Smax} on the heading angle $\angle K_i$.

The constraint (C) is a deviation from the original trajectory y_d, described by the membership function μ_{CLF} :

$$\mu_{CLF}(y_d) = \begin{cases} 1 & for \ y_d < y_{min} \\ 1 - \dfrac{y_d - y_{min}}{y_{max} - y_{min}} & for \ y_{min} \le y_d \le y_{max} \\ 0 & for \ y_d > y_{max} \end{cases} \tag{10}$$

where y_{min} and y_{max} are, respectively, the values of minimum and maximum deviations from the original trajectory acceptable by the navigators.

Moreover, it is recommended to take into account a visible manoeuvre. This means such a change in the ship's course that will be noticed by the target ship navigator. This constraint can be described by the membership function μ_{CC}

$$\mu_{CC}(\Delta\Psi) = \begin{cases} 1 & for \ \Delta\Psi = 0 \\ \dfrac{\Delta\Psi - \Delta\Psi_{min}}{\Delta\Psi_{RL} - \Delta\Psi_{min}} & for \ \Delta\Psi_{min} \le \Delta\Psi < \Delta\Psi_{RL} \\ 1 & for \ \Delta\Psi_{RL} \le \Delta\Psi \le \Delta\Psi_{RH} \\ 1 - \dfrac{\Delta\Psi - \Delta\Psi_{RH}}{\Delta\Psi_{RH} - \Delta\Psi_{max}} & for \ \Delta\Psi_{RH} < \Delta\Psi \le \Delta\Psi_{max} \\ 0 & in \ another \ case \end{cases} \tag{11}$$

where:

$\Delta\Psi$	– course change,
$\Delta\Psi_{min}$	– minimum course change,
$\Delta\Psi_R$	– recommended lower boundary of course change,
$\Delta\Psi_{RH}$	– recommended upper boundary of course change,
$\Delta\Psi_{ma}$	– maximum acceptable course change.

5.   MULTI-STAGE CONTROL IN A FUZZY ENVIRONMENT

The control process for the state space $X = \{x_1, \ldots x_n\}$ and control set $U = \{u_1, \ldots u_m\}$ consists in the selection of control variables u_j under constraints $\mu_{Cj}(x)$ with the goals $\mu_{Gi}(x)$ imposed on the states x_i in subsequent stages of control.

The following fuzzy decision (D) is taken as a quality criterion of multi-stage decision making process (control

$$D(x_0) = C^0 * G^1 * C^1 * G^2 * C^{P-1} * G^P \tag{12}$$

where:
P – number of control stages,
C^i – constraint at i-th stage of control,
G^i – goal at i-th stage of control,
x_0 – initial state of the process.

The above decision D is described by the membership functions:

$$\mu_D(u_0, \ldots, u_{N-1} \mid x_0) = \mu_{C0}(u_0) * \mu_{G1}(x_1) * \ldots * \mu_{CP-1}(u_{P-1}) * \mu_{GP}(x_p) \tag{13}$$

where x_i – process state at i-th state of control ($i = 1, \ldots, P$).

The (multi-stage) task of optimal control is then formulated as follows:

$$\mu_D(u_0^*, \ldots, u_{N-1}^* \mid x_0) = \max(\mu_D(u_0, \ldots, u_{N-1} \mid x_0)) \tag{14}$$

Then, the optimal strategy is made up of a series of settings u^*

$$u^* = (u_0^*, u_1^*, \ldots, u_{N-1}^*) \tag{15}$$

Problems of this type are often solved by dynamic optimization methods. One such example is an application of Pontryagin's maximum principle for the determination of an optimal safe trajectory at the minimized deviation from the preset (original) course [6]. The closest point of approach CPA_L has been taken as a safety criterion. Dynamic programming is also used for the determination of ship trajectory [7]. It is a standard method of dynamic optimization used in problems of multi-stage decision making and control. The optimal ship control in terms of a specified control quality indicator is performed with Bellman's optimum principle. The principle defines the basic property of optimal strategy, which says that, regardless of the initial state and decision, the other decisions have to create optimal strategies from the point of view of the state formed due to the first decision. The above problem can be solved by dynamic programming methods, the branch-and-bound method or using the theory of graphs.

6. GRAPH METHOD

The problem of determining an optimal trajectory of a ship can be effectively solved using the properties of a directed graph, where edges are oriented and the arrows indicate the direction of movement or the order of choice. The edges are called arcs, branches, a path or sections of a network of routes. This kind of graph is called a digraph. In a digraph a set of edges $E = \{e_1, e_2, ...\}$ consists of ordered pairs of vertexes. An edge can be connected with one vertex (v_i, v_i) and then it is called a node. There may be more than one edge connected with one pair of vertexes, e.g. rhumb line (loxodrome) and great circle.

A graph may be assigned an unlimited number of graphic representations. By means of graphs and digraphs one can present systems or structures, that may be considered as a set of elements, of which some pairs are combined in a certain way. It often becomes necessary to describe a graph geometrically by assigning the space co-ordinates to the nodes, and a specific distance to the edges. Such graphs are called geometrical graphs. Their properties result from the theory of graphs and the properties of a space in which they are considered.

Conditions are added to the digraph, resulting from the fact that it is a way of representing various possible tracks from starting to final point in a preset area. The digraph is developed in order to the shortest time route to be chosen. Such a digraph will be connected and acyclic. The connected digraph means that for each two vertexes belonging to a set of vertexes there exists a path connecting them. The acyclic digraph means that there is no route in which the first and last vertexes in a series determining the route were identical. The graph in question will not comprise a loop in any vertex if stops in a voyage have not been planned. The vertex illustrating the start of a voyage has only outgoing arcs, whilst the final vertex has only ingoing arcs. Other vertexes have both outgoing and ingoing arcs.

Numerous optimization problems are mathematically equivalent with seeking the shortest path in a certain graph. For this reason the algorithms for defining the shortest path have been given much attention. Several such algorithms have been proposed. The most common ones are those for the determination of the shortest path

— between two specific vertexes,
— between all pairs of vertexes,
— from a certain vertex to all the other vertexes,
— between specific vertexes that goes through some specific vertexes; and
— determination of the second, third etc. shortest path.

One of the most effective algorithms proposed for the determination of the shortest path between a given pair of vertexes is Dijkstra's algorithm [3]. In a given digraph G with n vertexes, labels are attributed to each vertex. The starting vertex is attributed with a fixed label with the 0 value, whereas the remaining vertexes obtain a temporary label denoted as ∞ (a very large number, e.g. larger than the sum of all weights attributed to graph edges).

In subsequent iterations the following operations will be repeated:
1. For each vertex v_j that has a temporary label, a new one is calculated whose value is:

$$\text{min [previous label } j, \text{ /label } i+d_{ij}/]$$

   where "i" is the last vertex with a fixed label determined in the previous iteration, whilst d_{ij} /$d_i \geq 0$/ is a distance attributed to the edge e_{ij} between vertexes v_i and v_j. It is assumed that when no edge e_{ij} exists, then $d_{ij} = \infty$.
2. From the set of all temporary labels the smallest one is chosen (or one of them, if they are equal. It becomes a fixed label of an appropriate vertex. Steps 1 and 2 are repeated alternately. The algorithm terminates its operation the moment the final vertex receives a fixed label.

The above algorithm guarantees finding the so called shortest route (the concept of shortest route in the theory of graphs is ambiguous and may mean the shortest distance, the shortest time of process duration, the highest or lowest profit etc.) between a specific pair of nodes in a finite number of steps. This results from a fact that after each iteration step the number of vertexes with fixed labels increases, therefore the procedure ends when there is a finite number of nodes. The algorithm does not specify directly the sequence of arcs making up the 'shortest route' between the starting and final vertexes, but the value of label assigned to the final vertex. In order to determine subsequent passages between vertexes forming the 'shortest route', while defining the label of each vertex one should note down the characteristics of that vertex in the previous vertexes. Having such a list and doing proper summing up, one can obtain the optimal route.

Dijkstra's algorithm is of the $O(n^2)$ complexity class, where "n" is a number of graph vertexes. While using a given algorithm for the optimisation of voyage time, one cannot specify in advance the weights d_{ij} referring to the times of passages between particular nodes. The weights depend on conditions which vary in time and can only be calculated in the process of algorithm implementation after the labels of particular nodes have been taken into account.

The solution obtained with a program based on the described algorithm is an optimal solution for a graph with specified vertexes and arcs between them. The accuracy of the solution is affected by the density of digraph vertexes positioned within an examined area between the starting and final points and the assumed internal and external degree of the vertexes. This means that a better solution can be obtained by expanding the digraph with a larger number of vertexes and the degree of vertexes (number of branches). If the area is covered with a denser network of routes to choose from and a larger number of vertexes, then the computation time will be longer.

7. RESEARCH

The research focused on ship encounter situations in an open area. The collision prevention regulations in force referring to good visibility conditions are taken into account [2]. The movement of a ship as a control object is described with a non-linear model of ship's dynamics [8]. The ship's dynamics is modelled for a vessel with a capacity of 5427 DWT, length 95 [m], beam [18.2] and draft 5.5 [m].

The expert research has been performed covering encounter situations of ships in an open area in good visibility. The participating navigators, captains and watch officers, differed in sea service time and experience. The research had a form of questionnaires. The navigators were told to define safe distances for a variety of ship encounter situations between their own and target ship. The following parameters were determined: closest points of approach CPA_L, CPA_{Lmin}, CPA_{Lmax}, and the domains: D_S, D_{Smin}, and D_{Smax}. These made up a basis for the defining of fuzzy criteria of manoeuvring assessment and the fuzzy closest point of approach CPA_{LF} and the ship fuzzy domain D_{SF}, described by the membership functions $\mu_{CPALF}(CPA)$ and $\mu_{DSF\angle Ki}(d_{Ki})$. Fuzzy constraints, i.e. deviations from the original trajectory μ_{CLF} and recommended course change μ_{CC} were determined and described with the membership functions.

Multi-stage control and multi-stage control in a fuzzy environment were executed with the use of the graph method (compare Chapter 6). The optimal route was computed.

Simulated ship encounter situations in an open area were based on the above presented models of decision making processes. For comparison, optimal trajectories were determined for crisp (non-fuzzy) conditions: *CPA* criterion and ship domain. In these cases the covered route was taken as a quality indicator of optimal trajectory selection, which in the applied model of ship dynamics corresponds with minimum-time control.

Figures 5, 6, 7 present determined ship trajectories and distances between ships recorded during the simulation.

The data of ship control for crisp (non-fuzzy) criteria of navigational situation assessment: closest point of approach and ship domain – are presented in Figure 5. The manoeuvres were performed in an acceptable manner (nearly correct), similar to those carried out in practice.

The results of the multi-stage control in a fuzzy environment for one constraint (deviation from the original trajectory) are shown in Figure 6. Those manoeuvres were performed too late so that the course had to be significantly altered.

The results of the multi-stage control in a fuzzy environment for two constraints (deviation from the original course and recommended course change) are presented in Figure 7. Those manoeuvres were also performed in an acceptable manner as often occurs in practice. The distances to the target ship during passing manoeuvres are shorter in comparison with the distances for crisp (non-fuzzy) criteria of a navigational situation assessment.

Both manoeuvres are characterized by the course changes causing a decrease in the distance between own ship and the target ship after the latter finds itself on the heading angle on the $(270°, 360°)$ interval.

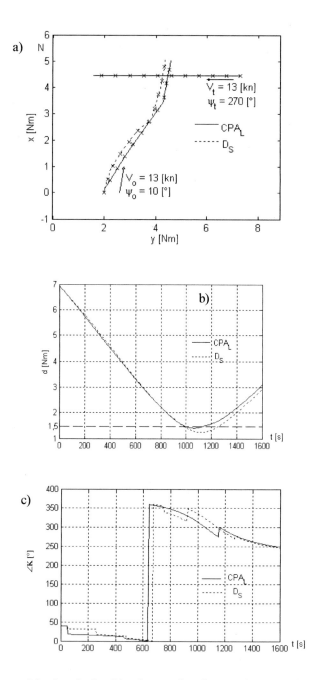

Fig. 5. Ship control for the criteria of the closest point of approach *CPA_L* and ship domain *D_S*; simulation time 1600 [s]: a) ships' movement trajectories – positions (x) on 150 [s] time intervals; b) distances from the target ship; c) heading angles on the target ship

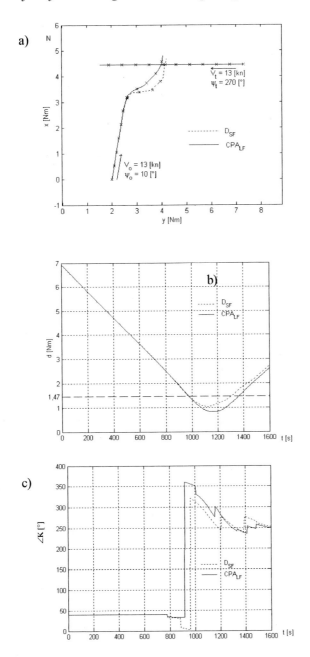

Fig. 6. Multi-stage control in a fuzzy environment for the criteria: fuzzy closest point of approach CPA_{LF} and ship's fuzzy domain D_{SF} and the fuzzy constraint C_{LF} of deviation from original trajectory; simulation time 1600 [s]: a) ships movement trajectories – positions (x) on 150 [s] time intervals; b) distances to the other ship; c) heading courses on the other ship

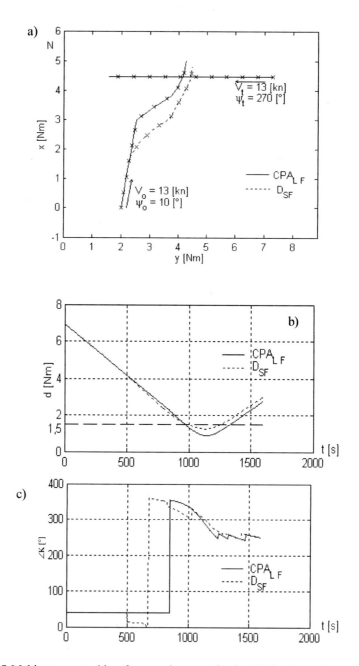

Fig. 7. Multi-stage control in a fuzzy environment for the criteria: fuzzy closest point of approach CPA_{LF} and ship fuzzy domain D_{SF} and the fuzzy constraints: C_{LF} of deviation from original trajectory and recommended course change C_{CC}; simulation time 1600 [s]: a) ships movement trajectories – positions (x) on 150 [s] time intervals; b) distances to the target ship; c) heading courses on the target ship

8. SUMMARY

The process of ship control should account for the applicable regulations, assure safe manoeuvring and be rational. This means, *inter alia*, that criteria used and accepted by the human being have to be applied. This is important from the point of view of the system reliability, and consequently, for the system to be used in practice. Ship control is connected with decisions to be made in the conditions of uncertainty, which results from difficulties in describing the control goals and constraints used by the navigator.

The presented problem of ship control is a problem of multi-stage control in a fuzzy environment. Criteria and methods of navigational situation assessment were implemented: fuzzy closest point of approach and ship fuzzy domain.

The methods and procedures herein discussed utilize the knowledge of expert navigators.

Simulation research of ship encounter situations in open areas is presented and the results are discussed and analysed.

The methods and tools for ship control can find applications in decision support systems used on board by navigators. They can well supplement shipboard collision avoidance ARPA systems.

REFERENCES

[1] Bellman R.E. and Zadeh L.A. (1970): Decision making in a fuzzy environment, Management Science, 17.

[2] COLREGs (1972): Convention on the International Regulations for Preventing Collisions at Sea, International Maritime Organization.

[3] Deo N. (1980): The Theory of Graphs and its Application in Technology and Computer Science, PWN Warszawa (in Polish).

[4] Goodwin E. M. (1975): A statistical study of ship domain, Journal of Navigation, 28.

[5] Kacprzyk J. (2001): Multi-stage fuzzy control, WNT, Warszawa (in Polish).

[6] Lisowski J. (1986): Ships collisions avoidance systems, Wydawnictwo Morskie Gdansk (in Polish).

[7] Lisowski J., Rak A.. (1999): Determining of dynamic trajectory with neural ship's domain, Sientific papers of Maritime University of Gdynia, No 37, 1999 (in Polish).

[8] Norrbin N. (1971): Theory and observations on the use of a mathematical model for ship maneuvering in deep and confined waters, SSPA Publ. 68, Goeteborg.

[9] Pietrzykowski, Z. (1999): Ship fuzzy domain in assessment of navigational safety in restricted areas, III. Navigational Symposium, Gdynia, Vol. I, (in Polish).

[10] Pietrzykowski Z. (2002): The analysis of a ship fuzzy domain in a restricted area, IFAC Conference Computer Applications in Marine Systems CAMS'2001, Elsevier Science Ltd.

Informative value of the possibilistic extension principle

ANDRZEJ PIEGAT
Technical University of Szczecin, Zolnierska 49, 71-210 Szczecin, Poland,
e-mail: Andrzej.Piegat@wi.ps.pl

Abstract: The present fuzzy arithmetic is based on possibilistic extension-principle of Zadeh. Fuzzy arithmetic is necessary to accomplish calculation in Computing with Words [6]. However, arithmetic operations carried out with the standard, possibilistic extension-principle often yield results which have small or no practical value. Sometimes the results are paradoxical ones. An example of such case is presented in the paper and also a new cardinality extension-principle in a version that enables regard for all additional constraints resulting from the context of the problem to be solved. The principle can be used only to fuzzy sets of numbers of probabilistic character which often occur in practical problems.

Key words: fuzzy arithmetic, extension-principle, constrained extension-principle, Computing with Words.

1. INTRODUCTION

Fuzzy arithmetic allows for accomplishment of arithmetic operations on fuzzy sets of numbers, operations such as addition of the sets (about 5) + (about 7). The operations can be carried out with use of the standard extension-principle of Zadeh [2], formula (1):

$$\mu_{A*B}(z) = \vee \left[\mu_A(x_A) \wedge \mu_B(x_B) \right], \quad \forall x_A * x_B = z, \tag{1}$$

where:
* stands for one of the operations: addition, subtraction, multiplication, division,
A, B are fuzzy sets of numbers which constraint possible values of the variables
$x_A, x_B, \quad x_A \in A, x_B \in B$

μ_A, μ_B - membership functions that define membership of variables x_A, x_B to the sets A, B.

Because the standard extension principle (1) takes into account only the basic constraints A and B imposed on variables x_A and x_B and does not regard for other possible constraints G.J. Klirr proposed in [3] *constrained fuzzy arithmetic* that enables regard for any constraints which can exist in the problem to be solved. Let $R(x_A, x_B)$ denote any constraint imposed on variables x_A, x_B then arithmetic operations * are accomplished according to formula (2).

$$\mu_{A*B}(z) = \bigvee [\mu_A(x_A) \wedge \mu_B(x_B) \wedge \mu_R(x_A, x_B)], \quad \forall x_A * x_B = z, \tag{2}$$

To realize the union operation $\vee$ s-norms [4] as Max can be used. For intersection operation $\wedge$ t-norms as Min, Prod can be applied. The union operation $\vee$ in formulas (1) and (2) means that both the standard extension-principle of Zadeh and the constrained extension-principle of Klirr are possibilistic principles because from any relation $x_A * x_B = z$ only one element is chosen: the element with the greatest membership grade (operator Max, Sup). The both extension-principles have not the feature of additivity. What comes of this fact?

Let us consider the candy example.

Example

Description of the problem
    A mother had a small number of chocolate candies and decided to give them to their children, Fig. 1.

Fig. 1. Ilustration for the candy example.

Each child took a small number of candies from the mother.
Query

How many candies were left (how large is the remainder)?

Solution

In Fig. 2 the membership function of the set small number of candies, which was identified by inquiry of the mother, is presented.

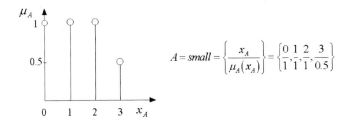

$$A = small = \left\{ \frac{x_A}{\mu_A(x_A)} \right\} = \left\{ \frac{0}{1}, \frac{1}{1}, \frac{2}{1}, \frac{3}{0.5} \right\}$$

Fig. 2. Membership function of the fuzzy set of numbers small number of candies used by the mother.

Because each of the 3 children took the small number A of candies the task consists in calculation of the fuzzy difference (2).

$$G(z) = A(x_A) - A(x_B) - A(x_C) - A(x_D) \tag{2}$$

To simplify calculations let us firstly calculate how many candies were left after the first child had taken his/her candies. Thus, the difference (small number - small number), formula (3) is to be calculated.

$$G(z) = A(x_A) - A(x_B) \tag{3}$$

The crisp number x_A of candies the mother had was limited. The constraint is expressed by the fuzzy set $small = A$. This constraint is defined by formula (4).

$$x_A \in A, \quad A = \left\{ \frac{x_A}{\mu_A(x_A)} \right\} = \left\{ \frac{0}{1}, \frac{1}{1}, \frac{2}{1}, \frac{3}{0.5} \right\}$$

$$x_B \in A, \quad A = \left\{ \frac{x_B}{\mu_B(x_B)} \right\} = \left\{ \frac{0}{1}, \frac{1}{1}, \frac{2}{1}, \frac{3}{0.5} \right\} \tag{4}$$

Because no child could achieve the crisp number x_B of candies that would be greater than the number x_A the other had the constraint (5) expressed by relation $R(x_A, x_B)$ imposed on the both variables (x_A, x_B) has to be taken into account.

$$(x_A, x_B) \in R, \quad \mu_R = \begin{cases} 1 & \text{if} \quad x_B \le x_A \\ 0 & \text{else} \end{cases} \tag{5}$$

Below the calculation of the difference $A(x_A) - A(x_B)$ (*small* number - *small* number) with use of the possibilistic constrained extension principle (2) of Klirr will be presented. The intersection of sets will be performed with Product and the union with Maximum.

Step 1

Calculation of all possible relations $x_A - x_B = z$.

$$A(x_A) - A(x_B) = \left\{ \frac{0}{1}, \frac{1}{1}, \frac{2}{1}, \frac{3}{0.5} \right\} - \left\{ \frac{0}{1}, \frac{1}{1}, \frac{2}{1}, \frac{3}{0.5} \right\} =$$
$$= \left\{ \left[\frac{0}{1}, \frac{0}{1}, \frac{0}{1}, \frac{0}{0.5} \right], \left[\frac{1}{1}, \frac{1}{1}, \frac{1}{0.5} \right], \left[\frac{2}{1}, \frac{2}{0.5} \right], \left[\frac{3}{0.5} \right] \right\}$$

(6)

Step 2

Determining in each particular relation $x_A - x_B = z^*$ the element with the greatest membership (operation $\vee$) as the relation representative.

$$A(x_A) - A(x_B) = \left\{ \frac{0}{1}, \frac{1}{1}, \frac{2}{1}, \frac{3}{0.5} \right\}$$

(7)

Fig. 3 illustrates the calculations.

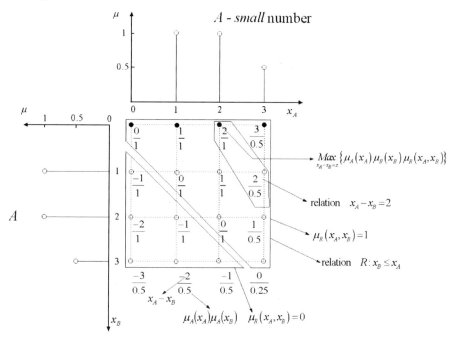

Fig. 3. Illustration of calculation of the difference $A(x_A) - A(x_B) = ($ *small* number - *small* number) with use of the possibilistic, constraint-extension principle (2) of Klirr.

After subtraction of the 2 equal possibilistic fuzzy sets (*small - small*) the difference $(A - A)_c$ shown in Fig. 4 was achieved.

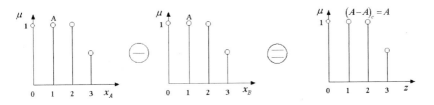

Fig. 4. Result of subtraction of two identical fuzzy sets $A(x_A) - A(x_B)$ (the number of candies the mother had – the number of candies the first child took) with the possibilistic constraint-extension principle (2).

As results from formula (6) and Fig. 4 the difference $(A - A)_c$ that stands for the possible number of candies which was left after the mother had given candies to the first child is identical with the fuzzy set A representing candies which the mother have had at the beginning. Thus, if the next, second child takes the small number of candies the remainder $(A - A - A)_c$ will also be identical with the original fuzzy set A. Continuing this process, independently of how many next children would take small number of candies from the mother the remainder of candies which is left will always be identical with the initial fuzzy set *small*: (*small - small - small-, ...,small*) = *small*.

This strange situation is shown in Fig. 5.

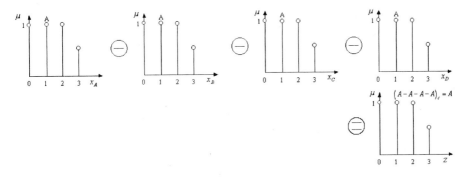

Fig. 5. Illustration of subtraction of fuzzy sets of numbers $(A - A - A - A)$ representing taking candies from themother by her 3 children.

The result of subtraction $(A - A - A - A)$ shown in Fig. 5 with use of the possibilistic extension principle (2) is correct and explainable though it seems paradoxical. It means the possible number of candies that was left to the mother after she had endowed her 3 children. It is possible that each child took 0 candies - therefore the possibility grade that the mother is left 3 candies is the same as at the beginning. It is also possible that only the first child took 1 candy and the next children took 0 candies - then the mother is left 2 candies. It is possible that two children took 1 candy each and the third took 0 candies - then the mother is left 1 candy, etc.

The above explains that the achieved strange result $(A - A - A - A)_c = A$ is correct in the possibilistic sense. Even when 1000000 or more children would take the *small* number of candies from the mother she would have the same *small* number at the end.

However, **how large is the practical use of such possibilistic subtraction of fuzzy sets of numbers?**

A very small one. The result $(A - A - A - A)_c = A$ we get says us almost nothing. The result does not react on subtraction of successive subtrahends A (the number of candies the successive children took). But intuitively we await that the number of candies the mother is left after endowment of successive children should (minuend) decrease more and more. In this case the possibilistic fuzzy arithmetic is insensitive. It is correct? Was in the course of the solution process of the problem made an error ?

2. PROBLEM OF CORRECT RECOGNITION OF THE CHARACTER OF FUZZY SETS OF NUMBERS

In the literature of fuzzy set theory fuzzy evaluations as *young, small* integer etc are treated as possibilistic ones. Professor Zadeh himself in his publication [5] gives the evaluations *young* and *small* integer as examples of possibilistic evaluations. However, let us consider how the membership function of the set *small* integer could be identified. To this aim a great number of persons should be asked whether the numbers 0, 1, 2, 3,... they consider as *small* or not. The ratio of number of persons which consider the particular number, e.g. 3 as *small* to the number of all asked persons has meaning of ease [4] to classify this number as *small*. Thus, the ease of classification means probability of classification to the set. Similarly as the membership of *small* integer the membership of *young* man or *medium* height can be identified. In the case, we want to identify membership function of not a group of persons but only of a one single person, this person should be asked many times, in different days about his/her classification of particular numbers 1, 2, 3, ..., etc. Only in this way we can identify how the person really understands meaning of the word *small* integer. Thus, possibility that the element x is in the fuzzy set A is probability of classification this element to the set. Because this probability referring to only one element, in the extreme case, can be equal to 1, the sum of probabilities of all elements being in the set A can be greater than 1.

If the mother informs us that she has the *small* number of candies and when we known her way she understands the word *small* expressed by membership function (8):

$$x_A \in A, \quad A = \left\{ \frac{x_A}{\mu_A(x_A)} \right\} = \left\{ \frac{0}{1}, \frac{1}{1}, \frac{2}{1}, \frac{3}{0.5} \right\} \tag{8}$$

then we can conclude that probability of the mother having 0 or 1 or 2 candies is the greatest one and equal for all these numbers and probability of 3 candies is two times smaller than that of 2 candies.

If the membership function of small integer is of probabilistic character the problem of candies can be solved in the framework of probability theory [1] or by use of cardinality extension-principle proposed by author of this paper.

3.   CARDINALITY EXTENSION-PRINCIPLE REGARDING FOR CONTEXT-DEPENDENT CONSTRAINTS

The cardinality extension-principle (9) formulates the way of calculation of the membership grade of a possible result z^* of the arithmetic operation $x_A * x_B$, where the mark * stands for addition or subtraction or multiplication or division.

$$\mu_{A*B}\left(z^*\right) = \frac{\sum\limits_{over\,S(R)} \mu_R\left(x_A * x_B = z^*\right)}{Max\left\{\sum\limits_{over\,S(R)} \mu_R\left(x_A * x_B = z\right)\right\}} \tag{9}$$

Where:

R - resulting constraint-relation regarding for all constraints imposed on variables x_A, x_B in the problem to be solved,

$R = A \cap B \cap C_{A1} \cap, \ldots, C_{Am} \cap C_{B1} \cap, \ldots, C_{Bn} \cap C_{AB1} \cap, \ldots, C_{ABp} \cap C_{C1} \cap, \ldots, C_{Cr}$

$S(R)$ - support of the resulting constraint-relation R

Membership function $\mu_R\left(x_A, x_B\right)$ of the resulting constraint-relation R is defined by formula (10).

$$\mu_R\left(x_A, x_B\right) = \left[\mu_A\left(x_A\right) \wedge \mu_B\left(x_B\right)\right] \wedge \left[\mu_{CA1}\left(x_A\right), \ldots, \mu_{CAm}\left(x_A\right)\right] \wedge$$
$$\wedge \left[\mu_{CB1}\left(x_B\right), \ldots, \mu_{CBn}\left(x_B\right)\right] \wedge \tag{10}$$
$$\wedge \left[\mu_{CAB1}\left(x_A, x_B\right), \ldots, \mu_{CABp}\left(x_A, x_B\right)\right] \wedge \left[\mu_{C1}\left(z\right), \ldots, \mu_{Cr}\left(z\right)\right]$$

Where:

$\mu_A\left(x_A\right), \mu_B\left(x_B\right)$ - membership functions of constraints imposed on variables x_A, x_B by fuzzy sets A and B being subject of the arithmetic operation * (addition, subtraction, division, multiplication),

$\mu_{CAi}\left(x_A\right)$ - additional constraint on variable x_A resulting from context of the problem to be solved,

$\mu_{CABj}(x_A, x_B)$ - additional constraint imposed simultaneously on both variables (x_A, x_B) resulting from context of the problem to be solved,

$\mu_{Ck}(z)$ - additional constraint imposed on the resulting variable $z = x_A * x_B$ resulting from context of the problem to be solved.

In formula (9) the expression $\sum\limits_{over\,S(R)} \mu_R$ stands for cardinality of a single concrete

relation $x_A * x_B = z^*$, whereas the expresion $Max\left\{\sum\limits_{over\,S(R)} \mu_R\right\}$ means the greatest

relation cardinality from all relations $z = x_A * x_B$ which occur in the problem.

The cardinality extension-principle (9) can be used only for fuzzy sets of probabilistic and not of possibilistic character. It seems complicated one but example of its application to solve the problem of candies will show that it is simple one. Let us calculate how many candies were left after the mother had endowed the first child who had taken the small number A of candies. Let us remember that on the variables x_A, x_B the constraints (4) and (5) are imposed.

Step 1

Determination of all possible and (by constraints) admissible relations $z = x_A - x_B$ with use of operator Product for intersection $\wedge$ and Maximum for union $\vee$.

$$A(x_A) - A(x_B) = \left\{ \frac{x_A}{\mu_A(x_A)} \right\} - \left\{ \frac{x_B}{\mu_B(x_B)} \right\} =$$

$$= \left\{ \frac{0}{1}, \frac{1}{1}, \frac{2}{1}, \frac{3}{0.5} \right\} - \left\{ \frac{0}{1}, \frac{1}{1}, \frac{2}{1}, \frac{3}{0.5} \right\} =$$

$$= \left\{ \left[\frac{0}{1}, \frac{0}{1}, \frac{0}{1}, \frac{0}{0.5} \right], \left[\frac{1}{1}, \frac{1}{1}, \frac{1}{0.5} \right], \left[\frac{2}{1}, \frac{2}{0.5} \right], \left[\frac{3}{0.5} \right] \right\}$$

Step 2

Determining cardinalities of particular relations $x_A - x_B = z$.

$$card(x_A - x_B = 0) = 3.25 = Max\ card(x_A - x_B = z)$$
$$card(x_A - x_B = 1) = 2.5$$
$$card(x_A - x_B = 2) = 1.5$$
$$card(x_A - x_B = 3) = 0.5$$

Step 3

Calculation of membership grades of particular admissible values of the result $z = x_A - x_B$.

$$\mu_{A\text{-}A}(z{=}0)=\frac{\text{card}\left(x_A-x_B=0\right)}{\text{Max card}\left(x_A-x_B=z\right)}=\frac{3.25}{3.25}=1$$

$$\mu_{A\text{-}A}(z{=}1)=\frac{\text{card}\left(x_A-x_B=1\right)}{\text{Max card}\left(x_A-x_B=z\right)}=\frac{2.5}{3.25}=0.769$$

$$\mu_{A\text{-}A}(z{=}2)=\frac{\text{card}\left(x_A-x_B=2\right)}{\text{Max card}\left(x_A-x_B=z\right)}=\frac{1.5}{3.25}=0.462$$

$$\mu_{A\text{-}A}(z{=}3)=\frac{\text{card}\left(x_A-x_B=3\right)}{\text{Max card}\left(x_A-x_B=z\right)}=\frac{0.5}{3.25}=0.154$$

Subtraction result *small* number - *small* number (of candies) is given by formula (11) and in Fig. 6.

$$A(x_A) - A(x_B) = \left\{\frac{z}{\mu_{A-A}(z)}\right\} = \left\{\frac{0}{1},\frac{1}{0.769},\frac{2}{0.462},\frac{3}{0.154}\right\} \tag{11}$$

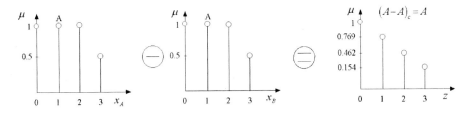

Fig. 6. Illustration of subtraction of two fuzzy sets of numbers A - A (*small* number - *small* number) with use of the cadinality extension principle (9).

After endowment of all three children the mother was left $(A-A-A-A)_c$ of candies. This set is expressed by formula (12) and shown in Fig. 7.

$$\left[A(x_A) - A(x_B)-A(x_C)-A(x_D)\right]_c = \left\{\frac{0}{1},\frac{1}{0.491},\frac{2}{0.175},\frac{3}{0.035}\right\} \tag{12}$$

As can be seen in Fig. 7 the result if subtraction $(A-A-A-A)_c$ standing for remainder of candies is not identical with the set A standing for the number of candies the mother had at the beginning . In the case of possibilistic extension principle, Fig. 5, both sets were identical. Now the subtraction result reacts on subtracting successive fuzzy sets of numbers (A) (taking candies by successive children). The results here are not paradoxical ones. In the case of possibilistic extension-principle such reaction did not occur. Therefore informative value of the result achieved with use of the cardinality extension-principle (9) is greater than of the result achieved with the possibilistic extension-principle of Zadeh(1) or of Klirr (2).

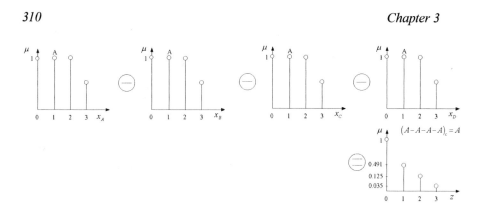

Fig. 7. Illustration of subtraction of fuzzy sets of numbers $(A - A - A - A)$ and result of that subtraction which informs about number of candies that was left after endowment of children.

4. CONCLUSIONS

The paper presents cardinality extension-principle of arithmetic operations from crisp numbers on fuzzy sets of numbers. The principle can be applied to sets of probabilistic character whereas the standard extension-principle of Zadeh to possibilistic sets. In any problem to be solved character of fuzzy sets has to be carefully identified, because mistakes are made here frequently and probablistic sets are often treated as possibilistic ones. When the possibilistic extension principle of Zadeh is used to probabilistic fuzzy sets of numbers the results achieved can be paradoxical and useless ones. It was shown in the paper on example with candies. Results achieved with the cardinality extension principle are free of this disadvantage.

REFERENCES

[1] Bronstein I.N., Siemiendiajew K.A.,1996, Handbook of Mathematics, (in Polish), Wydawnictwo Naukowe PWN, Warszawa
[2] Driankov D., Hellendorn M., Reinfrank M.,1993, An introduction to fuzzy control, Springer-Verlag, Berlin
[3] Klirr g.,L.,1997, Fuzzy arithmetic with requisite constraints, Fuzzy Sets and Systems 91, pp.165-175
[4] Piegat A.,2001, Fuzzy modeling and control, A Springer-Verlag Company, Heidelberg-New York
[5] Zadeh L.A.,1978, Fuzzy sets as a basis for a theory of possibility, Fuzzy Sets and Systems 1, vol.3, No.28
[6] Zadeh L.A., 2002, From computing with numbers to computing with words- From manipulation of measurements to manipulation of perceptions. Applied mathematics and computer science, vol.12, No.3, pp.307-324

Intelligent Marine Control Systems

ROMAN ŚMIERZCHALSKI
Gdynia Maritime University
Morska str. 83, 81-225 Gdynia, Poland, e-mail: roms@am.gdynia.pl

Abstract: The paper discusses current directions of development in marine control systems, special attention being paid to artificial intelligence methods. Taking into account tasks attributed to the control of particular processes on a ship, the control systems were divided into integrated sub-systems. The ship was defined as an intelligent machine making use of artificial intelligence to control processes.

Key words: integrated control system, artificial intelligent, ship control, evolutionary computation, intelligent machine,

1. INTRODUCTION

An automated vessel as an object of control represents a structure consisting of three main systems, which are: the navigational, power, and loading systems. Those systems, in turn, comprise sub-systems for ship guidance, stabilisation, propulsion, steam flow, electric power, air-conditioning, cooling, loading etc. (see: Fig. 1). The vital role in the overall ship operation is played by two systems intended for ship navigation and power. Technological development, especially noticeable in computer techniques and navigation systems, along with modern designs of main engines and electric motors have resulted in increased reliability of individual installations being in operation on the ship, and, consequently, in increased reliability of the ship. An important requirement concerning the safety of ship motion is continuous and reliable work of all those sub-systems. Automation introduced to them creates additional opportunities for more economical use of individual devices and installations via optimisation of their operating parameters. A crucial element in the strategy of reducing costs of automated vessel operation is crew reduction. Maritime world companies in their tendency to reduce operating costs have the dilemma whether to employ cheap, poorly trained crews, or reduce manning level by increasing shipboard automation. Since the latter involves certain capital investment, a short term solution for some is to employ cheap labour and/or to carry cargo in ill-maintained, poorly equipped vessels. Such operations are connected with increased risk of accidents, collisions and equipment failure, and frequently lead to loss of life and damage to the environment. For navigation system [23] the development of navigational automatic ship control system can be divided into the following stages: (I) course-keeping autopilots: (II) track-keeping controllers and (III) automatic berthing systems. Before 1980 almost all conventional autopilots used on sea-going vessels were designed for the course-keeping task. Using directional information taken from a gyrocompass, an autopilot is able to steer a ship on a predefined course. A more sophisticated type of autopilot is the track-keeping controller which not only controls the heading but also controls the ship's position with respect to a reference track. More recent studies on automatic ship guidance in harbours (such as automatic berthing systems) have been reported in many works.

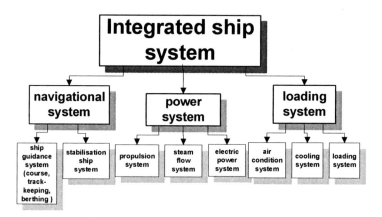

Fig. 1. System structure of the automated ship

2.   METHODS OF MARINE CONTROL SYSTEMS

From technical perspective, the majority (90%) of closed control systems bases on PID controllers, of various design forms. As a result, big potential of computer-aided control systems is, in fact, wasted, and the task of optimal control is in most cases reduced to tuning PI or PID controllers. Those solutions are only effective for selected, simple classes of tasks, and advanced techniques for controlling processes on a ship have to be applied in cases which require high precision of control, or are performed for changing dynamics of the controlled object. In those cases these techniques may considerably improve the quality of control, compared to a conventional single control loop. Although the number of difficult problems connected with controlling processes on the ship is, as a rule, limited, compared to total number of closed control systems, they have, however, key effect on the quality of control, safety and reliability of the ship. Taking into account methods of control [1] [8], ship control processes can be divided into four levels. Below is presented a classification of process control levels. Level I consists of conventional control ship's processes that are well known and have been widely used for several decades. The advanced control processes in Level II are referred to as classical because they have been used in ship automation for over 20 years. The process control processes in Level III have been widely used in ships and are described as current process control. Level IV contains both old and new control processes that include new approaches used in ship's systems.

Level I: Conventional control: Manual control, PID control, Ratio control, Cascade control, Feed forward control.

Level II: Advanced control: classical techniques: Gain scheduling, Time delay compensation, Decoupling control, Selective/override controllers.

Level III: Advanced control: widely used techniques, Model predictive control, Statistical quality control, Internal model control, Adaptive control.

Level IV: Advanced control: newer techniques with some ship applications [4][8]: Optimal control, Expert systems, Nonlinear control, Neurocontrollers, Genetic Algorithms, Fuzzy control, Robust control techniques.

The ship is to be treated as an integrated system of simultaneously co-operating sub-sytems. The total ship system integration requires that all shipboard instruments have a standard interface to a common data highway, and communicate using a standard protocol. The ship integration control system with network connection is presented in Fig. 2.

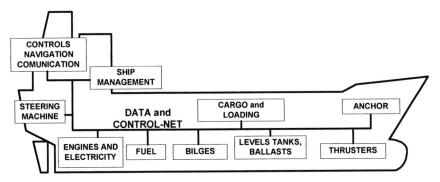

Fig. 2. Ship's data and control network

3. SHIP AS INTELLIGENT MACHINE

Conventional control systems are generally able to cope with relatively simple disturbance effects such as changes in load, or ambient temperature, for instance. However, a higher form of intelligent behaviour is required in an unstructured environment. Here, the machine needs to be capable of reasoning, which in turn requires access to knowledge on:

- goals and tasks,
- own capabilities,
- the environment in which the ship operates.

In the case of an expert system, part of this knowledge can be obtained from human operators who have performed similar tasks successfully, and have their expertise recorded in a suitable knowledge base. The ship as a intelligent machine may be regarded as a system that comprises a number of essential elements or sub-systems as perception, rules and knowledge, and execution, see Fig.3.

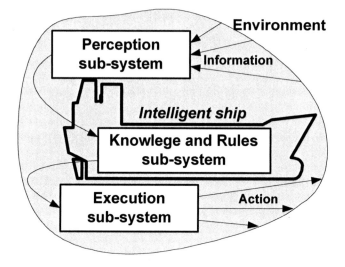

Fig. 3. Ship as a intelligent machine

3.1   Perception

This subsystem collects information about the environment, and the system itself. After that, it processes the information to provide data on the current state of the machine, and the world in which it operates. The essential elements are: sensors -provide raw data on the environment and the machine, signal processing - transforms the information into a suitable form, data fusion - uses multidimensional data spaces to build representations of the system and its environment. According to Burns [2]-[4], on a ship raw navigational data is detected from a range of navigation aids. The Global Positioning System (GPS) is now being employed internationally with hyperbolic electronic positioning systems such as Omega and Loran C, as back-up. In addition there is a move to provide coastal coverage in Europe using differential GPS with increased accuracy. Other marine sensors include ship's log, gyrocompass, Doppler sonar, radar, wind, current and depth under keel recorders. At present, this information is used by integrated bridge systems employing either an automatic radar plotting aid (ARPA) to help with collision avoidance or on more recent vessels using Electronic Chart and Data Information Systems (ECDIS). In the past there was an attempt to create data fusion using Kalman Filter techniques. An important aspect of artificial intelligence (AI) is the use of neural networks to model manoeuvring characteristics of surface vessels. Such techniques eliminate the need for differential equation description of system dynamics via mathematical techniques and provide a relatively simple and computationally efficient technique for multidimensional data fusion.

3.2   Rules and knowledge

This function in an intelligent machine is responsible for making decisions on actions to undertake in order to achieve specified goals. In order to do this the machine is to be able to model itself within its environment and predict results of its own actions, along with possible environment changes. Here, key activities include: reasoning - rule-based systems, fuzzy logic, neural network, evolutionary computation, strategic planning - optimal policy evaluation, adaptive search methods, path planning, learning - from past events, from examples, and/or by discovery.

For instance, weather routing has become a generally accepted technique in strategic planning a journey for an ocean-going vessel. Such procedures have in the past been land based but there have been increasing moves to produce shipboard systems including such techniques as dynamic programming or adaptive search algorithms to compute optimal routes based on minimum time or minimum fuel strategies. Such information is used conventionally as a decision support tool for the ship's master.

As another example, conventional ship autopilots are typically course-keeping and course-changing guidance systems using PID control algorithms. More and more often are being used track-keeping systems which employ cross-track error and lateral velocity as control variables. Much effort has been made in recent years to design intelligent autopilots based on fuzzy logic, self-organising fuzzy logic, neural network, and neuro-fuzzy algorithms [21][23]. All of these control schemes are designed to maintain robust control in conditions of changing ship variables or environmental changes. There have been attempts to integrate dynamic path-planning algorithms with ship guidance systems in order to produce compact automatic weather routing and guidance control systems. In tactical planning several attempts have been made to employ AI techniques in the area of collision avoidance by designing suitable decision support tools [5][9]. It has been suggested that such tools could be integrated with vessel guidance systems to produce an intelligent track management system that could cope with automatic collision avoidance. Still, much work is to be done in the area, particularly with the reliability of target identification. Currently, rapid development is observed in Vessel Traffic Services [7] [19] (VTS) in larger harbours, with increased emphasis on land based control of incoming and outgoing vessels. According to some future prognoses, control is likely to be handed over from the ship's master to the local VTS if accurate and reliable onboard guidance systems are in place. Another area of current research involves the use of AI in automatic berthing. Such systems have been found to work well in simulation and will eventually be integrated within the overall guidance system.

3.3   Execution

These need to be sufficiently flexible to allow for both high and low speed manoeuvres to be undertaken whilst under automatic guidance. This is usually achieved with a combination of control surfaces (rudders and fins) and thrusters (bow and main propellers). AI strategies tend to minimise rudder and engine perturbations when the ship is in an open seaway to reduce fuel consumption but also to provide maximum control in manoeuvring at low speed. In the future perspective, the advent is seen of the unmanned engine-room and direct control over the main engines from an integrated bridge. It is therefore necessary to integrate this technology with the automatic ship guidance system for both reduced fuel consumption passage in the open seaway and increased manoeuvring control in port approaches. Also as part of the propulsion systems AI techniques are being used in the areas of machine surveillance, performance monitoring and fault diagnosis.

4. INTELLIGENT SYSTEM TO AVOID COLLISION

The inner structure of the ship trajectory planning system was presented in detail in cited earlier works by Śmierzchalski [13,14], and Śmierzchalski et al. [16] There, an evolutionary environment was also defined, and the general formula for an evolutionary algorithm was presented, along with the description of an evolutionary procedure of optimum trajectory search. The structure of the system is divided into a number of levels (see: Fig. 4). The highest level is the trajectory planning. For the assumed evolutionary model and evolutionary method of safe trajectory computation, an exact trajectory is obtained as a solution. This trajectory is computed in two modes: off line, and on line. In the off line mode, the trajectory is estimated basing on an assumption that the parameters of approached targets (their speed and course) do not change in time. The ARPA (Automatic Radar Plotting Aids) system, however, controls whether this assumption is true i.e. whether the targets have not changed parameters of their motion during the time when the own ship is moving along the estimated trajectory. In case any changes of speed and/or course of moving targets are recorded, the already estimated trajectory is modified in on line mode. The trajectory, with possible on-line modifications, is then transmitted to a secondary adaptation guidance system, which leads the ship along the trajectory, disturbances such as sea-way, sea currents, wind, sea bottom profile etc. being taken into account. The last, lowest level is the direct control of the ship movements in real time. Here, the control instruments like main engine governor and automatic pilot are used to follow the earlier selected trajectory. Taking into account the common facts that any water region can be restricted by land, canals, shallows, water lines etc. and that it can be occupied by other moving ships, the problem of ship guidance can be reduced to the task of multi-criterion dynamic optimisation with static and dynamic constraints A solution method proposed here makes use of evolutionary algorithms, namely classes of algorithms with adaptation random search.

Their operation bases on probabilistic methods for creating a population of solutions. In the present system, they are used for creating the population of passing paths, with a subsequent search for the optimum solution within this population, i.e. the best possible path with respect to the fitness function. and finding the optimum solution within this population. The multiple iteration process of transforming and creating new individuals, accompanied by the creation of new populations, is carried on until any of the „stop" tests, for example: a number of generations, the fitness function accuracy, in the program are satisfied. In each generation, the operators modify the trajectory. A crucial step in the development of an evolutionary trajectory planning system was made by the introduction of dynamic parameters: time, and moving constraints. The moving constraints represent approaching ships, and the shape of each constraint depends on an assumed value of the safe approach distance, as well as on the speed, course, and bearing of the moving target. During the safe trajectory planning, the evolutionary algorithm should take into account both fixed constraints, and areas of danger connected with moving targets, which dynamically change their locations.

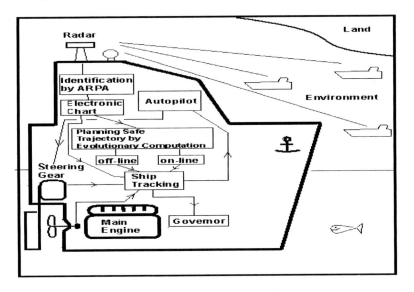

Fig. 4. The structure of the intelligent ship guidance system

The trajectories are treated in the population as individuals subject to genetic operations, turning points being genes of a particular individual. In the first version of the algorithm the own ship was assumed to move with a constant speed along a given trajectory. In some navigational situations the possibility of changing the speed along each individual trajectory section, accompanied by course changes, seems to be more effective than only course manoeuvres. To put it in practice, an additional genetic operator was introduced to the evolutionary algorithm (second version) to mutate the speed. For this reason, the gene of each individual was completed by a new parameter - ship's speed along a trajectory section defined by its turning points. The speed mutation operator acts by random selection of a speed from a set of permissible speed values, (defined, for instance, as slow, half and full ahead). A randomly selected trajectory section is given the speed and then, for the modified trajectory, the actual value of the fitness function is estimated. If this value is higher than that for any trajectory in the population, the new trajectory joins the population and undergoes further genetic transformations.

The system of evolutionary planning of the ship trajectory was tested for the numerous cases of passing fixed navigational constraints and moving targets. The analysis of cases displays the need for the introduction of an additional parameter to the evolutionary trajectory planning algorithm, namely the change of the own ship's speed along particular trajectory sections. In practice, the speed was modified using an additional genetic operator: the speed mutation. A set of permissible speed values was defined as $V=\{3,6; \ 8,6; \ 13,6 \ knots\}$ from which the mutation operator could take a speed at the trajectory section of concern. Additionally, the total time of trajectory passing was added to the function of the trajectory fitness, which took into consideration changes in the own ship's speed. After this modernisation of the evolutionary process of the trajectory search, a trajectory will be looked for which, besides meeting the formerly set safety and economy conditions, will represent the shortest time needed for covering the studied distance.

5. SUMMARY

Undoubtedly, the use of AI in all aspects of marine control is going to increase dramatically in the near future. The research direction for increased automation on the ship are connected with economic aspects as crew reduction, prevention of environment etc. Much of the work in these areas has been done in numerous economically leading countries all over the world. The most of governments of countries with developed marine industry understand that the importance of the work in this area, the benefits of which in terms of both economic and environmental considerations are of high importance to the international community.

REFERENCES

[1] Balchen J. G. 1995. Modelling, identification and control, Vol. 15, No. 3, Research Council of Norway.

[2] Burns R. S. 1992. An Intelligent Integrated Ship Guidance System. 2nd IFAC Workshop Control Applications in Marine Systems, Genova, Italy.

[3] Burns R. S. 1995. An intelligent automatic guidance system for surface ships. Marine Technology and Transportation, Coputational Mechanics Publications, Southampton, Boston, pp. 641-652.

[4] Burns R. S. 1995. The aplication of artificial intelligence techniques to modelling and control of surface ships. Eleventh Ship Control Systems Symposium, Coputational Mechanics Publications, Southampton, Boston Vol. 1, pp. 77-83.

[5] Dove M. J., Burns R. S., Stockel C. T. 1986. An Automatic Collision Avoidance and Guidance System for Marine Vehicles in Confined Waters. Journal of Navigation, Vol. 39.

[6] Furuhashi T, Nakaoka K, Uchikawa Y. 1996. A Study on Classifier System for Finding Control Knowledge of Multi-Input Systems F. Herrera, J.L.Verdegay Editors. Genetic Algorithms and Soft Computing, Phisica-Verlang.

[7] Hayashi S, Kuwajima S, Sotooka K, Yamakazi H, Murase H. 1991. A stranding avoidance system using radar image matching: development and experiment. Journal of Navigation, Vol. 44.

[8] Iijima Y, Hayashi S. 1991. Study towards a twenty-first century intelligent ship. Journal of Navigation, Vol. 44.

[9] Iijima Y, Hagiwara H. 1994. Results of Collision Avoidance Manoeuvre Experiments Using a Knowledge-Based Autonomous Piloting System. Journal of Navigation, Vol. 47.

[10] Lin HS, Xiao J, Michalewicz Z. 1994. Evolutionary Algorithm for Path Planning in Mobile Robot Environment. Proceeding IEEE Int. Conference of Evolutionary Computation, Orlando, Florida,.

[11] Michalewicz Z. 1996. Genetic Algorithms + Data structures = Evolution Programs. Spriger-Verlang, 3rd edition.

[12] Michalewicz Z, Xiao J. 1995. Evaluation of Paths in Evolutionary Planner/Navigator. Proceedings of the International Workshop on Biologically Inspired Evolutionary Systems, Tokyo, Japan.

[13] Śmierzchalski R, The Decision Support System to Design the Safe Manoeuvre Avoiding Collision at Sea. 14th International Conference Information Systems Analysis and Synthesis, Orlando, USA, 1996.

[14] Śmierzchalski R, Multi-Criterion Modeling the Collision Situation at Sea for Application in Decision Support. 1996. 3rd International Symp. on Methods and Models in Automation and Robotics, Miedzyzdroje, Poland.

[15] Śmierzchalski R. 1997. Trajectory planning for ship in collision situations at sea by evolutionary computation. 4th IFAC Conference on Manoeuvring and Control of Marine, Brijuni, Creotia.

[16] Śmierzchalski R. 1997. Dynamic Aspect in Evolutionary Computation on Example of Avoiding Collision at Sea. 4th International Symp. on Methods and Models in Automation and Robotics, Międzyzdroje, Poland.

[17] Śmierzchalski R. 1997. Evolutionary Guidance System for Ship in Collisions Situation at Sea. 3rd IFAC Conference Intelligent Autonomous Vehicle, Madrid, Spain.

[18] Śmierzchalski R, Michalewicz Z. 1998. Adaptive Modeling of a Ship Trajectory in Collision Situations. 2nd IEEE World Congress on Computational Intelligence, Alaska, USA.

[19] Sudhendar H, Grabowski M. 1996. Evolution of Intelligent Shipboard Piloting Systems: A Distributed System for the St Lawrence Seaway. Journal of Navigation, Vol. 49.

[20] Trojanowski K, Michalewicz Z. 1998. Planning Path of Mobil Robot (in Polish). 1st Conference Evolutionary Algorithms, Murzasichle, Poland.

[21] Witt NA, Sutton R, Miller KM. 1994. Recent Technological Advances in the Control and Guidance of Ship. Journal of Navigation Vol. 47.

[22] Xiao J, Michalewicz Z, Zhang L. 1996. Evolutionary Planner/Navigator: Operator Performance and Self-Tuning. Proceeding IEEE Int. Conference of Evolutionary Computation, Nagoya, Japan.

[23] Zhang Y., Hearn G.E., Sena P. 1995. Neural network approaches to a class of ship control problems. Part I and II. Eleventh Ship Control Systems Symposium, Coputational Mechanics Publications, Southampton, Boston Vol. 1, pp. 115-150.

How to deal with the data in a bankruptcy modelling

REJER IZABELA
Uuniversity of Szczecin
Mickiewicza 64, Szczecin, e-mail: i_rejer@uoo.univ.szczecin.pl

Abstract: This article presents results of a survey that has been led in this year in the University of Szczecin. The aim of the survey was to find a neural model that would be able to predict a bankruptcy of a firm with a high rate of precision. The problem of bankruptcy prediction is broadly discussed in the economic literature and a lot of highly efficient models built via different modelling techniques have been developed in this field so far. The reason why this problem is once more touched in this article is connected with the data involved to the model.

Key words: neural modelling, bankruptcy prediction, clusters computing,

1. INTRODUCTION

There are a lot of problems that can be encountered in a process of modelling. Most of them have their source in the data used to describe an analysing system. Sometimes the data are incomplete, sometimes uncertain and sometimes they even remain in contradiction to the theory. There has been a lot of work done in the field of dealing with incomplete data but the problem how to deal with data unsuited to the theory still remains open.

The bankruptcy prediction is a typical example of the aforementioned problem. It is not a rear situation that a firm which should bankrupt a long time ago is artificially kept in life. Sometimes also an opposite situation can come out – a very stable firm suddenly fails without any previous signals. Of course in every real system exceptions can appear. However, in the bankruptcy problem these "exceptions" turn up quite often, which makes the problem very difficult to model.

There is one more problem which can be encountered during a process of bankruptcy modelling. This time it is not connected with the possibility of misclassification but with the "outliers" existed in the input data. A very common approach taken to deal with this problem is to cross out the outliers from the original data set. It is sometimes a good solution, especially when only a few of them exist and when the data set is fairly large. This solution, however, cannot be taken when most of the input variables have their own outliers and when the system is placed in a very high-dimensional input space, like the system analysed in this article.

The common approach, which allows to deal with both aforementioned problems, taken in many researches on bankruptcy modelling, is to choose from the whole data set some typical examples of bankrupt firms and some typical examples of sound firms. This approach allows to omit the main problems connected with the data but on the other hand it simplifies the whole system. Moreover, it can cause also an improper model's performance in a future application. Why is it so? The bankruptcy problem is described in an economic literature by about 100 crucial factors. It is impossible for a human to properly evaluate such big set of factors, especially for a large number of firms. In most cases when such task is given to the expert he is able to analyse only a very narrow subset of the whole factor's set. As there is no agreement in theory which factors are the vital ones [1], it can turn out that the factors analysed by the expert were not the most crucial in the examined system. In such cases a model created on the base of typical bankrupt and sound firms, chosen from the whole data set, can perform very well on the training set (and also on the testing set) but might not be able to operate properly on the data formerly eliminated from the original set.

2.   THE BACKGROUND OF THE SURVEY

The goal of the survey was to predict whether a firm described by a chosen set of financial ratios would fail in a next year or not. The data set that was used in the survey contained 61 input variables and one output variable. Among input variables were financial ratios chosen from a bankruptcy literature [1][4]. Some of them are shown in the tab. 1. As the aim of the survey was to predict a state of the firm in the next year, the output variable represented the condition of the firm in a year $k+1$. This variable could take only one of two possible values: 0 or 1. Value 0 pointed that according to the law the firm failed in the year $k+1$ and value 1 pointed that according to the law, the firm was still alive in the year $k+1$. The whole set of data consisted of 694 examples of bankrupt firms and of 397 examples of sound firms (total: 1091 examples).

cash/current liabilities	long term debt/equity
cash flow/current liabilities	net income/total assets
cash flow/total assets	total debt/total assets
cash/net sales	working capital/equity
current assets/current liabilities	working capital/total assets

Tab.1. Some ratios used in the survey

First problem that appeared during the survey was the outlier problem, discussed in the introduction to this article. Unfortunately this problem could not be solved via standard approach because in each studied dimension existed too large fraction of outliers. Tab. 2 shows some examples of typical and untypical values taken by chosen input variables.

Name of variable	Typical interval	Untypical interval	% of typical values	% of untypical values
net income/total sales	<-2; 0.2>	<-1140; 16.9>	96,88%	3,12%
interests/total sales	<0; 300>	<-83.49; 5072>	97,71%	2,29%
working capital/ (costs-amortisation)	<-100; 0.5>	<-1067; 68>	96,15%	3,85%
(debts-cash)/total sales	<-1; 2>	<-213; 21060>	95,51%	4,49%

*Tab.2.*Typical and untypical intervals of chosen input variables

In order to eliminate the outliers problem, the data from the original set were transformed via exponential function, presented in the fig. 1.

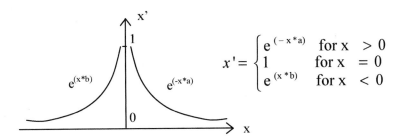

$$x' = \begin{cases} e^{(-x*a)} & \text{for } x > 0 \\ 1 & \text{for } x = 0 \\ e^{(x*b)} & \text{for } x < 0 \end{cases}$$

Fig. 1. The exponential function used for transforming the original data

Since each variable took values from different intervals the values of a and b parameters had to be chosen individually for each variable. In order to gain a maximum diversity of the data, the parameters were established via stepwise visual technique. Fig. 2 shows an example of process of matching the a and b parameters for the variable *net income/total sales*.

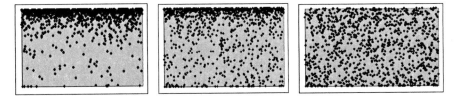

Fig. 2. A process of matching the a and b parameters for the variable: *net income/total sales*; a) a=1, b=1; b) a=1, b=5; c) a=28, b=5

3.   EXPERIMENT NO. ONE

The first step of the modelling process is to choose these variables from the whole set of variables which are the most important for behaviour of the modelling system. This step is very important because only a model containing the most important variables can perform well not only for typical data but also for untypical ones. The problem is how to find out which variables are the vital in the analysed system. The only possibility to be sure that the most important subset of factors was chosen is to examine all possible combinations of factors. Of course such approach could not be taken in the describing survey because of too large number of possible input variables.

The significance of input variables was analysed via a hierarchical method [5]. The hierarchical method is an example of a stepwise procedure. The main idea of it is to analyse the significance of the input variables by building sets of models consisted of some of these variables. Hence, in the hierarchical method the process of determining the input significance is made simultaneously with the process of modelling. Since the hierarchical method examines all input variables at every step of the modelling process, the results obtained with this method have very high rate of reliability.

The algorithm of the hierarchical method can be summarized as follows:
- Build a complete set of one-input models, where each model contained one of the analysing factors.
- Compare the errors of all models and choose the model with the smallest error.
- Build a set of two-input models consisted of the variable from the model chosen in the second step and one of the remaining variables.
- Choose the model with the smallest error. If the error of the two-input model is smaller than the error of the one-input model, build a set of three-input models. If not - stop the process.
- Continue the process as long as the model's error decreases.

The models created at every stage of the modelling process were constructed via neural network technique. The parameters of neural networks used in the survey were as follows: flow of signals: one-way, architecture of connections between layers: all to all, hidden layers: 1 hidden layer with 6-10 sigmoid neurons, output layer: 1 sigmoid neuron, training method: backpropagation algorithm with momentum and changing learning rates.

The neural models were trained on the base of 80% of data chosen randomly from the whole data set. The remaining 20% of data were used in the testing process. Each neural model was trained five times. The overfitted models were at once eliminated from the survey.

According to the hierarchical method at the beginning of the modelling process 61 one-input models were build. The best of them contained the variable *total debt/total assets* thus this variable was used in the next step. In the second stage 60 two-input models were built and once again the best model was chosen (variable - *total costs/total sales*. The process was continued for three, four and five-input models. The variables chosen at every stage of the modelling process and the training and testing errors of consecutive models are shown in the tab. 3.

Name of chosen variable	training error %	testing error %
total debt/total assets	26,92	25,38
total costs/total sales	22,03	21,37
EBIT/total assets	18,48	18,13
net income/current liabilities	15,78	17,53

Tab. 3. Errors of consecutive models – experiment 1

As it can be observed (tab. 3), the results obtained during the first experiment were very bad. The only variable that was able to induce the decrease in model's error at the fourth step of the modelling process caused its overfitting. As a result of this situation the whole process of modelling had to be stopped at the third step with the three-input model characterised by the error of 18,48%. Such a big error of the model aimed at the bankruptcy prediction was a big flop.

In this stage of the survey a question arose – why such bad results were obtained? After a careful study it occurred that the improper model's performance had its source in the data set. The original set of data contained firms that received (or not) the bankruptcy status only from the law point of view. At first look such distinction of the data seemed to be very clear and reliable. Unfortunately it was not true. When the data were presented to the expert it occurred that among firms classified (from the law point of view) as well-working firms were a lot of firms which should be regarded as bankrupt ones. Moreover, also among firms which were classified as bankrupts were some firms with so good financial and economical results that they should exist without any problems for a few next years.

Eventually, the reason of not very precise model's performance occurred to be typical: the classes existed in the data set were not fully separable. Mentioned problem is illustrated in the fig. 3 in a three-input subspace of the analysed system (used in the second experiment). As it can be observed in the figure it is possible to divide roughly the whole data space into two classes. Unfortunately the data of bankrupt and sound firms existed in the middle area of the data space are mixed together so much that usage them in the neural network training had to bring unsuccessful results.

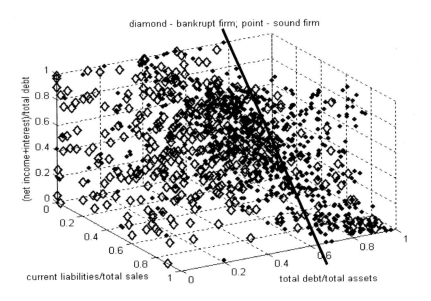

Fig. 3. Three-input subspace of the analysed system showing the problem of not fully separable classes

In order to reorganize the data set a cluster analysis was performed. The aim of this analysis was to find such set of clusters which would be characterised by the greatest discrimination abilities. The measure of the discrimination abilities was defined as an average difference between number of failed and non-failed firms existing in each cluster from the analysing set of clusters. A c-means method was used as a method of determining the clusters' location [3].

The cluster analysis was performed many times with different number of clusters and different starting positions of each cluster. At the end of this analysis the set of 10 clusters characterized by the greatest discrimination abilities was chosen (tab. 4). After the cluster analysis had been made, the new values for output variable had to be found. They were established according to the rule: all firms classified to the clusters consisted in more than 66,67% of bankrupt firms were regarded as bankrupt (class 0), all firms classified to the clusters consisted in less than 33,33% of bankrupt firms were regarded as sound (class 2), the rest firms were regarded as "difficult to determine" (class 1).

Number of cluster	Number of failed firms	Number of non-failed firms	% of failed firms	Number of class
1	50	20	71,43%	0
2	66	27	70,97%	0
3	21	115	15,44%	2
4	36	55	39,56%	1
5	13	103	11,21%	2
6	54	141	27,69%	2
7	53	36	59,55%	1
8	36	16	69,23%	0
9	35	83	28,57%	2
10	32	99	24,43%	2

Tab.4. Set of clusters with the greatest discrimination abilities

After new classification the set of data consisted of 215 failed firms, 696 non-failed firms and 180 firms of an unknown state. As it can be observed via chart presented in the fig. 4, the process of the data set reorganisation brought large improvement in the data classification (compare fig. 3 and 4).

As in the first experiment a hierarchical method was used to determine the most significant input variables. This time five steps of the modelling process had to be made. The results of them are shown in the tab. 5. The modelling process was stopped with the five-input model because there was no variable which added to this model would cause the reduction of its error.

As it is presented in the tab. 5 the results obtained during the second experiment were much more interesting than the results of the first one. Such good performance of a model was achieved thanks to the reordering of the data set which allowed to find real classes existing in this set.

The testing process of the final model was made in two steps. At the first step the performance of the model was verified on the testing data. The result was quite good because the testing error was only slightly bigger than the training error (0,09% - tab. 5).

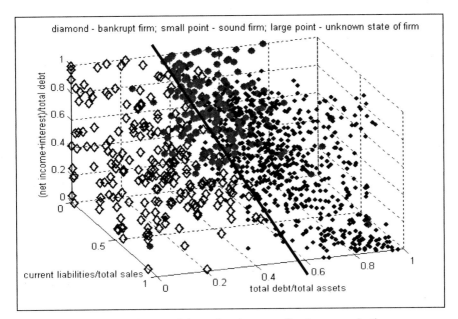

Fig. 4. Three-input subspace of the analysed system after the reorganization process (comp. fig. 3)

Name of chosen variable	training error %	testing error %
total debt/total assets	15,98%	15,62%
current liabilities/total sales	10,41%	10,30%
(net income + interest)/total debt	7,79%	7,80%
invested capital (logic variable)	5,80%	4,85%
EBIT/current liabilities	3,47%	3,56%

Tab. 5. Errors of consecutive models – experiment 2

The second step of the testing process was made with the participation of an expert. During this step 25 new examples were presented to the expert and to the model. It occurred that the model's performance was in 92% in agreement with the expert's evaluation. Such good result proved that the reorganization of the data set gave some benefits and that the final model can be used in practical applications.

4. CONCLUSION

Most economic systems are very difficult to examine because of data involved to these systems. The data mostly are not only very inaccurate but also irregularly scattered and sometimes even not properly arranged.

The presented article showed how to deal with two main data problems existed in the bankruptcy modelling. First problem was connected with the outliers existed in the data set and was solved by exponential transformation. The second problem was connected with the improper data classification. The only way to solve that problem was reorganization of the original data set. The reorganization was made by identifying clusters consisted of similar firms. Afterwards the original values of the output variable were changed according to this partition. As it was shown via two experiments the reorganization of the data set allowed to build very accurate model of the bankruptcy problem.

REFERENCES

[1] Back B. Laitinen T. Sere K. Wezel M. 1996. 'Choosing Bankruptcy Predictors Using Discriminant Analysis, Logit Analysis, and Genetic Algorithms'. *Technical Raport No 40*. Turku Centre for Computer Science.

[2] Demuth H. Beale M. 2000 'Neural Network Toolbox User's Guide'. *The Math Works Inc.* Natick MA USA.

[3] Piegat A. 1999. 'Fuzzy Modelling and Control'. *Physica-Verlag*. New, York.

[4] Poddig T. 1995. 'Bankruptcy Prediction: A Comparison with Discriminant Analysis'. *Neural Networks in the Capital Markets*. John Wiley$Sons. Chichester.

[5] Sugeno M. Yasukawa T. A. 1993. 'A Fuzzy-Logic-Based Approach to Qualitative Modelling'. *IEEE Transaction on Fuzyy Systems*. vol. 1, no. 1, February.

Dependency Mining in Large Sets of Stock Market Trading Rules

PIOTR LIPINSKI
Institute of Computer Science, University of Wroclaw, Wroclaw, Poland
LSIIT, CNRS, Université Louis Pasteur, Strasbourg, France
Email: lipinski@ii.uni.wroc.pl

Abstract: This paper addresses the problem of dependency mining in large sets. The first goal is to determine and reduce the dimension of data using principal component analysis. The second is to group variables into several classes using Kohonen's self-organizing maps and then the K-means algorithm. Evaluations have been performed on 350 financial trading rules (variables) observed in a period of 1300 instants (observations). It was shown that the rules are strongly correlated, all of which can be reproduced from 150 generators with an accuracy of 95%. Moreover, the initial set of 350 rules was subdivided into 23 classes of similar rules.

Key words: data mining, time series, trading rules, dependency analysis, PCA

1. INTRODUCTION

This paper addresses the problem of dependency mining in large sets. The problem is shown in the context of financial time series. Tables of the data used consist of over one thousand rows (time instances). Each row (one data vector) is characterized by several hundreds of traits (variables), herein referred to as *trading rules*.

The **first goal** is to investigate the dependencies among the trading rules in the circumstance when there are several hundreds of them. What is the true (effective) dimensionality of the data characterized by so many traits? Could this dimensionality be effectively reduced? For example, is it possible – instead of the presently used 350 trading rules – to use only, say, half the number of them, without loosing essential information contained in the data? To answer these questions principal component analysis is used.

The **second goal** is to subdivide variables into several classes to group them with the aim of discovering similarities among them. To achieve this goal

Kohonen's self-organizing maps [3] and K-means clustering of the derived codebook vectors are used.

This paper is structured in the following manner: Section 2 describes the financial data from the Paris Stock Exchange. Section 3 considers the first problem, dimensionality reduction. Section 5 considers methods for subdivision of the entire large set of trading rules into some subgroups. The methods introduced in Section 3 and Section 5 are illustrated in Section 4 and Section 6 respectively using real data from the Paris Stock Exchange (the data set concerning Peugeot presented in Section 2). Section 7 shows some further applications and their results. Finally, Section 8 concludes the paper.

2.   DATA DESCRIPTION

Traders on the stock market observe quotations of stocks with the aim to sell an item if it tends to lose value, to buy an item if it tends to gain value, and to take no action in the remaining cases. Traders often assume that future values can be, more or less accurately, predicted on the basis of past observations. Many methods that analyze past data behavior were introduced [1, 6, 8]. These methods attempt to detect trends or discover contexts leading to occurrences of particular events, which for instance might cause a rise or fall in stock prices.

Let K_t denote the knowledge available at time t. This knowledge may represent historical data, previous stock quotes, or other information on the considered stock. The concept of a stock market trading rule may be formalized by a function f, which computes a decision $f(K_t) \in \{0.0 \equiv sell, 0.5 \equiv do\ nothing, 1.0 \equiv buy\}$ on the basis of the knowledge K_t available at the time t. Naturally, the function f may be defined in a variety of ways.

Let d denote a number of considered trading rules $f_1, f_2, ..., f_d$. For a given stock, at a given instant t all these d functions may be evaluated producing a data vector $x_t = (x_{t1}, x_{t2}, ..., x_{td})$. This is a vector composed from values 0.0, 0.5 and 1.0 appropriately. Taking N time instants in such a way a data matrix X of size N x d is obtained. The i-th column of the matrix corresponds to the i-th rule (variable), and the j-th row corresponds to the j-th instant of the time period (observation).

This paper concerns a large set of rules observed over long time periods. Evaluation was performed on a set of 350 trading rules computed on five data sets. Each data set consists of a financial time series from the Paris Stock Exchange in a period of about 1300 instants. Each financial time series includes daily quotes of a given stock in a period from January 2, 1998 until May 12, 2003.

Details on input data for the experiments are presented in Table 1. The first column, d, denotes the number of rules, and the second column, N, denotes the length of the time period. Although there were 350 trading rules, d can be less than 350, because, for each stock, columns with constant values in all the N time instants were removed from the input data. The time period was the same for all experiments. However, the number of observations N can also differ, because for some stocks no quotes were recorded on some specific days.

Stock	d	N
AXA	348	1302
Credit Lyonnaise	350	1290
Peugeot	348	1292
Renault	348	1292
Sodexho	348	1290

Table 1. Input data summary

The large size of data, variables, as well as observations, poses a major problem for many currently available methods.

3. 1ST GOAL: DIMENSIONALITY REDUCTION

The method of linear dependency detection and dimensionality reduction is based on principal component analysis (PCA) [2]. It provides a technique that linearly transforms a number of correlated variables into a smaller number of new variables, called principal components. The first principal component explains as much of the variability in the data as possible, while each subsequent component explains as much of the remaining variability as possible.

The direction of the first principal component is determined by the eigenvector associated with the largest eigenvalue of the data correlation matrix. Eigenvectors associated with succeeding eigenvalues define directions of succeeding principal components.

The analysis is performed using the correlation matrix $\boldsymbol{R} = \{ r_{ij} \}$, $i, j = 1, 2, ..., d$ calculated for the data set. Let $\lambda_1 \geq \lambda_2 \geq ... \geq \lambda_d$ denote eigenvalues, and $v_1, v_2, ..., v_d$ corresponding eigenvectors of the matrix $\boldsymbol{R}$. Then the matrix $\boldsymbol{R}$ can be reproduced according to the formula:

$$\mathbf{R} = \sum_{i=1}^{d} \lambda_i v_i v_i^T . \tag{2}$$

Although the sum (2) has actually d components, truncating it on the k-th position can produce a satisfactory approximation of the matrix $\boldsymbol{R}$. Let

$$\mathbf{R}^{(k)} = \sum_{i=1}^{k} \lambda_i v_i v_i^T . \tag{3}$$

The matrix $\boldsymbol{R}^{(k)} = \{ r^{(k)}_{ij} \}$, $i, j = 1, 2, ..., d$ represents an approximation of the original matrix $\boldsymbol{R}$. It may be shown [2] that

$$\left\| \mathbf{R} - \mathbf{R}^{(k)} \right\| = 1 - \frac{1}{d} \sum_{i=1}^{k} \lambda_i .$$

Thus, if the sum of truncated eigenvalues constitutes a small amount of the entire sum $\lambda_1 + \lambda_2 + \dots + \lambda_d$, one may assume that in fact the matrix R may be effectively reproduced by k first principal components, i.e. approximated by $R^{(k)}$. For the sake of simplicity, let $C(k)$ denote the sum of k greatest eigenvalues, i.e. $C(k) = \lambda_1 + \lambda_2 + \dots + \lambda_k$. Since R is a correlation matrix, $C(k)$ is a non-decreasing function of k and $C(d) = d$. In order to present the value on a percentage basis, let $c(k) = C(k) / d$. An example of the behavior of the function $c(k)$ for the Peugeot data is shown in Figure 1.

The reasoning presented so far was concerned with reproduction of the entire matrix R. Another interesting problem is see to what extent the individual variables may be approximated by the derived principal components. In order to better assess the quality of the approximation, a few indices are introduced.

Let $A(k, p)$ denote the number of diagonal elements of the matrix R, which are at least $p\%$ approximated by diagonal elements (i.e. variances of variables) of the matrix $R^{(k)}$. Formally,

$$A(k, p) = \# \{i : | r_{ii} - r^{(k)}_{ii} | < (1 - p) | r_{ii} | \}.$$

In other words, a number $A(k, p)$ of diagonal elements of the matrix R is at least $p\%$ approximated by diagonal elements of the matrix $R^{(k)}$. In order to present the value on a percentage basis, let $a(k, p) = A(k, p) / d$. Then, $0 \le a(k, p) \le 1$, $a(k, p)$ is non-decreasing with increasing k, and $a(d, p) = 1$. For this reason it can be depicted at the same graph as $c(k)$. An example of the behavior of the function $a(k, p)$ for the Peugeot data is shown also in Figure 1.

Let $b(q) = \min\{k : a(k, 0.95) \ge q N\}$. In other words, $b(q)$ denotes the number of components, which is sufficient to reproduce at least $q\%$ of diagonal elements at least in 95%.

4.   EXAMPLE OF A REDUCTION IN THE NUMBER OF TRADING RULES FOR THE PEUGEOT DATA

In this section, details of the results obtained are presented for the data set concerning Peugeot. Other calculations gave results quite similar; thus, because of size constraints, they are only summarized in Section 7.

The thick black line in Figure 1 presents $c(k)$ – the ratio of the sum of k greatest eigenvalues to the total of all eigenvalues of the correlation matrix R. One can see that the sum of 105 greatest eigenvalues accounts for more than 95% of the total of all eigenvalues. Therefore, one may assume that all variables can be approximately reproduced from 105 components created from initial variables.

In order to analyze the dimension more precisely, the reproduction of the original matrix R by k first principal components is studied. The red line in Figure 1 presents $a(k, 0.95)$, for $k = 1, 2, \dots d$. It is easy to see that $b(0.95) = 148$, i.e. 148 components can approximate the original matrix to a satisfactory degree of 95% properly approximated diagonal elements (i.e. variances of variables).

This suggests that all 348 rules are strongly correlated. All variables can be reproduced from about 150 components with the accuracy of 95%.

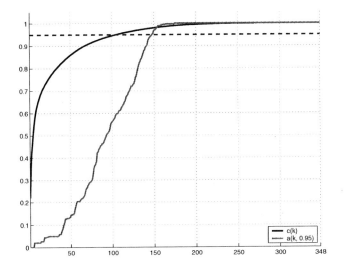

Figure 1. The ratio of the sum of k greatest eigenvalues to the total of all eigenvalues and the percent of the number of variables for which variance was at least 95% approximated by k first principal components.

5.   2ND GOAL: CLUSTERING OF VARIABLES

The second goal is to divide variables into several classes. After dimensionality reduction, each variable is well-approximated by a linear combination of 150 first principal components. Thus, each variable can be defined by 150 coordinates, constituting an entry point to further analysis. Variables are grouped on the basis of these coordinates. Input data consists of the set of initial variables each described by 150 coordinates (new traits).

First, a Kohonen's self-organizing map is created, with 88 units. After the learning process the map covers the data space, and each variable is assigned to the nearest codebook vector. Thus, variables are grouped in 88 classes defined by codebook vectors [3].

Next, the K-means algorithm is used to group codebook vectors into a smaller number of classes. In such a way, a second partition of initial variables is obtained. The number of classes is chosen so that the Davies-Bouldin index for the clustering is as small as possible [7].

6.   EXAMPLE OF CLUSTERING TRADING RULES FOR THE PEUGEOT DATA

This section presents in detail results for the data set concerning Peugeot. Other calculations are summarized in Section 7.

Figure 2 presents the clustering obtained by applying the K-means algorithm to the Kohonen's map. Hexagons represent map units. The clusters obtained are marked by different colors. Labels inside hexagons denote numbers of variables, which are assigned to the map unit represented by the given hexagon.

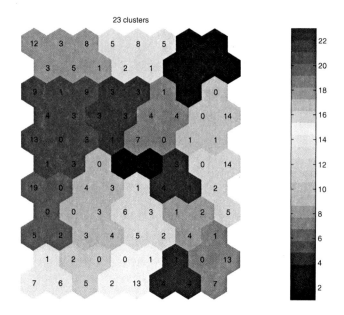

Figure 2. Variable Clustering

7. FURTHER EXAMPLES OF APPLICATIONS

Evaluations have been performed on five financial time series from the Paris Stock Exchange (see Table 1). The final results are similar for all cases considered.

Stock	*M*	*M'*	*b(0.60)*	*b(0.80)*	*b(0.90)*	*b(0.95)*
AXA	103	103	105	127	138	144
Credit Lyonnaise	106	106	107	131	142	147
Peugeot	105	105	107	131	142	148
Renault	103	103	105	129	138	145
Sodexho	105	105	105	131	141	149

Table 2. Summary of dimensionality reduction

Table 2 presents a summary of the dimensionality reduction. Although the number of variables is large, all can be reproduced on the basis of about 150 components. The second column, *M*, presents the minimal number of eigenvalues whose sum is greater than 95% of the total of all eigenvalues. The third column, M', presents the minimal number of components necessary to reproduce the correlation matrix R with a mean ratio of elements of the matrix $R^{(k)}$ to the corresponding elements of R greater than 95%. The next columns present the minimal number of components sufficient to reproduce 60%, 80%, 90%, 95% of diagonal elements of the correlation matrix R (i.e. variances of variables).

Table 3 summarizes clustering after dimensionality reduction. In all cases, the rules were grouped in about 22 classes using the method described in Section 5. Surprisingly, for all five data sets similar numbers of classes were obtained.

Stock	Classes
AXA	23
Credit Lyonnaise	22
Peugeot	23
Renault	21
Sodexho	21

Table 3. Summary of variable clustering

This investigation was performed to study dependencies among trading rules. The PCA analysis enabled a large dimensionality reduction. Dependencies between particular rules can be obtained from principal components definitions. The dimension reduction enabled further study and the division of rules into several clusters.

8. CONCLUSIONS

In this paper, studies of dependencies among trading rules were presented. Experiments made on the basis of a set of 350 rules observed in a period of about 1300 days showed strong dependencies. The large set of rules was reduced to linear combinations of only 150 generators. After dimensionality reduction, rules were grouped into roughly 22 clusters. Clusters were created according to rules represented in the space defined by the first 150 principal components.

The main problem concerning investigations presented in this paper was the size of the data considered. Although principal component analysis is widely known, it is usually applied to much smaller data sets.

Although the result yields a significant reduction in data dimension, further study using the GTM model and self-organized Kohonen's maps can improve the results obtained. Discovery of non-linear analysis can introduce more dependencies among trading rules.

The large size of the set of rules is often a bottleneck for expert systems, which build experts based on these rules. Significant reduction in dimension of the rule space may enable optimization and a notable decrease in computation time. The idea presented may be used in decision support expert systems, such as described in [4, 5].

Table 4 shows results of a few tests performed with the decision support expert system presented in [4, 5]. This system generates stock market trading expertise built on the basis of a set of trading rules. The table presents computation time necessary to build the expertise using the original set of rules (before dimensionality reduction) and using the reduced set of rules (after dimensionality reduction). Experiments showed large decrease in computation time without significant decline in quality of the expertise obtained.

Stock	Before	After
AXA	18 s	9 s
Credit Lyonnaise	21 s	12 s
Peugeot	19 s	11 s
Renault	23 s	18 s
Sodexho	20 s	14 s

Table 4. Results of application in a decision support system.

ACKNOWLEDGEMENTS

The author would like to thank Prof. Anna Bartkowiak from the Institute of Computer Science, University of Wroclaw, Wroclaw, Poland for her helpful comments on preliminary versions of this paper.

REFERENCES

[1] Colby, W., Meyers, T., "The Encyclopedia of Technical Market Indicators", Down Jones-Irwin, 1990.
[2] Jolliffe, I., T., "Principal Component Analysis", Springer, 1986.
[3] Kohonen, T., "Self-Organizing Maps", Series in Information Science, Vol. 30. Heidelberg, Springer, Second ed. 1997.
[4] Korczak, J., Lipinski, P., Roger, P., "Evolution Strategy in Portfolio Optimization", Artificial Evolution, ed. P. Collet, Lecture Notes in Computer Science, vol. 2310, Springer, 2002, pp. 156-167.
[5] Korczak, J., Roger, P., "Stock timing using genetic algorithms", Applied Stochastic Models in Business and Industry, 2002, pp. 121-134.
[6] Murphy, J., "Technical Analysis of the Financial Markets", NUIF, 1998.
[7] Vesanto, J., Himberg, J., Alhoniemi E., Parhankangas, J., "SOM Toolbox for Matlab 5", SOM Toolbox Team, Helsinki University of Technology, Finland, Libella Oy Espoo (http://www.cis.hut.fi/projects/somtoolbox).
[8] Weigend, A., S., Gershenfeld, N., A., "Time Series Prediction: Forecasting the Future and Understanding the Past", Addison-Wesley, 1993.

Choosing representative data items: Kohonen, Neural Gas or Mixture Model?
A case study of erosion data

ANNA BARTKOWIAK[1], JOANNA ZDZIAREK[1],
NIKI EVELPIDOU[2], ANDREAS VASSILOPOULOS[2]

[1] *Institute of Computer Science, University of Wrocław,*
Przesmyckiego 20, Wrocław 51-151 Poland, e-mail: aba@ii.uni.wroc.pl
[2] *Remote Sensing Laboratory, Geology Dept., University of Athens,*
Panepistimiopolis Zografou, Athens 15-784, Greece, e-mail: evelpidou@geol.uoa.gr

Abstract: When analyzing the erosion risk of Kefallinia, Greece, we have faced the problem, how to choose representatives (prototypes) for a big data set. We consider 3 methods serving this purpose: 1 - *Kohonen's self-organizing map* (SOM), 2 - *Neural gas* (NG), and 3. *Mixture model* (MM) of Gaussian distributions. The representativeness of the derived prototype vectors is measured by the quantization error, as defined by Kohonen (1995). It appears that neural gas and mixture models surpass quite steadily the SOM method in providing better representatives. To obtain a more thorough insight into the results, we map the obtained prototype vectors onto planes obtained by the *neuroscale* mapping, which seems to be a convenient alternative to Sammon's mapping. The SOM codebook vectors are visualized in the same planes and linked by *threads*. This is shown for the Kefallinia erosion data from Greece.

Key words: Self-organizing maps, Neural gas, Mixture models, Neuroscale mapping, Thread plotting, Kefallinia Island

1.   INTRODUCTION

Nowadays we obtain very large data sets containing thousands of data vectors. A proper statistical analysis of such data may cause some problems not only in computing time but also with accuracy of the calculations due to rounding errors. However, in many cases it is not necessary to use **all** the data during the analysis – very often a representative sub-sample would be sufficient.

How to choose a representative sample from a huge data set?

The most popular methods serving this purpose appear under the watchword "vector quantization". The methods work as follows: The entire data space is subdivided into adjacent regions. Each region has a representative, called prototype or codebook vector. Then, all data vectors belonging to a given region may be, to some extent, substituted by their representative prototype.

The most eminent methods used for vector quantization are: Kohonen's *self-organizing maps* (SOM) [5, 12, 1] and the *neural gas* method [7, 8, 2]. The *mixture model* [10], based on a complete different philosophy, may serve the same goal.

Our aim is to compare the results of the three methods mentioned above. We will do it using the Kefallinia erosion data [15, 1]. From this data set, we will use only 3 variables – to make our results more transparent and evident. The results of the comparisons will be illustrated by planar graphs obtained by the *neuroscale* transformation [6, 14, 11].

In Section 2 we present the Kefallinia data. In Section 3 the found representatives are shown in 3D plots. In Section 4 we compare the found representatives using the neuroscale mapping. Section 5 contains some closing remarks concerning the investigated methods.

2.   PRESENTATION OF THE DATA

The total area of the investigated island (Kefallinia, Greece) was subdivided into $n = 3422$ adjacent units (squares) of fixed area. For further analysis, we will consider only 3 variables for each territorial unit:

- $X1$, drainage density,
- $X2$, slope, and
- $X3$, - vulnerability.

A more detailed description of the data and of the variables may be found in [1, 15, 4]. The data contain 2 very big outliers that were really observed.

3.   THREE METHODS OF SEARCH FOR REPRESENTATIVES

We will consider three methods:
1. Kohonen's SOM as described in [5]. The found representatives are called codebook vectors. They are restricted by a neighborhood function defined when constructing Kohonen´s map.
2. Neural gas (NG) described e.g. in [7, 8]. The sought representatives, called prototype vectors (shortly: prototypes) are found by competitive learning.
3. Mixture model (MM) [10, 11]. The method aims at providing a formula for the density distribution of the observed data points. We assume that the entire density is a sum of M independent Gaussian distributions. The centers of the derived distributions constitute the representative prototypes.

The representatives found by these three methods are shown in Figure 1.

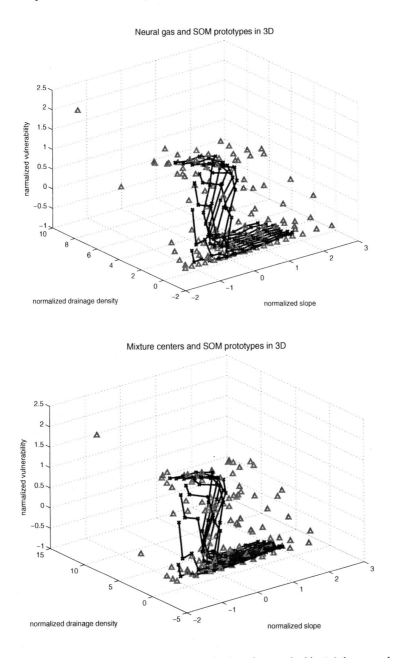

Fig. 1. M=120 representatives found by three methods. Points marked by 'x' denote codebook vectors obtained from the 12x10 SOM. The x points are bound by threads to reflect the · column structure of the corresponding SOM. Prototypes found independently by neural gas (top exhibit) and mixture model (bottom exhibit) are added to the plot as loose triangles. One may observe the inadequacy of coverage of the data space by the SOM codebook points.

Figure 1 depicts the results of search for M = 120 representatives. This amount (=120) resulted from establishing a SOM of size 12 x 10, which was the default in the package somtoolbox2 [16]. We have considered also a map of size M = 19 x 15 which yielded M = 285 representatives. Correspondingly, in the two mentioned situations, the data space was subdivided into M = 120 and 285 regions. Thus we were seeking for M = 120 and M = 285 representatives of the entire data set counting n = 3422 data vectors.

The three applied methods yielded the following quantization errors (*iters* in the table is abbreviation for *iterations* carried out during the process of training):

Map size	Method					
	SOM		MM		NG	
	Default tr.	Long training	20 *iters*	50 *iters*	10 *epochs*	30 *epochs*
12 x 10	0.301	0.290	0.222	0.201	0.196	0.185
19 x 15	0.199	0.193	0.159	0.141	0.138	0.122

One may see in that table, that both neural gas (NG) and mixture models (MM) yield smaller quantization errors as the SOM does. This means that the data items are better represented by the NG and MM prototypes as by the SOM codebook vectors.

4. COMPARISON OF THE REPRESENTATIVES USING THE NEUROSCALE MAPPING

The neuroscale mapping was proposed by Lowe and Tipping [6, 14]. Similarly as Sammon's method [13], also the neuroscale mapping permits to visualize multivariate data points in lower dimensions. The main underlying principle is to preserve the distances between pairs of points.

The Sammon's algorithm [13] finds the coordinates of the derived points as parameters undergoing the optimization process. This makes the Sammon's algorithm computational expensive. Moreover, after enlarging the set of the projected data, we have to start the optimization process anew.

In the neuroscale algorithm, "a feed-forward neural network is utilized to effect a topographic, structure preserving, dimension-reducing transformation of the data" (quoted after [6]). The transformations formulae derived from one data set may work on other arbitrary data set with the same number of columns (variables). The algorithm uses the concept of a RBF network with parameters obtained from the RBF network architecture.

A neuroscale mapping needs a training data set – referred to as *the base*. During the training the mapping $\{\Phi : R^p \to R^q, q < p\}$ is found. Using the derived mapping, we usually display firstly the base set. Next, using the same mapping Φ, we may project additional data sets.

In the following, we will apply the neuroscale algorithm to produce a mapping from the data space to a plane, i.e. to a subspace of dimension 2.

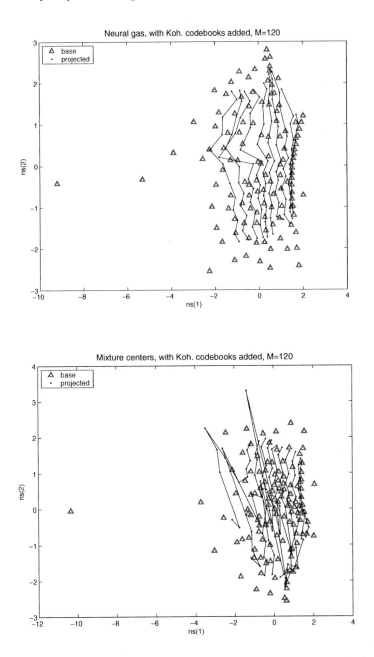

Fig. 2. Neuroscale mapping of prototypes (marked by triangles) and SOM codebook vectors (dots), the latter bound column-wise. *Top*: Projections of NG prototypes and SOM codebook vectors obtained using the Φ_{NG} mapping. *Bottom*: Projections of mixture centers and of the SOM codebook vectors, obtained by the Φ_{MM} mapping. The mapping based on NG prototypes seems t o reflect more of the SOM structure as the mapping based on MM centers.

In Figure 2 we show two such mappings: In the first exhibit, located at the top of the figure, the neural gas prototypes were used as the base data set – yielding the mapping Φ_{NG}. Using the derived Φ_{NG}, firstly the NG prototypes and next the SOM codebook vectors were displayed. The second exhibit in Figure 2 has used the mapping Φ_{MM} obtained from mixture centers taken as the base.

The SOM codebook vectors visualized in both exhibits are bound with threads. The last reflect the column structure of the respective SOM. It is known that the codebook vectors appear in the data space in some order; this is conceivable in the graphical representation using bounding of projected points.

Explaining the bounding in few other words: It is known that the columns (or rows) of the SOM designate some directions in the data space. Thus, codebook vectors belonging to one column are supporting a trajectory across the data space. It is interesting to inquire, whether (how much) such a trajectory is distorted when its supports are projected to the plane $< ns(1), ns(2) >$, where $< ns(1), ns(2) >$ denotes the coordinates of the planar Φ mapping. Looking at Figure 2, one may see that the mapping Φ_{NG} has, in principle, preserved the spatial trajectories. What concerns the Φ_{MM} mapping, it has acted in a different way: the spatial trajectories are in some parts of the exhibit confused and intersected.

Another neuroscale mapping is shown in Figure 3. The base mapping Φ_{MM} was obtained from the MM centers; the respective projections are denoted in the figure by triangles. Next, using the derived Φ_{MM} mapping, we projected the NG prototypes onto the same plot. It is interesting to notice that now the set of the projected NG prototypes shows 3 considerably outlying points, while among the MM prototypes one may find only one such point.

5. DISCUSSION AND CLOSING REMARKS

We have stated, that the Neural gas (NG) and the Mixture models (MM) yield better representatives of the data set than the codebook vectors derived by Kohonen's SOM method.

We stated also, that the neuroscale mapping of multivariate data points to a subspace (in our case: to a plane) works much faster than the Sammon's mapping. The neuroscale mapping is more convenient because it allows for mapping additional data sets to the same subspace.

The NG and MM methods use principles of quite different philosophies; it is not clear, which of the two methods is preferable. We think this depends on the intended interpretation of the results.

We might state here that – when using the NG method – it is more likely to obtain prototypes positioned at singleton points, which might represent outliers. The MM method tends to model the data by subdividing them into subgroups. Each of the subgroups has then an individual distribution (Gaussian or other). The used algorithm [11] (deriving mixture prototypes) is unable to establish a distribution for a solitary point; the algorithm tends to cluster at least few points and get for them a representative. A more thorough method is needed to detect outliers. We think, this point is worth of further elaboration.

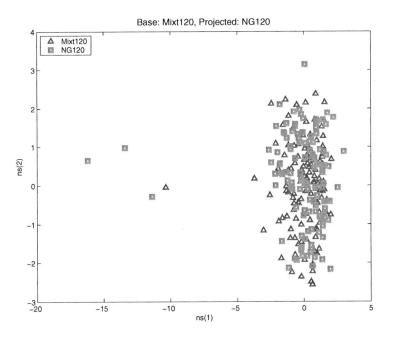

Fig. 3. Neuroscale mapping obtained from M=120 mixture centers; projections of these centers are shown as triangles. Using the derived mapping formula, additional M=120 neural gas prototypes, marked by squares, were projected onto the same plane. One may notify that from the MM centers only one appears as an distinct outlier. The NG prototypes, projected onto the same plane, exhibit 3 outliers.

A novelty in our approach is the thread plotting. It is combined with the neuroscale mapping. It permits to get an idea, how the points visualized in the planar graphs reflect directional tendencies in the input space. We may rely here on both the column and the row structure of the SOM. For clarity of exposition, we have exploited in Figure 2 only the column structure of the obtained SOM.

REFERENCES

[1] Bartkowiak A., Vassilopoulos A., Evelpidou N. 2003. 'Choosing data vectors representing a huge data set: Kohonen's SOM applied to the Kefallinia erosion data'. Proceedings of the *First Int. Conf. on Environmental Research and Assessment*, Bucharest, Romania, March 23–27, 2003, pp. 505–522, ISBN 973-558-077-2, print on CD–ROM, © Ars Docendi Publishing House, Bucharest, Romania.
[2] Bartkowiak A., Szustalewicz A., Evelpidou N., Vassilopoulos A. 2003. 'Choosing data vectors representing a huge data set: a comparison of Kohonen's maps and the neural gas method'. Proceedings of the *First Int. Conf. on Environmental Research and Assessment*, Bucharest, Romania, March 23–27, 2003, pp. 561–572, ISBN 973-558-077-2, print on CD–ROM, © Ars Docendi Publishing House, Bucharest, Romania.

[3] de Rider D., Duin R. P. W. 1997. 'Sammon's mapping using neural networks:
   A comparison'. *Pattern Recognition Letters* 18, pp. 1307–1317.

[4] Gournellos T., Evelpidou N., Vassilopolous A. 2003. 'Developing an erosion risk map
   using soft computing'. *Natural Hazards,* Kluwer, to appear.

[5] Kohonen T. 1995. *Self-Organizing Maps.* Series in Information Science. Vol. 30.
   Heidelberg, Springer. Second Edition. 1997.

[6] Lowe D., Tipping M. 1996. 'Feed-forward neural networks and topographic mappings for
   exploratory data analysis'. *Neural Computing and Applications* 4, pp. 83–95.

[7] Martinetz M., Berkovich S., Schulten K. 1993. 'Neural-gas' network for vector
   quantization and its application to time series prediction. *IEEE Trans. Neural Networks*
   V. 4, pp. 558–569.

[8] Martinez T. M., Schulten K.J. 1994. 'Topology representing networks'.
   Neural Networks 7, pp. 507–522.

[9] Matlab: The Language of Technical Computing. 2002. Version 6p5. The Mathworks Inc.,
   Natick MA USA.

[10] McLachlan G., Peel D. 2000. *Finite Mixture Models.* Wiley, New York, Chichester.

[11] Nabney I. T. 2001. *Netlab: Algorithms for Pattern Recognition.* Springer London, Berlin,
   Heidelberg. Springer Series: Advances in Pattern Recognition.

[12] Osowski S. 1996. *Sieci neuronowe w ujęciu algorytmicznym.* WNT Warszawa.

[13] Sammon J. W. (Jr.). 1969. 'A nonlinear mapping for data structure analysis'.
   IEEE Trans. on Computers C-18 (5), pp. 401–409.

[14] Tipping M. E., Lowe D. 1997. 'Shadow targets: A novel algorithm for topographic
   projections by radial basis functions'. In: Proceedings of the *Int. Conf. on Artificial
   Neural Networks* 440, pp. 7–12, IEE.

[15] Vassilopoulos A. 2002. 'Coastal geomorphological classifications in GIS environment of
   Kefallinia Island'. Proc. *6th Pan-Hellenic Geographical Congress of the Hellenic
   Geographical Society,* Thessaloniki 3-5.10.2002, Vol. 1., pp. 388-394.

[16] Vesanto J., Himberg J., Alhoniemi E., Parhankangas J. 2000. *SOM Toolbox for Matlab 5.*
   Som Toolbox Team. Helsinki University of Technology, Finland, Libella Oy Espoo.
   See also:http://www.cis.hut.fi/projects/somtoolbox/ .

Application of the Ant Colony Algorithm for the Path Planning

MARCIN PLUCIŃSKI

Technical University of Szczecin, Faculty of Computer Science and Information Systems,
ul. Żołnierska 49, 71-210 Szczecin, Poland,
tel. (+48 91) 449 55 80, e-mail: mplucinski@wi.ps.pl

Abstract: The paper presents the ant colony algorithm and its application for the path planning. Ant algorithms were designed on the base of the behaviour of real ant colonies. Real ants can always find the shortest way between the nest and the food so one of the most "natural" is the application of the ant colony algorithm in the path planning. Described algorithm was implemented in some off-line experiments.

Key words: Ant colony optimisation, ant algorithms, trajectory planning, natural computation

1. INTRODUCTION

The path planning is very popular optimisation task, which must be solved for example in a case of small mobile robots and large sea vessels. The main idea of the path planning problem for mobile robots was presented in [5]: given a robot and a description of an environment, plan a path of the robot between two specified locations, which is collision-free and satisfies certain optimisation criteria.

There are many ways to solve the problem described above. It can be solved off-line when the environment (mainly the location of all obstacles) is exactly known or on-line when we try to find a path without such knowledge. Sometimes the solution is a combination of off-line and on-line methods when the environment is known only partially. Different methods must be used in the static environment and in the dynamic environment when some of obstacles move.

One of the approaches to the problem is an application of artificial intelligence methods. For example, the problem can be solved with help of evolutionary algorithms [4, 5]. In the paper there will be presented ant colony algorithm and its application for the path planning.

2.   ANT COLONY ALGORITHM

Ant algorithms were designed on the base of the behaviour of real ant colonies. There are of course many differences between artificial and real ants but the main idea of colony behaviour is the same.

Each ant performs very simple tasks independent from one another. But all ants acting in group can solve quite complex problems like selecting and picking up materials, nest building or finding and storing foods. Ants are capable of finding the shortest path between food source and the nest without the use of visual information, and they are also capable of adapting to changes in the environment [3]. Such process is a kind of distributed optimisation. It is very interesting that, although a single ant is in principle capable of building a solution (i.e. of finding path between nest and food), it is only the ant colony that presents the shortest path-finding behaviour. This behaviour is an emergent property of the ant colony. Ants can perform this specific behaviour using a simple form of indirect communication achieved by the pheromone laying, known as stigmergy [1].

Ant colony algorithms can be used in many optimisation tasks. For the first time they were used as a multi-agent approach to difficult discrete optimisation problems such as the travelling salesman problem or the quadratic assignment problem [1]. There are examples of ant colony algorithm applications in job scheduling problem, bus stop allocation problem, numeric optimisation, dynamic routing in telecommunication networks or even in classification rule discovery [2,3].

One of the most "natural" is the application of ant colony algorithm in path planning. Real ants can always find the shortest way between the nest and the food. During moving, each ant leaves a certain amount of special chemical substance called pheromone and in this way it marks its path and communicates with other ants.

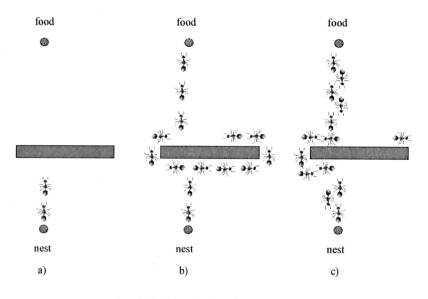

Fig. 1. Real ants finding the shortest path

Ants try to follow pheromone trails and with the greater probability, they will choose a path where the amount of pheromone is large. The more ants follow the trail, the more attractive the trail becomes to be followed by other ants. This process can be described as a loop of positive feedback, where the probability of choosing the path by an ant increases as the number of ants that already passed by that path increases [3]. The main idea of the algorithm is presented in Fig. 1.

We can see in the Fig. 1b that ants, which choose the left side of the obstacle, reach the food faster. They choose the same side in their way back to the nest because there are pheromone trails (ants from right side didn't reach the food yet). In this way on the left side of the obstacle there is much more pheromone and this side is chosen more frequent then the right one (Fig. 1c).

Artificial ants can be defined as agents that imitate the behaviour of real ants. Each one has same features listed below.

1. Artificial ants live in the discrete environment and in discrete time.
2. Artificial ants know the direction to the food (end of the path) and to the nest (start of the path).
3. Artificial ants have no information about the environment. They can see a small area around them and in that area, they can detect an amount of pheromone.
4. Artificial ants have short memory – they can only remember the direction they came from.
5. Artificial ants choose probabilistically the direction of movement and the probability is larger for the direction with larger amount of pheromone. It means that the solution in the algorithm is found in a probabilistic way.

The environment is divided into discrete cells and an ant can move only to neighbouring cells, Fig. 2. An ant chooses this cell on the base of the state of the neighbouring environment and applying its local search strategy.

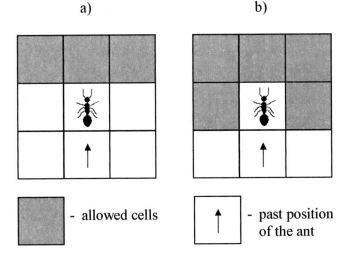

a)   b)

- allowed cells   - past position of the ant

Fig. 2. Two strategies of the next cell choosing

There are two strategies of the next cell choosing. The "narrow" strategy –
presented on Fig. 2a and the "wide" one – presented in Fig. 2b. State of each cell
mainly depends on an amount of pheromone deposited earlier and on the distance to
the end point of the path. In each strategy the next cell is chosen probabilistically.
The highest probability of being chosen has always the cell with the highest value of
the cell state value (1).

$$c = f(d) + w_p \cdot p,\qquad\qquad\qquad (1)$$

where: c – cell state value,
    $f(d)$ – function of the distance to the end point of the path,
    w_p – pheromone weight coefficient,
    p – pheromone amount in the cell.

Stochasticity in the ant moving ensures searching of new cells and enables
finding new paths. Thanks to this component of strategy ants can explore new cells –
unvisited earlier by any ant (with no pheromone). After each step of the optimisation
algorithm, the pheromone trails can evaporate:

$$p(t+1) = p(t) \cdot \alpha,\qquad\qquad\qquad (2)$$

where: t – discrete time,
    α – evaporation coefficient, $\alpha \in (0,1]$.

$\alpha = 1$ means no evaporation and α close to 0 means strong evaporation. The
level of updates in the pheromone trail (like the level of stochasticity in the search
policy) determines the balance between the exploration of new areas in the
environment and the exploitation of knowledge accumulated in cells [1].
Evaporation of pheromone allows adapting to changes in the environment.
    The whole algorithm can be shortly presented in the form of pseudo-code:

```
while (stop_criterion_not_fulfilled)
    {
    move_ants();
    pheromone_evaporation();
    ants_drop_pheromone();
    }

move_ants()
    {
    for (each_ant)
        {
        detect_possible_cells();
        find_obstacles_in_possible_cells();
        count_probability_of_move_for_each_cell();
        choose_cell_probabilistically();
        move_an_ant_to_next_cell();
        }
    }
```

To find the shortest path, each ant counts cells visited in the way from the start point. Each cell has the special cell index and in the beginning of the algorithm all this indexes are set to infinity. When an ant come to a cell, the cell index is compared with the number of cells counted by the ant. When it is less it is replaced by this number. Hence, to draw the shortest path we must start in the end point and move always to the neighbouring cell with the least cell index until we reach the start point.

The way the whole algorithm behaves depends on many parameters. The most important are:
- the number of ants,
- the number of ants that can stay in one cell at the same time,
- pheromone weight coefficient wp,
- function of the distance to the end point of the path f(d),
- evaporation coefficient α.

Moreover, it is very important which searching strategy is applied in the algorithm and how the stochastic selecting of the next cell is realised. Good solutions can be found in short time only when mentioned parameters and strategies are chosen properly.

3. EXPERIMENTS AND RESULTS

Described algorithm was implemented in off-line experiments.

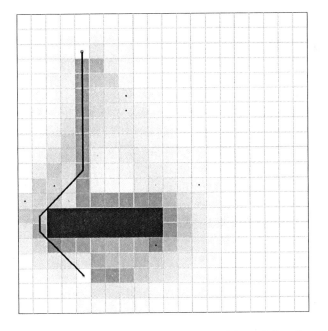

Fig. 3. First experimental environment and the path found

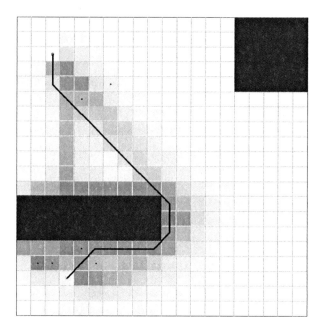

Fig. 4. Second experimental environment and the path found in 6240 step

Fig. 5. Third experimental environment and the path found in 21800 step

There were prepared environments with polygonal obstacles from simple ones to more complicated. In the first experiment the environment was very simple and similar to one presented in Fig. 1. Results of this experiment are presented in Fig. 3.

In the figure, we can see the shortest path found (in 3440 step of the algorithm), the obstacle and the pheromone amount in the each cell (darker cell means more pheromone). The population size was set to 20 in all experiments.

Results of next experiments are presented in Figs. 4, 5, 6.

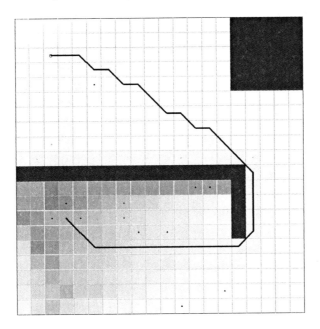

Fig. 6. Fourth experimental environment and the path found in 237000 step

4. CONCLUSIONS

The proposed algorithm proved to be efficient and fast tool in path planning. It can be used in off-line planning and it was shown in experiments but without any modification it can be used in on-line planning too. It results from the fact that ants have no knowledge about the whole environment and they can "see" only the closest neighbourhood.

Choosing proper values of all algorithm parameters we can use it in dynamic environments and it will be the direction of future research.

REFERENCES

[1] Dorigo M., Di Caro G., Gambardella L.M.: Ant algorithms for discrete optimization, Artificial Life, vol. 5, No. 2, pp. 137-172, 1999
[2] Krishnaiyer K., Cheraghi S.H.: Ant algorithms: review and future applications, Industrial Engineering Research Conference IERC'02, Orlando, Florida, USA, May 2002

[3] Parpinelli R.S., Lopes H.S., Freitas A.A.: An ant colony algorithm for classification rule discovery, H Abbass, R. Sarker, C. Newton (Eds.): Data Mining: a Heuristic Approach, pp. 191-208, London: Idea Group Publishing, 2002

[4] Śmierzchalski R.: Evolutionary algorithm in problem of avoidance collision at sea, Proceedings of the 9th International Conference 'Advanced Computer Systems' ACS'2002, Międzyzdroje, Poland, October 23-25, 2002

[5] Xiao J., Michalewicz Z., Zhang L., Trojanowski K.: Adaptive evolutionary planner/ navigator for mobile robots, IEEE Transactions on Evolutionary Computation, vol. 1, No. 1., pp. 18-28, 1997

Application of fuzzy logic for track corrector formation into flight simulator

VICTOR J. MAMAEV, DMITRY A. JUDIN
Saint-Petersburg University of Aerospace Instrumentation, Department of Aviation instrument making (caf.11)67, B.Morskaya st., Saint-Petersburg,190000
e-mail: vera@aanet.ru (for Mamaev V.J.)

Abstract: The main problem of pilot training is to learn the student of distance and course correction. The way of standard course corrector using fuzzy logic is discussing below. In flight simulator navigator operations will be compared with corrector functioning.

Key words: Track corrector, fuzzy logic, navigation system, flight simulator

There are many different navigational aid aboard to course correction and determining aircraft position. There is no universal navigational aid and depending on circumstances navigator is to determine optimal navigation system. In non-automatic flight the problem of navigation corrector determination is usually decided by means of navigator experience, knowledge, intuition. But the decision time is often limited by circumstances. So we see the necessity of intellectual sensor making. Such sensor is intended for optimal navigation system selection and replacing human navigator in this situation.

Our method of path corrector construction we will illustrate by means of example of two radio navigational aids. Two distances D_I and D_{II} from beacons and two beacon bearings A_I and A_{II} may be the measuring navigational quantities. Fix error in latter version depends on angle ω of line of equal bearings intersection. Thus, the trainee's task is to make a decision about radio navigational system (RNS) configuration selection using 3 main parameters: ω, D_I, D_{II}. RNS configuration selected will determine potential aircraft fixing error (root-mean-square error σ (RMSE)). RNS configurations for 2 radio beacons (RB) are shown in tab.1.

Denomination of RNS configuration	1st radio beacon	2nd radio beacon
S1	azimuth channel	azimuth channel
S2	distance-measuring channel	distance-measuring channel
S3	azimuth channel	distance-measuring channel
S4	distance-measuring channel	azimuth channel

Tab. 1. RNS configurations for 2 radio beacons.

Let's assign linguistic variables according to the fuzzy logic theory by means of several terms.

ω = {„parallel azimuth lines" (ω_1), „angle of 45 degree" (ω_2), „orthogonal azimuth lines" (ω_3)};

D_I, D_{II} = {„very close to" (D_1), „nearby" (D_2), „average distance" (D_3), „far" (D_4), „very far" (D_5)};

σ = {„very high" (σ_1), „high"(σ_2), „average"(σ_3), „low"(σ_4), „very low"(σ_5)}.

Accuracy evaluation rule's base developed by navigator consists of derivation rules "if ω =... D_I =... and D_{II} =... , then $\sigma(S_1)$=..., $\sigma(S_2)$=..., $\sigma(S_3)$=..., $\sigma(S_4)$=...". It is convenient to present this base in a table form (tab.2,3).

Functional scheme to illustrate information conversion sequence according to foregoing thesis is shown in fig.1.

Let's consider system functioning for one step of training. Navigator work with system via user's interface and he give to system parameters ω^*, D^* and RNS configuration he decided to use in this navigation situation. In fuzzyfication block teaching system compares ω^*, D^* with linguistic variables ω_1 ... ω_3 and D_1 ... D_5. Then in decision block according to fuzzy rules (tab.2,3) and initial values system give us possible accuracy of this navigation system for different RNS configurations. I.e. expression like "if ω = ω_1, D_I = D_2 and D_{II} = D_4 , then $\sigma(S_1)$=σ_5, $\sigma(S_2)$=σ_5, $\sigma(S_3)$= σ_2, $\sigma(S_4)$= σ_4" is "if RB1 and RB2 bearing lines is parallel, RB1 is nearby, RB2 far away then we have very low accuracy with S_1 and S_2 RNS configuration (see tab.1), configuration S_3 provide high accuracy and S_4 – low accuracy". In defuzzyfication block, system converts linguistic values σ_i in specific values $\sigma^*(S_i)$ of four RNS configuration according to Mamdani's algorithm.

Block of reference RNS configuration selection selects the best RNS configuration in terms of accuracy.

Estimation, error analysis explanation forming block compares reference RNS configuration (S^*_{REF}) with RNS (S^*_{NAV}) navigator selected, find the error in coordinate definition and source of this error, forms and displays recommendation to trainer (navigator) about his decision to use this RNS configuration to aircraft track correction.

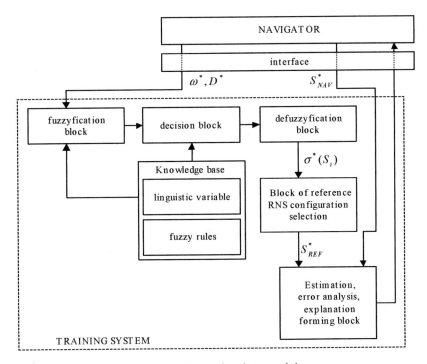

Fig. 1. Functional scheme of navigator training system.

		D_{II}				
		D_1	D_2	D_3	D_4	D_5
	D_1	$\sigma(S_1)=\sigma_5$ $\sigma(S_2)=\sigma_5$ $\sigma(S_3)=\sigma_1$ $\sigma(S_4)=\sigma_1$	$\sigma(S_1)=\sigma_5$ $\sigma(S_2)=\sigma_5$ $\sigma(S_3)=\sigma_1$ $\sigma(S_4)=\sigma_2$	$\sigma(S_1)=\sigma_5$ $\sigma(S_2)=\sigma_5$ $\sigma(S_3)=\sigma_1$ $\sigma(S_4)=\sigma_3$	$\sigma(S_1)=\sigma_5$ $\sigma(S_2)=\sigma_5$ $\sigma(S_3)=\sigma_1$ $\sigma(S_4)=\sigma_4$	$\sigma(S_1)=\sigma_5$ $\sigma(S_2)=\sigma_5$ $\sigma(S_3)=\sigma_1$ $\sigma(S_4)=\sigma_5$
	D_2	$\sigma(S_1)=\sigma_5$ $\sigma(S_2)=\sigma_5$ $\sigma(S_3)=\sigma_2$ $\sigma(S_4)=\sigma_1$	$\sigma(S_1)=\sigma_5$ $\sigma(S_2)=\sigma_5$ $\sigma(S_3)=\sigma_2$ $\sigma(S_4)=\sigma_2$	$\sigma(S_1)=\sigma_5$ $\sigma(S_2)=\sigma_5$ $\sigma(S_3)=\sigma_2$ $\sigma(S_4)=\sigma_3$	$\sigma(S_1)=\sigma_5$ $\sigma(S_2)=\sigma_5$ $\sigma(S_3)=\sigma_2$ $\sigma(S_4)=\sigma_4$	$\sigma(S_1)=\sigma_5$ $\sigma(S_2)=\sigma_5$ $\sigma(S_3)=\sigma_2$ $\sigma(S_4)=\sigma_5$
D_I	D_3	$\sigma(S_1)=\sigma_5$ $\sigma(S_2)=\sigma_5$ $\sigma(S_3)=\sigma_3$ $\sigma(S_4)=\sigma_1$	$\sigma(S_1)=\sigma_5$ $\sigma(S_2)=\sigma_5$ $\sigma(S_3)=\sigma_3$ $\sigma(S_4)=\sigma_2$	$\sigma(S_1)=\sigma_5$ $\sigma(S_2)=\sigma_5$ $\sigma(S_3)=\sigma_3$ $\sigma(S_4)=\sigma_3$	$\sigma(S_1)=\sigma_5$ $\sigma(S_2)=\sigma_5$ $\sigma(S_3)=\sigma_3$ $\sigma(S_4)=\sigma_4$	$\sigma(S_1)=\sigma_5$ $\sigma(S_2)=\sigma_5$ $\sigma(S_3)=\sigma_3$ $\sigma(S_4)=\sigma_4$
	D_4	$\sigma(S_1)=\sigma_5$ $\sigma(S_2)=\sigma_5$ $\sigma(S_3)=\sigma_4$ $\sigma(S_4)=\sigma_1$	$\sigma(S_1)=\sigma_5$ $\sigma(S_2)=\sigma_5$ $\sigma(S_3)=\sigma_4$ $\sigma(S_4)=\sigma_2$	$\sigma(S_1)=\sigma_5$ $\sigma(S_2)=\sigma_5$ $\sigma(S_3)=\sigma_4$ $\sigma(S_4)=\sigma_3$	$\sigma(S_1)=\sigma_5$ $\sigma(S_2)=\sigma_5$ $\sigma(S_3)=\sigma_4$ $\sigma(S_4)=\sigma_4$	$\sigma(S_1)=\sigma_5$ $\sigma(S_2)=\sigma_5$ $\sigma(S_3)=\sigma_4$ $\sigma(S_4)=\sigma_5$
	D_5	$\sigma(S_1)=\sigma_5$ $\sigma(S_2)=\sigma_5$ $\sigma(S_3)=\sigma_5$ $\sigma(S_4)=\sigma_1$	$\sigma(S_1)=\sigma_5$ $\sigma(S_2)=\sigma_5$ $\sigma(S_3)=\sigma_5$ $\sigma(S_4)=\sigma_2$	$\sigma(S_1)=\sigma_5$ $\sigma(S_2)=\sigma_5$ $\sigma(S_3)=\sigma_5$ $\sigma(S_4)=\sigma_3$	$\sigma(S_1)=\sigma_5$ $\sigma(S_2)=\sigma_5$ $\sigma(S_3)=\sigma_5$ $\sigma(S_4)=\sigma_4$	$\sigma(S_1)=\sigma_5$ $\sigma(S_2)=\sigma_5$ $\sigma(S_3)=\sigma_5$ $\sigma(S_4)=\sigma_5$

Tab. 2. RNS accuracy determination rule's base for ω_1 („parallel azimuth lines").

		D_{II}				
		D_1	D_2	D_3	D_4	D_5
D_I	D_1	$\sigma(S_1)=\sigma_1$ $\sigma(S_2)=\sigma_1$ $\sigma(S_3)=\sigma_5$ $\sigma(S_4)=\sigma_5$	$\sigma(S_1)=\sigma_2$ $\sigma(S_2)=\sigma_1$ $\sigma(S_3)=\sigma_5$ $\sigma(S_4)=\sigma_5$	$\sigma(S_1)=\sigma_3$ $\sigma(S_2)=\sigma_1$ $\sigma(S_3)=\sigma_5$ $\sigma(S_4)=\sigma_5$	$\sigma(S_1)=\sigma_4$ $\sigma(S_2)=\sigma_4$ $\sigma(S_3)=\sigma_5$ $\sigma(S_4)=\sigma_5$	$\sigma(S_1)=\sigma_5$ $\sigma(S_2)=\sigma_5$ $\sigma(S_3)=\sigma_5$ $\sigma(S_4)=\sigma_5$
	D_2	$\sigma(S_1)=\sigma_2$ $\sigma(S_2)=\sigma_1$ $\sigma(S_3)=\sigma_5$ $\sigma(S_4)=\sigma_5$	$\sigma(S_1)=\sigma_3$ $\sigma(S_2)=\sigma_1$ $\sigma(S_3)=\sigma_5$ $\sigma(S_4)=\sigma_5$	$\sigma(S_1)=\sigma_4$ $\sigma(S_2)=\sigma_1$ $\sigma(S_3)=\sigma_5$ $\sigma(S_4)=\sigma_5$	$\sigma(S_1)=\sigma_5$ $\sigma(S_2)=\sigma_4$ $\sigma(S_3)=\sigma_5$ $\sigma(S_4)=\sigma_5$	$\sigma(S_1)=\sigma_5$ $\sigma(S_2)=\sigma_5$ $\sigma(S_3)=\sigma_5$ $\sigma(S_4)=\sigma_5$
	D_3	$\sigma(S_1)=\sigma_3$ $\sigma(S_2)=\sigma_1$ $\sigma(S_3)=\sigma_5$ $\sigma(S_4)=\sigma_5$	$\sigma(S_1)=\sigma_4$ $\sigma(S_2)=\sigma_1$ $\sigma(S_3)=\sigma_5$ $\sigma(S_4)=\sigma_5$	$\sigma(S_1)=\sigma_5$ $\sigma(S_2)=\sigma_1$ $\sigma(S_3)=\sigma_5$ $\sigma(S_4)=\sigma_5$	$\sigma(S_1)=\sigma_5$ $\sigma(S_2)=\sigma_4$ $\sigma(S_3)=\sigma_5$ $\sigma(S_4)=\sigma_5$	$\sigma(S_1)=\sigma_5$ $\sigma(S_2)=\sigma_5$ $\sigma(S_3)=\sigma_5$ $\sigma(S_4)=\sigma_5$
	D_4	$\sigma(S_1)=\sigma_4$ $\sigma(S_2)=\sigma_4$ $\sigma(S_3)=\sigma_5$ $\sigma(S_4)=\sigma_5$	$\sigma(S_1)=\sigma_5$ $\sigma(S_2)=\sigma_4$ $\sigma(S_3)=\sigma_5$ $\sigma(S_4)=\sigma_5$	$\sigma(S_1)=\sigma_5$ $\sigma(S_2)=\sigma_4$ $\sigma(S_3)=\sigma_5$ $\sigma(S_4)=\sigma_5$	$\sigma(S_1)=\sigma_5$ $\sigma(S_2)=\sigma_4$ $\sigma(S_3)=\sigma_5$ $\sigma(S_4)=\sigma_5$	$\sigma(S_1)=\sigma_5$ $\sigma(S_2)=\sigma_5$ $\sigma(S_3)=\sigma_5$ $\sigma(S_4)=\sigma_5$
	D_5	$\sigma(S_1)=\sigma_5$ $\sigma(S_2)=\sigma_5$ $\sigma(S_3)=\sigma_5$ $\sigma(S_4)=\sigma_5$	$\sigma(S_1)=\sigma_5$ $\sigma(S_2)=\sigma_5$ $\sigma(S_3)=\sigma_5$ $\sigma(S_4)=\sigma_5$	$\sigma(S_1)=\sigma_5$ $\sigma(S_2)=\sigma_5$ $\sigma(S_3)=\sigma_5$ $\sigma(S_4)=\sigma_5$	$\sigma(S_1)=\sigma_5$ $\sigma(S_2)=\sigma_5$ $\sigma(S_3)=\sigma_5$ $\sigma(S_4)=\sigma_5$	$\sigma(S_1)=\sigma_5$ $\sigma(S_2)=\sigma_5$ $\sigma(S_3)=\sigma_5$ $\sigma(S_4)=\sigma_5$

Tab. 3. RNS accuracy determination rule's base for ω_3 („orthogonal azimuth lines").

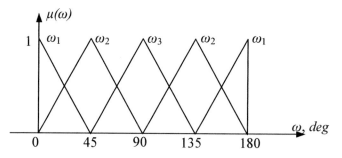

Fig. 2. Characteristic function of "azimuth lines intersection angle" variable.

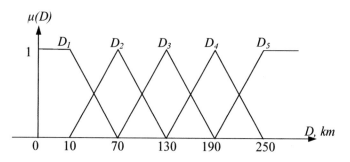

Fig. 3. Characteristic function of "distance" variable.

Characteristic function of variables "distance", "azimuth lines intersection angle" and "accuracy" are shown in fig.2-4.

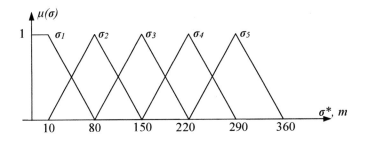

Fig. 4. Characteristic function of "accuracy" variable.

According to the fuzzy logic theory we have assigned linguistic terms for all input and output variables. These terms correspond with exact value's ranges. We have also produce the rule's table based on conditional expressions. So we have the full mathematical model of aircraft track corrector variant selector.

Let's test this model for specific navigational conditions: $\omega^* = 85°$; $D_I^*=83\ km$, $D_{II}^*=200\ km$ (see fig. 5).

Conforming to the characteristic functions (fig. 2-4) values of this variables are the following:

$\omega_1(\omega^*)=0$; $\omega_2(\omega^*)=0,11$; $\omega_3(\omega^*)=0,89$;
$D_1(D_I^*)=D_4(D_I^*)=D_5(D_I^*)=0$; $D_2(D_I^*)=0,75$; $D_3(D_I^*)=0,25$;
$D_1(D_{II}^*)=D_2(D_{II}^*)=D_3(D_{II}^*)=0$; $D_4(D_{II}^*)=0,85$; $D_5(D_{II}^*)=0,15$.

According to the fuzzy logic theory we produce the tables of restrictions for output variables (tab.4,5).

		D_{II}				
		D_1	D_2	D_3	D_4	D_5
	D_1	0	0	0	0	0
	D_2	0	0	0	0,11	0,11
D_I	D_3	0	0	0	0,11	0,11
	D_4	0	0	0	0	0
	D_5	0	0	0	0	0

Tab. 4. Table of restrictions for ω_2 variable.

		D_{II}				
		D_1	D_2	D_3	D_4	D_5
	D_1	0	0	0	0	0
	D_2	0	0	0	0,75	0,15
D_I	D_3	0	0	0	0,25	0,15
	D_4	0	0	0	0	0
	D_5	0	0	0	0	0

Tab. 5. Table of restrictions for ω_3 variable.

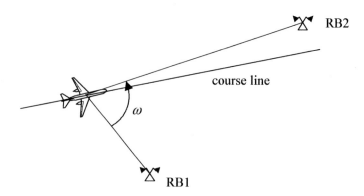

Fig. 5. For navigational conditions determination.

Characteristic functions for output variables are shown in fig.6-9.

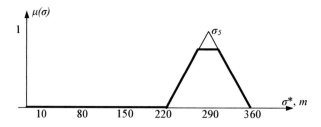

Fig.6. Characteristic function of RNS configuration S_1 variable.

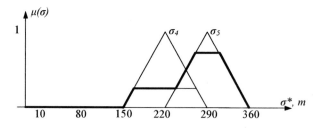

Fig.7. Characteristic function of RNS configuration S_2 variable.

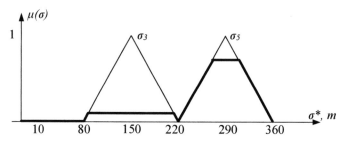

Fig.8. Characteristic function of RNS configuration S_3 variable.

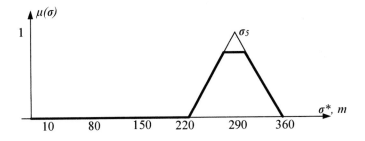

Fig.9. Characteristic function of RNS configuration S_4 variable.

As a result of defuzzyfication we have:

$\sigma^*(S_1)$= 290 m;
$\sigma^*(S_2)$= 255 m;
$\sigma^*(S_3)$= 275 m;
$\sigma^*(S_4)$= 290 m.

We can conclude that in current navigational situation using RNS configuration S2 (employing distance-measuring equipment with RB1 and RB2) preferably because of its higher accuracy for aircraft position fixing.

REFERENCES

[1] Judin D.A. 2001. 'Intellectual system of moving object fixing'. *IV SPGSS*, SPbSUAI.
[2] Petrov S.J., Shifrin B.M. 'Model of system for cellulose forming using fuzzy logic. *Devices and Systems. Control and diagnostics*. 2/2002.
[3] Zmitrivich A.I. 'Intellectual information systems'. *Tetra Systems*. 1997. 36

Algorithm for Automatic Definition of Validated and Non-Validated Region in Multi-Dimensional Space

PRZEMYSŁAW KLĘSK

Institute of Artificial Intelligence and Mathematical Methods, Faculty of Computer Science and Information Systems, Technical University of Szczecin
Żołnierska Street 49, e-mail: przemyslaw.klesk@bellstream.pl

Abstract: When having a set of measurement samples Θ at disposal , it is useful to create a definition of the region enclosing the samples — the domain of discourse. If the samples represent a system performing $\mathbb{R}^n \to \mathbb{R}$ mapping, then this is about defining such region within $\mathbb{R}^n$. In the case of clustering, the outcome region should be the sum of regions defined for single clusters. After having defined numerically this region, one can check if a certain testing sample (newly acquired), to be used as input to a ready model, is placed inside the *validated region* (VR) or outside it — in *non-validated region* (nVR). Such test allows to state whether the model output for this sample should be considered interpolation or extrapolation effect, and hence, how credible it is. This paper shows what approaches to VR definition could be chosen. Also, the paper presents the algorithm, the implementation of which would automatically define VR by producing a set of inequalities, forming the minimal convex region.

Key words: validated and non-validated region, convex region, input-output modeling, extrapolation, interpolation

1.   INTRODUCTION

In system modeling tasks, when having a set of measurement samples Θ at disposal, it is useful to create a definition of the region enclosing the samples — the domain of discourse. For some modeling algorithms the ideal case is to have uniform regular distribution of samples. By uniform and regular, the rectangular grid is often meant. True-to-life problems, in which cause-effect relations are vague or not known at all, show however that distribution of samples can be far from ideal rectangular case, see Fig. 1[1]. Many various and obvious reasons for this can be enumerated. One could be the fact that there can be dependencies between input variables (sometimes such dependencies are too weak to be clearly stated and assessed). Another reason could be the fact that often modelers perform a casting of samples (a projection) onto a certain set of chosen input variables. There are of course more reasons, and often specific to the particular problem, see e.g. [5].

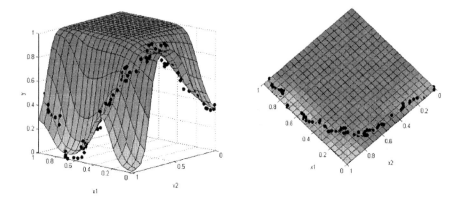

Fig. 1. Distribution of samples in real-life problem — unemployment rate in Poland. Exemplary model with 2 inputs: population size, money supply.

Defining the domain of discourse for a system on samples basis, means that one should specify a certain subset of the space being the Cartesian product of all chosen inputs. If the samples represent a system performing $\mathbb{R}^n \to \mathbb{R}$ mapping, then the task is to define such region within $\mathbb{R}^n$. For small $n = 1, 2, 3$ this task can be fairly simple, and one can still draw the samples and graphically represent the VR (*validated region*). There can be however practical problems when the modeler must cope with really many inputs, tens or in extreme cases even hundreds, and really many samples; see e.g. [5]. It is not possible then for a human to define the VR by depicting it. This must be done automatically, by a computer implementation of wanted algorithm.

Clustering of samples is popular approach in modeling. Various clustering methods can be met in literature (hierarchical, iterative, evolutionary), see e.g. [2], [3, pp. 331-352]. If doing the clustering, the outcome validated region should be the sum of validated regions defined for single clusters.

Finally, after having this region numerically defined, one can check if a certain testing sample (newly acquired), to be used as input to a ready model, is placed inside the *validated region* (VR) or outside it — in *non-validated region* (nVR). In the second case it is also helpful to assess the sample closeness to the border of VR. Such test — stating the location of sample either in VR or in nVR— allows to answer whether the model output for this sample should be considered interpolation or extrapolation effect, and hence, how credible it is.

---

[1] Illustration taken from [5]

Obviously, the more far from the border the worse credibility; see too [1], [4]. Fig. 2 and Fig. 3 depict the considerations hereby[2].

This paper shows what approaches to VR definition could be chosen. The paper presents as well the algorithm, the implementation of which would automatically define VR by producing a set of inequalities, forming the minimal convex region.

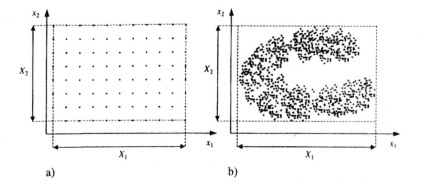

a)   b)

Fig. 2. Samples distribution: -a- regular grid, -b- exemplary non-regular distribution.

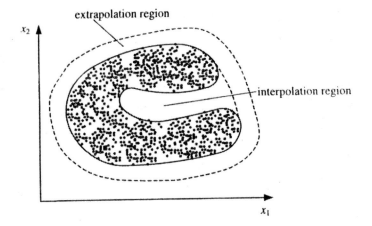

Fig. 3. Interpolation (approximation within VR), extrapolation (approximation within $\cap$VR).

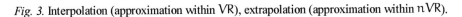

[2] Illustrations taken from [3]

2.   SAMPLES CLUSTERING

The approach to clustering task and concrete clustering methods are not the actual focus of this paper. The focus is how to define the VR. Hence, from now on let us assume that the modeler is given a large set of samples in $\mathbb{R}^n$, and he is at the stage of clustering already done. So, all the samples are grouped into known clusters. Any method could have been used for this purpose: Ward method (hierarchical agglomeration), C-means method (iterative), evolutionary algorithm, see [2]. For further considerations it does not matter. The point is that the task of defining the VR can be now brought to every single cluster independently. At the end, the outcome VR should be considered the sum of validated regions found for all single clusters.

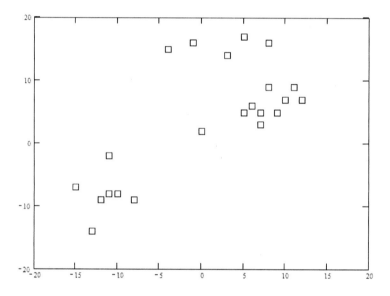

Fig. 4. Exemplary distribution of samples in $\mathbb{R}^2$ before clustering.

3.   CONVEX REGIONS. CUBE IN $\mathbb{R}^n$, SPHERE IN $\mathbb{R}^n$, MINIMAL POLYHEDRON IN $\mathbb{R}^n$.

The convex region in $\mathbb{R}^n$ is the region in which any two points can be joined by a segment line completely enclosed within this region. To enclose the samples within such region, the possible easy-to-find candidates could be, e.g. cube or sphere (in $\mathbb{R}^n$). But, that would not be exactly the wanted precise result. The overhead of border space not covered by the samples could be too large, depending on concrete distribution.

To find the cube, one must iterate through all the samples and find the minimum and the maximum values for every input, between which the samples are spread.

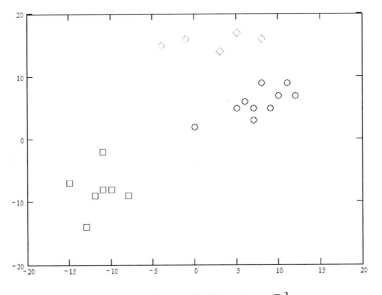

Fig. 5. Exemplary result of clustering in $\mathbb{R}^2$.

To find the sphere, one must iterate through all the samples and calculate the center point (for every input, the arithmetic mean from all the samples). The distance from the center point to the most remote sample, would be the radius.

As for the credible $\mathfrak{n}$VR region (extrapolation), the scale coefficient can be introduced. Let's denote it by α. The modeler can decide for example to have $\alpha = 1.30$, i.e. he would decide that the acceptable closeness to VR, on each side, should not be greater than approximately 15% of VR's size (measured along certain axis); see also [3, pp. 331-352], [4], [1].

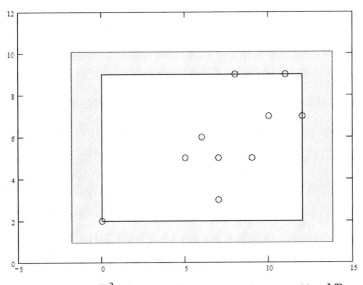

Fig. 6. Cube in $\mathbb{R}^2$. The gray region represents the acceptable $\mathfrak{n}$VR.

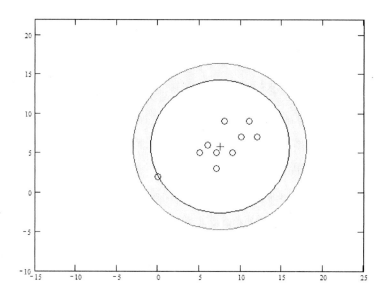

Fig. 7. Sphere $\mathbb{R}^2$. The gray region represents the acceptable $\mathsf{n}VR$.

As already stated, for the considered region enclosing the samples it would be more satisfactory to find something better than a cube or a sphere. This could mean to find the minimal convex region for the given set of samples. This region would be a certain polyhedron in $\mathbb{R}^n$.

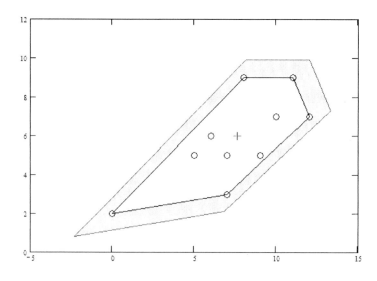

Fig. 8. Minimal convex polyhedron in $\mathbb{R}^2$. The gray region represents the acceptable $\mathsf{n}VR$.

One is always able to find the minimal convex for any finite set of samples $\Theta \subset \mathbb{R}^n$, providing that the following two conditions are met:

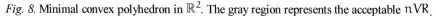

(1) the cardinality of the set is greater than the dimensionality of considered space, i.e. $\#\Theta > n$,
(2) samples do not lie on the same hyperplane, i.e.

$$\nexists_{a_0,a_1,\ldots,a_n;a_i \in \mathbb{R}} \; \forall_{\theta_i \in \Theta} \quad a_0 + a_1\theta_{i1} + \cdots + a_n\theta_{in} = 0,$$

where θ_{ij} denotes the j-th input of i-th sample.

In other words, the number of samples must be sufficient, and there must be at least one sample that is not in the same hyperplane as others (for $\mathbb{R}^1$ the samples must not be the very same scalar point, for $\mathbb{R}^2$ the samples must not lie on the same one line, for $\mathbb{R}^3$ the samples must not lie on the same one plane, an so on.).

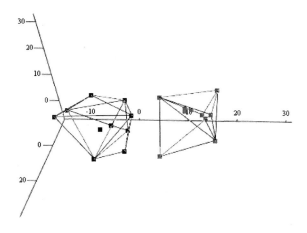

Fig. 9. Minimal convex regions (polyhedrons) for two clusters in $\mathbb{R}^3$.

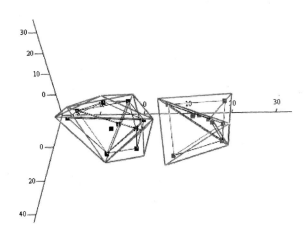

Fig. 10. Minimal convex regions (polyhedrons) for two clusters in $\mathbb{R}^3$ with their close acceptable nVRs.

4. THE ALGORITHM

Again, it is assumed that a finite clustered set of samples $\Theta \subset \mathbb{R}^n$ is given. The following is the algorithm to find the minimal convex polyhedron, listing the steps to be taken for a single cluster.

(1) Find the set Ω containing all possible $\binom{\#\Theta}{n}$ hyperplanes built from Θ, where each hyperplane is set upon n samples θ_i from Θ. I.e. for $\mathbb{R}^1$, Ω will contain scalar points; for $\mathbb{R}^2$ — lines, for $\mathbb{R}^3$ — planes, and so on. In generic case, for each hyperplane $a_0, a_1, \ldots, a_n$ coefficients can be found, such that for all those n samples forming the single hyperplane:
$$a_0 + a_1\theta_{i1} + \cdots + a_n\theta_{in} = 0.$$

(2) From Ω, choose hyperplanes, only those that divide $\mathbb{R}^n$ into two subspaces; one subspace containing the whole Θ, the other not containing any element from Θ. Let the set of hyperplanes found this way be denoted by Ω'.

(3) Let us introduce a matrix M, with $\#\Omega'$ rows and $n+1$ columns, where in every row j, coefficients $a_0, a_1, \ldots, a_n$ of j-th hyperplane are kept. If necessary, the coefficients can be multiplied by -1, so that the row could be interpreted as an inequality with default sign '$\leq$', i.e.
$$a_0 + a_1x_1 + \cdots + a_nx_n \leq 0.$$

(4) Let v_M represent the function $v_M: \mathbb{R}^n \to \{0, 1\}$. Let v_M return 1 if all inequalities (from every row in M) are true for a certain testing sample θ_*. Otherwise, let it return 0.

(5) Hence, the VR can be defined this way
$$VR = \{(x_1, \ldots, x_n); x_i \in \mathbb{R} \mid v_M(x_1, \ldots, x_n) = 1\}.$$

5. EXAMPLE

For exemplary cluster from Fig. 8, such M is obtained:

$$M = \begin{pmatrix} -2.286 & -1 & 1.143 \\ 14 & 1 & -7 \\ -9 & 0 & 1 \\ -3.25 & 1 & -1.25 \\ -15.5 & 1 & 0.5 \end{pmatrix}.$$

This corresponds to the following set of inequalities:

$$VR = \begin{cases} -2.286 - 1x_1 + 1.143x_2 \leq 0 \\ 14 + 1x_1 - 7x_2 \leq 0 \\ -9 + 0x_1 + 1x_2 \leq 0 \\ -3.25 + 1x_1 - 1.25x_2 \leq 0 \\ -15.5 + 1x_1 + 0.5x_2 \leq 0 \end{cases}.$$

Now, the center point for this cluster is found, and the region gets scaled around it, using the scale $\alpha = 1.3$. This results in the following set of inequalities, which represents the VR with close acceptable nVR:

$$VR \cup nVR = \begin{cases} -3.194 - 1x_1 + 1.143x_2 \leq 0 \\ 7.88 + 1x_1 - 7x_2 \leq 0 \\ -9.9 + 0x_1 + 1x_2 \leq 0 \\ -4.195 + 1x_1 - 1.25x_2 \leq 0 \\ -16.97 + 1x_1 + 0.5x_2 \leq 0 \end{cases}.$$

Summing up all the clusters, the result would look like on Fig. 11 (see also Fig. 10).

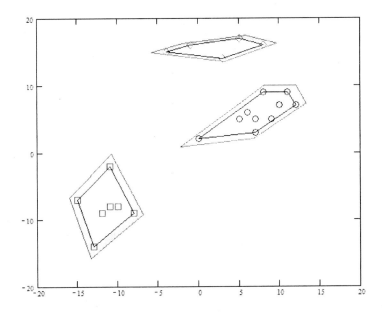

Fig. 11. Three exemplary clusters with their VR and nVR regions.

6. CONCLUDING REMARKS

No matter what approach to input-output modeling is chosen — be it conventional methods, neural networks, fuzzy logic, or any other — it is helpful to start with the definition of *validated* and *non-validated* regions. This means, the region tightly enclosing the samples, and the region very close to it — acceptable neighbourhood. When having a large set of samples and dealing with really many inputs, a computer implementation of the algorithm described in this paper could be used to do these definitions automatically, rather than e.g. trying to depict it traditionally (if doable at all). Having those regions defined allows to do further modeling tasks: classifying testing samples, assessing crediblity of samples and model results (interpolation, extrapolation).

REFERENCES

[1] Lászlo Kóczy and Kaoru Hirota. Interpolative reasoning with insufficient evidence. In *Information Sciences,* pages 169-201. Elsevier Science Publishing Co., 1993.
[2] Marcin Korzeń. Zastosowanie algorytmu ewolucyjnego w analizie skupien. In *Materiały VII sesji naukowej informatyki,* volume 2, Faculty of Computer Science and Information Systems, Technical University of Szczecin, Szczecin, Poland, 2002.
[3] Andrzej Piegat. *Fuzzy Modeling and Control.* Physica Verlag Heidelberg, Germany, 2001.
[4] Anthony Ralston. *Wstęp do analizy numerycznej.* PWN, Warszawa, Poland, iii edition, 1983. Title of the original: *A First Course in Numerical Analysis.*
[5] Izabela Rejer. *Metoda modelowania wielkowymiarowego systemu z użyciem metod sztucznej inteligencji na przykładzie bezrobocia w Polsce.* Szczecin, Poland, 2002. Ph.D. thesis.

Adaptive simulation of separable dynamical systems in the neural network basis

WALERY ROGOZA
Faculty of Computer Science & Information Systems, Technical University of Szczecin
49, Zolnierska st., 71-210 Szczecin, Poland, wrogoza@wi.ps.pl

Abstract: A technique for the computer analysis is considered as applied to simulation of complex dynamical systems using the neural network basis. The technique is essentially grounded on the decomposition of separable differential equation sets with small parameters (singularly perturbed sets).

Key words: complex systems, simulation, singularly perturbed differential equations, model reduction, parallel computation, neural network basis.

1. INTRODUCTION

The problem of complex object model simplification is one of the primary topics of system analysis [1]. Difficulties emerging in such an analysis are associated for the most part with the problem stiffness and rigorous restrictions on the integration step lengths. As a consequence, this causes the accumulation of round-off errors, affects adversely the convergence rate of numerical procedures and may require huge computer time to solve the problem.

To overcome these difficulties, it is appropriate to decompose and reduce the entire mathematical model of a complex object into the number of submodels, which can be analyzed independently or/and concurrently. A.Tikhonov, the Russian academician, has pioneered analytical properties of one important class of reducible models, namely, the set of ordinary differential equations (ODEs) with small parameters on derivatives, or, the set of singularly perturbed ODEs [2]. As it seems, this approach is particularly promosing, since it is shown [3] that an arbitrary reducible model given in the form of the set of ODEs can be transformed to the singularly perturbed set of equations. Unfortunately, this theory does not suggest constructive methods applicable to the computer implementation.

This paper discusses the method of motion separation of complex object models based on the Tikhonov's theory and proposes an algorithm for the numerical implementation of this method using the neural network basis.

2. MATHEMATICAL GROUND

Mathematical models of dynamical systems used in various engineering applications are frequently represented in the form of the Cauchy problem – the set of differential and algebraic equations (DAEs) with the initial condition

$$\Phi(x, \dot{x}, t) = 0, \qquad x(0) = x_0, \tag{1}$$

where $x = x(t)$ is the n-dimensional vector of variables which represents the object states in time within the given observation time interval $t \in [0, T]$ (the state variable vector), $\dot{x}(t) = dx / dt$ is the n'-dimensional vector of state variable time derivatives reflecting behavioral dynamics; x_0 is the vector of the given initial conditions. Further it is assumed that $n' = n$.

The dimension of $\dot{x}(t)$, called the system order, can reach hundreds and thousands. At the same time, numerous experiments lead us to the conclusion that within a rather wide observation interval $[0, T]$, subintervals exist, where some variables vary fast and others slowly. The separation of the x vector into "fast" and "slow" variables is much more simpler if (1) is transformed to the form resolved for derivatives. The algorithm allowing such a transformation is proposed in [3]. It transforms the general model (1) to the Tikhonov's set of differential equations – the set of equations with parameters on derivatives:

$$a) \mu \frac{dz}{dt} = F(z, y, t); \qquad z(0) = z_0;$$

$$b) \quad \frac{dy}{dt} = f(z, y, t); \qquad y(0) = y_0; \tag{2}$$

where $z(t)$ is the M-dimensional, and $y(t)$ – m-dimensional state subvectors; $M + m = n$; μ is a $(M \times M)$ diagonal matrix of parameters. In cases being of practical interest, parameters μ reflect some weak influences between the parts of a complex object, and also second order and parasitic effects of different kinds. Due to their nature, parameters are small enough in magnitude, and (2) can be considered as the set of singularly perturbed differential equations.

The algorithm of model (2) reduction at $\mu \to 0$ can be built on the basis of analytical properties of the above model [2, 4] as follows. An important property of (2) is that with reasonably small values of μ there exists a boundary layer $[0, \tau_\eta]$ in the neighborhood of point $t = 0$, whose width is in inverse proportion to the values of parameters $\tau_{II} = O\left(\dfrac{1}{\mu}\right)$, in which $z(t)$ vary fast and $y(t)$ remain practically steady. It is evident that if there are a number of parameters, then a number of boundary layers could be selected each has its own width. But for the sake of simplicity, we'll consider only one boundary layer as if it is a single small parameter in (2). Thus, due to transformation (1) to (2), we are able to select the groups of relatively "fast" and "slow" variables in the explicit form. It should be noted that a possibility exists to realize a reduction algorithm without such a transformation because these groups of variables could be directly selected in the course of computation. Nevertheless, if the above transformation has been done, we are able to represent the algorithm of processing model (2) in the analytical form obtained below.

For ease of notation we'll consider model (2) as if it is the case of two equations and two variables $z(t)$ and $y(t)$. Let's represent $z(t)$ and $y(t)$ in the form of two formal series – regular and boundary series (by x we denote both z and y)

$$x = \bar{x}(t,\mu) + \Pi x(\tau,\mu), \tag{3}$$

where regular series terms depend depended on time t

$$\bar{x}(t,\mu) = \bar{x}_0(t) + \mu\bar{x}_1(t) + \dots \tag{4}$$

and boundary series terms depend on the scaled time $\tau = \dfrac{t}{\mu}$

$$\Pi x(\tau,\mu) = \Pi_0 x(\tau) + \mu\Pi_1 x(\tau) + \dots \tag{5}$$

Substituting (3) and (4) into (2) and multiplying the both sides of the second equation by μ, we can obtain

$$
\begin{aligned}
&a)\,\mu\frac{d\bar{z}}{dt} + \frac{d\Pi z}{d\tau} = F(\bar{z} + \Pi z, \bar{y} + \Pi y, t); \\
&b)\,\mu\frac{d\bar{y}}{dt} + \frac{d\Pi y}{d\tau} = \mu f(\bar{z} + \Pi z, \bar{y} + \Pi y, t);
\end{aligned}
\tag{6}
$$

The right-hand sides in (6) can also be expanded into the formal series in the μ powers. To obtain the expressions in a compact form, let's introduce values $\overline{F}$ и ΠF assuming

$$\overline{F} = F\big(\bar{z}(t,\mu), \bar{y}(t,\mu), t\big),$$

$$\Pi F = F\left(\begin{array}{l} \bar{z}(\tau\mu,\mu) + \Pi z(\tau,\mu), \bar{y}(\tau\mu,\mu) + \\ + \Pi y(\tau,\mu), \tau\mu) - F(\bar{z}(\tau\mu,\mu), \bar{y}(\tau\mu,\mu), \tau\mu) \end{array}\right).$$

Introducing values $\bar{f}$ and Πf in the same manner, we can rewrite (6) as follows

$$a)\,\mu\frac{d\bar{z}}{dt}+\frac{d\Pi z}{d\tau}=\bar{F}+\Pi F;$$

$$b)\,\mu\frac{d\bar{y}}{dt}+\frac{d\Pi y}{d\tau}=\mu(\bar{f}+\Pi f).$$

$$(7)$$

To obtain the final form of these equations, expand formally $\bar{F}$ and ΠF in powers of μ (coefficients of these expansions are functions of t and τ, respectively). Rewriting (7) first for variables t and then for variables τ, we can obtain:

$$a)\,\mu\frac{d}{dt}\left(\bar{z}_0(t)+\mu\bar{z}_1(t)+\mu^2\bar{z}_2(t)+...\right)=$$
$$=\bar{F}_0(t)+\mu\bar{F}_1(t)+\mu^2\bar{F}_2(t)+...;$$

$$b)\,\mu\frac{d}{dt}\left(\bar{y}_0(t)+\mu\bar{y}_1(t)+\mu^2\bar{y}_2(t)+...\right)=$$
$$=\mu\left(\bar{f}_0(t)+\mu\bar{f}_1(t)+\mu^2\bar{f}_2(t)+...\right);$$

$$c)\,\frac{d}{d\tau}\left(\Pi_0z(\tau)+\mu\Pi_1z(\tau)+\mu^2\Pi_2z(\tau)+...\right)=$$
$$=\Pi_0F(\tau)+\mu\Pi_1F(\tau)+\mu^2\Pi_2F(\tau)+...;$$

$$d)\,\frac{d}{d\tau}\left(\Pi_0y(\tau)+\mu\Pi_1y(\tau)+\mu^2\Pi_2y(\tau)+...\right)=$$
$$=\mu\left(\Pi_0f(\tau)+\mu\Pi_1f(\tau)+\mu^2\Pi_2f(\tau)+...\right);$$

$$(8)$$

Equating coefficients of the same powers of μ in the right-hand and left-hand sides of these equations separately for the terms being functions of t and τ, we can obtain equations in the required separated form:

$$a)\,\frac{d\bar{z}_{k-1}}{dt}=\bar{F}_k,\qquad\qquad b)\,\frac{d\bar{y}_k}{dt}=\bar{f}_k;$$

$$c)\,\frac{d\Pi_kz}{d\tau}=\Pi_kF,\qquad\qquad d)\,\frac{d\Pi_ky}{d\tau}=\Pi_{k-1}f,$$

$$(9)$$

where numbers $k=0,1,2,...$ can be treated as the approximation orders of the reduced model.

The above set of equations is decomposed with respect to the "fast" and "slow" variables and with respect to the components of different approximation orders. The remarkable properties of the final model can be expressed as follows:

1. The *k*-th order approximation can be obtained using the lower order approximations.
2. The *0*-order approximation ($k = 0$) takes the special form

$$(a)\ 0 = \overline{F}_0 \equiv F(\overline{z}_0, \overline{y}_0, t); \quad (b)\ \frac{d\overline{y}_0}{dt} = f(\overline{z}_0, \overline{y}_0, t) \tag{10}$$

that is, in this case (2) degenerates to the subset of algebraic equations and subset of differential equations of a lower dimension.

3. Equations (9b) and (9c) are resolved and linear with respect to the desired state variables.
4. (9a) and (9d) are separated by indices, namely, they include discrepant indices on the left-hand side derivatives and right-hand side. As a consequence, equation (9a) is not a differential equation with respect to $\overline{z}_{k-1}(t)$, and there is no need to recalculate the right-hand side of (9d) in the course of computation since it is independent of the current index *k*.

To solve (9), initial conditions should be calculated for new variables. The calculation technique is trivial. Expanding (3) into series by μ at the vicinity of $t = 0$ and equating the obtained expression to the initial condition vector, we can obtain

$$\overline{x}_0(0) + \mu\overline{x}_1(0) + ... + \Pi_0 x(0) + \mu\Pi_1 x(0) + ... = x^0.$$

Next, equating terms on the same powers of μ and considering limiting properties of terms at $t \to \infty$ [4], we can obtain the following expressions for the zero and first order approximations:

$$\overline{y}_0(0) = y^0;\ \Pi_0 y(0) = 0;\ \ \overline{z}_0(0) = \phi(\overline{y}_0(0), 0);$$
$$\Pi_0 z(0) = z^0 - \overline{z}_0(0),$$
$$\Pi_1 y(0) = -\int_0^\infty \Pi_0 f(s)ds;\ \ \overline{y}_1(0) = -\Pi_1 y(0);\ \ \overline{z}_0(0) = \overline{z}_1(t)\big|_{t=0};$$
$$\Pi_1 z(0) = -\overline{z}_1(0) \tag{11}$$

in which $\overline{z}_0(t) = \phi(\overline{y}_0(t), t)$ is the solution of the nonlinear (in the general case) algebraic equation (10a), and the infinite upper integration limit in $[0, \infty]$ can be changed by the finite limit $[0, \tau_\Pi]$.

3. SOLUTION ALGORITHM

Taking into account the above consideration, the algorithm for the solution of the original problem (2) can be formulated in the form given step by step in Table 1.

Table 1. Steps of computation and computer savings required for the realization of the motion separation method per one integration step

Step	Procedure	Function to be calculated or the equation to be solved	Number of "long" operations	Remark
1	2	3	4	5
1	Determination of the initial m-vector $\bar{y}_0(0)$	$\bar{y}_0(0) = y^0$	-	-
2	Calculation of the vector-functions $\bar{y}_0(t)$ and $\bar{z}_0(t)$ of the m and M dimensions, respectively	a) $[\partial F(\cdot)/\partial z]^{-1}$; b) $z_{\eta+1}^{p+1} - z_{\eta+1}^{p} = -[\partial F(\cdot)/\partial z]^{-1} F(\cdot)$; c) $d\bar{y}_0/dt = \bar{f}_0(t)$.	a) $(1/3)(M^3+3M^2 - M)$; b) $3M^2$; c) $3m$	η is the integration step number; p is the iteration number; $F()$ is the M-vector; $[\partial F(\cdot)/\partial z]^{-1}$ is the (M x M)-reciprocal Jacobi matrix.
3	Calculation of the initial M-vectors $\bar{z}_0(0)$ and $\Pi_0 z(0)$	a) $\bar{z}_0(0) = \phi(\bar{y}_0(0),0)$; b) $\Pi_0 z(0) = z^0 - \bar{z}_0(0)$;	-	Vector $\bar{z}_0(0)$ is calculated at the first iteration at step 2.
4	Calculation of the M-vector $\Pi_0 z(\tau)$	$\dfrac{d\Pi_0 z(\tau)}{d\tau} = F(\bar{z}_0(0) + \Pi_0 z(\tau), y^0)$;	M	A single iteration is required.
5	Calculation of the m-vector $\Pi_0 f(\tau)$	$\Pi_0 f(\tau) =$ $= f(\bar{z}_0(0) + \Pi_0 z(\tau), \bar{y}_0(0),0) -$ $- f(\bar{z}_0(0), \bar{y}_0(0),0)$	-	

#	Description	Formula		Comment
6	Calculation of the M-vector $\overline{F}_1$	$\overline{F}_1 = \overline{F}'_z(t)\overline{z}_1 + \overline{F}'_y\overline{y}_1 = \dfrac{d\overline{Z}_0(t)}{dt} \approx \dfrac{\overline{Z}_{0,\eta+1} - \overline{Z}_{0,\eta}}{t_{\eta+1} - t_\eta}$	M	This vector is determined as $\overline{Z}_0(t)$ with $t=0$ at step 2.
7	Calculation of the m-vector $\Pi_1 y(0)$	$\Pi_1 y(0) = -\displaystyle\int_0^\infty \Pi_0 f(s)ds$	m	Integration limits $[0, \infty]$ are changed by $[0, \tau_{TI}]$
8	Calculation of the m-vector $\Pi_1 y(\tau)$	$\dfrac{d\Pi_1 y(\tau)}{d\tau} = \Pi_0 f(\tau)$	m	A single iteration is required.
9	Determination of the initial m-vector $\overline{y}_1(0)$	$\overline{y}_1(0) = -\Pi_1 y(0)$	$\overline{y}_1(0) = -\Pi_1 y(0)$	
10	Calculation of the m-vector $\overline{y}_1(t)$	a) $\overline{F}_z^{-1}$; b) $\overline{f}_z(t)\overline{F}_z^{-1}(t) = \Phi_0$; c) $\Phi_0 \overline{F}'_y(t) = \Phi_1$; d) $[\overline{f}'_y(t) - \Phi_1]\overline{v}_1(t) = \Phi_3$; e) $\Phi_0 \dfrac{d\overline{Z}_0(t)}{dt} = \Phi_4$; f) $\overline{f}_1(t) = \Phi_3 + \Phi_4$; g) $\dfrac{d\overline{y}_1(t)}{dt} = \overline{f}_1(t)$.	a) $\dfrac{M^3 + 3M^2 - M}{3}$; b) $M^2 m$; c) Mm^2; d) m^2; e) Mm; f) 0; g) m.	A single iteration is required to solve (g).
11	Calculation of the M-vector $\overline{Z}_1(t)$	$\overline{Z}_1(t) = \overline{F}_z^{-1}(t)\left[\overline{F}_1 - \overline{F}'_y(t)\overline{v}_1(t)\right]$	M^2	All the components in the right-hand side are given at step 10.

12	Calculation of the initial M-vector $\bar{z}_1(0)$	$\bar{z}_1(0) = \bar{z}_1(t)$, $t = 0$.	-	Determined at step 11 with $t = 0$
13	Determination of the initial M-vector $\Pi_1 z(0)$	$\Pi_1 z(0) = -\bar{z}_1(0)$	-	
14	Calculation of the M-vector $\Pi_1 z(\tau)$	$a)\ F'_z(\tau)\Pi_1 z(\tau) = \psi_0$; $b)\ F'_y(\tau)\Pi_1 y(\tau) = \psi_1$; $c)\ \left(F'_z(\tau) - \bar{F}'_z(0)\right) \times \left(\bar{z}'_0(0)\tau + \bar{z}_1(0)\right) = \psi_2$; $d)\ \left(F'_y(\tau) - \bar{F}'_y(0)\right) \times \left(\bar{y}'_0(0)\tau + \bar{y}_1(0)\right) = \psi_3$; $e)\ \left(F'_t(\tau) - F'_t(0)\right)\tau = \psi_4$; $f)\ \Pi_1 F = \psi_0 + \psi_1 + \psi_3 + \psi_4$; $g)\ \dfrac{d\Pi_1 z(\tau)}{d\tau} = \Pi_1 z(\tau) = \Pi_1 F(\tau)$.	a) M^2; b) Mm; c) M^2; d) Mm; e) M; f) 0; g) M.	Solution of (g) requires a single iteration

Remark: M and m are the numbers of "fast" and "slow" variables, respectively.

The estimations of "long" operations (multiplications and divisions) given in the third column have been obtained for the following numerical methods: the Runge-Kutta's first order method for the solution of ordinary differential algebraic equations (DAE), the iterative Newton's method for the solution of a nonlinear algebraic equations (NAE), and the Gauss's method for the solution of linear algebraic equations (LAE) [5].

The steps of computation of terms of the zero and first approximation orders are given in Table 1 as the example of the approach discussed. In the same manner we can obtain separated equations to calculate the terms of expansion (8) of any approximation order.

4. SYNTHESIS OF NEURAL NETWORKS FOR THE SOLUTION OF SEPARATED SETS OF EQUATIONS

To explore the benefits of the decomposed model (9), let us consider a question in what manner this form of equations can be used to optimize computation.

As can be seen, the total dimension of (9) is greater than that one of the original model (2). Thus to take advantage of the decomposition, a parallel computation scheme is preferable to be used. In this connection the question arises whether a possibility exists to solve the above problem concurrently using parallel computation inherent in the neural network basis? By the neural network basis it is meant the arithmetic operations of weighted summation of input signals followed by the transformation of this sum using formal neuron activation functions.

As can be seen from Table 1, the solution of (9) involves computations of the two kinds – the solution of ODEs and the solution of LAEs formed at each iteration and each integration step. Let us consider these problems in detail.

Adaptive neural network algorithm for the solution of DAEs

As a possible adaptive method of ODEs solution, we can explore that one proposed in [6]. This is an iterative method for the solution of a matrix ordinary differential equation of the first order. As can be seen from Table 1, all the ODEs to be solved are resolved as respect to derivatives

$$\dot{x} = f(x,t), \qquad x(0) = x_0. \tag{12}$$

Let $\hat{x}(t)$ be an exact solution of (12). The solution iterative procedure involves the calculation of the approximate solution vector and the error vector:

$$a)\, x^m = x^m(t); \qquad b)\, \delta^m = \left| \hat{x}(t) - x^m(t) \right|_{L2} = \left| f - f^m \right|_{L2}, \tag{13}$$

where x^m and ε^m are the approximation and error vectors, respectively, calculated in the L_2 norm of the Banach space obtained at the m-th iteration. The desired iterative process

$$a)\, d(x^m)\,/\,dt = f^{\,m}(x^m); \qquad b)\, x^{m+1} = \varphi^m(x^m), \tag{14}$$

can be built using an approximation function $\varphi^n(x^m)$ to be obtained.

It is evident that $\varphi(x)$ should be chosen to provide calculation convergence $\lim_{t \to \infty} \delta^m \to 0$. We can use, for example, a piecewise linear approximation: $\Phi(t) =$ $c_i t + d_i$ with $t_i \le t \le t_{i+1}$, where $t_1, ..., t_i, ..., t_N$ are the set of time points which divide the observation interval $[0, T]$ into subintervals. In this case, $\Phi(.)$ is a linear function of time t and parameter vector $p = (c_1, c_2, ..., c_{N-1}, d_1, d_2, ..., d_{N-1})^t$ (here, the upper t is the transposition index): $\Phi = \Phi(t, p)$.

To calculate Φ and solve the stated problem, we can use a two-layer neural network given in Fig. 1, with the first layer activation function of the form:

$$y(x) = \begin{cases} 1, & if \ x > 1; \\ x, & if \ -1 \le x \le 1; \\ -1, & if \ x < -1. \end{cases} \tag{15}$$

We'll find the unknown parameter vector p using the condition of the δ^m error minimization. To do this, the following optimization problem should be solved:

$$\delta^m(x, p) \to \min_p, \tag{16}$$

which can be represented as the learning task for the neuron network given in Fig. 1. Thus the learning and solution process can be given by the following steps:

1. Select arbitrarily a random parameter vector p.
2. Put the pattern vector $x^m = (x^m_1, x^m_2, ..., x^m_n)$ to the network input component by component. This vector is the set of n learning examples. Evidently, a nature way of the selection of vector x^m components is to use the solutions of equations obtained at the previous integration steps.
3. Select the total number of learning examples E (the greater the number of layers, the greater the number of possible parameters could be used to tune the network).
4. Determine the NN output for each input

$$x^{m+1}_{out} \approx \Phi(x^m, p).$$

5. Calculate the vector-function $f^{\,m+1}(x^{m+1}(t))$ using $x^{m+1}(t)$.

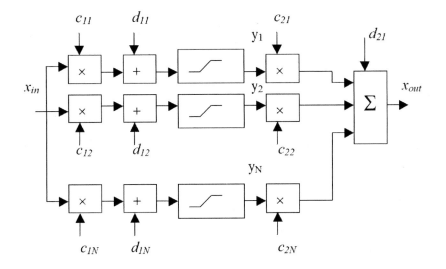

Figure 1. Neural network structure to calculate $\Phi(x)$: c_{ij} is the i-th layer weight coefficient for the j-th state variable; d_{ij} is the threshold value of the j-th neuron of the i-th layer; x_{in} is the network input; y_i is the first layer i-th neuron output; x_{out} is the network output [6].

6. Form the error vector $\delta^m = \left| f - f^m \right|_{L2}$ as the L_2 norm estimation and implement learning according to (16):

$$\delta^{m+1} = \frac{1}{L} \left(\sum_{i=1}^{E} \left(f(x_i) - f^{m+1}(x_i^{m+1}) \right)^2 \right) \to \min_p .$$

7. If the desired solution is obtained within the admissible error, assume that $\hat{x}(t) \approx x^{m+1}(t)$, and terminate the iterative process; otherwise increment $m := m+1$ and make the next iteration.

Adaptive neural network algorithm for the solution of LAEs

This algorithm is based on the iterative scheme, proposed in [7,8] and the basic scheme of the neuron network, which corresponds to this scheme, is given in Fig. 2.

The LAEs given at steps 2, 10, 11, and 14 of Table 1 can be written in the general matrix form as follows:

$$Ax = b, \tag{17}$$

where x is the n-dimensional vector of the desired variables, b is the n–dimensional vector of real numbers, and A is the $(n \times n)$ -matrix of real coefficients $\left[a_{ij} \right]_{n \times n}$.

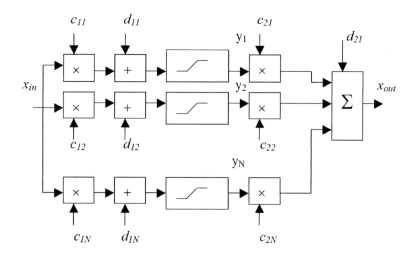

Figure 2. Structure of NN for the solution of the set of LAEs with the minimization error squared (T is the one-clock delay) [7].

Since the residual vector-function of (17) $\delta = |Ax - b|$ allows us to estimate whether the approximate solution x is in the vicinity of the accurate solution $\hat{x}$, the numerical solution of (17) can be formulated as the problem of minimization of the functional

$$F = (\Psi(Ax - b))^2, \tag{19}$$

where the activation function Ψ can be selected in such a manner that provides a simple way to calculate its gradient.

Summarizing our discussion, we can build the desired iterative scheme based on the relationship:

$$y^{m+1} = y^m - 2hAA^t y^m, \tag{19}$$

where the step h^m at the m-th iteration can be chosen using the dichotomy method or any other wide-use approach.

Finally, the algorithm of solution of (17) is as follows:
1. $x(0) = 0;$
2. $y^m = \Psi(Ax^m - b);$
3. $x^{m+1} = x^m - 2hA^t y^m.$

The desired NN structure given in Fig.2 allow us to minimize the error squared and to represent one of possible network solutions.

5. NUMERICAL ESTIMATIONS

To estimate the total number of "long" operations (multiplications and divisions) of the reduction algorithm given in Table 1, we should take into account the number of subintervals N' within the boundary layer $[0, \tau_{II}]$, the number of subintervals N within the entire observation interval $[0, T]$, the number of "fast" variables M, and the number of "slow" variables m, which are present in the state model (2). To do this, the number of operations estimated at steps 4, 8 and 14 should be multiplied by N', and the number of operations estimated at steps 2, 6, 10, and 11 – by N. Thus the total number of "long" arithmetic operations is

$$\Sigma_1 = \left[\frac{1}{3}\left(M^3 + 3M - M\right) + 3M^2 + 3m\right]N + MN' + MN + mN' +$$

$$+ \left[\frac{1}{3}\left(M^3 + 3M^2 - M\right) + M^2m + Mm^2 + m^2 + Mm + m\right]N +$$

$$+ M^2N + 2\left(M^2 + Mm + M\right)N'$$

Analyzing Table 1, we can observe that calculations performed at steps 6 and 11 and also at steps 3 – 4 – 5 – 7 – 9 – 10 can be carried out independently. In addition, calculations performed at step 8 can be performed separately of those at steps 9–10–11–12–13–14. Assume that we've got a parallel computing system, which perform one "long" operation per clock. Such a system will perform calculation concurrently, and the total time required to perform the entire cycle will be governed by the longest path, that is, by the total time of calculation over steps $1 - 2 - 3 - 4 - 5 - 7 - 9 - 10 - 11 - 12 - 13 - 14$. This yields the number of "long" operations that is less only by MN.

Now, let us consider the situation when the structure of a computer system is adjusted to the fine-grained algorithmic structure, that is, one operation is performed per time clock. We can adopt that each "long" operation is carried out using a separate neuron (one operation per neuron), and therefore the number of operations will be determined by the number of iterations (clocks) but not the number of equations:

$$\Sigma_2 = 15N + 8N'.$$

The benefits of the neural network approach are readily illustrated in Fig. 3, which exhibits the relation between the volumes of computations for the serial and neuron computers.

These histograms demonstrate the fact that the computation time is smaller by a factor of 10^4 when the neural computer is used instead of the serial computer, and in addition, this time even grows in the second case with increase in the relative number of fast variables.

Another relation is given in Fig. 4 in the form of histograms of Σ_1 and Σ_2 as functions of the number of integration steps N' within the boundary layer. It is quite evident that the number of integration steps within the boundary layer should grow with increase in the width of this layer.

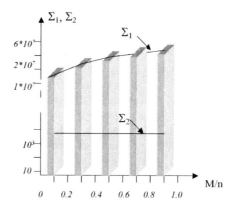

Figure 3. The volumes of computation in the serial computer Σ_1 and "idealized" neuron computer Σ_2 versus the relative number of "fast" variables M/n estimated for the problem with N=100, n=100, and N'=5

In the special case, if the boundary layer expands over the whole time interval, the problem is not stiff at all. As can be seen from Fig. 4, the use of the neural basis is especially efficient just for the stiff problems, because in this case computational expenses are minimal.

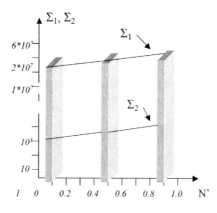

Figure 4. The volumes of computations in the serial computer Σ_1 and "idealized" neuron computer Σ_2 versus the relative width of the boundary layer N' estimated for the problem with N=100, n=100, M=70, and m=30

6. CONCLUSIVE DISCUSSION

The proposed algorithm has been tested using problems of different dimensions and stiffness. The three approaches have been checked: (a)direct solution of problem (1, 2) through the application of the Gear's implicit methods of the 1...5 orders with the automatic control of integration steps and orders; (b)solution of decomposed problem (9) through the application of the explicit Runge-Kutta's methods of the 2...4 orders; and (c) simulation of process solution of problem (9) in the neural network basis using the iteration procedures described in Section 4.

The qualitative analysis of the laboratory research allows us to make the following conclusions:

1. Approach (a) allows the reduction of the total number of integration steps. For example, a stiff problem (fundamental frequencies differed by 9 orders) with 70 differential equations, 8 fast variables and 62 slow variables, was solved by method (a) within 63 integration steps, whereas 102 integration steps were needed to solve this problem by method (b).

2. Nevertheless, the total volume of calculations in approach (b) may be far less than in approach (a) since the computation cost of each iteration step in (a) is much greater - it requires 3...7 iterations for the solution of the set of nonlinear algebraic equations to provide convergence, and each iteration which realizes the Newton's iteration method, requires, as a rule, the re-formation of the Jacobi (n x n) matrix (where n is a problem dimension).

3. In spite of the fact that the number of integration steps is greater in method (b) than in method (a) (it is quite understandable – implicit integration methods are preferable in the solutions of stiff problems), but approach (b) being applied to the solution of the decomposed problem (9) allowed the substantial reduction of the total volume of arithmetic operations.

4. Of special interest is the use of the neural network basis. A neuron computer had not at the author's disposal, and therefore the analysis has been carried out using a serial computer used to simulate the neuron computer computation. Approach (c) possessed practically all the advantages of approach (b), but, in addition, it allows to reduce substantially the number of machine clocks for the solution of a separate set of equations - each integration step can be performed within one machine clock (instead of n clocks in approach (b), where n is the problem dimension).

Another factor that favors the use of neuron computers, is that in many instances they are good alternative to the high-cost multi-computer and multi-processor systems. The number of artificial neurons may reach thousands with relatively low cost of a computer system.

The above reasoning as well as the fact that neural networks exhibit unique capability for learning also argues for developing soft- and hardware for computation in the neural network basis. This modern scientific direction can be called neurocomputing.

REFERENCES

[1] Rogoza W., Ishchenko A. Complicated Systems: Fuzziness and Adaptation. –Proc. of the 9th Int. Conf. on Advanced Computer Systems "ACS'2002", part 1, 2002. – P.239 – 244.

[2] Tikhonov A.N. Sets of differential equations containing small parameters on derivatives. – Math. Collection, 31 (73), №3, 1952.- P.575-586 (In Russian).

[3] Rogoza W. Methods for the analysis of state models containing parameters. – Kiev: KPI. 1999. (In Russian).

[4] Vasilieva A.B., Butuzov V.F. Asymptotic expansions of solutions of singularly perturbed equations. – Moscow: Nauka. – 1973. (In Russian).

[5] Bakhvalov N.S. Numerical Methods. – Moscow: Nauka. – 1980. (In Russian).

[6] Logovski A.S. Methods for the solution of ordinary differential equations in the neural network basis. – Moscow: Neuron computers: development and application, #2, 1992. (In Russian).

[7] Galushkin A.I. and Sudarikov V.A. Adaptive neuron network algorithms for the solution of linear algebra problems. – Moscow: Neuron computers: development and application, #2, 1992. (In Russian).

[8] Sudarikov V.A. Investigations of adaptive neuron network algorithms for the solution of linear algebra problems. – Moscow: Neuron computers: development and application, #3,4, 1992. (In Russian).

Improvement of the processors operating ratio in task scheduling using the deadline method

KOICHI KASHIWAGI, YOSHINOBU HIGAMI,
SHIN-YA KOBAYASHI
EHIME Uuniversity,
3 Bunkyo-cho, Matsuyama, Ehime, 790-8577 Japan,
e-mail: {kashiwagi, higami, kob}@koblab.cs.ehime-u.ac.jp

Abstract: Task scheduling technique which allocates some tasks to some processors is essential to high performance computing. Scheduling to the processors is crucial for optimizing performance. The objective of scheduling is to minimize the overall completion time or schedule length of the parallel program. On the other hand, a processors operating ratio may fall with the algorithm which pursued only this purpose unfortunately. For improvement of a processors operating ratio, there are the limitation method and the deadline method which we have proposed. In those methods, we limit the number of available processors. In this paper, we propose the method of improving the deadline method, by changing the limitation value of the number of available processors.

Key words: task scheduling, processors operating ratio, multi-processor system, parallel processing

1. INTRODUCTION

Task scheduling is one distinguishing features of parallel versus sequential programming. Many list scheduling algorithms have been proposed, however, they considers shortening tasks processing time primarily, because scheduling aims at minimizing the overall completion time of the parallel program. As a result, these traditional scheduling algorithms try to use all available processors, and then, processors operating ratio extremely decreases[1]. The other side, it is also a just claim to use limited resources effectively.

For example, in CP/MISF[3], in case of there are ready tasks and idle processors, these tasks are allocated to the idle processors even if this allocation shortens processing time little. On the other hand, some processor works only few time intervals during tasks are executed. This situation brings unfortunately decrement of operating ratio of processors. One more processor carries no more improvement of processing time and only reduction of operating ratio of processors.

So, We had proposed `deadline method' in order to resolve the problem[2]. In this method, available processors are restricted by the limitation that is calculated from property of tasks set. In this paper, we propose the improving method for the deadline method by change of the limitation.

We explain about target multi-processor system. Job that is inputted by user is divided into several tasks. Scheduling algorithm allocates these tasks to processors. Number of processors that are necessary for executing tasks is determined by scheduling algorithm. All processors that are allocated tasks are exclusively reserved during the tasks are executed.

2. DEADLINE METHOD

2.1 Property of tasks set

Let $T = \{T_1, T_2, ..., T_N\}$ denote a set of tasks T_i into which job is divided, where N is number of tasks. All tasks have one or more predecessors and successors except for start tasks and end tasks. A s_i be a task size of T_i , i.e., it is also amount of computation needed by T_i .

The set of tasks is conveniently represented as a directed acyclic graph called a task graph[4]. An arc (i, j) between two tasks T_i and T_j specifies that T_i must be completed before T_j begins. Then, T_i is one of predecessors of T_j and T_j is one of successors of T_i. Now pl_i denotes the longest path among paths from T_i to end task in the task graph. The critical path (CP) of set of tasks is the longest path among pl_i in the task graph, i.e., it is the maximum of pl_i[5].

The task can be processed only after all predecessors of the task have been done, and then each task cannot start before certain time. The lower bound of this time when available processors are enough is called `earliest starting time (EST)'. We refer est_i as the earliest starting time of T_i . On the other hand, task must be done before certain time in order to achieve the shortest processing time of set of tasks. In other words, if task has not finished by the certain time, it takes longer time than CP to complete execution of all tasks. We call the time `latest completion time (LCT)' and refer lct_i as the latest completion time of T_i [1].

2.2 Limitation of available processors

Now we define `execution probability' of each task as probability if the task is processed or not at any instant[1]. Anyway, if execution probability of T_i is 1 at some point, T_i must be processed in order to achieve the shortest processing time of set of tasks.

We can determine the execution probability of task with its EST and LCT. We let $f_i(t)$ be the task execution probability of a T_i at time t.

The $f_i(t)$ is defined zero before the est_i or after the lct_i, and the $f_i(t)$ is not zero between the est_i and the lct_i. Next, in case of $lct_i - est_i \leq 2s_i$, the $f_i(t)$ is determined by the following formula from Fig. 1 (a).

$$f_i(t) \equiv \begin{cases} 0 & : \ t < est_i, lct_i \leq t \\ \dfrac{t - est_i}{lct_i - est_i - s_i} & : \ est_i \leq t < est_i + s_i \\ \dfrac{s_i}{lct_i - est_i - s_i} & : \ est_i + s_i \leq t < lct_i - s_i \\ \dfrac{lct_i - t}{lct_i - est_i - s_i} & : \ lct_i - s_i \leq t < lct_i \end{cases}$$

Similarly, in case of $lct_i - est_i > 2s_i$, the $f_i(t)$ become following from Fig.1 (b).

$$f_i(t) \equiv \begin{cases} 0 & : \ t < est_i, lct_i \leq t \\ \dfrac{t - est_i}{lct_i - est_i - s_i} & : \ est_i \leq t < est_i + s_i \\ \dfrac{s_i}{lct_i - est_i - s_i} & : \ est_i + s_i \leq t < lct_i - s_i \\ \dfrac{lct_i - t}{lct_i - est_i - s_i} & : \ lct_i - s_i \leq t < lct_i \end{cases}$$

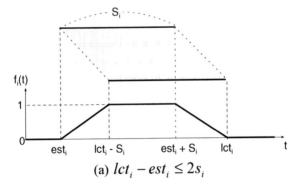

(a) $lct_i - est_i \leq 2s_i$

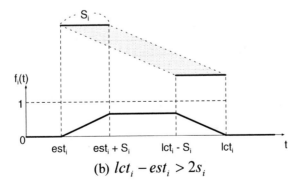

(b) $lct_i - est_i > 2s_i$

Fig. 1. time t vs. $f_i(t)$

So, we can consider the summation of the $f_i(t)$ from i = 1 to N, i.e., $\sum_{i=1}^{N} f_i(t)$ as expectation of required number of processors at time t in order to complete set of tasks for the shortest time. We refer F(t) as $\sum_{i=1}^{N} f_i(t)$. In other words, at time t, number of tasks that are processed is expected F(t). And we make the maximum of F(t) from time 0 to time CP the limitation of available processors

2.3   Release of the limitation

First, we define the time that subtract task size from LCT as 'latest starting time (LST)' and refer to $lct_i - s_i$ as lst_i. All tasks $\{T_1, T_2, ..., T_N\}$ are allocated at each lst_i at the latest when processors exist infinitely and communication time is zero, then processing time should be CP. When available processors are limited to the limitation, some tasks may not be allocated to available processors at each lst_i because of the limitation. When such tasks exist, processing time increases from CP.

So, for task T_i which was not allocated at lst_i, the limitation is canceled temporarily and it allocated to the processor which could not be used because of the limitation, at lst_i. We call these processors temporarily available processors. In this way, since all tasks are allocated by LST at the latest, processing time become CP. This is the fundamental part of the deadline method[2].

On the other hand, the processor that can be used now with this way is not used in time before LST. Consequently, if task T_i can be allocated before lst_i then it can be allocated at its time. As a result, idle time of the processor may be reduced. In scheduling, $availTime_i$ defined by the earliest time which can perform an allocation of T_i. AvailTime$_i$ satisfies $est_i \leq availTime_i \leq lst_i$.

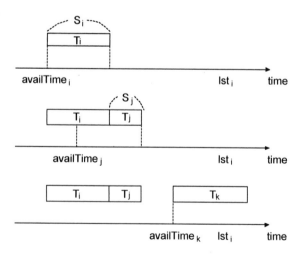

Fig. 2. Example of allocation by the deadline method

For example, when tasks T_i, T_j and T_k with the same LST (i.e. $lst_i = lst_j = lst_k$) are not allocated to the available processors at the LST, at first, T_i is allocated temporarily available processor. If the processor is not used until availTime$_i$, T$_i$ is allocated at availTime$_i$. Next, when availTime$_i$ + s$_i$ ≤ lst$_j$ and T$_j$ is chosen as a following task for allocation, if availTime$_j$ ≤ availTime$_i$ + s$_i$ then T$_j$ is allocated at availTime$_i$ + s$_i$. Finally, when availTime$_i$ + s$_i$ + s$_j$ ≤ lst$_k$, T$_k$ is allocated the same processor. If availTime$_i$ + s$_i$ + s$_j$ < availTime$_k$ then T$_k$ is allocated at availTime$_k$. Fig. 2 shows this allocation.

3. SIMULATION

We apply our deadline method to pseudo tasks sets that are generated with random series in order to evaluate our method. We use CP/MISF as scheduling algorithm and four series of pseudo tasks sets for evaluation. We create pseudo tasks sets with the following algorithm.

First of all, we create sets of fundamental tasks. These sets of tasks are prescribed by four parameters, N, bp, ep and prob. N is number of tasks. Task T$_i$ might depend on task T$_j$ (i + bp ≤ j < i + bp + ep) at probability prob. Anyway, task T$_i$ has (ep - 1) × prob successors expectantly. Average of task size is 100 (probability distribution is exponential distribution).

Secondly, duplicates are made using two parameters r and m. N × r tasks are chosen and those averages of m duplicates are made (probability distribution is P(X = x) = 1/(2m + 1), x = 0,1,...,2m). The duplicated tasks has same predecessors and successors that original task has. This duplication means loop iteration.

However, this tasks generation algorithm has unacceptable problem. The problem is that tasks are divided into some groups that are independent of each other; moreover there might be a task that has no predecessor and successor. In order to avoid this problem, we impose the following restrictions on tasks generation algorithm. Each task is forced to have one predecessor or successor at least. We consider the following four series.

Series 1

- $N = \{200, 400, 600\}$
- $bp \in \{1, 10, 50\}$
- $ep \in \{10, 50, 100\}$
- $prob \in \{0.1, 0.3, 0.5\}$
- $r \in \{0.0, 0.1, 0.3\}$
- $m \in \{5, 10\}$

This notation means that N takes one value out of 200, 400, or 600. Similarly bp, ep, prob and r take one value out of 3 values respectively and m takes one value out of 2 values. Namely, number of these combinations is 3 × 3 × 3 × 3 × 3 × 2 = 486. Moreover we generate 10 different tasks sets for each combination. Consequently number of tasks sets of Series 1 is 4860.

Similarly the following Series 2, 3, 4 are generated. N, r, m are the same as Series 1.

Series 2
- bp = 1
- ep takes an integer from 1 to N - i at random for each task T_i
- $prob \in \{0.1, 0.3, 0.5\}$

Series 3
- bp = 1
- ep is N - i for each task T_i
- prob takes a real number from 0.1 to 0.5 at random for each task T_i

Series 4
- bp = 1
- ep takes an integer from 1 to N - i for each task T_i
- *prob* takes a real number from 0.1 to 0.5 at random for task T_i

We scheduled these tasks sets by using CP/MISF and CP/MISF with deadline method. Tab. 1 shows average of processors operating ratio by each scheduling. As these results, to pseudo tasks that we made deadline method is effective for improvement of processors operating ratio.

Next, Tab. 2 shows average of ratio of the number of tasks allocated to temporarily available processors by the deadline method. It was found that there are few tasks allocated to temporarily available processors by the deadline method. In other words, this means that the algorithm of section 2.3 is not used for most of tasks sets.

methods	Series1	Series2	Series3	Series4
CP/MISF	0.26902	0.23787	0.21142	0.20751
CP/MISF with deadline	0.50113	0.31356	0.26766	0.26801

Tab. 1. Average of processors operating ratio by CP/MISF and deadline method

Series1	Series2	Series3	Series4
0.9%	0.7%	0.4%	0.6%

Tab. 2. Average of ratio of the number of tasks allocated to temporarily available processors by deadline method

4. PROPOSAL METHOD

We propose changing the limitation that is used by the deadline method. The result of section 3 shows that most of tasks are allocated to available processors before LST. This implies that the limitations for each tasks set are too large. So, we reconsider how to calculate the limitation.

We have defined the limitation as maximum of F(t) ($0 \leq t \leq CP$) in section 2.2, where $F(t) = \sum_{i=1}^{N} f_i(t)$, N is number of task and $f_i(t)$ is execution probability of a T_i at time t. This is only one value to a tasks set. We call this limitation L_m. On the other hand, we have proposed the limitations for every tasks as follows[6]. The limitation L(i) of each task T_i is

$$L(i) \equiv \max_{est_i < t \leq lct_i} \{F(t)\}$$

L(i) satisfies $0 < L(i) \leq L_m$. A new limitation L_r is defined using the limitations L(i). We define L_r as average of L(i). Namely, L_r is

$$L_r = \frac{\sum_{i=1}^{N} L(i)}{N}$$

L_r is smaller than L_m because L(i) satisfies $0 < L(i) \leq L_m$. We use L_r as a new limitation used by the deadline method.

5. EVALUATION

We scheduled pseudo tasks sets of section 3 by using CP/MISF with deadline method which changed the limitation into L_r. Tab. 3 shows average of processors operating ratio by this method. We see from Tab. 1 and Tab. 3 that average of processors operating ratio is improved by change of the limitation in all series.

On the other hand, Tab. 4 shows average of ratio of the number of tasks allocated to temporarily available processors by the deadline method using L_r. Tab. 2, 3 and 4 indicate that using new limitation L_r makes more tasks allocated to temporarily available processors. In other words, the algorithm of section 2.3 is applied much more times.

These results presents that this algorithm is effective for the improvement of processors operating ratio and usage of new limitation L_r caused it.

Series1	Series2	Series3	Series4
0.56269	0.36606	0.30731	0.30250

Tab. 3. Average of processors operating ratio by deadline method using L_r

Series1	Series2	Series3	Series4
3.6%	5.7%	6.0%	5.5%

Tab. 4. Average of ratio of the number of tasks allocated to temporarily available processors by deadline method using L_r

6.   CONCLUSION

We had proposed the deadline method for the improvement of processors operating ratio, and we could obtain high operating ratio.

In this paper, we have proposed the new limitation for the deadline method. The new limitation L_r was made into the average value of the limitations for every task.

We applied former deadline method and deadline method with L_r to pseudo tasks sets to evaluate these method. The deadline method using L_r achieves higher processors operating ratio that former deadline method.

REFERENCES

[1] K. Kashiwagi and S. Kobayashi, "Limitation of used processor for task scheduling," Proc. 19st IASTED International Multi-Conf. Applied Informatics, pp.122-126, Innsbruck, Austria, Feb. 2001.

[2] K. Kashiwagi and S. Kobayashi, "Consideration of task's deadline for cheduling method with used processors limitation," Proc. Advanced Computer Systems, no.VII-9, pp.487-496, Mielno, Poland, Oct. 2001.

[3] H. Kasahara and S. Narita, "Practical multiprocessor scheduling algorithms for efficient parallel processing," IEEE Trans. Computers, no.33(11), pp.1023-1029, 1984.

[4] Albert Y. Zomaya, Parallel & distributed computing handbook, McGraw-Hill, New York, 1996.

[5] Thomas H. Cormen, Charles E. Leiserson, Ronald L.Rivest, Introduction to algorithms, The MIT Press, Massachusetts, 1994.

[6] H. Hashimoto, K. Kashiwagi, Y. Higami and S. Kobayashi, "How to limit the number of available processors for every task in scheduling", Proc. SJCIEE2001 (Japanese), Sept. 2001.

Author Index